Agenda for Reform

Other books by William B. Gould IV

Black Workers in White Unions: Job Discrimination in the United States. Cornell University Press, 1977.

Japan's Reshaping of American Labor Law. MIT Press, 1984.

Strikes, Dispute Procedures, and Arbitration: Essays on Labor Law. Greenwood Press, 1985.

Labor Relations in Professional Sports (with Robert C. Berry and Paul D. Staudohar). Auburn House, 1986.

A Primer on American Labor Law. MIT Press. Third edition, 1993.

Agenda for Reform

The Future of
Employment Relationships
and the Law

William B. Gould IV

The MIT Press
Cambridge, Massachusetts
London, England

© 1993 Massachusetts Institute of Technology

All rights reserved. No part of this book may be reproduced in any form by any electronic or mechanical means (including photocopying, recording, or information storage and retrieval) without permission in writing from the publisher.

This book was set in Palatino by .eps Electronic Publishing Services and was printed and bound in the United States of America.

Library of Congress Cataloging-in-Publication Data

Gould, William B.
  Agenda for reform : the future of employment relationships and the law / William B. Gould IV.
    p. cm.
  Includes bibliographical references and index.
  ISBN 0-262-07151-7
  1. Labor laws and legislation—United States. 2. Industrial relations—United States. I. Title.
KF3369.G63 1993
344.73'01—dc20
[347.3041]   93-19031
                                                                                                      CIP

to the late Kurt Hanslowe

Contents

Preface   ix

1 Introduction   1

2 How We Got from There to Here in the Era of Modern Labor Legislation   11

3 The Development of Job Security Law and Practice in the United States: Wrongful Discharge Law and Collective Agreements   63

4 The Variety and Vagaries of Workers' Participation: Labor-Management Cooperation or Co-optation   109

5 The National Labor Relations Act: The Reform of Labor Law   151

6 The Strike Weapon and Other Forms of Economic Pressure: Self-help for the Workers in a Democratic Society   181

7 Canada and the United States: A Tale of Two Contiguous Countries   205

8 The Civil Rights Act of 1991: The Law and Politics of Race   235

9 Conclusion   259

Notes   265
Index   303

Preface

This book addresses labor issues which I perceive to be the central issues confronting the employee-employer relationship today. Many of these issues I have reflcted upon and addressed in my teaching and practice during the past thirty-two years, since my graduation from Cornell Law School. Of cource some of them, particularly the wrongful discharge issue, are matters that came to the forefront only in the late 1970s.

The book's beginnings are in a series of lectures given at the Australian National University in Canberra while I was a visiting professor of law there in 1985. I have already presented aspects of this book in the Fourth Annual Farr Lecture, which I delivered at the J. Reuben Clark Law School, Brigham Young University, in November 1986, as well as in a series of lectures from 1986 to 1991 at Arizona State College of Law, the University of Wisconsin Law School, and the University of Wyoming Law School.

I have benefited from comments provided to earlier drafts by Robert Flanagan of the Stanford School of Business and James Gross of the New York State School of Industrial Labor Relations at Cornell University. I am grateful to both of them for their willingness to read this manuscript and to provide helpful critiques. I also benefited considerably from discussion with Brian Bercusson when I gave a series of lectures as a visitng professor of law at the European University Institute in Florence, Italy, in May 1988.

My research was aided by a 1988 Faculty Research Grant provided by the Canadian government as part of their Canadian Studies Program. This allowed me to travel and conduct interviews throughout Canada in 1988 and 1989. I express my gratitude to the government of Canada for their assistance.

Preface

I also thank the Deutscher Akademischer Austausch Dienst for providing me with a research travel grant to Germany in 1987 to renew my investigation of German industrial relations in general and works councils in particular. I am further grateful to a number of students who provided research assistance for me. At the top of the list is Henry Dinsdale, a distinguished Canadian labor lawyer, who arrived at the Stanford Law School in the fall of 1992 to begin work on a doctorate and provided not only standard research help but also comments about chapter 7, "A Tale of Two Contiguous Countries" and additional information about new legislation in a number of the Canadian provinces. Special thanks also go to Kathleen Schneider, Santa Clara Law School 1994, who, while working as my assistant here, has provided research assistance as well as typing and retyping the full-length manuscript.

I also express appreciation for research assistance to Robert Lazo, Stanford Law School '89, Tom Thompson, Stanford Law School '90, Paul Schmidtberger, Stanford Law School '91, Christy Haubegger, Stanford Law School '92, and Timothy S. Gould, University of California at Davis Law School '94.

This book is dedicated to the memory of Kurt Hanslowe of Cornell Law School who was my teacher of labor law there. I am forever in his debt for his generous and wise counsel and assistance.

# Agenda for Reform

1 Introduction

It is not simply the economic trough in which the United States and much of Europe find themselves lodged in the last decade of this twentieth century. It is not simply the dramatic, painful and emotionally charged layoff of more than 70,000 workers of the General Motors Corporation, for years the centerpiece of the American industrial economy—50,000 more workers already dismissed in the years immediately preceding the innovative 1990 collective bargaining agreement entered into by that company. Significant though they are, it is much more than those events, and the loss of public confidence in its wake, that plague the country and its workers.

The declining fortunes of workers are succinctly summarized by Peter Kilborn in a 1991 Labor Day column. Says Kilborn:

From the end of World War II until the start of the 1970's, when spending on the Vietnam War and inflation pushed the country into the recession of 1974–75, labor unions and Democrats collaborated to build the world's richest working class, one in which a blue collar factory hand could own a home, and support a family on one paycheck. Since then, more inflation, changes in the tax system, the growth of the budget deficit and the rise of foreign competition, have combined to depress most people's income.

Lawrence Mishel, economist at the pro-labor Economic Policy Institute . . . calculates that the typical production or nonsupervisory worker's average wage in July of $10.30 is 6.8 percent less than 10 years ago in terms of what it will buy. He said that young males with high school diplomas but no college, the backbone of the organized work force, had lost even more during the decade—20 percent of their wages.

In contrast, Pearl Meyer & Partners an executive recruiting firm in New York, reports that the average salary of chief executives of the nation's 200 biggest companies doubled over the last decade to $800,000.[1]

The decline in living standards is inevitably linked to productivity—a critical consideration that is central to good labor-management relationships:

As the [1992] economic slump extends from months to years, Americans worry increasingly that the nation requires not short-term fixes but long-term prescriptions. Bruised by recession and foreign competition, G.M., I.B.M., and other stalwarts of corporate America are laying off thousands of workers, helping to create a palpable eagerness to cure the competitiveness malady before more high-paying jobs vanish.

Evidence of the illness is everywhere. The weekly wages of the average American factory worker have fallen 9 percent since 1973. In recent years, productivity—the key to improved living standards—has grown at one-third the 1960 rate and one-quarter the Japanese rate, although America still leads the world in output per worker.[2]

Three factors coincide with these developments. The first is change in the employment relationship discussed in chapter 2, the rise of part-time work and a peripheral work force, which is excluded from benefits essential to a civilized society such as pensions and health care. These employees are ". . . counted as working but facing the hardships and insecurity of the jobless . . . probably numbering more than three million [they include] many temporary and freelance workers, older men pushed into lower paying jobs, consultants and single mothers who cannot work as many hours as they would like."[3]

The second factor is the continuing divisiveness of race, notwithstanding the landmark constitutional and statutory case law of recent years, a phenomenon that is at once as pernicious for worker solidarity as the changing nature of work itself. The Bush administration's skillfulness in exploiting this issue in order to combat enactment of the Civil Rights Act of 1991 under the "quota" rubric (until its perceived insensitivity to sexual harassment matters induced retreat) left no doubt about the abiding nature of racism in our society. A two-year effort by the Democratic party, and some elements of the Republican party, to reverse what Justice William Brennan properly called "cramped" interpretations of civil rights legislation, and to restore Supreme Court precedents of the 1970s, consistently ran up against an attempt to deliberately confuse the nature of the legislation so as to exacerbate racial divisiveness and harm our societal fabric.

Third, it is the decline of the labor movement itself—a kind of free-fall descent during the 1980s and 1990s, the decimation of manufacturing industries in which the unions possessed strength—that has made workers more vulnerable than at any time since the Great Depression of the 1930s. The plight of many workers coupled with the inability of unions to represent them at the bargaining table is a volatile combination. It is one that erodes the fabric of democratic institutions and is thus profoundly worrisome to all who value pluralism and a system of checks and balances in the workplace where "workers compete for jobs and management competes for labor."[4]

This book is about institutional practices and the law of the workplace. For years I and others have advocated labor law reform that would facilitate trade union organization and collective bargaining. These views, developed in chapters 2, 5, and 6 are based upon my belief in both the values of industrial democracy and the principle that our society must promote employee participation and involvement in the economy as well as in the political process. I am alarmed by deficiencies in the administration of our federal labor law that have made it more difficult to achieve such objectives and by interpretations of the National Labor Relations Act provided both by the National Labor Relations Board and the U.S. Supreme Court—interpretations that, in my judgment, are at odds with these values. Some of my concerns extend to the content of the relevant law as well as its administration.

A number of points need to be made that underscore some of my assumptions about labor policy. The first is that, so far as I am aware, the case for the idea that the National Labor Relations Act is primarily responsible for organized labor's decline has not been made. The corollary to this position is that enactment of labor law reform will not necessarily reverse the process of decline. Absent substantial changes in the political or economic environment, the downward trend will probably continue. The reasons for union decline appear to be numerous and complex. Leo Troy has persuasively made the case that factors such as the market are far more important than the law itself.[5] My view is that Troy has had the better of this particular argument, notwithstanding the fact that considerations other than the market appear to have triggered union decline.

What is particularly instructive about the impact of the National Labor Relations Act upon trade union decline in the United States is the relationship between the law and the unions in the public sector. Public employee trade unionism has come to the United States, by comparative standards, relatively recently. In a number of countries, such as Japan, trade unionism first took root in the public sector. The opposite is true in the United States, where an explosive growth began in the 1960s.[6]

From the late 1960s onward, a majority of jurisdictions in this country have enacted comprehensive labor relations statutes that attempt—

except for their intervention to resolve disputes through mediation, fact-finding, and sometimes interest arbitration over unresolved issues at the expiration of a collective bargaining agreement—to replicate the National Labor Relations Act. The general view appears to be that these statutes have been "a prime determinate" in promoting collective bargaining for public employees.[7]

It may seem obvious that a major reason trade unions have developed with the aid of labor law in the public sector—the very same labor law exists in the private sector—is that employer opposition frequently does not exist or is not of an intensity comparable to that in the private sector. But the main reason, as Troy has noted,[8] is that the same market pressures presently applicable to the private sector have not prevailed for public employers to date. Without market pressures similar to those of the private sector employers, the main source of pressure for public sector employers is public employee unionism's resort to the political process.[9] Again the experience in the public sector suggests that the role of labor law has been, at best, secondary and that a reversal of the trend cannot be realized in the absence of the alteration of other factors.

Beyond my proposals set forth in chapter 5, I have devoted a great deal of argument to the reasons for revising our law as it relates to the right to strike for private sector workers under the NLRA. The idea that employers can permanently replace workers when they strike has long seemed to me to be both anomalous and hypocritical in a system in which the law purports to protect the worker's right to withhold his or her labor in order to resolve differences with the employer if all other efforts fail. Most probably public policy should promote third-party intervention as an alternative to the strike—just as it does in disputes arising during a collective bargaining agreement involving that instrument's interpretation. Legislative proposals, particularly the so-called Packwood-Metzenbaum amendment introduced in 1992, are a step down the road toward promoting dialogue on this issue. But with or without such policies the law relating to the strike simply does not make sense.

This does not mean that the strike is likely to be the preferred weapon of unions unable to resolve their differences with employers. Although assessments vary depending upon an employer's need to fill business orders or its concern with excessive inventory, generally unions are not interested in using the strike unless other alternatives prove unattractive. Again the focus should be upon both the strike and its substitute. Indeed, while the right to strike is integral to a democratic society, the primary thrust of labor policy ought to be upon more rational and cooperative avenues for labor and management to pursue.

In the organized sector, particularly in the immediate post–World War II period, grievance-arbitration procedures through which a third-party neutral provided a binding interpretation of the existing terms of the collective bargaining agreement when the parties themselves could not agree upon one, have been the primary substitute for industrial warfare.[10] Some relationships, steel being the most prominent example in the private sector, have attempted to use the same procedure for interest disputes over the terms of a new agreement.[11] But the processes' sometimes confrontational and adversarial form, as well as its increased domination by lawyers, has sharpened the focus upon more informal institutions.

This is not to say that arbitration is inappropriate in the employment arena. Quite to the contrary, alternate dispute resolution procedures that include arbitration, explicitly encouraged by the Civil Rights Act of 1991, are at the heart of the proposals set forth in chapter 3, and they remain important elements in reforming the employment relationship. Damage liability, which has been expanded by the Civil Rights Act of 1991, the Americans with Disabilities Act of 1990, and common-law wrongful discharge litigation, has concentrated the minds of employers marvelously and sharpened their interest in procedures outside of litigation. This is as it should be because of the abuses that inevitably flow from unfettered discretion for any actor in the employment relationship, particularly the employer. The Bill of Rights in the Constitution makes this point well in connection with governmental entities. The task is to devise an analogue to the private sector and to accomplish this with both economy and informality.

The search for informal methods of addressing mutual concerns in the employment relationship is one of the reasons why the cooperative model described in chapter 4 can be so significant for the organized sector of the economy. The approaches undertaken at both New United Motors Manufacturing, Inc. (NUMMI) in Fremont, California, and at the new General Motors Saturn facility in Spring Hill, Tennessee, appear to have had a good and successful run at achieving some mutual objectives.

Still the cooperative model, while a radical modification of much of the American industrial relations past, cannot serve as a complete substitute for a more adversarial framework in which the strike and arbitration remain integral. It may diminish resort to dispute resolution procedures if it is designed and administered well, but grievance-arbitration machinery will remain important. So will the right to strike, especially if the reforms adopted in chapter 6 become law at some point in the future. Democratic collective bargaining can best facilitate the fine balance between autonomy and independence—more cherished in the West (particularly in the United States) than in Japan—and loyalty and efficiency that further the firm's competitive interest.

Again it is unlikely that collective bargaining will spread, let alone hold its own in the foreseeable future. True, the democratic secret ballot-box election of new leadership in the International Brotherhood of Teamsters can purge corrupt and criminal elements from the ranks of organized labor's leadership and consequently boost its public image. It is even possible that the 1991 election in which President Ron Carey prevailed will mean the adoption of new, more democratic direct election procedures in other unions, thus undermining the heavily layered bureaucracy in which organized labor has ossified.[12] Until these results are realized, however, it is imperative to devise a set of proposals that have applicability to the nonunion as well as the unionized sector. Clearly the principle that all workers, whether represented by unions or not, should have protection retains its vitality even if the scope of union representation is expanded considerably. The fact that this is not likely to happen in the near future makes adoption of my proposals for the nonunion sector particularly pressing.

Even those unions that find objectionable the idea of protection for both union and nonunion workers ought to realize that an imperfect system of protection or representation promoted or mandated by statute may ultimately serve as a kind of building block for collective bargaining because of the likelihood of employee dissatisfaction with the nonunion systems' comparative imperfections. As collective bargaining recedes, along with the labor and employment trends already noted, a new vacuum has emerged in which a new public policy is being forged. In the area of cooperation and participation, one approach to take is that which has been pursued by the European Community which, with dissenting Britain standing at one side, seems to be moving toward a European-wide works council system. Beyond the merits of this idea—and in my view, they are considerable—it is unlikely that such an approach will be followed in the United States, and this is even more unlikely than labor law reform promoting trade union growth.

American employers would be even more obdurate about a system that would provide for representation without unions, which after all became acceptable in the post–World War II era because they are institutions that impose responsibilities and obligations upon the workers that they represent. Accordingly American management will be tenacious in fighting the idea of works council legislation. Such an effort would be a wasteful diversion from the protection of employment conditions generally—labor law reform that promotes collective bargaining and obligates employers to recognize unions in circumstances other than those in which the union establishes a majority status.

More important is the fact that inevitably the works council idea conflicts with this country's concept of exclusive bargaining status, that is to say, the principle that the union bargains for all employees in an appropriate grouping as the exclusive agent. Even if subject matter demarcation lines are drawn between the roles to be given the unions and the works councils (e.g., involvement in sales or pricing for works councils and wages, hours and working conditions for unions), my sense is that more than fifty years of experience with duty-to-bargain issues under the NLRA make clear the synthetic and arbitrary nature of such a dividing line. In the American system, without elimination of the exclusive bargaining representative concept, works councils are an idea whose time has not and should not come.

On the other hand, to give employee participation a role in the nonunion sector through works councils would entice antiunion employers to use state apparatus as a device with which to thwart the NLRA's public policy of freedom of association. This seems to me to be an undesirable and probably unintended consequence of those who support such ideas.

At the same time the problem of representation for employees in the nonunion sector should be addressed. I am of the view that the principal legal obstacle to labor-management cooperation is the anti-company-union unfair labor practice provision of the NLRA. This provision makes it an unfair labor practice for an employer to dominate, interfere with, or assist a labor organization except in connection with pay for negotiations or grievance administration during working hours. The effect of this has been to frequently impede constructive communication between employees and employers as well as discussions about the performance of the corporation and the connection between the employment relationship and the firm's ability to sell its product in the marketplace.

One irony here is that company unions were regarded by the authors of the National Labor Relations Act to be the principal obstacle to trade union organization. The employee representation plans of the 1920s and 1930s constituted a major aspect of the abuses and evils at which the NLRA was aimed. This is no longer a problem for unions—or at least today not the same problem that it was more than fifty years ago. As I point out in chapter 5, in some instances, the company unions at which the statute was originally aimed became the framework for autonomous trade unions that obliged management to engage in good-faith collective bargaining.

The labor movement would generally object to interpretations or amendments to the statute that would allow the employer to facilitate such structures through time off from work, provision for office space, company equipment, and so forth, on the ground that it would be used to keep unions out. Surely many employers would engage in such tactics and do so today. Yet unless antiunion motivation can be shown through, for instance, remarkable coincidences between the timing of such a structured entity or institution and the appearances of a union organizational campaign, employer involvement is intrinsically worthwhile and could provide employees with more protection than they otherwise enjoy. As I noted earlier, it might ultimately promote their interest in unions and real collective bargaining.

My views about job security, particularly the so-called wrongful discharge issue which generally involves the commencement of common-law litigation by individual employees, are similar to those expressed about employee participation. Again it is the nonunion model that has driven innovation and change in this area. Again sound labor policy dictates protection of employees, whether or not they are represented by unions and participate in the collective bargaining process. This is why I would like to see adoption of a comprehensive wrongful discharge statute, at either the federal or state level, that protects workers effectively. The erosion of standards and the increased vulnerability of workers are phenomena that are not well suited to a democratic society. The Chicago classicists notwithstanding, even though the market has overwhelmed the unions, it has not put something equitable in their place.

This is then what this book is about. It attempts to set forth a series of proposals that are practicable and workable in the employment relationship and balance sensibly the interests of both management and worker. The reform agenda put forward here does not reject the paradigm of collective bargaining that emerged from The New Deal, the War Labor Board during World War II, and the postwar period of the 1940s and 1950s. Quite the contrary, some of my proposals—particularly those set forth in chapters 4 and 6—are designed to make these institutions and procedures work more effectively. My belief continues to be that unions are the most effective advocates and representatives of employee interests in the workplace. But the proposals here do assume that, with or without reform, most workers are not likely to be represented by unions and protected by collective bargaining agreements in the foreseeable future.

The Employee Retirement Income Security Act of 1974, which protects worker interests in pensions, as well as the Occupational Safety and Health Act of 1970, which protects the health and safety of workers so far as practicable, are good examples of lawmaking designed to shore up collective bargaining where it exists and to provide a kind of rough substitute where it does not. The Civil Rights Act of 1964, as amended through the Equal Opportunity Act of 1972 and the Civil Rights Act of 1991, as well as antidiscrimination legislation such as the Equal Pay Act of 1963 (equal pay for roughly equal work) and the Americans with Disabilities Act of 1990, all proceed upon the assumption that the collective bargaining process cannot be effective in shaping employment conditions that are compatible with the public policies enshrined in these statutes.

This book then proceeds upon the assumption that collective bargaining is likely to remain less important than it has been for most of the post–World War II era. This is a factor—and a fairly important one—in promoting the agenda set forth here, namely the protection of employee participation and job security in the workplace. No abiding treatment of these two critical issues can be fashioned in the absence of labor law reform that promotes collective bargaining as the best forum within which differences should be resolved. Organized labor and the work force cannot behave responsibly when the continued existence of institutions that represent employees is at issue or threatened.

2 How We Got from There to Here in the Era of Modern Labor Legislation

The roots of the American labor law system are in the Great Depression. They were formed in an attempt to modify and renew the capitalist system of the 1920s and 1930s. The War Labor Board operating under the emergency conditions of World War II gave these reforms much of the shape that they possess today, as the twentieth century is about to close. Whatever the contemporary assessment of this effort, quite clearly success in this respect was obtained.

The mass production system, the rise of industrial unionism in the form of the Congress of Industrial Organizations (CIO) as a challenge to the still influential craft union federation,[1] the American Federation of Labor—now a merged federation since 1955—along with the job control system espoused by the American labor movement are all well known and embedded in American labor law policy. A basic ingredient in the statutory framework promoted by the New Deal was the idea that consumption of the workers would stimulate the economy, the purchasing power philosophy that serves as a rationale for the promotion of trade unionism.[2]

But much has changed in the fifty-eight years since the Act was approved by Congress at Senator Robert Wagner's initiative and signed into law by President Franklin D. Roosevelt. The economy has now become globalized, and trade unions that functioned in industries previously oligopolistic are now no longer immune to foreign and domestic competition. The parties can no longer operate in an environment that is cocooned and where unions are always able to point to profits and gains that can be shared with workers.

Beyond foreign competition the same process has been engendered in the transportation industry of trucking, railroads, and airlines—union strongholds all. The new competitive environment demands a system that is more flexible than that required by mass production where workers were engaged in a more segmented process. Flexibility means that employees must be both committed and more knowledgeable about the purposes of production. It brings with it reforms in pay and work rules, a departure from automatic percentage wage increases supplemented with cost-of-living adjustments (COLAs), and numerous job classifications that are designed to ensure a measure of job security.

Four major developments overshadow the American industrial relations landscape as this century comes to a close. The first and most important of all is the fact that the American industrial relations environment no longer exists in vacuo, so to speak, without reference to the outside world. The United States is now part of a global economy.[3] After a breathing space of approximately fifteen to twenty years provided by the victories that this country obtained in World War II, the United States has found itself in an international environment that manifests itself in a number of forms.

One is an increased awareness of international obligations and international organizations. The International Labor Organization, and now disappearing Cold War, trading relationships, and competition inevitably require this country to be concerned with international obligations as well as with developments in the European Community relating to workers' participation arrangements in corporate hierarchical structures. Yet the United States has only ratified approximately a dozen of the ILO conventions, and none of those that bear upon the fundamentals of collective bargaining or the employment relationship in this country. Thus the American labor movement, through the American Federation of Labor–Congress of Industrial Organizations (AFL-CIO), has found itself protesting domestic law relating to the right to strike in the private sector under conventions to which the United States is not a signatory.

A second facet of international developments relates to foreign competition. Increased competition has come from not only the vanquished of World War II, namely Germany and Japan, but also rising Third World countries, the young tigers like Singapore, Taiwan, Hong Kong, and Brazil. The advent of the multinational corporation has alarmed the unions, and whatever the merits of the debate about the impact of multinational corporations upon industrial relations,[4] it is clear that foreign competition has wreaked havoc through the unemployment that has been visited upon the basic American manufacturing union strongholds like automobile, steel, electrical appliance, and machine tool. This has made the unions circle the wagons to retreat from erstwhile proclaimed fidelities to free trade in support of new tariff walls, to actively agitate for protectionist policies, and most recently to oppose "fast-track" authority for President George Bush in this country's trade negotiations with Mexico and Canada about the North American Free Trade Agreement (NAFTA).

The NAFTA represents a continuation of the trade liberalization that has emerged through the various rounds of the General Agreement on Tariffs and Trade (GATT). From the 1950s through the 1980s the share of foreign manufactured products as a percentage of the goods produced in the United States has more than quadrupled. Fueled by the perception that a healthy Mexico is good for the American economy, that economies of scale can be obtained through cross-border investment, and that the flow of illegal immigrants to the United States can be slowed, the NAFTA would facilitate increased trade and investment already in place.[5] Mexican compensation is approximately one-tenth of that in the United States on average, and the NAFTA may substitute Mexican imports for Asian competitors whose compensation is higher than that of Mexico. It is estimated that the NAFTA will produce on balance 60,000 jobs for the United States, but by any calculation the treaty will cost considerable dislocation, particularly among low-skilled workers in labor-intensive industries.[6] The Clinton administration has stated that it will negotiate labor and environmental agreements with Mexico in order to protect labor standards and the environment. NAFTA represents further steps toward elimination of tariff barriers to a global economy.

The key to an effective labor standards agreement will be a supernational monitoring and enforcement mechanism or institution staffed by representatives of the United States, Canada, and Mexico. The goal of such an institution should be that of compressing some of the existing labor standards differentials so as to effectuate a kind of harmonization of practices, as the European Community is attempting to do.[7]

The increased focus upon international labor standards and free-trade negotiations recognizes the need to protect labor through standards on both sides of the border. In this way it is closely related to the second of the three modern developments: the decline of the trade union movement in the United States. The American labor movement is in the depths of a self-acknowledged crisis that has gathered momentum over more than thirty years, reaching whirlwind proportions

Table 2.1
Union membership in selected OECD countries (percent of total civilian wage and salaried employees)

	1955	1960	1965	1970	1975	1976	1977	1978	1979	1980
United States[a]	33	31	28	30	29	28	27	26	25	25
United States[b]	—	—	—	—	22	22	23	22	23	22
Canada	31	30	28	31	34	36	36	37	—	35
Australia[a]	64	61	46	43	48	47	47	47	47	47
Australia[b]	—	—	—	—	—	42	—	—	—	—
Japan	36	33	36	35	35	34	33	33	32	31
Denmark	59	63	63	64	72	75	79	83	84	86
France	21	20	20	22	23	22	22	21	20	19
Germany	44	40	38	37	39	40	40	41	40	40
Italy[e]	57	34	33	43	56	60	60	62	62	62
Netherlands	41	42	40	38	42	42	43	43	42	41
Sweden	62	62	68	75	83	85	88	90	87	88
Switzerland	32	33	32	31	35	37	36	36	36	35
United Kingdom	46	45	45	50	53	55	57	58	57	56

Source: Bureau of Labor Statistics (C. Chang and C. Sorrentino), *Monthly Labor Review* 114, 12 (1991).
a. Data from biennial surveys of labor unions and employee associations headquartered in the United States. For 1955, 1968, and 1965 data exclude members of employee associations. In 1978, excluding employee associations, union membership as a percentage of civilian wage and salary emplyees was 27 percent.
b. Data from Current Population Survey. For 1975 and 1976 data excluded members of employee associations. For 1975–80 data are for May. For all other years data are annual averages.
c. Data from reports from unions and confederations. For 1955–84 data are for December 31, and coverage in some unions was limited to dues-paying

in the hostile environment of the Reagan 1980s. The movement, in its contemporary form of the AFL-CIO and some approximately one hundred affiliates, remains a potent political force at both the federal and state level. But its precipitous numerical decline in percentage of workers represented in the work force, its unwillingness or inability to use its traditional strike weapon, and, more important, its failure to devise a credible substitute for the strike have left the movement bereft in a sea of self-analysis, self-criticism, and lethargy. Particularly ominous is the fact that just 9 percent of 18–24 year olds were in unions in the United States compared with 35 percent of 18–24 year olds in other countries. The reason for this is that in the 1970s and 1980s U.S. unions failed to organize new workplaces where young people are more likely to be employed.[8]

	1981	1982	1983	1984	1985	1986	1987	1988	1989	1990
United States[a]	—	—	—	—	—	—	—	—	—	—
United States[b]	—	—	19	18	17	17	17	16	16	16
Canada	35	38	37	37	36	36	35	35	35	36
Australia[a]	47	47	47	47	47	46	45	44	44	43
Australia[b]	—	40	—	—	—	37	—	34	—	34
Japan	31	31	30	29	29	28	28	27	26	25
Denmark	91	94	96	93	92	89	91	88	90	88
France	19	18	18	17	17	—	—	—	11	—
Germany	40	40	40	40	40	40	40	39	39	—
Italy[e]	62	62	62	63	61	61	63	65	—	—
Netherlands	39	39	38	36	34	34	33	33	33	28
Sweden	89	91	92	93	95	96	97	96	95	—
Switzerland	35	35	35	35	32	32	32	31	31	31
United Kingdom	55	54	53	52	51	49	49	46	—	—

members, while other unions covered various other members—unemployed, retired, and honorary members, as well as members whose dues were in arrears. Beginning in 1985, data are for June 30 and include all persons regarded as members by unions.

d. Data derived from household surveys include only employed union members and exclude persons aged seventy years and over. For 1976 data are for February; for 1982 data are for March–May; and for 1986, 1988, and 1990 data are for August.

e. Data exclude independent unions, which in the late 1980s represented an estimated four million members (including pensioners and self-employed and unemployed members).

The trade union movement now represents only approximately 16 percent of the eligible work force (see tables 2.1 and 2.2). True, some unions have enjoyed considerable membership growth. For instance, the Service Employees Union has acquired 119,000 members just over the past two years for a 881,000 total membership.[9] The American Federation of State County Municipal Employees Union (AFSCME) has moved up to 1.19 million members, having organized 101,000 workers over the same period of time. The American Federation of Teachers, dwarfed by the far larger unaffiliated National Education Association (it boasts nearly two million members), has organized 29,000 more workers.

But the heart of the trade union batting order for the past half century has suffered a precipitous decline. For instance, the United

Table 2.2
Total paid membership of the AFL-CIO for 1955 and subsequent two-year periods

Period	Membership	Period	Membership
1955	12,622	1975	14,070
1957	13,020	1977	13,542
1959	12,779	1979	13,621
1961	12,553	1981	13,602
1963	12,496	1983	13,758
1965	12,919	1985	13,109
1967	13,781	1987	12,702
1969	13,005	1989	13,556
1971	13,177	1991[a]	13,933
1973	13,407		

a. The 1991 figures are based on the two-year period ending June 30, 1991 (in thousands of members). Eighteen affiliated organizations paid a reduced monthly per capita tax on 270,200 additional association members during the two-year period ending June 30, 1991.

Auto Workers, once with well over one million members, now has 840,000. The worst is yet to come for this union because of its failure to organize even one of the approximately 300 Japanese-owned auto supplier firms now located in the United States.

Similarly the Amalgamated Clothing and Textile Workers Union, once headed by Sidney Hillman[10] (of whom President Franklin Roosevelt said during the debate about Harry Truman's nomination as vice president at the 1944 convention, "clear it with Sidney"), has declined to 154,000 from more than three times that number because many of its jobs have been shifted to the Third World. The United Steelworkers of America, seventeen years ago with a membership in excess of one million, has had its ranks cut in half. Even the mighty International Brotherhood of Teamsters, within the past decade reaffiliated with the AFL-CIO after a period of corruption-related ostracism and exclusion, has lost membership.

A decade and a half ago, Peter Drucker predicted that ". . . by 1990 union membership in the private sector will be back to where it was before the tremendous unionization wave of the 1930's or around 1/8 of the work force and in old and stagnate industries."[11] In 1991 John Sweeney, president of the Service Employees International Union, said: "We face the prospect that in 10 short years, we will represent only 5% of the private-sector work force."[12] In the early 1990s private sector membership in unions is threatening to move into single-digit territory.

No other industrialized countries, except France and Spain (which is after all just emerging from isolation), have a smaller trade union presence. Other countries, however, have seen their trade union movement decline, Japan and the Netherlands being two of the most prominent examples in the past decade. (Japan went from 32 to 25 percent and the Netherlands from 42 to 28 percent.) Moreover Britain, after an increase in membership beyond 50 percent in the friendly 1970s dominated by Labor governments, has dropped to approximately 46 percent. The rebound of the German trade union movement—it now represents 39 percent of the work force—and the pronounced increase in membership in Sweden and Denmark (to 95 and 88 percent, respectively) compels one to examine the peculiarities of the American circumstance—though the retreat of labor is surely an international phenomenon, extending even to much-cited Canada (discussed in chapter 7).

A Look Back at Previous Ebbs and Flows

First the modern labor movement must be placed in perspective. Although the unions have declined, this is hardly the first time that it has happened. From 1897 to 1914 the labor movement was in a steady period of growth, recruiting approximately 125,000 members a year. By 1914, as Leo Wolman has noted, the unions had achieved a level that ". . . bore the earmarks of solid and permanent development,"[13] demonstrating strength in coal mining, building, and railroads in particular, with the rapid development of craft unions in manufacturing. "The peak in the rise of union membership was reached in the postwar inflation of 1920 . . . ."[14] But a persistent decline began in the recession of 1921, which was interrupted only slightly in 1927 and ended in 1933. The decline during this period was from roughly five million to a little less than three million workers. Indeed in 1933 the unions were only able to show 3,622,000 members.

It was this period, with twelve years of uninterrupted Republican administrations (from 1921 to 1933), that most closely resembles the situation of the 1980s and early 1990s. As Rees has said:

From 1923 to 1929 the economy experienced a fortunate combination of prosperity and stable prices. The unions, however, failed to benefit from these conditions. Instead of growing as in earlier prosperous periods, they gradually lost strength. In some cases the losses resulted from mistakes by the unions themselves. For example, the United Mine Workers which had won a very high wage scale in the northern bituminous coal industry, lost strength as production shifted rapidly to the non-union fields of the South. In most cases, however, employer policy was more important in the 1920's than union policy.[15]

Irving Bernstein, speaking of the 1920s, has referred to the "paralysis of the labor movement." In the twenties, as in the eighties and early nineties, "uneven prosperity" had a disparate impact upon the well-being of trade unionism. But a fundamental difference between the two eras is that real wages remained stable in the twenties but have declined in the last decade.[16] Bernstein notes that the business cycle "neutralized the prospect for union growth" in that the ". . . cost of living remains stable" and "real wages rose somewhat [and therefore] . . . tended to divert workers' interest from unionization."[17]

As Bernstein said, "great segments of American industry were either totally devoid of unionization or showed only a trace."[18] And so it is today. Indeed the unions have made no effort to reach most of the Silicon Valley firms in California because no union, within or without the AFL-CIO, seems to have the staff, understanding, and knowledge to mount such an effort.[19] The theory that trade union membership expanded in good times and contracted in bad ran up against contrary facts. Expansion, albeit in uneven prosperity, has been a phenomenon of the twenties, the eighties, and the early nineties.[20] In the Reagan-Bush-Thatcher 1980s, union manufacturing and transportation jobs were edged out by service jobs as a matter of economic policy,[21] which, for instance, deprived manufacturing of adequate training.[22]

According to Bernstein, the heterogeneity of the work force was its consequent division—the labor movement being composed ". . . predominantly of older white stocks, skilled workmen in the manual trades and males" possessed "little appeal" to the new prewar wave of immigrants from southern and eastern Europe, as well as displaced farmers and blacks migrating to the cities from the south.[23] Today much of the new work force consists of women and recent immigrants from Asia and Central and South America. For the most part illegal or undocumented workers, paid the minimum wage or less, are beyond the reach of trade unions.

The composition of unions was also a factor in the decline in unionism. In the twenties craft unions became "structurally obsolete." The craft unions refused to organize the semiskilled and unskilled workers in mass production, characterizing them as unorganizable, or not suitable, for recruitment. It took the rise of a new federation, the Congress of Industrial Organizations, to perform the task during the Great Depression that the American Federation of Labor had been previously unwilling or unable to do.

A similar transformation may have to take place within the trade union movement before the new work force can be unionized. As we note in chapter 3, there really is not an appropriate union to organize workers in Silicon Valley and in some of the other unorganized arenas. Another illustration of the problem is the illegal immigrant workers. In southern California the AFL-CIO has funded organizations such as the California Immigrant Workers Association (CIWA) and Labor Immigrant Assistance Project (LIAP), and the International Ladies Garment Workers Union has been very active in attempting to reach immigrant workers. Yet a more considerable effort will be needed to make a dent in the swelling sector of unorganized workers.

There are two other labor problems of the twenties described by Bernstein that still loom large in the employment relationship today. The first is the phenomenon of welfare capitalism, and the use of the company union through which employers attempted to dominate unions and squash any movement toward an authentic arm's-length relationship with an independent organization. While in the eighties and nineties, there has been no proliferation of company unions, employee committees in nonunion establishments there have been aplenty.

The National Labor Relations Act, which contains unfair labor practice prohibitions applicable to both employers and labor organizations, seems to have fairly well dealt with the problem of company unions. Employers no longer attempt to "expropriate" the collective bargaining process and limit a company union to one firm. Although unions limited to one firm, and thus company unions in that sense of the word, continue to exist in such corporations as Proctor & Gamble. In contrast, representation plans, sponsored by companies fostering company unions, were the order of the day sixty to seventy years ago.

The company union may exist in a slightly altered modern form, however. Today union leaders are frequently heard advocates of cooperative initiatives—though frequently rebuffed by nonunion employers threatened by union organizational efforts. The most determined drive for cooperative efforts has come from quality of work life programs in the nonunion sector, particularly in large unionized firms like the GM-Saturn division, New United Motors Manufacturing, Inc. (the General Motors-Toyota joint venture in Fremont, California), and Mazda.

Whatever the merits of the company union issue, a related fundamental problem in American industrial relations is a "me-and-them" environment in which both parties adopt a self-defeating blinkered and limited vision of their relationship. This is well-illustrated by the Bluestones when they state that both labor and management have frequently adopted the view that "if it's good for the other side, it must be bad for us."[24] Whatever the legacy of the past in this regard, my sense is that, on balance, the cooperative initiatives are positive and helpful.

The second alleged similarity lies in the law itself. A series of Supreme Court decisions in which Chief Justice William Howard Taft set an antilabor, liberty of contract tone, said yellow-dog contracts were enforceable; federal and state legislation prohibiting them were characterized as unconstitutional restraints upon both personal liberty and private property.[25] In the landmark Supreme Court decision of *Duplex Printing Press Company v. Deering*,[26] the secondary boycott—stoppages, picketing, and boycotts of employers who had business relationships with the "primary" employer with whom the union had a dispute—engaged in for the purpose of organizing the employees of the primary employer, was held to be in violation of both the Sherman and Clayton Antitrust Acts and therefore the object of a remedy that became more important for employers in the twenties—the labor injunction.

In *Truax v. Corrigan*[27] the Court struck down a statute that prohibited an injunction of peaceful picketing as inconsistent with both due process and equal protection under the Fourteenth Amendment. In essence the idea of trade unionism, while theoretically lawful, was under attack in all its forms of activity. Here also there are some threads to modern times that mirror the pattern of the twenties.

A decade ago I testified before a congressional committee about the failure of American labor law to redeem its promise of protecting workers against conduct that is designed to discriminate against union members, discourage union activity, and to erode the collective bargaining process.[28] Four prominent illustrations of reversals or modifications of existing authority that have tilted the balance of power against labor were set forth in my testimony, as well as in that of others.[29]

Most of the harm to the collective bargaining process was done between 1983 and 1986. In one area the Board reversed its previous position, once a majority of Reagan appointees were on the agency, and interpreted the statute narrowly so as to preclude a bargaining order for a union as exclusive representative even where employer tactics were said to have deprived the union of majority status. This made it impossible for unions to compete effectively in Board-conducted representation proceedings designed to determine whether a union has represented a majority of the workers. The debate here stems from the Warren Court's decision in *NLRB v. Gissel*[30] where the Court held that a finding of unfair labor practice violations—dismissals of union members, surveillance of union activity engaged in by employees, various forms of intimidation, and the like, against union members—could be the basis for imposing a bargaining obligation upon an employer without the traditional representation proceeding and secret ballot-box election. In *Gissel* the union had obtained majority status from authorization cards signed by workers. In the cases adjudicated by the Reagan Board, the unions involved had been unable to acquire majority status because of the employer's egregious unfair labor practices.

A second area of concern is the Supreme Court and Labor Board's genuflection to management prerogatives. Bargaining about decisions to institute plant closures and massive layoffs that eliminate jobs is deemed to be beyond the bargaining process.[31] The irony here is that in the 1970s and 1980s throughout basic manufacturing in the United States employers have sought to obtain wage and work rule concessions from unions and that part of the quid pro quo has been a modification or relinquishment of management prerogatives in the collective bargaining process. In the automobile industry, for instance, the parties bargain and negotiate without reference to the demarcation lines between bargaining about mandatory subject matter about which they are obliged to negotiate—such as wages, fringe benefits, seniority, and vacations—and nonmandatory subject matter which labor and management are not required to address through bargaining. Although the law restricts the roles of the parties at the bargaining table in these vital areas, the subject of plant closures and layoffs, as well as investment and design decisions, can be addressed—as at the GM-Saturn division in Tennessee, where the collective bargaining process has spawned committees that deal with these issues. Nonetheless, the Supreme Court ruled in 1981 that plant closures that have a "direct impact on employment, since jobs [are] inexorably eliminated by the termination" were a management prerogative set "wholly apart from the employment relationship." If industry is to move toward a more democratic structure, inevitably all decisions—including, as at Saturn, those involving investment—will have to be discussed.

Another example of the pro-employer and antiunion approach to job security is the Court's decision in *NLRB v. Bildisco & Bildisco*[32] where a 5–4 majority, over Justice Brennan's strong dissent, concluded that a collective bargaining agreement cannot be enforced against an employer that has petitioned for bankruptcy. Justice Brennan noted in dissent that there is no provision in the bankruptcy code for an employer to terminate its collective bargaining agreement, and indeed the National Labor Relations Act obligates an employer not to terminate or modify the agreement. The Court in *Bildisco* ignored both the policy of autonomous self-regulation through collective bargaining and the explicit language of the statutes. As in the plant closure cases, job security of workers represented by unions is at issue. Here also it was subordinated to other considerations by the Court, though eventually that decision was partially reversed by Congress.[33]

The fourth illustration of a parallel between the 1920s, the 1980s, and the 1990s is Labor Board and Supreme Court decisions that declare that the employee has a right to resign union membership under the National Labor Relations Act.[34] Neither the Board nor the Court took into account the unions' solidaristic interest in utilizing the strike weapon. The absolute right to resign made it impossible to resolve differences with the employer and the right of employees engaged in concerted activities under the Act to pressure the employer to modify its position. Granted, union members should have the right to walk out of the union under a statute that protects the right to refrain from union activity—but as with all things in life, at an appropriate time and in appropriate circumstances.[35]

It is certainly true that the Board, particularly under the leadership of Chairman Donald Dotson between 1983 and 1986, was preoccupied with a mission to reverse a series of decisions that might promote the collective bargaining process. The appointments made to the Labor Board were one-sided and promanagement—often consisting of management labor lawyers (union lawyers have not been selected for the Board by Democratic administrations)—and this made the Board's appointment process an unusually significant part of the labor movement's political agenda. Of course Board policy changes with each new administration, which generally makes the appointments for a five-year term. However, criticism of the Board in the Reagan administration far exceeded anything that the unions had generated at the time of the so-called "Eisenhower Board," or that employers had argued at the time of the Kennedy and Johnson Boards which tended to favor unions.[36]

Thus the unions looked to the law as the primary basis for their decline. Indeed, in an unusually self-analytical study, *The Changing Situation of Workers and Their Unions,* published by the AFL-CIO in 1985, one of the first problems mentioned was the "failure of the law." But the facts are slightly more complicated and require us to look beyond the law for an explanation for union decline.

After all, since 1986 the Board has handed down a number of decisions that may facilitate trade union growth. For instance, the Board in the *Deklewa*[37] decision has issued a series of rules that have promoted recognition of construction unions by contractors. (The Supreme Court has further facilitated construction industry recognition agreements by holding that the National Labor Relations Act does not preempt state enforcement of a collective agreement when the state acts as owner of a construction project.[38]) The Court in *American Hospital Association v. NLRB*[39] approved a Board rule that establishes eight bargaining units in the health care industry and thus eliminates the delay inherent in case-by-case litigation of the appropriate unit or grouping of employees issue. Moreover the Court in an opinion that is far-reaching has held that secondary handbilling by unions is an appropriate organizational weapon, notwithstanding the secondary boycott prohibitions contained in the Taft-Hartley amendments.[40] This decision has made it easier for unions, unable to wage effective strikes or other forms of economic pressure, to publicize their corporate campaigns so as to attract community support in labor-management conflict.

In 1988 the unanimous Board in the landmark *Jean Country*[41] decision, protected union access to organize employees or publicize labor disputes on company property against the employer's property interest and held that access will be provided where there are no reasonable means of communicating with the audience elsewhere. The Board held that in assessing reasonable alternatives, the union would not have to actually try them all. Said the Board: "We note however that, in general, it will be the exceptional case where the use of newspapers, radio, and television will be feasible alternatives to direct contact." In an era of shopping-center malls, the Board commented that "denial of access will more likely be found unlawful when property is open to the general public than when a more private character has been maintained."

But the impact of *Jean Country* was substantially eviscerated by the Supreme Court in *Lechmere v. NLRB*[42] where the Court, in Justice Clarence Thomas' first authored opinion, held that the rule exceeded the protections afforded the workers under the National Labor Relations Act. The Court, by a 5–3 vote, held that there is a strong presumption against access to private property for nonemployee union organizers. Nonetheless, in states like California where protection is given to picketing and leafletting on private property in shopping malls,[43] handbilling and picketing of corporate campaigns has been available to the unions.

Penultimately the Board, though it has been sometimes unsuccessful in obtaining judicial enforcement,[44] held that a full-time union official is an employee who has protection under the Act even though he or she sought employment only for the purpose of organizing employees. The recent record of "testers" (they apply for jobs with employers to determine whether the firm's response will be different to comparable black and white applicants) in connection with employment discrimination litigation makes it clear that the role of such individuals is important to effective enforcement of the statute. Enforcement of labor law and antidiscrimination law is promoted through the use of sophisticated full-time representatives of unions or civil rights organizations, whose purpose in the employment relationship involves more than assuming the role of applicant or employee.

Finally, the Board, notwithstanding the strong presumption to management prerogatives that the Court in *First National Maintenance* has provided in plant closing and partial plant closing involving job security, has articulated a more balanced approach in plant relocation cases. Said the Board in *Dubuque Packing Co., Inc.*:[45]

. . . we announced the following test for determining whether the employer's decision is a mandatory subject of bargaining. Initially, the burden is on the General Counsel to establish that the employer's decision involved a relocation of unit work unaccompanied by a basic change in the nature of the employer's operation. If the General Counsel successfully carries his burden in this regard, he will have established *prima facie* that the employer's relocation decision is a mandatory subject of bargaining. At this juncture, the employer may produce evidence rebutting the *prima facie* case by establishing that the work performed at the new location varies significantly from the work performed at the former plant, establishing that the work performed at the former plant is to be discontinued entirely and not moved to the new location, or establishing that the employer's decision involves a change in the scope and direction of the enterprise. Alternatively, the employer may proffer a defense to show that by a preponderance of the evidence: (1) that labor costs (direct and/or indirect) were not a factor in the decision or (2) that even if labor costs were a factor in the decision, the union could not have offered labor cost concessions that could have changed the employer's decision to relocate.[46]

The significance of *Dubuque* remains to be seen. If unions are obliged to offer labor cost concessions comparable to the wages enjoyed by Mexican workers, for instance, where a company plans to relocate to that country, the bargaining process will be meaningless. On the other hand, it may be that concessions in other areas coupled with ideas about business decisions—perhaps unrelated to labor costs themselves—can provide the basis for genuine dialogue.

It may nonetheless be said that the Supreme Court's view of labor law is more pro-employer and anticollective bargaining than that of the Board—even the Board of the Reagan-Bush era. It is quite possible, for instance, that this Rehnquist Court will reverse the expert administrative agency in cases involving plant relocation disputes, just as it did in cases involving nonemployee organizer assistance to union organizational campaigns in *Lechmere*.

The Supreme Court, on which President Richard Nixon's appointee, Warren Burger, was chief justice, fashioned opinions promoting management prerogatives and the right of workers to resign from unions. The Court also restrained secondary picketing, notwithstanding some of the precedents established by the Warren Court. These decisions were long before the new conservative Rehnquist Court.

As I have written elsewhere, if it is a beat that the Courts presided over by both Chief Justices Burger and Rehnquist respond to, it is a "beat that goes on—*marcato*." Even the Warren Court,[47] which has been viewed as "liberal" in the areas of racial discrimination and due process for criminal defendants, has not been particularly prounion or procollective bargaining. A comparable point cannot be made about the Taft Court which was the ultimate arbiter of labor disputes (without the intervention of any Labor Board) in the period of earlier decline, the 1920s. The Taft Court's decisions are not doctrinal descendants of previous authority, as in both the Burger and Rehnquist Courts.

The third significant change or development—one that is hardly unrelated to the decline of unions—is the emergence of a variety of new relationships between employer and employee. Nontraditional employment—part-time, temporary, contract, and other kinds of flexible work arrangements—constituted 24 percent of the work force in

1988. The Bureau of Labor statistics has estimated that this work force will increase by 18 million by the year 2000 and that part-time employment will increase most dramatically in the service sector, which has been an area of difficulty for union organizational activity. In 1988 part-time workers made up 36 percent of workers in service occupations.[48]

Illegal aliens, who reportedly number between one and twelve million employees in the work force and whom the Supreme Court has declared to be within the coverage of the National Labor Relations Act,[49] do not appear to possess the will to protest, and their numbers continue to increase substantially.[50] These factors mean that the work force will possess a greater percentage of more vulnerable workers who have fewer protections, health and pension benefits in particular, as well as lower incomes. For instance, in 1988, 29 percent of part-time workers who were single parents lacked medical insurance coverage from any source, and another 29 percent relied upon the Medicaid program. Only about 10 percent of part-time workers had pension coverage, and even where employers provide pension plans, the Employee Retirement Income Security Act of 1974 obliges pension coverage only for employees who have worked 1,000 hours or more in a year.[51] More than half of part-time workers worked fewer hours in 1988. Moreover, although most of the increase in involuntary part-timers happened in the 1970s, in the first part of 1991 there were one million more part-time workers than in 1990. Much of the growth in involuntary part-timers took place in retail businesses.[52] Complicating their plight is the fact that, according to the General Accounting Office, thirty-three states deny unemployment compensation benefits to part-time workers unless their earnings exceed $2,000 a year and 21 percent of part-time employees are below the poverty line, compared to 5 percent of families headed by full-time workers.

Some unions, particularly in Los Angeles, are now trying to reach workers by employing bilingual organizers.[53] Yet quite frequently the union's staff does not include individuals who speak the language of the workers who are being recruited as new members. Indeed labor has provoked rank-and-file litigation against labor organizations by refusing to provide Spanish language translation and internal union meetings for Spanish-speaking members.[54]

The unions and potential members are not always a good match in terms of structure. As noted earlier, there is no union truly suited to recruit workers in the Silicon Valley. Arguably the International Brotherhood of Electrical Workers emerges as the union with the appropriate charter from the AFL-CIO, but it is a craft union with a principal focus upon the construction industry and, to a lesser extent, craft occupations in manufacturing and public utilities. In the higher echelon, managerial employees are completely beyond the reach of unions, a fault attributable to the law through its exclusion of managers and supervisors.[55] Very few of the Silicon Valley employers are organized, and almost as few have been the object of organizational campaigns.

Thus structural problems and the lethargy that flows from them have meant that an insufficient number of union organizers are in the field recruiting new members. Paula B. Voos has written extensively about the long-range decline in the supply of union-organizing services to nonunion workers and dues expended for such purposes.[56] Indeed, though the Supreme Court's important *American Hospitals Association* decision, discussed above, has facilitated trade union organization in the hospitals, the growth rate of union membership in the industry has been much less than was anticipated.[57] One reason for union decline is the inactivity of the labor movement.

The fourth major development relates to discrimination in the workplace, a persistent phenomenon. The contemporary manifestation of racial discrimination was dramatized by the debate between President Bush and the Democratic Congress over the quota issue that preceded enactment of the Civil Rights Act of 1991. The United States was the first of any major industrialized country to enact comprehensive legislation prohibiting discrimination on the account of race, sex, religion, and national origin in the workplace by employers or unions under title VII of the Civil Rights Act of 1964. A year before its enactment, the Equal Pay Act of 1963 prohibited pay discrimination on the basis of sex, where equal work was being performed, or more precisely work that was substantially equal.

The fact is that this legislation is the product of another generation. Three Republican presidents, Nixon, Reagan, and Bush, have all run successfully for the White House on the race issue, feeding off the politics of resentment against blacks in particular—those who are perceived to have benefited excessively from the new legal framework.[58] In 1989 the Supreme Court handed down a series of rulings that emasculated central portions of the law against employment discrimination,[59] thus providing judicial validation for the politics of race, and a repudiation of President Lyndon Johnson's Great Society. The stalwart resistance of politicians, much more than business managers, to reforms that would mostly reinstate the law as it was is vivid testimony for this proposition. President Bush's obsession with the quota issue, and his characterization of legislation designed to strengthen the law against employment discrimination as a measure that would impose "quotas," dramatizes the political profit and high stakes to be gained in this area.

The race issue—as well as sexual harassment case law,[60] the thus far unaccepted comparable worth theory (unaccepted in the United States but not in Europe), and the ongoing emotionally charged debate about compensation for past wrongs—is an essential part of the workplace thirty years after the law first became a factor. The Americans with Disabilities Act (ADA), enacted in 1990, which obliges employers to accommodate themselves to handicapped applicants and employees, promises to promote a profound impact and ultimately considerable controversy.

Quotas of course are not mandated by any versions of the Civil Rights Act. One of the ironies here is that the Democratic party leadership made a calculated judgment in late 1989 to remain aloof from the entire affirmative action debate and to legislatively attack the Supreme Court decisions of 1989 that related to job bias issues distant from the affirmative action debate. Until the October 1991 Anita Hill–Clarence Thomas hearings, in which the sexual harassment issue was dramatized by allegations against the Supreme Court nominee, President Bush found it politically profitable to make it difficult for the Democrats to position themselves in this manner. Bush, who had opposed the Civil Rights Act of 1964 as well, would not allow the Democrats to reverse the 1989 decisions through legislation by a skillful use of the argument that the Democrats were really supporting quotas.

In contrast to the quota rhetoric, a real issue in the Civil Rights Act debate relates to damages. In the final compromise between the White House and Congress agreed upon in October 1991, a graduated series of "caps" dependent upon the number of employees employed by the particular employer was instituted. That is to say, the larger employers, with more than 500 employees, can be liable in the instance of intentional and willful discrimination for punitive and compensatory damages not to exceed $300,000. The cap for smaller employers decreases depending upon their size.[61] (This issue is spelled out in more detail in chapter 9.)

Employment Discrimination and Wrongful Discharge Litigation

In a sense the debate about the provisions of the fair employment practices laws mirrored the war of words that has occurred over the past decade regarding multimillion dollar punitive and compensatory damage awards in wrongful discharge actions. A disproportionate percentage of these cases are tried in state court before juries. An integral part of both title VII and wrongful discharge policy debates is the presence of the trial lawyers' bar and the prevalence of contingency fee arrangements through which lawyers recover, if they are successful, 30 to 40 percent and sometimes more of the total award.

Monetary relief clearly is an essential element of reform. Damages awards in both employment discrimination and wrongful discharge actions can sting effectively. But from a policy perspective there are differences between the merits of their availability in employment discrimination as opposed to wrongful discharge cases.

In the first place there are institutional, state-sponsored investigation and conciliation procedures in the employment discrimination arena. Namely, there is the potential for resolving disputes about what constitutes discrimination, factually and legally, before the matter gets to the courts, available under the auspices of the Equal Employment Opportunity Commission at the federal level and its state counterparts. In the one state that has enacted wrongful discharge legislation—as we see in chapter 4 most of the debate takes place today within the context of common-law actions—there has been no provision for an administrative agency like that established by title VII. Unless proponents of social legislation are successful in amending the National Labor Relations Act and making it an unfair labor practice at a federal level to unfairly dismiss workers (a fairly remote possibility at this writing), it is unlikely that any state will have an incentive to create a comparable administrative apparatus in the wrongful discharge arena. Accordingly in employment discrimination cases (and *not* in the wrongful discharge area) a forum exists in which conciliation without the likelihood of substantial punitive damages may be exhausted before judicial combat. True, there is a potential for frivolous litigation fueled by the contingency fee arrangements made by plaintiff's lawyers in both situations, but it seems to me that the availability of conciliation machinery helps argue for monetary damages beyond back pay, given both the opportunity for resolution as well as the delay involved in remedying meritorious cases.

But more than institutional differences are involved in justifying monetary damages in employment discrimination cases. Discrimination, particularly race discrimination, is different from garden variety wrongful discharge actions because of the stigmatization that is frequently associated with it. It is easier to credit testimony relating to emotional distress in race and sex cases than it is in wrongful discharge cases generally, although the potential for emotional harm where *any* job loss is involved, a point developed in chapter 3, cannot be gainsaid.

Indeed an equally important and related development is the rising sense or consciousness of fairness among workers—namely the view that workers ought not to be treated in an arbitrary manner and dismissed when they have done a proper job unless economic circumstances dictate such a result. In a sense this attitude has its roots in a number of institutions that have been accepted in this country for some time, notably the grievance-arbitration machinery which is negotiated in collective bargaining agreements and provides for review of the propriety of a worker's dismissal by a third-party neutral. Out of this has developed an arbitral common law that established substantive protections for employees, absent contract language in the collective agreement to the contrary. Employers have been obliged to follow principles of progressive discipline that require counseling and suspensions before discharge, as well as procedural due-process-type guarantees such as the right to be notified of the reason for the dismissal and the right to confront one's accuser. The latter has become part of an evolving constitutional law, fashioned by the U.S. Supreme Court, which declared that public sector employees possess a kind of property interest in employment as well as basic or minimal due process guarantees.[62]

The evolution of civil rights legislation in the early 1960s, in particular title VII of the Civil Rights Act of 1964, was closely related to these concepts of due processes and job protection. The landmark ruling in this respect was the unanimous decision of *Griggs v. Duke Power Co.*[63] in which the Court held that neutral practices such as written examinations and educational qualifications that disproportionately exclude minorities—later the Court was to include women[64]—violated employment discrimination law, even though there was no finding of an intent to discriminate. Subsequently, in 1989, the Court was to emasculate this holding,[65] prompting Congress to pass the Civil Rights Act of 1991, designed to restore *Griggs* to its original state, an effort that was first vetoed by President Bush in 1990 but ultimately acceded to in 1991.

These developments are frequently discussed under the rubric of individual rights or the individual in the employment relationship. Yet the collective relationship (upon which many of these developments have a direct bearing) and what is now regarded as traditional labor law, which emerged during the Great Depression, are hardly unimportant. History has shown us that unions, notwithstanding the severity of their current plight, are a part of any society with democratic institutions, and this ebb too will ultimately pass. The National Labor Relations Act of 1935, notwithstanding the Taft-Hartley amendments of 1947 which addressed purported union abuses and placed consequent restrictions upon organized labor, proclaims its support for collective bargaining. The preamble to the statute observes that "without full freedom of association or *actual* liberty of contract" employers would attempt to depress competitive wage rates and working conditions, producing conflict which would disrupt commerce. Support for collective bargaining remains public policy in the 1990s—and properly so.

Public Policy for Collective Bargaining

Considerably more than a half-century away from the enactment of the NLRA and its Bill of Rights for workers,[66] which still provides a central framework for modern labor law, it is permissible to decline complete acceptance of the statute's rationale for collective bargaining and yet to subscribe to the process itself. Indeed collective bargaining is the best model through which to address the modern employment relationship. It does not mean that the law should not be concerned with nonunion enterprises. To the contrary, the law must concern itself, if only because the work environment is a growing one, with enveloping almost 90 percent of the work force.

Nor does a preference for collective bargaining mean that public policy should proceed upon the assumption that unions do not engage in misdeeds and abuses. They do. The undemocratic and corrupt conduct of some union officials, notably the national leadership of the International Brotherhood of Teamsters for the past forty years, makes it clear that the labor movement is not without sin. Their sometimes tardy adherence to civil rights laws—a matter that I have addressed earlier[67]—is further evidence. Indeed a vibrant and well-populated trade union movement—a phenomenon not present in the United States today—can pose difficulties for economic policy designed to suppress inflation and the need of any society for vital supplies. The close relationship between the trade union movement (LO) and the Social Democratic party in Sweden facilitates the resolution of problems in the former arena in that country. Taft-Hartley's provision for an eighty-day injunction in national emergency strikes and lockouts—this prompted the statute's critics to speak of the entire law as the "slave labor act"—are aimed at the latter issue, though it may not be the best vehicle through which they should be addressed.

Although I view the emphasis that collective bargaining places upon spontaneity and self-determination as two of its most formidable justifications, I do not hold the position that wide-open, unbridled collective bargaining is always the best approach to the employment relationship. For a number of reasons the ideas presented here in this chapter and throughout this book frequently mean more state intervention or regulation than is presently mandated, and sometimes less. But my own judgment is that collective bargaining, operating within an appropriate framework, is better than the alternative, to paraphrase Winston Churchill in his comments about democracy.

The first is that democratic values are important in the workplace, and collective bargaining is an effective manner through which they can be realized. Real participation in industrial society is critical to a democratic society. Regrettably in the United States the concept of economic democracy has lagged considerably behind political democracy.

Second, employees, both skilled and unskilled, sometimes professional and managerial, are often in a position to do collectively what they cannot do individually. As Otto Kahn-Freund has said:

Typically, the worker as an individual has to accept the conditions which the employer offers. On the labour side, power is collective power. The individual employer represents an accumulation of material and human resources, socially speaking the enterprise is itself in this sense "collective power." If a collection of workers (whether it bears a name of a trade union or some other name) negotiate with an employer, this is thus a negotiation between collective entities, both of which are, or may at least be, bearers of power. But the relation between an employer and an isolated employee or worker is typically a relation between a bearer of power and one who is not a bearer of power. In its inception it is an act of submission, in its operation it is a condition of subordination, how much of the submission and the subordination may be concealed by that indispensable figment of the legal mind known as the "contract of employment."[68]

Employees, particularly those who have an investment in the firm acquired through seniority or tenure, will often be afraid to speak out in protest over the unfairness of working conditions when their view is a solitary one because of the fear of dismissal or some other sanction that could harm their standard of living. Even if free competition means that other employers stand ready to hire the dismissed worker away from the previous employment relationship, it is unlikely that seniority, implicit or explicit, will be transferred to the other firm or that something that can be translated into a comparable benefit will be obtained.[69] This is why unions have traditionally attempted to appeal to workers on the ground that a collective bargaining agreement can protect them against arbitrary dismissal, an argument that has been to some extent logically undercut by the development of wrongful dismissal law (discussed in chapter 4) and the host of layoffs instituted for economic reasons throughout most of basic manufacturing.

Unions in bargaining relationships with management have attempted to address such concerns through the grievance-arbitration machinery, through which a variety of employee complaints can be heard, as well as with seniority provisions, which serve as an objective basis for the allocation of jobs at the time of layoff and, less frequently and fully, promotion and transfer. In organized labor-management relationships, this is one of the principal examples of a voice through which workers are able to express their concerns to the employer without exiting from or leaving the firm altogether. Collective dealings rather than individual discussions with management are able to utilize voice effectively because much of the employment relationship involves so-called public goods that affect the well-being of all employees in a way that tempts them to utilize the benefits at no cost by relying upon their fellow workers to protest. State Freeman and Medoff:

Safety conditions, lighting, heating, the speed of the production line, the firm's formal grievance procedure, a pension plan, and policies on matters such as layoffs, work-sharing, cyclical wage adjustment, and promotion, all obviously affect the entire workforce in the same way that defense, sanitation, and fire protection affect the community at large. One of the most important economic theorems is that competitive markets will not provide enough of such goods; some form of collective decision making is needed. Without a collective organization, the incentive for the individual to take into account the effects of his or her actions on others, to express his or her preferences, or to invest time and money in changing conditions, is likely to be too small to spur action.[70]

Penultimately the existence of a strong and independent trade union movement has an important public policy function in a democratic system. Unions are able to promote not only labor legislation, which is designed to further their own interest and that of workers who wish to affiliate with the movement, but also initiatives in such arenas as unemployment compensation, social security, and workers' compensation—issues that improve as well the standards of the general working community which consists principally of nonunion employees. Nonunion employees have no minimum standards in any of these areas (except as imposed by law) and thus experience a relatively greater benefit than employees covered by and enjoying the benefits of collective bargaining agreements.

Unions have pushed for legislation in the area of domestic civil rights, such as the Civil Rights Acts of 1964 and 1991, the Voting Rights Act of 1965, and the various renewals of that statute. Again the beneficiary is society at large. True, the unions have a monopoly wage effect that has undesirable consequences for resource allocation. Wage and fringe benefit increases induce employers, particularly in capital-intensive industries, to engage in technological innovation. This forces the exit of workers into the nonunion sector, decreasing the wages and benefits paid there because of the consequent greater competition between the workers. Yet the available data indicates that the lower turnover attributable to the exit-voice role of the union outbalances the monopoly wage effects and costs of trade unionism.[71]

Finally, the absence of unions and collective bargaining means that the state, through legislation or common-law litigation, is more directly involved in fashioning employment conditions than the parties themselves. This seems to be one of the lessons to be derived from recent wrongful discharge litigation, health and safety and fringe benefit protections, and prevailing wage legislation and efforts at the state and local level to mandate industrial relations procedures through government contractor regulations.[72] As collective bargaining recedes, it leaves a vacuum that nature inevitably abhors. Direct state regulation, which is the substitute, is frequently inferior to the expertise that can be brought to bear on employment conditions by labor and management.

The arguments in favor of collective bargaining clearly outweigh the disadvantages. But there are a number of other developments besides those discussed earlier that may have consigned these arguments about trade unionism to near irrelevance. The first of course is the precipitous and rapid decline of the labor movement throughout most of the industrialized world. Unions have had difficulty even in the manufacturing work force—witness the defeat of the United Auto Workers at the Nissan plant in Tennessee in the summer of 1989.[73] Where the unions have been successful, the heavily unionized manufacturing and transportation sectors have taken an enormous hit during the past two decades, producing layoffs that have decimated the ranks of major industrial unions like the United Auto Workers, United Steelworkers, and the International Brotherhood of Teamsters (see table 2.3), foreign competition and deregulation being the main culprits. This has meant that the unions have lost their bastions of strength.

Contrarily, in countries such as Germany and Sweden, nonunion U.S. employers frequently presume that they will be unionized. The employer is pressured by virtue of the predominance of employer associations, tariffs, or agreements that include a large number of employers if it is not party to the association agreement.

While employer associations are not alien to American soil, they are the exception, and even the de facto industrywide arrangement in basic steel has recently dissolved and the national freight agreement has declined in importance. By the standards of Europe (which has had multiemployer regional bargaining on the Continent) and Japan (while decentralized in that trade union structure is on a companywide basis, it promotes national wage bargaining through *shunto*, the spring offensive), the United States has always been decentralized in its industrial relations. Plant bargaining has been the rule on this enormous and heterogeneous continent of North America. Indeed, to the extent that relatively sophisticated grievance-arbitration machinery is a central feature of the system, it provides the parties with procedures that are strong in the sense that they are tailored to the peculiarities of the relationship, both implicit and explicit.[74]

The absence of multiemployer associations or industrywide bargaining means that there is no structure or organization for new enterprises that exclude employers, as in Sweden or Germany, where American multinationals have thus far unsuccessfully attempted to retain their nonunion environment. In the United States there is no national or regional system (as in Germany and Japan) through which collective bargaining agreements can be applied to the nonunion sector. This phenomenon logically ought to pose difficulties for labor because "free riders" who get the benefits of the union agreement have no incentive

Table 2.3
AFL-CIO statistics on paid membership of union affiliates

Organizations	\multicolumn{8}{c}{Thousands of members}
	1955	1965	1975	1985	1987	1989	1991
Actors and Artists of America, Associated	34	61	76	100	95	97	99
Air Line Pilots Association	9	18	47	33	31	31	31
Aluminum, Brick and Glass Workers, International Union				49	45	44	42
Asbestos Workers, International Association of Heat and Front Insulators	9	12	13	12	12	12	12
Automobile, Aerospace and Agricultural Implement Workers of America, International Union, United	1,260	1,150	a	974	998	917	840
Bakery, Confectionary and Tobacco Workers International Union				115	109	103	101
Boilermakers, Iron Ship Builders, Blacksmiths, Forgers and Helpers, International Brotherhood of	131	108	123	110	90	75	66
Bricklayers and Allied Craftsman, International Union of	120	120	143	95	84	84	84
Broadcast Employee and Technicians, National Association of	4	4	5	5	5	5	5
Carpenters and Joiners of America, United Brotherhood of	750	700	700	609	609	613	494
Chemical Workers Union, International	79	70	58[b]	40	35	34	40
Clothing and Textile Workers Union, Amalgamated				228	195	180	154
Communications Workers of America	249	288	476	524	515	492	492
Coopers International Union of North America	3	2	2	1	1	1	1
Distillery, Wine and Allied Workers International Union, AFL-CIO/CLC				14	13	11	10
Electric, Electrical, Salaried, Machine and Furniture Workers AFL-CIO, International Union of					185	171	160
Electrical Workers, International Brotherhood of	460	616	856	791	765	744	730
Elevator Constructors, International Union of	10	12	13	20	21	22	22
Engineers, International Union of Operating	200	270	300	330	330	330	330

Table 2.3 (continued)

Organizations	Thousands of members						
	1955	1965	1975	1985	1987	1989	1991
Farm Workers of America, AFL-CIO, United			14	12	9	11	15
Fire Fighters, International Association of	72	87	123	142	142	142	151
Firemen and Oilers, International Brotherhood of	57	44	40	25	25	25	25
Flight Attendants, Association of				17[c]	20	21	24
Flight Engineers' International Association	1	1	2	1	1	1	1
Food and Commercial Workers International Union, United				989	1,000	999	997
Garment Workers of America, United	40	35	32	28	26	24	21
Garment Workers Union, International Ladies'	383	363	363	210	173	153	143
Glass, Molders, Pottery, Plastics and Allied Workers International Union				72	65	86	80
Glass Workers Union, American Flint	28	31	35	24	22	20	22
Government Employees, American Federation of	47	132	255	199	157	156	151
Grain Millers, American Federation of	33	25	29	30	28	28	27
Graphic Communications International Union				141	136	124	113
Horseshoers of United States and Canada, International Union of Journeymen	1	1	1	1	1	1	1
Hospital and Health Care Employees, National Union of				23[d]	60	58[d]	
Hotel Employees and Restaurant Employees International Union	300	300	421	327	293	278	269
Industrial Workers of America, International Union, Allied		71	93	63	61	60	53
Iron Workers, International Association of Bridge, Structural and Ornamental	133	132	160	140	122	111	101
Laborers' International Union of North America		403	475	383	371	406	406
Laundry and Dry Cleaning International Union, AFL-CIO		22	20	15	14	14	14
Leather Goods, Plastics and Novelty Workers Union, International	30	34	39	21	19	15	12

Table 2.3 (continued)

Organizations	\multicolumn{7}{c}{Thousands of members}
	1955	1965	1975	1985	1987	1989	1991
Leather Workers International Union of North America	2	5	2	1^e			
Letter Carriers, National Association of	100	130	151	186	200	201	210
Locomotive Engineers, Brotherhood of						3^f	20
Longshoremen's Association, AFL–CIO, International		50	60	65	64	62	60
Longshoremen's and Warehousemen's Union, International						16^g	45
Machinists and Aerospace Workers, International Association of	627	663	780	520	509	517	534
Maintenance of Way Employees, Brotherhood of	159	77	71	61	38	48^h	42
Marine and Shipbuilding Workers of America, Industrial Union of	27	22	22	17	12		
Marine Engineers' Beneficial Association, National	9	9	20	22	22	48^i	53
Maritime Union of America, National	37	45	35	17	18		
Mechanics Educational Society of America	49	37	23	5	4	4	3
Metal Polishers, Buffers Platers and Allied Workers International Workers	13	11	9	5	5	5	4
Mine Workers of America, United	67	50	50	32	32	^{j}	
Molders and Allied Workers Union, AFL–CIO, International							82^k
Musicians of the United States and Canada, American Federation of	250	225	215	67	60	54	51
Newspaper Guild, The	21	23	26	24	25	25	25
Novelty and Production Workers, International Union of Allied				23	23	23	23
Office and Professional Employees, International Union	44	52	74	90	86	84	89
Oil, Chemical and Atomic Workers International Union	160	140	145	108	96	71	90
Painters and Allied Trades of the United States and Canada, International Brotherhood of	182	160	160	133	128	128	124
Paperworkers International Union, United			275	232	221	210	202
Pattern Makers League of North America	11	10	10	8	8	7	7

Table 2.3 (continued)

Organizations	1955	1965	1975	1985	1987	1989	1991
Plasterers' and Cement Masons' International Association of the United States and Canada, Operative	60	68	55	46	43	39	39
Plate Printers, Die Stampers & Engravers Union of North America, International	1	1	1	1	1	1	1
Plumbing and Pipe Fitting Industry of the United States and Canada, United Association of Journeymen and Apprentices of the	200	217	228	226	220	220	220
Police Associations, International Union of				14	13	15	18
Postal Workers Union, AFL-CIO, American			249	232	230	213	228
Professional Athletes, Federation of				2	1	1	1
Professional and Technical Engineers, International Federation of			14	19	20	21	21
Radio Association, American	2	2	1	1	1	1	1
Retail, Wholesale and Department Store Union	97	114	118	106	140	137	128
Roofers, Waterproofers and Allied Workers, United Union of				26	25	23	21
Rubber, Cork, Linoleum and Plastic Workers of America, United	163	153	173	106	97	92	89
School Administrators, American Federation of			7	9	9	9	9
Seafarers International Union of North America	42	80	80	80	80	80	80
Service Employees International Union, AFL-CIO			480	688	762	762	881
Sheet Metal Workers International Association	50	100	120	108	108	108	108
Siderographers, International Association of	1	1	1	1	1	1	1
Signalmen, Brotherhood of Railroad	15	11	10	11	11	10	10
Stage Employees and Moving Picture Machine Operators of the United States and Canada, International Alliance of Theatrical	46	50	50	50	50	50	50
State, County and Municipal Employees, American Federation of	99	237	647	997	1,032	1,090	1,191

Table 2.3 (continued)

Organizations	Thousands of members						
	1955	1965	1975	1985	1987	1989	1991
Steel Workers of America, United	980	876	1,062	572	494	481	459
Stove, Furnace and Allied Appliance Workers International Union of North America	10	9	3	3	3	4	5
Teachers, American Federation of	40	97	396	470	499	544	573
Teamsters, Chauffeurs, Warehousemen and Helpers of America, International Brotherhood of						1,161[1]	1,379
Textile Workers of America, United	49	36	36	23	20	20	18
Tile, Marble, Terrazzo, Finishers, Shopworkers and Granite Cutters, International Union, AFL-CIO				7	8	m	
Train Dispatchers Association, American		3	3	3	3	2	2
Transit Union, Amalgamated		98	90	94	94	96	98
Transport Workers Union of America	80	80	95	85	85	85	85
Transportation Communications International Union					113	86	73
Transportation Union, United			134	88	n	n	64
Utility Workers Union of America	53	50	52	52	54	51	55
Woodworkers of America, International	91	49	52	34	26	23	21
Writers Guild of America, East, Inc.						o	3

Source: From AFL-CIO Executive Council report to nineteenth constitutional convention.
Note: The average per capita membership of current affiliates paid to the AFL-CIO for the year 1955, two-year periods ending in 1965, 1975, 1985, and subsequent conventions. The 1991 figures are based on the two-year period ending June 30, 1991.

a. Disaffiliated 7/1/68, Reaffiliated 7/1/81.
b. Chemical Workers charter revoked by convention 10/3/69, reinstated by Executive Council 5/12/71.
c. Flight Attendants charter granted 2/23/84.
d. Hospital and Health Care Employees charter granted 10/1/84. Merged into Service Employees International Union and American Federation of State, County and Municipal Employees on 6/1/89.
e. The membership figure shown is based on one month's per capita tax and this union was suspended in accordance with article xv, section 5, of the AFL-CIO Constitution.
f. Locomotive Engineers charter granted 4/1/89.
g. Longshoremen's and Warehousemen's Union charter granted 8/22/88.
h. Marine and Shipbuilding Workers of America merged with International Association of Machinists and Aerospace Workers 10/17/88.
i. Maritime Union of America, National, merged with National Marine Engineers' Beneficial Association on 3/29/88.
j. Mine Workers of America, United affiliated 10/1/89.
k. Molders and Allied Workers Union merged with Glass, Molders, Pottery, Plastics, and Allied Workers International Union 5/1/88.
l. Teamsters, Chauffeurs, Warehousemen and Helpers of America affiliated 11/1/87.
m. Tile, Marble, Terrazzo, Finishers, Shopworkers and Granite Cutters International Union merged with United Brotherhood of Carpenters and Joiners of America 11/10/88.
n. Transportation Union reaffiliated 8/1/89, date of disaffiliation 4/1/86.
o. Writers Guild of America, East, Inc. affiliated 8/19/89.

to join the labor organization that negotiated it. On the contrary, here each new enterprise or employer tests anew the worker's allegiance to trade unionism and the collective bargaining process through a secret ballot-box election conducted within an appropriate unit or grouping of workers among whom there is a community of interest.

There are many other contributing factors to labor's decline. Though federal labor law prohibits employer promises of benefits,[75] and threats, to dissuade workers from joining unions, the fact is that employers have been able to convince workers not to join union workers by providing them with benefits comparable in most respects (and sometimes superior to them) to those contained in collective bargaining agreements negotiated by unions. Thus, except for job security and provision for impartial arbitration, a kind of benevolent paternalism has helped to succeed in making workers disinterested in unions. By providing benefits, employers have been able to show workers that the payment of dues and initiation fees to the union would leave the now unorganized in an inferior economic position. This tactic has been a particularly formidable employer technique.[76]

But there are other factors as well. The strike is now almost obsolete in capital-intensive industries like telephone and oil refining. Indeed, although the employer tactic of permanent replacements, in response to the strike weapon, remains an important public-policy issue (see chapter 6), the fact is that a goodly number of the industries that were thought to contain emergency strike potential at the national and local level no longer meet that standard. Nationally bituminous coal has been pushed to one side by nonunion rivals—the United Mine Workers has had limited success with surface mining organizational activity in the West—as well as by competing energy products. The impotency of the strike is thus attributable to such considerations. Resort to the weapon itself has declined appreciably (see chapter 6).

President Reagan's dismissal of illegally striking air controllers in 1981 represents—some would say has promoted—a labor-management environment in which established relationships are more frayed and fragile and organizational efforts less effective. True, the stoppage itself was something of an aberration, poorly planned and initiated by a union that was isolated from the rest of the labor movement—a disability ironically exacerbated by the air controller's "against-the-labor-grain" support of Ronald Reagan's successful candidacy in 1980.

Why had employer opposition to union organizational campaigns—as evidenced through unfair labor practice litigation—increased during

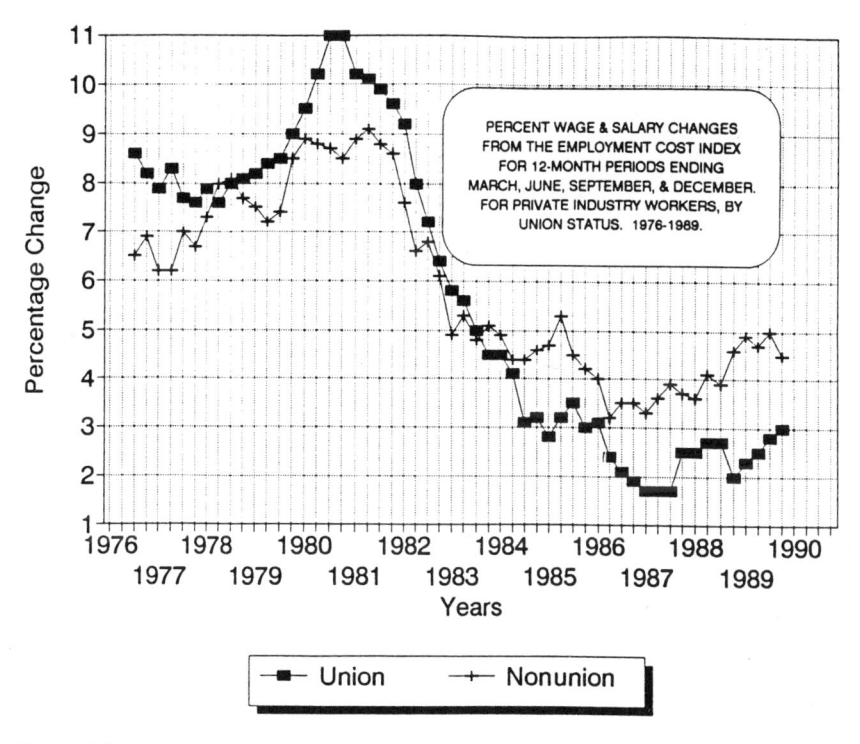

Figure 2.1

the decades of the 1970s and 1980s?[77] Although it has now declined, Robert Flanagan has seen the union-nonunion differential to be a major cause of employer resistance (see figures 2.1 and 2.2).[78]

In his important book, *Labor Relations and the Litigation Explosion*,[79] Flanagan makes the point that institutionally there is likely to be employer resistance to unionization in the United States because of the decentralized form in which bargaining takes place in this country. That is to say, the decentralized basis for collective bargaining in this country makes employers more competitive and thus less likely to be able to pass on costs that cannot be absorbed through productivity gains. Moreover American workers represented by unions have relatively high fringe benefits for their members, and this raises the competitive threat from the nonunion sector. Since many fringe benefits are established by law in Europe, the same dynamics do not apply there. Blancheflower and Freeman have subsequently maintained that trade union density lags in the United States, vis-à-vis Europe, because

Percentage Change In Compensation (wages, salaries & employer costs for employer benefits) From the Employment Cost Index for 12 Month Periods. 1980 - 1989

— Union   + Nonunion

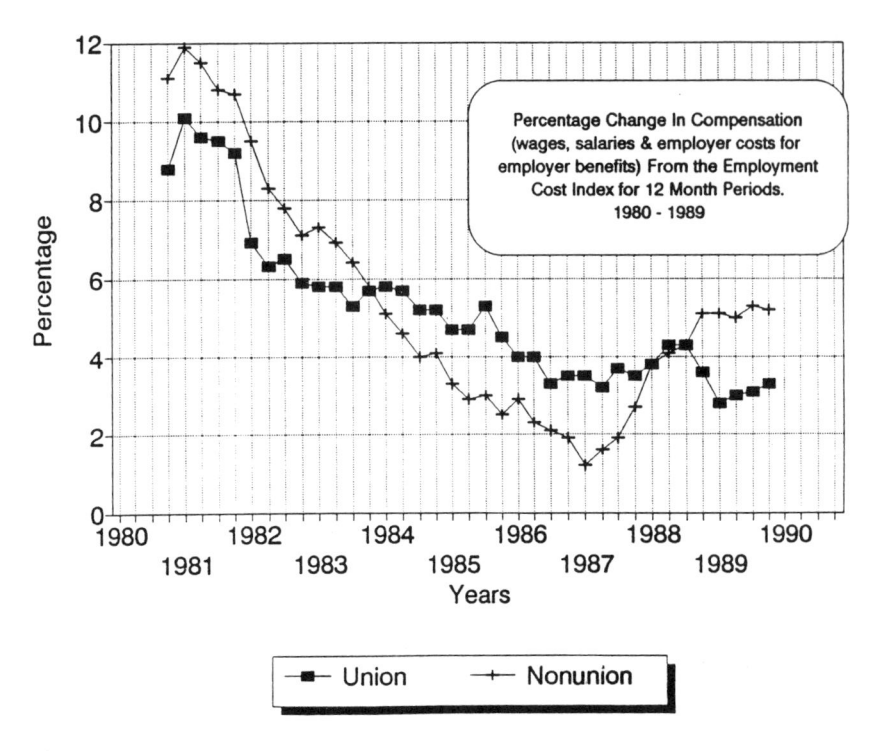

Figure 2.2

of the wage differential. They state that "... at any given differential, management has a greater monetary incentive to keep unions out than workers have to organise."[80]

While it is reasonable to assume that employers would utilize the law more for economic reasons, the fact is that workers ought to be attracted to the unions that offer a premium that they will obtain as the result of successful collective bargaining. There are a number of reasons why this has not happened so as to enhance trade unionism.

First, while on the supply side more workers will be interested in being employed in union jobs if a differential is substantial, on the demand side a large union-nonunion wage differential provides incentives for employers to economize on union labor by substituting capital for labor, relocating plants, and resisting unionization more vociferously. The demand side effects reduce the number of union jobs available, so the net result of these two forces is an increased number of applicants or employees who seek union labor who are not able to obtain such employment and high-wage union jobs. This is why, notwithstanding the attractiveness of trade unionism, the differential appears to have an inhibiting effect on trade unionism.

A second reason why this phenomenon is not helping the unions is rooted in the change in the work force composition available to union organizational efforts. In smaller establishments, where union organizational activity constitutes a more formidable task because of personal relationships, it is congregated disproportionately, and a worker is made more vulnerable by his or her relatively exposed position, since the employer is able to observe and discern each worker's attitude.

Meanwhile, the unions, through reports such as the AFL-CIO's 1985 *The Changing Situation of Unions and Workers,* have expressed concern and looked for new answers. This is in sharp contrast to the attitude presented in former President George Meany's expressed belief that the state of worker affiliations with unions had nothing to do with labor's viability.[81] The decline, while particularly visible and prominent in the 1980s, reflects a rising tide of employer resistance to unionization which is of a long-standing nature. The fact is that American employers have never accepted trade unionism to the extent that their counterparts have in other industrialized countries throughout the world, a phenomenon sometimes encapsulated by the term "American exceptionalism." While the current decline is traceable to the mid-1950s, the idea of American exceptionalism has contained the view that the movement's foundations have been extraordinarily shaky since the business unionism approach promoted by American Federation of Labor's first president, Samuel Gompers, won the day against the radicals, Socialists, and Wobblies who advocated a labor party, as well as ambitious state intervention (though the Wobblies were antistatist) and regulation of employment conditions, both of which were anathema to the Federation.[82] (While American labor's view of union involvement with politics has changed considerably, it continues to hold the same position about a labor party.)

Thus American exceptionalism would have it that the defeat or alienation of labor radicalism in the United States has made unnecessary the buyout of European labor's revolutionary spirit and its accommodation, which apparently induced the European employers to come to terms with an established labor movement and accept its existence. No such incentive existed in America. As the theory goes, the absence of the buyout inducement has its roots in the turn of the century and the rise of the AFL.

Whatever the strength or validity of this idea—its responsibility for American labor's contemporary state seems diminished by other factors as well as the point that labor's decline is an international phenomenon—the fact is that American trade unionism arrived on the scene at a relatively late period. Whether this is attributable to the individualism bound up with the frontier, the Horatio Alger myth or, as maintained by Forbath, the law itself, is problematical.[83]

Forbath holds the view that law has historically played a major role in the inability of unions to function effectively in the United States. Confounding the argument that the decline phenomenon is international, he states:

In the early twentieth century, state coercion and violence against strikers was substantially greater in the United States than in other industrial nations. Elsewhere, by the early 1900s, strikes, secondary actions, and labor protests were no longer in a legal twilight. Strikers were no longer semi-outlaws, and police and troops arrested, injured and killed significantly fewer of them than in the United States.[84]

Whatever the cause, law or cultural characteristics, the mass of semiskilled and unskilled workers remained beyond the reach of union recruitment efforts until the catastrophic Great Depression of the 1930s. One obtains some sense of the time lag in noting that the rise of the "new unionism" in Britain sought out a similar constituency a full half century before John L. Lewis and the Congress of Industrial Organizations rose to the same or comparable challenge in the Great Depression.

American exceptionalism then dismisses or makes subordinate the law—at least the contemporary legal approach of labor-management relations to the question of what ails labor. This view is supported by both the apolitical nature of the Federation and the existence of employer practices, such as employee representation committees under the American Plan and the velvet glove of company unionism alongside the iron fist of yellow-dog contracts that forbade workers to join unions as a condition of employment. Yet, as argued by Forbath, law has been a factor, both historically and today—although its precise impact cannot be quantified. States Forbath:

During the late nineteenth and early twentieth centuries, courts legal ideology and legal violence played a decisive part in shaping the consciousness and aspirations of organized labor in the United States.[85]

Historically criminal conspiracy doctrines, the declaration that picketing was unlawful intimidation, even sometimes a "nuisance" tort theory designed to protect employer property, antitrust law that characterizes unions and their conduct as an unlawful restraint of trade, and especially the injunction, were all legal devices used by the courts to suppress unions in this country. In 1842 the Supreme Judicial Court of Massachusetts, in *Commonwealth v. Hunt*[86] introduced a balancing test to determine whether the union had engaged in an unlawful conspiracy. But the key was whether the union was pursuing an unlawful objective—a resolution to be made by a hostile judiciary. Moreover in the wake of the *Hunt* decision, subsequent to the Civil War, civil damages became a prominent way to thwart unions.[87]

While, as we have seen, the Clayton Anti-Trust Act of 1914 was thought to have removed the more draconian features of the Sherman Anti-Trust Act, the Supreme Court's decisions soon established the proposition that labor's "bill of rights" was more ephemeral than substantive, the Supreme Court relying upon common law that antedated antitrust legislation to restrict union power and ushering in a new round of labor injunctions against unions that was only dissipated by the laissez-faire philosophy of the Norris-LaGuardia Act of 1932, which deprived the federal courts of jurisdiction to issue labor injunctions.

The historical record of legal repression is obvious—as is the fact that it was more long lasting than in other western democracies like Britain and Sweden. On the other hand, the evidence on the role of law in modern labor relations is a little less clear-cut. Much of the evidence marshalled by Forbath consists of statements by union officials, characterizing the impact of the law on union conduct. But in the previous century as well as the 1980s and 1990s, law can be a convenient scapegoat, an explanatory crutch for other more discomforting factors. Statements made on the floor of union conventions as well as press commentary consist frequently of posturing rather than providing a genuine assessment of law in labor-management relations.

The Wagner Act of 1935 (as amended, it is most often called the National Labor Relations Act) provided labor with a bill of rights in the form of an unfair labor practice code of conduct or good behavior for employers, as well as a representation procedure through which workers could express their free choice about unionism in a secret ballot-box election. (It was and is an unfair labor practice to discriminate against workers on the basis of union membership, to retaliate against them for engaging in the collective activity or for cooperating with the Labor Board, to refuse to bargain in good faith, and to create or assist a so-called company union.)

As Justice Robert Jackson said for the Supreme Court in the landmark 1944 *J.I. Case* decision:

> ... advantages to individuals may prove as disruptive of industrial peace as disadvantages. They are a fruitful way of interfering with organization and choice of representatives; increased compensation, if individually deserved, is often earned at the cost of breaking down some other standard thought to be for the welfare of the group, and always creates the suspicion of being paid at the long range interest of the group as a whole. Such discriminations not infrequently amount to unfair labor practices. The workman is free, if he values his own bargaining position more than that of the group, to vote against representation; but the majority rules, and if it collectivizes the employment bargain, individual advantages or favors will generally in practice go in as a contribution to the collective result.[88]

The aegis for case handling was one of President Roosevelt's expert alphabet administrative agencies, the National Labor Relations Board whose principal virtues were deemed to be a possession of expertise along with sympathetic, swift, efficient, and informal procedures that had been found wanting in an inexpert, unsympathetic, and hostile judiciary. At least until the late 1950s or early 1960s, these mechanisms seemed to be more help than hindrance in implementing the Act's self-proclaimed goal of freedom of association for the workers—a goal that had been previously adopted by Congress when it enacted the Norris-LaGuardia Act of 1932.[89] Indeed, when the Civil Rights Act of 1964 was debated in Congress, its proponents assumed that the NLRA structure and the Board were the ideal that new legislation should seek to emulate. (*Partial* adoption of this scheme—a division, for instance, between the General Counsel and the commissioners who do not have the writing responsibilities that is that of the Labor Board members—is one of the things that accounts for the Equal Employment Opportunity Commission's rather awkward structure.[90])

In 1947 Congress comprehensively amended the statute through the Taft-Hartley Act. The thrust of the statute was to impose responsibilities and regulations upon unions as well as employers, since the 1935

Wagner Act had fashioned restrictions only for employers. These amendments outlawed, among other things, the secondary boycott, the closed shop through which workers were compelled to be union members prior to employment, and national emergency strikes affecting the country's health and safety. Did this law cause or promote the decline of organized labor? This is the view readily put forward by union lawyers.[91] But is it truly accurate?

Clearly a substantial number of employers readily grasped the view that the tools now made available by the 80th Republican Congress could be used by them to deflect union organizational activity. The highly vaunted and advertised CIO "Operation Dixie" was the first of a series of such uniformly unsuccessful ventures designed to organize the South. It sputtered badly in the wake of Taft-Hartley and the greater scope that it provided for employer "free speech," an enhanced ability, for instance, to interrogate workers about their union sympathies provided by Taft-Hartley. Yet the actual decline of representation throughout the entire work force did not commence until almost a decade after the amendments.

Tracing the impact of Taft-Hartley on union membership is a task as formidable as determining the relationship, on the other side of the Atlantic, between the Thatcher government's labor legislation enacted between 1980 and 1990 (discussed below) and the British movement's previously noted precipitous, if not entirely comparable, decline to 45 percent of the work force. The five statutes enacted by the Conservative government, in power now for nearly a decade and a half, outlaw secondary boycotts and picketing in a more sweeping fashion than that employed by the Americans and have undoubtedly made unionization a more arduous task. But it seems clear that unemployment and union conduct toward employers as well as the public—and perhaps some union lethargy similar to that witnessed in the United States—have also played an extremely significant role.

The Left and the NLRA

The modern left wing or neo-Marxist view of the factors relating to union decline in this country, however, is more subtle. It raises questions about the propriety and underlying assumptions of labor law—like the Wagner Act which provided a representation procedure—and ultimately the question explored in chapter 5 of whether a repeal of modern American labor-management legislation in its entirety rather than a reform should be at the top of the labor law agenda. The view propounded by the far left is that the Wagner Act is a device to control or cabin the labor movement, to make it an organ of the state, and thus to provide the justification for state constraints upon otherwise lawful union activity, a position first put forward in the 1930s.[92]

Until the 1959 Landrum-Griffin amendments to the Act, it would have been difficult to consider this argument seriously given the fact that the unions, as the Supreme Court had held in the *Curtis Brothers* decision,[93] could lawfully use picket line pressure to induce an employer to bargain with it even though the union did not represent a majority. That is to say, the law did not impose restraints upon organized labor and its use of economic weaponry for the first quarter of a century of the statute—and allowed unions to resort to self-help to obtain recognition without any requirement to invoke the Board's processes. Indeed the Supreme Court held that antitrust law could not constrain union self-help through damage liability and criminal prosecution under the Norris-LaGuardia Act and expressed a public policy of judicial laissez-faire in labor disputes.[94]

On the other hand, a persuasive argument in favor of the view that the NLRA constrained labor is rooted in the idea that unions became accustomed to the statutory requirement of majority rule, campaigned to gain it as the litmus test of success and abandoned other forms of representation when it was not obtained. The unions could be said to have been forced into a legal procrustean mold established by the state in the sense that they could be forced to rely exclusively upon the ballot box and certification as a binding alternative to self-help.

For the past thirty years, however, the minority picketing—engaged in with the objectives to obtain recognition—at issue in *Curtis Brothers* has been disallowed by prohibitions contained in Landrum-Griffin. But it has remained possible for those prohibitions to be circumvented by unions that engage in so-called informational picketing where employees or others carry placards stating that the employer is "unfair" to labor, to utilize area wage standard picketing that advertises that the employer does not provide compensation and standards comparable to that afforded others in the relevant labor market, and more recently to engage in secondary handbilling.[95] The United Food and Commercial Workers Union has employed this tactic during the past decade as it has grown increasingly disillusioned with the decisions of the Reagan Board.

Some foreign experience on the relationship between law and the labor movement is instructive in any examination of union decline. As

Andrew Shonfeld stated in a Note of Reservation filed in the Royal Commission Donovan Report issued in Britain in 1968:

> . . . It is no longer possible to accept the traditional notion of the individual workplace as a separate and largely autonomous estate where employers and employees are able to conduct their quarrels with little or no regard to the effects of what they do on other workplaces. In recent years we have seen how a large complex of interrelated industrial operations located in different concerns may suddenly be placed at the mercy of the impulse of some small work group somewhere along the line. The degree of industrial interdependence is certain to increase. . . . [I]ts [the plant and management] willingness to accept the risks of heavy investment in the production of specialized products dependent on the chain of other operations will be influenced by the view that it takes on the reliability of the engagements made by its suppliers of essential goods and services. If the flow is constantly subject to unpredictable interruption, business initiative in important fields of activity is likely to be discouraged. There is also the effect on wage-earnings, the demand for total autonomy by a work group which has banded together to stop or slow down production in one place results in the loss of wages and the disruption of the working lives of many times their number elsewhere. These workers and their employers have a right to expect the effective intervention of trade unions in plants where labour is organised, to insure that frivolous or minor disputes are not allowed to cause excessive damage.
>
> . . . They have no right to demand that the strike weapon shall never be used. The existence of a threat of this kind, whether it is the complete withdrawal of labour or a change in work practices, such as a go-slow to the detriment of the employer, will continue to be a necessary element in the bargaining power of wage and salary earners for as far ahead as one can see. But all those who have to rely on the output of a particular body of workers for their livelihood are entitled to a clear assurance about the status and purposes of the organisations in whose name the order to use the strike or other weapons of industrial dispute is issued, and about the responsibilities of those in charge of them.[103]

Regulation of organized labor's tactics and procedures in the public's interest is appropriate. But it is in the arena of protection (i.e., freedom of association) that American labor law has failed. I do not believe that this is attributable to inherent failings or deficiencies in the NLRA or Wagner Act, though the past twenty years have made the statute's procedures and processes archaic and more difficult to implement.

To repeat, experience abroad and in this country supports the idea of trade union regulation through one approach or another as hardly undemocratic. It has been accepted in the form of peace obligations embodied in German, Scandinavian, and Japanese law, as well as the under the Wagner Act logically provided a basis for Taft-Hartley's restrictions was advanced as an argument—just as the immunities accorded unions by the Trades Disputes Acts of 1906 and 1965 served as a rallying cry for the view that unions held themselves above the law in Britain. In America the argument was that the provision of positive rights translated itself into a basis for state regulation.

But it was the attitude and conduct of the labor movement in both countries (in Britain especially) that provided some of the basis for regulation rather than the logic of regulation itself. In America it was a tumultuous rash of stoppages in 1946–47 in most basic industries arising out of demands that were pent up by World War II restraints and the perceived view that unions' contractual obligations voluntarily given in the form of no-strike pledges were being flouted with impunity. America's miners' strikes of the 1940s and the consequent confrontation between the United Mine Workers' President John L. Lewis and Presidents Roosevelt and Truman during and immediately after World War II placed into focus the frequently asymmetrical nature of union power and public interest. A similar reaction is even more easily comprehensible with the 1979 "winter of discontent" in which a rash of strikes disrupted services, essential and otherwise. Unions that had gained in considerable measure from the Labor government's Social Contract, persisted in behavior far more inflammatory than persuasive.

The Need for Balanced Regulation

Despite the overreaching nature of the American amendments contained in the 1947 and 1959 statutes and the British Employment Acts of 1980, 1982, 1988, and 1990,[102] the fact is that regulation of union behavior in the form of limitation upon strikes, the enforcement of collective bargaining agreements (with, it should be remembered, peaceable procedures designed primarily for the benefit of employees and their representatives), and legal protection for democratic procedures are by no means inherently incompatible with the idea of an autonomous trade union movement. Indeed balanced internal regulation and rational dispute resolution procedures may well be a prerequisite for it. A balanced approach to labor-management relations in a democratic society translates into reasonable limits on union power.

A modern economically interdependent society ought to be able to protect itself against union abuses while simultaneously promoting freedom of association for the workers in an effective fashion. As

British unions which had succeeded in pursuit of their narrow and parochial interests until the May 1979 elections in that country. In neither the Labor government of Harold Wilson nor the Conservative regime of Edward Heath did the labor movement brook any discussion of accommodation or compromise—until, that is, the political reaction of 1979 stripped the unions of all their cards and made dialogue between the unions and government well nigh impossible. As Henry Phelps Brown has said:

History has distorted the presentation to the British people of the relation between trade unions and the law. This is a great misfortune. The belief that trade unions, alone among the institutions of the country, are inherently entitled to immunity from parliamentary regulation has no reasonable foundations. It exerts an anomalous constraint on public policy towards industrial relations.[99]

Well before the "winter of discontent" in which a rash of both private and public sector strikes repudiated the Trades Union Congress–Labor government's "Social Contract," and in the process alarmed a vulnerable public, this attitude became ever more pronounced. The TUC campaigned against and boycotted successfully the provisions of the Heath government's Industrial Relations Act of 1971—a law that at least superficially resembled both the Wagner Act and the Taft-Hartley Act.[100] The result was a repeal in the second Wilson government elected, as it was, in a campaign fought over the 1974 miners' strike.

The 1974 strike—Prime Minister Edward Heath put the issue in terms of who "rules the country," unions or government—had nothing to do with the Industrial Relations Act. But the myth that the Act was the issue in the dispute, the mishandling of it by the Tories, and the message inherent in the election returns' reprimand meant that the resolution of the miners' strike was nevertheless propagated as a defeat for law in industrial relations. With it came the new conventional wisdom that while law could effectively play a role in promoting trade unionism,[101] it could not control the movement's abuses and excesses. Therein were sown the seeds for Britain's infamous 1979 "winter of discontent" and the public hostility to labor's "barons" who soon conveniently obliged Mrs. Thatcher by assuming the role of whipping boys for her government.

In the events preceding enactment of Taft-Hartley in this country, a law passed by both houses of Congress by margins sufficient to override President Harry Truman's veto, there is a similar, though more distant, ring. Again the idea that the rights acquired by organized labor it happens, the British unions have suffered a decline almost as dramatic as that experienced by the American labor unions simultaneous with the introduction of a series of labor laws that have imposed restraints upon labor. Though many of the unions in Britain now apparently would like such reforms, the law does not provide for any kind of recognition procedure or system of exclusivity through which unions might be said to be cabined.

Mrs. Thatcher and the British Unions

The sweeping attack upon the National Labor Relations Act's framework and approach fails to take into account the antiunion and repressive Thatcher legislation of 1980, 1982, and 1988 (by contrast to the 1984 Trade Union Act which properly imposes democratic obligations upon labor unions) and the absence of a comparable statutory scheme in that country. A system of establishing certification of unions as bargaining agents, while hardly necessary to provide a justification for that country's new laws, was flirted with ever so briefly and tentatively under the Heath government's Industrial Relations Act of 1971[96] but ultimately rejected. The British experience invites the view that the tender trap of exclusivity is hardly a prerequisite for the imposition of legal limits upon union power. Indeed, in contrast to their American counterparts, the British unions have until recently vigorously opposed labor law of any kind other than that which imposed some kind of floor for collective bargaining, for most of this century—a kind of *collective laissez-faire,* as Kahn-Freund put it.[97]

Of course the existence of a favorable legal climate for union growth serves as a logical argument for legal limitations upon union power. The state can take away more justifiably when it has provided in the first instance. But that need not take the American form of an exclusive bargaining representative system. The most obvious proof for this proposition is Canadian labor law, discussed in chapter 7, which in relevant respects mirrors the American National Labor Relations Act both at the provincial and federal level.[98] The Canadian trade union movement, by no means any more free from regulation than unions south of the forty-ninth parallel, has been gaining influence and members (at least until recently) as they have marched up the hill, while their American counterparts have been moving in the opposite direction.

If one looks to the origins of the Thatcher labor law reform, it must be said that they are to be found in the unbounded arrogance of the regulation of union internal procedures in Japan. The debate in a democratic society ought to be about the *form* of regulation and the need for a balanced approach, not about regulation itself. Again this view is in no way incompatible with significant protection of the right to organize and engage in collective bargaining.

The Alleged Peculiarities of the American Certification System

If the Wagner Act has licensed unions so as to immobilize them, one would assume that the American trade union decline would be an aberration on the international trade union scene. Although, with the possible exception of France, the American trade union decline may be the most precipitous, for the most part the pattern in this country can hardly be regarded as an aberration. With the exception of the German and Scandinavian labor movements and the somewhat uncertain and peculiar experience of Canada (outlined in chapter 7), decline has set in everywhere.

Previously discussed Britain, as well as Italy, France, and Japan are obvious cases in point. Those countries have no certification or procedures through which to bestow a set of good conduct rules upon labor, although British unions would argue that the Thatcher government's new world of labor law is a major factor responsible for that movement's decline from approximately 55 to about 45 percent during the past decade.

To one degree or another, all of the industrialized countries in Europe, Japan, and North America have experienced roughly the same difficulties. Indeed, as noted above, the one country besides the nordic group to experience growth has the Wagner Act and that is Canada itself!

The point is that the law may have something to do with trade union decline—that is why the Canadian features that differ from those prevailing in this country are discussed in chapter 7. But it is not the peculiar legacy of Wagner that is at fault. No evidence supports that idea. The source of union decline, as well as the remedy for it, is more complex than an examination of the law will yield.

Union Decline and Regulation of the Employment Relationship

In a sense, as the trade union presence has receded, statutory regulation of wrongful discharge, employment discrimination, and a variety of employment relationship issues have begun to fill the vacuum. Although some have argued that this too is a factor in the labor movement's decline, the fact is that it seems to be more of a response, and thus an effect, as opposed to a cause. If employees see no need for unions because of the availability of various forms of protection outside the collective bargaining process, one wonders why Scandinavia and much of the rest of Europe have a higher union density than that enjoyed by American unions. The correlation between employee protection and union density seems to be antithetical to what it would be if there was a connection between these two phenomena.

Of course it could be argued that the European experience has no relevance to that of the United States because of the different role of the labor movement in this country. That is to say, legislation that provides employees with benefits in Europe would be less likely to be harmful to the movement because of union involvement in the enactment and administration of the legislation. The unions have been "social partners" in northern Europe, and the availability of benefits outside of collective bargaining in such circumstances would not disparage labor or collective bargaining as institutions. Yet, notwithstanding the differences between America and Europe, the case for some kind of connection between decline for unions and individual employee protections does not seem to have been made out. Not only does the decline antedate the regulation of the employment relationship—in this country it occurred in the 1970s except for the Civil Rights Act of 1964—but there is simply no evidence that employees are rejecting unions because of the floor that has been provided them in areas such as pensions, health and safety, and job security, beyond antidiscrimination matters.

Whatever the cause of this development, it appears that the argument for state regulation has never been more forceful. Developments here in the United States mirror but lag behind those of other industrialized countries in Europe and Japan. However, the difference is that in America state regulation appears to be moving into an arena more obviously abdicated by the collective bargaining process.

In Great Britain and even more so on the continent of Europe, the 1970s saw a series of statutory enactments sought by the unions that provided statutory rights in such fields as occupational health and safety, job security, and union access to employees and employers on plant premises at the work site. The new legislation, frequently opposed in Europe by both domestic and foreign businesses—particularly in the codetermination area where labor attempted to expand its beachhead of parity on the boards of directors established in German coal and steel in the early 1950s—was seen as shifting the balance of power from management to labor. The goals and interests of local works councils elected by workers at the enterprise level in Germany, for instance, became more effectively harmonized and integrated with union influence in key industries like metals and paper, notwithstanding the participation of nonunion personnel in the electoral process.

In the United States, however, the legislative developments of the 1970s, while not inconsiderable by any standard, were hardly equal to European developments in the same period. Thus far they appear to have produced an entirely different effect, notwithstanding that the American labor movement had also assumed the role of a vigorous legislative proponent. In America the 1970s as well as the 1980s were seen as an era where individual rights accorded by statutes would diminish the significance of collective rights afforded employees by the collective bargaining process, a view given increased credibility by labor's steady decline during this same period. The employment contract between worker and management has become more individualized, particularly as it relates to job security.

Actually legislation promoting individual rights commenced in the 1960s with the enactment of title VII of the Civil Rights Act of 1964, which prohibited discrimination in employment on account of race, sex, religion, color, national origin, and, through 1967 legislation, age. Here the AFL-CIO supported antidiscrimination law applicable to labor, as well as employers in 1963, even before the Kennedy administration was willing to include this feature in its comprehensive omnibus civil rights bill. (Later of course the AFL-CIO was to experience difficulties with title VII as it related to seniority disputes between black and white workers and the movement's defense of the former[104]—but that is another and somewhat separate story.) The labor movement was similarly supportive when the Act was strengthened by amendments, effective March 24, 1972, providing for judicial enforcement of antidiscrimination prohibitions. It adopted the same posture in the debate about the Civil Rights Act of 1991.

The 1970s witnessed the passage of such laws as the Occupational Safety and Health Act of 1970 and the Employee Retirement Income and Security Act of 1974, the latter providing for expanded employee pension rights. State legislatures frequently replicated such statutes, and states pioneered with new protection in the 1970s and 1980s and with regulations relating to invasion of employee privacy, sometimes relating to controversial matters such as lie detectors, polygraphs, drug tests, and the right to inspect personnel records. Sexual harassment cases, at the heart of the debate about the Civil Rights Act of 1991 because of the inability of women to obtain effective monetary relief for such practices, began to figure prominently in the title VII litigation in the 1980s and 1990s. Some states have enacted legislation that protects the rights of pregnant women against dismissal.

The Supreme Court's landmark 1991 decision, *UAW v. Johnson*,[105] held that women could not be excluded from jobs where toxic materials posed the potential for harm to their reproductive capabilities. The point of the decision was that women could not be singled out for special treatment when their male counterparts had not undergone similar scrutiny, or indeed any at all. While constituting a victory for women workers in many industries, the decision may result in a more healthy environment in the workplace for all employees.

In 1988 Congress enacted polygraph legislation of its own.[106] The same year, with considerable more conflict and debate, Congress enacted, over President Reagan's opposition, plant-closing legislation in the form of the Workers' Adjustment, Retraining and Notification Act.[107] The statute provides for a sixty-day notice for some workers affected by substantial layoffs and plant closings.

Finally, parental leave legislation was twice vetoed by President Bush in the form of the Family and Medical Leave Act of 1990 and 1991,[108] but was ultimately signed into law by President Clinton in 1993. The problems of working mothers in particular are affected by the lack of corporate provision, particularly for temporary and part-time employees, for parental leave.

These developments, continuing through the 1980s, moved the state into a collective bargaining vacuum caused by the labor union decline, and thus gave Congress and the state legislatures jurisdiction by default. Paradoxically in the Reagan era of deregulation, near abdication of the bargaining process helped to sow the seeds and to nurture those already planted in the 1970s of legislative intervention and regulation of conditions of employment.

Employee Participation and Union Decline

Employee participation is an issue of abiding importance to the state and status of trade unions today.[109] Somewhat paradoxically the most determined drive for workers' participation, particularly in the form of quality work circles, quality work life (QWL), and the team leadership concept, has come from the nonunion sector. Yet significant participation in shaping one's employment relationship in the nonunion sector remains the exception and not the rule. Although these ideas were imported to Japan by Americans at the conclusion of World War II, the impetus for their acceptance in this country has come from Japan where their experience has been so successful.

Another irony is to be found in the convergence between protections afforded the organized and unorganized in this country. As we have noted here and in chapter 3, the sudden emergence of wrongful discharge litigation has made unions think again about the adequacy of the remedies contained in their own collective bargaining agreements. But it is job control and the relatively rigid sense of job classification and occupation, which previously drove the unionized sector, that has triggered the need for employee involvement, participation, and flexibility.

The point here is that employee participation needs to be encouraged for both the organized and unorganized sectors of the economy. This would signify a less adversarial approach to industrial relations generally, a development that needs promotion in America where, except for countries like Britain and Australia, the mentality on both sides of the bargaining table has been more destructively adversarial in the form of "them and us" than elsewhere. The important question for policymakers is how can the law or public policy encourage this process. In my view, there are two basic options available.

The first is a view that seems to be gaining wide acceptance in the AFL-CIO. It has its roots in despair of an effective system through which collective bargaining can flourish and be encouraged through law. It would mandate works councils of the kind that have become law in Germany and most of Europe. This would ensure some form of participation on a comprehensive and relatively uniform basis. One difficulty is that this idea runs up against the grain of the American system, which provides for exclusivity in terms of bargaining rights over wages, hours, and working conditions for unions that have gained the allegiance of a majority of workers in an appropriate unit. It is difficult for another entity, which purports to represent the employees in some sense of the word, to coexist with the traditional trade union structure and American labor laws. On the other hand, one might limit such a works council approach to the nonunion sector. But this simply would provide an additional incentive for employers to seek coverage of the works councils as an alternative to genuine and independent trade unionism.

There is no easy alternative to the idea of mandated systems. The one practical alternative is to encourage (without statutory mandate) voluntary workers' participation systems where no form of representation exists. The difficulty here is that federal labor law, because it is still rooted in the Great Depression reaction to company unions through which employers controlled labor organizations, prohibits financial assistance by employers to any labor organization that might affect employment conditions and additionally that the term "labor organization" has been provided with a definition so broad as to include, potentially, employee quality work circles, other employee groups, "teams," and the like.[110]

True, some of the courts have now allowed assistance that would otherwise be prohibited where employees perceive the process to be for the betterment of their employment conditions.[111] But such efforts operate in the shadow of the law. The employee committees that are the object of contemporary litigation are not the equivalent of company unions of the 1920s and the 1930s. They may be designed to take the place of authentic unions. When the evidence shows that employers have instituted mechanisms so as to interfere with the concerted activity of union adherents or discourage union activism, the law ought to intervene and prohibit such conduct. But, whether it be financial or otherwise, assistance to any groups that are involved in employment conditions ought not to trigger an unfair labor practice proceeding under the National Labor Relations Act. Amendments to the Act that allow for cooperative relationships between employees and the employer are desirable.

Moreover a by-product of the approach advocated here is the clarification of legal ambiguities where there is an incumbent union already on the scene negotiating for workers it represents in the appropriate unit. As I discuss in chapter 4, legal questions about the propriety of some aspects of relations between the United Auto Workers and the General Motors Saturn and New United Motors Manufacturing (NUMMI), the California General Motors-Toyota joint venture, for instance, remain formidable because of the close relationship between the parties and assistance provided by the employers in question.

One of the major obstacles to cooperative relationships is executive pay and the amount of compensation that CEOs are receiving. In the 1980s, CEO compensation jumped by 212 percent, while the factory worker received 53 percent, engineers 73 percent, and teachers 95 percent. In 1990 the average chief executive of a major corporation was paid 85 times the pay of a typical factory worker. In Japan the Japanese counterpart is paid 17 times as much as an ordinary worker. American executive compensation, awarded by boards of directors, appears to be far more generous than that provided in other countries, doubling during the past decade in the larger corporations to an average of $800,000 average per annum. The immediate practical consequence, as General Motors learned to its regret when its management officials were awarded bonuses as soon as the ink was dry on the first of the concession agreements in 1982, is both bitterness and resentment. This mix is dynamite. It can derail the most rational and sensible plans for cooperation and productivity that labor and management can devise.

Particularly in the organized sector, the issue of job security is inextricably bound up in employee participation. If workers are required to exhibit new found flexibility, their concerns about loss of employment may be exacerbated. It is to this matter that we turn next.

3

The Development of Job Security Law and Practice in the United States: Wrongful Discharge Law and Collective Agreements

. . . we do not agree . . . that employment security agreements are so inherently harmful or unfair to employers, who do not receive equivalent guarantees of continued service, as to merit treatment different from that accorded other contracts. On the contrary, employers may benefit from the increased loyalty and productivity that such agreements may inspire.
—Chief Justice Malcolm Lucas' majority opinion for the California Supreme Court in Foley v. Interactive Data Corp.[1]

Over the past decade numerous initiatives through law, practice and the implicit understandings that are associated with it, as well as collective bargaining, have enhanced employee job security and limited the employer's discretion. True, some of the protection, like last-hired-first-fired seniority provisions that accord protections to workers when layoffs are instituted (a feature contained in 90 percent of collective bargaining agreements in the organized sector of the economy) gained their impetus at the time of World War II and the creation of the World Labor Board in the wake of the Great Depression. The same time-honored tradition surrounds the principle that a disciplinary dismissal may not be instituted against a worker who is discharged under a collective bargaining agreement for reasons other than those that satisfy a "just cause" standard. In other words, if a worker is dismissed in violation of the contractual just cause standard, the employee is generally entitled to reinstatement with or without back pay, an award that is issued by a third-party neutral arbitrator selected jointly by labor and management. Such processes are contained in approximately 95 percent of the collective bargaining agreements negotiated in the United States.

The concepts of due process, which permit a worker to confront his or her accuser in a disciplinary proceeding, and progressive discipline, which obliges an employer to counsel and, if necessary, to suspend a worker prior to discharge (or, as some arbitrators characterize it, "industrial capital punishment") have become firmly entrenched as part of the arbitral common law that has evolved under collective bargaining agreements. Said the Court, in a constitutional context that is borrowed from the arbitral common law: ". . . the minimum due process for the employer . . . requires notice of the employer's allegations, notice of the substance of the relevant supporting evidence, an opportunity to submit a written response, and an opportunity to meet with the investigator and present statements from rebuttal witnesses."[2]

Supplemental unemployment benefits (SUB), providing workers, particularly in manufacturing, with between 90 and 95 percent of their wage for a designated period of time, were first negotiated in the automobile industry in 1955. Civil service arrangements protecting public-sector employees have existed for as long as this century. Both protections are designed to buttress unemployment compensation legislation enacted first in the states and then at the national level earlier in the period between sixty and eighty years ago.

But the law's limitations upon the circumstances under which plants may be closed and mass layoffs instituted have only come into play during this past decade. More innovative collective bargaining agreements in the automobile industry, for instance, now provide income rather than job security for the three-year period of the collective bargaining agreement, although the payouts that the employers are obliged to provide are limited by economic circumstance. General Motors was liable for up to four billion dollars between 1990 and 1993, in addition to (1) full compensation provided to employees placed in a "jobs bank" under the Jobs Bank program where workers are laid off for reasons that are within the control of the corporation such as technological change, corporate reorganization outsourcing, and negotiated productivity improvements, and (2) SUB benefits that constitute between 90 and 95 percent of a worker's wage. In 1991 as many as 75,000 workers were receiving full compensation under the four-billion-dollar General Motors liability, for which General Motors is contractually liable. The planned layoffs announced by General Motors in December 1991—with a total of another 74,000 workers—means that the fund could be drained by the time that the agreement expires in

1993. This has placed pressure on the union to renegotiate the agreement in the interim. Whatever the outcome, the matter will continue to vex the parties beyond the expiration of the agreement in 1993.

Perhaps the most important development lies in so-called wrongful discharge litigation, whose origins are to be found in the nonunion sector, despite the fact that some of its principles now have implications for the unionized arena as well. The wrongful discharge area—its holdings apply to disciplinary discharges as well as layoffs or economic dismissals, a demarcation that is less sharp in Europe than it has been traditionally in America—represents the most sweeping and radical change in American labor law.

A recent study by the Rand Corporation[3] estimates that 20,000 of these cases were filed in various court dockets throughout the country, both state and federal. In the late 1980s, some believed that of the two million nonprobationary, nonunion, noncivil service employees who are not protected by existing procedures but are dependent upon wrongful discharge action theories, between 150,000 and 200,000 would have legitimate claims under a "good cause" standard. Appropriately then, this is the first issue discussed in this chapter.

In a comparative sense the American employment relationship is ripe for regulation. Job tenures are typically shorter than those observed in both Europe and Japan.[4] Moreover, whereas quit rates are lower in the unionized sector of the American economy than in the nonunion sector, layoffs are higher. As we note below, to a limited extent both statutes and the collective bargaining process have responded. But one aspect of collective bargaining appears to have promoted the layoff as opposed to work sharing as a response to economic difficulty—the use of seniority. As Flanagan has noted:

. . . Random selection for promotion and transfer decisions, and worksharing—equal reductions in hours of work—could be used instead of layoffs by seniority. The ascendancy of seniority is probably a direct consequence of determining employment arrangements by voting (e.g., contract ratification votes) rather than hierarchical decision-making. Since the median union voter will generally be older than the most mobile worker in a nonunion firm, the tendency to emphasize seniority over mechanisms involving a more equal sacrifice is understandable in the union sector. The development of unemployment insurance systems in individual states beginning in the 1930's became another reason for preferring layoffs by seniority over work sharing. Union leaders argued that the total wage income of workers would now be larger under a layoff system, for those losing their job could now collect unemployment benefits.[5]

The Wrongful Discharge Litigation

At common law in the United States—that is, law made by judges and not the legislature—the contract of employment between employee and employer has been terminable at will, though some jurisdictions, like California, have enshrined the doctrine in statutory form. That is to say, absent explicit provision in a written document, the employee could be discharged at any time for any reason unless the decision was motivated by such considerations as race, sex, religion, national origin, age, or union membership, the prohibition contained in the modern labor legislation of the 1930s and the 1960s.

The 1980s have transformed this rule of law fundamentally, notwithstanding the defeat of numerous legislative proposals designed to guarantee worker rights against dismissal in a number of the state legislatures across the country. It is the courts fashioning common law, and perhaps even more important, the juries administering their own form of both due process and justice, that have changed legal developments in recent years. The legal roots of these developments are to be found in U.S. Supreme Court decisions involving constitutional rights for public employees arising out of wrongful discharge. The result has been an uneasy coexistence between two systems of dispute resolution in the organized and unorganized sectors of the economy, the former taking the form of the arbitration process and the latter consisting of litigation in the courts.

In the public-sector cases the Court declared a property right for public employees protected by civil service legislation and the like.[6] In 1985 the Court, speaking through Justice Byron White, held that the due process clause of the Constitution mandates that some pretermination process must be accorded public employees who can be dismissed only for cause. The Court noted that the need for "some form of pretermination hearing" was evident from a balancing of the competing interest at stake, namely "the private interest in retaining employment, the government interest in the expeditious removal of unsatisfactory employees and the avoidance of administrative burdens, and the risk of any erroneous communication."[7] Said Justice Thurgood Marshall in connection with such procedural guarantees: "the longer a discharged employee remains unemployed, the more devastating are the consequences to his personal financial condition and prospects for re-employment."[8] But such worker protection against dismissal simply did not exist in the 1970s, especially in the private sector to which the U.S. Constitution does not apply.

Recently, however, a number of jurisdictions have enacted so-called "whistleblower" statutes, which protect employees who have been dismissed because they have spoken out publicly on such matters as health and safety or corruption in government.[9] Some states, like California, have circumscribed at-will presumptions by statute by, for instance, prohibiting discrimination on account of political activity[10] or retaliation for serving on a jury.[11]

Montana has now enacted legislation protecting employees from dismissals that are without cause, although the dismissed employees must sue in court to obtain compensatory damages for emotional distress, which were previously available, and with limitations placed upon the availability of punitive damages.[12] Puerto Rico and the Virgin Islands have statutes[13] that provide employees with severance pay for unjust dismissal. But for the most part the courts have adhered to the view that the contract of employment continues to be terminable at will and that relief is only available where there is an exception to this principle. Montana stands alone in directly confronting the at-will issue with substantive wrongful discharge legislation—though it is limited in the sense that an employee must engage in time consuming judicial proceeding without compensatory damages for emotional distress in any situation. Puerto Rico and the Virgin Islands provide a kind of severance pay surrogate.

Essentially three exceptions have emerged in most jurisdictions. Although at least forty-five states have accepted one of the three theories, only eight have utilized all three of the new legal doctrines, with twenty-five states applying two of them.[14] By contrast, in 1980 only thirteen states placed some kind of limitation upon the terminable at-will principle. What follows is a representative overview rather than an exhaustive or encyclopedic chronicling of all wrongful discharge litigation in the United States.

Public Policy

One of the most prominent and widely accepted exceptions to the terminable at-will doctrine—if not of practical significance to most employees—arises with dismissals that are deemed to be inconsistent with "public policy." All of these cases involve situations where no statute prohibits a dismissal. But a statute may condemn a practice that an employer insists upon as a condition of employment. For instance, the easiest cases in which the courts find liability are those in which the employer requires the employee to engage in illegal conduct such as price fixing or, to take the matter one step further, requires the employee to engage in conduct that is inconsistent with his or her public duties such as insisting that the employee come to work rather than perform jury service duties. Where the employee is the corporation spokesperson and speaks against the interest of the employer, the employee may be dismissed, notwithstanding the public policy exception as an "ineffective at will employee."[15]

The more difficult issue, and one left specifically unaddressed by the Supreme Court of California in the landmark *Foley*[16] decision, is whether public policy can be offended where the violation of a statute is not at issue. The Court in *Foley* reiterated its view that the public policy basis for a cause of action must be "firmly established" or "fundamental" and "substantial." The interest must be a public one and not merely of a private character. Said the court:

... in the previous cases asserting a discharge in violation of public policy, the public interest at stake was invariably one which could not be properly circumvented by agreement of the parties. For example ... a contract provision purporting to obligate the employee to comply with an order of the employer directing the employee to violate the antitrust laws would clearly have been void as against public policy ... a contract provision which purported to obligate the employee to commit perjury at the employer's behest would just as obviously have been invalid.[17]

The Supreme Court of California found that the duty of an employee to disclose information to the employer (about alleged embezzlement by his or her supervisor) serves only the private interest of the employer and is therefore not within the public policy exception. The divided Court of Appeals for the Seventh Circuit has held that arguably criminal activity is within the public policy exception.[18]

As the Massachusetts Supreme Judicial Court has said: "An employee, even one in a socially important occupation, who simply disagrees with her employer's policy decisions, may not seek redress in the courts."[19] In the Court of Appeals for the Third Circuit, it was held that a cause of action does not exist because the employer dismisses the employee in retaliation for expressing views about the employer's operations where the employee is not "... charged either by the employer or by law with the specific responsibility of protecting the public interest and [is not] ... acting in that role when engaging in discharge causing conduct."[20]

On the other hand, the California Supreme Court, in *Rojo v. Kliger*,[21] has used antidiscrimination law, notwithstanding the existence of its own statutory remedies, to declare a public policy against sex discrimination and sexual harassment in employment. Said the court: "no extensive discussion is needed to establish the fundamental *public* interest in workplace free from the pernicious influence of sexism."[22]

Some of the state supreme courts—and it is state law that is critical here whether the matter is heard in state or federal court—have been wide-ranging, and somewhat far-reaching, in defining public policy. For instance, the Supreme Court of Arizona has held that an employee who alleged that she was required to "moon" at a company recreation outing, stated a public policy cause of action even though no statute prohibited such conduct.[23] Nevertheless, the court analogized to penal statutes that prohibit lewd and lascivious behavior as a basis for prohibiting such employer action.

A New Jersey court,[24] as well as one in California, has held that an employer dismissal of an employee for extramarital conduct was inconsistent with his privacy and that it was against public policy to inquire into such matter. In Philadelphia the Court of Appeals for the Third Circuit held that an employer could not dismiss an employee for refusing to lobby for an initiative that was against the employee's conscience. The court reasoned that freedom of conscience is protected by the Constitution and that state public policy was to be defined in light of the Constitution.[25]

Notwithstanding the breadth of these decisions, the trend, as demonstrated by some of the earlier cases discussed under the public-policy rubric, seems to be toward narrowing the exception to the terminable at-will principle. Having rushed in, in a startling and dramatic fashion, the courts seem to be drawing back somewhat here and in connection with other wrongful discharge theories.

The Implied Contract

A second exception to the terminable at-will principle is that an implied contract has been shaped between employer and employee that limits the employer's discretion in discharge disputes. The Dan Rathers and Reggie Jacksons of this world, of course, have elaborate agreements with explicit guarantees.[26] But generally speaking, the contractual relationship involved in wrongful discharge litigation is implied from the employer's course of conduct in its dealings with the employee. That is to say, if the employer has provided commendations, promotions, increases in pay, and other benefits to the employee over a period of time, a promise against nonarbitrary behavior in regard to job security on the part of the employer can be implied. Lawyers characterize this kind of contract as one that is implied in fact. The assumption is that an employee would not assume or have an understanding that the employyer could dismiss without reason or cause at any time under such circumstances. Said the California Supreme Court in *Foley:*

> In the employment context, factors apart from consideration and express terms may be used to ascertain the existence and content of an employment agreement, including the personnel policies or practices of the employer, the employee's longevity of service, actions or communications by the employer reflecting assurances of continued employment, and the practices of the industry in which the employee is engaged.[27]

A variation on the contract theme relates to personnel manuals, handbooks, and the like, which are sometimes distributed to employees and sometimes only to the supervisory work force. The Supreme Court of Michigan in the *Toussaint*[28] decision has led the way in implying a contractual obligation under such circumstances, though that court has limited the scope of its holding in the last few years.[29] The Supreme Court of Iowa has said that the ". . . handbook language must be sufficiently definite in its offer of continued employment in that a fact finder is not left adjudicating the alleged breach of 'contract' for which the fact finder has supplied its own terms . . . claims premised on unilateral contract theory frequently fail because the handbook's dismissal or disciplinary provisions are too indefinite to meet [the] . . . standard of definiteness."[30]

Another group of cases have emerged in the contract arena. Oral contracts are often intertwined with the implied in fact and the handbook or personnel manual cases. There are situations where it is alleged by the worker that some representative of management, perhaps a supervisor, has made an oral representation that provides for job security. It may be said that the supervisor has stated that "so long as you do a good job, you will not be dismissed or let go." The courts have sometimes been receptive to a contract based upon such an oral representation, sometimes where it is in conflict with other written representations. But the Court of Appeals for the Second Circuit has said:

> . . . we note that, as a matter of common sense, every employment contemplates periodic reviews of performance as an aspect of normal employment practices. Such reviews, without more, do not convert an "at-will" contract

into one that can be terminated only on a showing of good cause or honest dissatisfaction.[31]

Both in the implied contract in fact cases where the contractual obligation is inferred from a course of conduct, as in *Foley*, and in the personnel manual situations and those involving alleged oral representations, employers have begun to counterattack. The weaponry employed are so-called at-will clauses that purport to allow employers to dismiss the worker at will regardless of the employer's conduct, representations, or oral representations, implied or explicit.[32] Frequently this is accomplished through so-called application agreements.

But such methods have encountered some resistance from the judiciary. For instance, one court has taken the view that since no exception has been carved out to an implied in fact or contractual theory, ". . . the court declines to pronounce to a rule that employment at-will disclaimers categorically preclude an argument based on implied in fact contract or contract modification."[33] A California Court of Appeal has rejected an application agreement contained in a form on the ground that an employee's salary and position were not set forth in the "standardized two-page form."[34] The court also noted that while the application agreement stated that the employee could be dismissed at any time, it did not say that the employee could be dismissed for any reason.

The Wyoming Supreme Court has taken this position where the disclaimer simply states that the handbook or manual is not a contract. Said the court:

. . . an employee is entitled to enforce a representation in an employee handbook if he can demonstrate that: (1) the employer should have reasonably expected the employee to consider the representation as a commitment from the employer; (2) the employee reasonably relied upon the representation to his detriment; and (3) injustice can be avoided only by enforcement of representation . . . Unless the employee can make this factual showing to overcome the presumption of an employment terminable at will of either party, the employee's cause of action will fail.[35]

The Wyoming Supreme Court also noted that the typical unilateral offer to an employee is to an individual who is "untutored in contract law." The court said that if an employer sought to offset the contractual tenor of its handbook with a disclaimer, "equitable and social policy concerns demand that the disclaimer be presented clearly so that employees are not mislead by the handbook." The court indicated that it would require that a manager not only explain that the handbook was not a contract but that the employee should sign the cover page below the disclaimer in order for it to be effective. Only then, said the court, would it be viewed as sufficiently "conspicuous."

Finally, a minority of jurisdictions have held that employers have a duty of covenant of good faith and fair dealing. Generally the covenant has been regarded as a tort and is therefore like the public policy cases, a cause of action that can lead to an award of punitive damages. Sometimes the tort of intentional infliction of emotional distress is plead in the same action, although states such as California have recognized this tort as constituting an independent cause of action. (But the same court has diminished the impact of such damages by holding that workers' compensation statutes—which do not provide for tortious damage relief—preempt the field and displace such actions in the state courts.[36])

The large amount of damages awarded by the courts in California seems to have prompted the courts to be cautious in accepting the covenant of good faith and fair dealing as a tort, and the *Foley* opinion, which rejected a line of intermediate authority to the contrary,[37] is representative of this approach. The court in *Foley* reasoned, in part, that the covenant was necessarily vague and amorphous and therefore would permit juries to fashion excessive damage awards that would lead to uncertainty in business relationships and a climate not conducive to sound commercial relationships. Chief Justice Lucas, writing for the majority, rejected the dissenters' reliance upon insurance cases in which the covenant has been deemed applicable because the employees, in contrast to the insured individual who was dealt with in bad faith, could obtain employment elsewhere and that there was no inherent employer-employee conflict as in the insurance cases since employers are interested in retaining good employees. The court therefore dismissed the argument that the duty constituted a tort, though it allowed the duty of covenant to be plead as a contract cause of action.

Notwithstanding the court's pronouncements about the amorphous nature of the duty, Justice Marcus Kaufman, who dissented in *Foley*, had carefully delineated the duty in an earlier case as a judge in the court of appeal,[38] the intermediate California state court. Said Justice Kaufman:

What then in the employment discharge cases distinguishes a mere breach of contract from a breach of the covenant of good faith and fair dealing?

... There is little difference, in principle, between a contracting party obtaining excess payment in such a manner, and a contracting party seeking to avoid all liability on a meritorious contract claim by adopting a "stonewall" position ("see you in court") without probable cause and with no belief in the existence of a defense. Such conduct goes beyond the mere breach of contract. Acceptance of tort remedies in such a situation is not likely to intrude upon the bargaining relationship or upset reasonable expectations of the contracting parties.... [T]he standard developed ... is appropriate to distinguish between the simple breach of an employment contract by discharge of the employee without good cause and a breach of the implied covenant of good faith and fair dealing affording tort remedies. If the employer merely disputes his liability under the contract by asserting in good faith with probable cause that good cause existed for discharge, the implied covenant is not violated and the employer is not liable in tort. If, however, the existence of good cause for discharge is asserted by the employer without probable cause and in bad faith, that is, without a good faith belief that good cause for discharge in fact exists, the employer has tortiously attempted to deprive the employee of the benefits of the agreement, and an action for breach of the implied covenant of good faith and fair dealing will lie.[39]

On the court's handling of the insurance issue in *Foley*, Justice Kaufman said the following in dissent:

It is, at best, naive to believe that the availability of the "marketplace," or that a supposed "alignment of interest," renders the employment relationship less special or less subject to abuse than [other relationships]. ... Indeed, I can think of no relationship in which one party, the employee, places more reliance upon the other, is more dependent upon the other, or is more vulnerable to abuse by the other, than the relationship between employer and employee. And, ironically, the relative imbalance of economic power between employer and employee tends to increase rather than diminish the longer that relationship continues. Whatever bargaining strength and marketability the employee may have at the moment of hiring, diminishes rapidly thereafter. Marketplace? What market is there for the factory worker laid off after 25 years of labor in the same plant, or for the middle-aged executive fired after 25 years with the same firm?[40]

But, sensing the rise of employee challenges to employer decisions in the employment relationship, the court rejected Justice Kaufman's line of reasoning without seriously considering it on the merits. The question of whether the court's reasoning applies to tort causes of action, such as intentional infliction of emotional distress, has not yet been resolved, although applicability of the workers' compensation statute to such actions have subsumed this issue as a practical matter, removing many such issues from courts of general jurisdiction, where juries can fashion damages. In the wake of *Foley*, the Court has concluded that the worker compensation statute excludes civil actions because it covers the matter of a worker's injuries at the workplace, whether psychological or physical, and this compensation is provided on a no-fault basis without a determination of liability, removing the cause from the courts and juries where larger damages can be awarded.[41]

My own judgment is that the *Foley* view was a misfortune not only because of the fact that the Kaufman view made more sense as a matter of logic and law but also because his position would have both galvanized the business community to adopting more effective reform, as well as the legislature toward the enactment of comprehensive and sensible legislation.

Factors That Have Wrought Change in Wrongful Discharge

Today a major debate rages regarding whether the state legislatures or Congress should enact wrongful discharge legislation that can either substitute for or serve as an adjunct to the common-law litigation that has evolved during the past decade. Montana is the only state that has taken the plunge.[42] Basic to any discussion about this debate, and indeed the idea of a wrongful discharge cause of action under the common law, are the factors that have prompted reform here.

The most important consideration relates to the fundamental significance of employment in modern society noted by Justice Kaufman. In a modern industrialized economy it is difficult to view many matters, even marital relations and religion, as significantly more fundamental than employment opportunities. Employment opportunities determine one's future prospects in all aspects of life and the prospects and aspirations of one's own family. As the Court of Appeals for the Fifth Circuit has said:

> Racial discrimination in employment is one of the most deplorable forms of discrimination known to our society, for it deals not with just an individual's sharing in the "outer benefits" of being an American citizen, but rather the ability to provide decently for one's family in a job or profession for which he qualifies and chooses.[43]

Similarly, the Supreme Court of New Jersey said the following:

> Job security is the assurance that one's livelihood, one's family's future, will not be destroyed arbitrarily; it can be cut off only for "good cause," fairly determined. [The employer's] commitment here [an employment manual pro-

viding that an employee would be terminated only for cause] was to what working men and women regard as their most basic advance. It was commitment that gave workers protection against arbitrary termination.[44]

This is why the loss of employment is particularly harmful and traumatic to employees, a point especially central to the debate about the Civil Rights Act of 1991. The traumatic nature of the injury, like the loss of a limb or bodily injury, is what has induced the courts and the juries to adopt an expansive approach to damages, both punitive and compensatory. This feature has made the courts receptive to the applicability of tort causes of action such as the intentional infliction of emotional distress to the employment arena. If this aspect of life is fundamental, the loss of it can affect one's mind and emotional state, as well as physical health. Indeed studies of plant closings have established a nexus between job loss and mental and physical health.

Yet it is said that protection for the employee under such circumstances is asymmetrical. After all no one expects that the employee will have an obligation to the employer that will be comparable. The employee does not promise commitment to the job. Why shouldn't the courts, as they did previously, protect freedom or liberty on both sides, namely the freedom to quit and the freedom to be fired?

One answer to this point is the thirteenth amendment to the Constitution, which prohibits involuntary servitude or slavery. Since the end of the Civil War employees cannot be obliged constitutionally to work for an employer, and so sensitive are the common-law courts to the undesirability of an obligation to perform personal services that even where the employee has explicitly obligated him- or herself to continue to work, damages will be the appropriate relief.

It is further unlikely that the parties will address the job security issue in their own bargaining when the employee is hired. The employee, if anxious to obtain the position, is likely to assume that his or her focus on this problem will be likely to make the employer reconsider the hire. Suppose that the employee says, "What will happen if I perform poorly?" or even, "Will you guarantee me that I will not be dismissed for lack of just cause, or that I will receive the same protection as an employee represented by a union under a collective agreement?" What reactions would be triggered on the part of the employer? What would an employee be likely to assume about the employer's reactions under such circumstances? The realities of the relationship make implied restrictions upon the employer's discretion a reasonable interpretation of the relationship, given the fact that it is unlikely that the parties would explicitly address the issue on their own initiative in most relationships other than through application forms which purport to negate either a cause standard or the assumption that there is an implicit contract.

But to some extent these kinds of considerations go directly to the equality of the relationship itself.[45] Just as unpleasant problems will not be raised by the employee at the time that he or she is hired, so also the employee, if employed for some period of time, will be more vulnerable and dependent. As the National Labor Relations Board has said in a case involving refusal to bargain violations under the National Labor Relations Act:

> [The employee has a stake in the enterprise because he has spent] years of his working life accumulating seniority, accruing pension rights, and developing skills that may or may not be salable to another employer. And just as the employer's interest in the protection of his capital investment is entitled to consideration in our interpretation of the Act, so too is the employee's interest in the protection of his livelihood.[46]

This is the point made so eloquently by Justice Kaufman in dissent in *Foley*. From the employer's perspective there are economic factors that bond them to employees, particularly the value involved in training investments that is lost if the worker exits from the employment relationship prior to the realization of the investment. This is why in the United States seniority and the wage increases that are associated with it are rooted in not simply principles of fairness that the unions emphasize but also in productivity considerations. Productivity in some measure correlates with length of service, as witnessed by the fact that nonunion employers frequently give weight to seniority as criteria for promotions and other forms of wage increases.

Yet all too frequently the employer has an incentive to hire another qualified employee who will work more for less, chiefly because he or she is less senior. There is an abiding incentive to renege on the implicit contract between employer and employee, a problem that is magnified by both the duration of the employment relationship[47] and the fact that the senior employee may have trained the junior worker and, when the task is completed, the former is expendable and thus discarded. Aside from the fact that most employees do not wish to create the impression that they are marginal and therefore in need of special protection in their dealings with management, the asymmetrical nature of the relationship between employer and employee is highlighted by the fact that employer actions to restrain employees who attempt dissolution of the employment relationship seem to be mainly focused upon the unique value of the employee, as in professional sports, or entertainment, or the potential for the solicitation of competitors or dissemination of trade secrets to them by the employee.

One does not read cases dealing with *employees* compelling *employers* to engage in illegal conduct or conduct that is offensive to public policy. The nature of the relationship suggests something very different. But the Supreme Court of California in *Foley* has stated that because it is generally to the ". . . employer's economic benefit to retain good employees," the interests of employer and employee are ". . . most frequently in alignment."[48] This position is both curious and otherworldly, given the realities noted above.

My sense is that the collective bargaining relationship is a more effective way to protect job security for a number of reasons explored in chapter 2. Yet, due to the considerations delineated in that chapter, the legal environment is likely to be one in which most workers will not be protected by just cause provisions in collective agreements calling for impartial or neutral arbitration.

The continued decline of the unions makes that a remote possibility. In part this is a reason why the courts have begun to afford employees protection, in contrast to the 1960s and 1970s when the judiciary had not yet created the above-noted exceptions to the terminable at-will principle.

What other considerations have produced judicial intervention? The first is the constitutional authority that emerged in the public sector in the early 1970s. More than twenty years ago the Supreme Court recognized a property interest for workers in public-sector jobs to which the Constitution is applicable. While the private sector presented issues that are legally distinct in the sense that the Constitution is not applicable to this segment of the work force, the Court's reasoning about the importance of jobs and income has had implications for the private sector as well.

Second, in all other industrialized countries some protection of this kind is afforded, although there is considerable dissatisfaction with the operation of unfair dismissal legislation in Britain and France.[49] Canada (at least in Quebec, Nova Scotia, and among federally covered employees)[50] and Japan[51] provide for some limitation upon employer discretion in dismissal. Rather than provide for trials before judges and juries, Europe has established labor courts or industrial tribunals that resolve controversies about whether the dismissal is "unfair" or "socially unwarranted." Canada uses arbitration to resolve these types of disputes.

Germany and Japan pioneered in the protection afforded workers against dismissal and simultaneously enjoyed an economic competitive advantage that is the envy of other nations. It would seem as though in Germany and Japan there is no inconsistency (indeed the opposite may be true) between offering a measure of security for employees and striving for efficiency in the workplace. The loyalty to the firm and its product and consequent productivity demonstrated by the workers seems to bear some relationship to job security present in these countries.[52] This is the nexus articulated by Chief Justice Lucas in the California Supreme Court's *Foley* opinion. It is an important part of the reasoning involved in workers' participation initiatives described in chapter 4—institutional machinery which is regrettably not generally linked to the protection of job security, particularly in the nonunion area.

Yet another consideration in the erosion of the terminable at-will principle is the recent rash of corporate mergers that have been smiled upon benignly by the free-market buccaneers of the Reagan administration. Whatever the merits of the Reagan administration's merger policy, it is clear that one of its by-products has been the displacement of middle-level management personnel in unprecedented numbers. This no doubt helps to account for the disproportionately high number of managerial and professional employees who have utilized one of the theories referred to above and instituted dismissal actions in the courts. Because of the subjective nature of the work involved in jobs at this level, these cases have frequently proved to be particularly vexatious and ill-suited to resolution by judge and jury, a picture that contrasts with the bulk of arbitral adjudications of dismissals under collective bargaining agreements.

A fifth factor to be taken into account is that the antidiscrimination protest of the 1960s and 1970s has increased the public's awareness of issues relating to fairness and due process in the work place generally. Title VII of the Civil Rights Act of 1964 represented a significant incursion upon employer discretion in the hiring, firing, and promotion of employees, a policy furthered significantly by the Supreme Court's landmark *Griggs* decision and its restoration in the Civil Rights Act of 1991. In so doing, these statutes raised expectations and created challenges to employer decision making and managerial authority. One consequence has been that minority and female employees whose complaints have been deemed unmeritorious under antidiscrimination standards for lack of proof have nevertheless frequently challenged personnel unfairness that had nothing to do with race or sex discrimination and that sometimes have been successful in prompting policy changes in such areas. (A regrettable but understandable flip side to this is the obvious incentive for employees to characterize wrongs visited upon them as race or sex bias: "They must have done it because of my race or sex. What else could it be?" If unfair dismissals were outlawed altogether, that incentive might of course dissipate.)

Moreover court decisions fashioned under antidiscrimination law that, for instance, condemned non-job-related tests and other qualifications established by employers and labor organizations have benefited *all* employees in the work force, not just minorities. Again increased awareness has produced challenges to personnel policies that had not been carefully thought out.

Also tied to the rash of wrongful discharge protests is the rise of reverse discrimination litigation. As harmful as such actions have been to the societal fabric of the United States—and this will be a growing problem in the 1990s barring the remote eventuality that the Reagan–Bush Supreme Court's decisions in this arena are reversed by Congress[53]—in some respects they represent an attempt by those who have not benefited directly from fair employment practices legislation to find a forum to resolve complaints. (The Bush administration's exploitation of the quota issue in the Civil Rights Act of 1991 debate dramatizes the tensions that are likely to remain with us in this arena.)

Thus far the final decades of the twentieth century have seen the development of the internal labor market through which job ladders or lines of progression within the corporation or firm itself have become increasingly important to future employment opportunities. This makes more significant the comments of the Supreme Court of New Jersey: "We are a nation of employees. Growth in the number of employees has been accompanied by increasing recognition of the need for stability in labor relations."[54] Another consideration relating to employee expectations is that of fairness itself. The fact is that workers of the 1990s are simply willing to tolerate less in the way of arbitrary behavior on the part of the employer. The traditional employment contract was presumed to be payment of wages and other benefits for labor. Until the modern cases dealing with contracts, the view was that cause or some other standard of protection for job security interests could not be recognized by the law because no consideration—an exchange or bargain that is one of the law's prerequisites to recognition of a contract—had been given for the promise of job security. All that was involved in the bargain, reasoned the courts, were wages and other economic benefits for labor. The modern cases have seen this equation to be a shortsighted and narrow one and have not required separate consideration for the implied promise by the employer that the employee will not be dismissed for reasons other than cause or in good faith.

Today the average employee enters into the employment relationship with the expectation that if he or she does a fair day's work, that he or she will not only receive compensation but also fair treatment. Consider, in this connection, how frequently employers will state, perhaps through the informal comments of the supervisory work force, "If you do a good job, you will be dealt with fairly."

A better grasp of this can be more effectively obtained if one considers the opposite situation. Would an employer state—and would an employee assume the relationship is such—that if the employee behaves in a responsible, efficient manner, he or she can be dealt with arbitrarily? The answer seems obvious. The basic assumption in the employment relationship on the part of both sides is to the contrary.

All of this has produced a very different state of law relating to job security throughout the United States than that which existed in the decade of the 1970s. But the law, as it has evolved in the 1980s, contains considerable limits and unsatisfactory elements from the perspective of employees, employers, labor unions, and the public itself. This has made the idea of legislation at both the federal and state level an ongoing debate. As noted above, no comprehensive legislation has yet been enacted. But discussion and debate there are aplenty. It is to this matter that we turn.

Wrongful Discharge Legislation

The contractual relationship between employer and employee has been a significant factor in the development of the common law of wrongful discharge. Yet, given the considerations referred to above, it hardly seems an appropriate basis for statutory regulation of the relationship. That is to say, the legislatures ought not to be content to merely ratify the prevailing judge's common-law view that policies of the employer, implied or explicit, provide the exclusive basis for limiting managerial discretion. In some circumstances this would simply ratify employment abuses that have triggered the legislative demand.

The rise of the so-called at-will clauses, through which an applicant or employee agrees that they may be dismissed without cause, and the consequent litigation about their validity makes it clear that a contractual basis for regulation, whatever its common-law merit, is anachronistic. So long as the intent of the parties is basic to the employer's obligation, there will be ceaseless litigation about the meaning of such clauses and disputes about what else was represented to the dismissed worker. Just as the "yellow-dog" contract, under which a worker promised not to join a labor organization, was outlawed by modern labor legislation, so also should contractual provisions through which workers strip themselves of job security protection be condemned.

There is an additional and related development in the U.S. Supreme Court's 1991 *Gilmer*[55] decision that appears to enable employers to remit wrongful discharge as well as employment discrimination cases to arbitration proceedings where damages are limited rather than to civil actions before juries where the contrary is true. Employers have been traditionally reticent about sharing decision-making authority in the dismissal area with others, let alone arbitrators, and it is unclear that *Gilmer* will have a major impact in either the employment discrimination or wrongful discharge areas. But it bears watching.

In this case the Court held that an arbitration clause contained in a form application agreement signed by the applicant would mandate arbitration of a lawsuit instituted by an employee under the Age Discrimination Act of 1967. The Court held that arbitration could be mandated to the exclusion of litigation, notwithstanding arguments relating to the unequal relationship between employer and employee and questions about the impartiality of the process itself. The Court has not yet answered the question of whether safeguards, such as those that were urged for arbitration of employment discrimination cases under collective bargaining agreements, will be required.[56] In *Alexander v. Gardner-Denver*,[57] the Court, while refusing to deny plaintiff the opportunity to litigate as it has done in *Gilmer*, suggested that great weight could be given to the arbitration award in court if the arbitrator was knowledgeable about employment discrimination law and procedural safeguards were afforded the employee.

It might nevertheless be said that the common law, given the protections afforded, is the appropriate mechanism for intervention. But the common law is not well-suited to employment disputes. While I am of the view that the California Supreme Court came to the wrong conclusion about the covenant of good faith and fair dealing in *Foley*, nevertheless, its pronouncements about the superior expertise of the legislature—views previously advanced by New York's high court, the Court of Appeals[58]—in this arena are sound ones. For instance, the contract cases such as *Foley*—and cases in most of the jurisdictions that have recognized this theory—have focused upon the longevity of employment as one of the factors through which an implied contract can be imposed.

But how much longevity? Under what circumstances? The common law must be necessarily vague. It cannot speak with precision. On the other hand, a statute fashioned by the legislature that defines a specific eligibility period, and addresses the employer's interest in maintaining a probationary period during which it may have complete discretion, plays a constructive role in allowing the parties to know precisely the time at which rights and liability come into play.

What is the standard to be employed? Is it to be just cause, frequently used by arbitrators under collective bargaining agreements? Does this mean that the courts will employ any or all of the practices generally associated with the just cause standard under the common law of arbitration? Or will the courts utilize cause as it has been defined by the common-law courts historically? Some of the same questions apply in judicial adoption of a good faith or honest judgment standard.

Another problem with the common law is the use of juries in employment disputes. In some respects this approach provides for a refreshing reexamination of sometimes inflexible, arbitral reviews of employee misconduct. For instance, it has become an article of faith with arbitrators that an employee can be dismissed for a first offense if it involves theft or dishonesty, regardless of the *de minimus* nature of employee wrongdoing.

Yet too often it appears that juries are taking into account factors that seem to have attracted their attention in other areas of the law, such as the deep pockets of the employer. This makes banks and public utilities and other entities that have contact with the community at large particularly vulnerable even in circumstances where arbitral precedent is clearly against the employee, an undesirable state of affairs for law that must command respect in a democratic society.

A further consideration arguing for legislation relates to the handling of dismissal cases under collective bargaining agreements negotiated between labor and management which contain just cause contractual provisions. In 1988 the Supreme Court in *Lingle v. Norge Division*[59] held unanimously that workers may maintain actions in state courts on a public-policy theory regardless of the availability of contractual grievance-arbitration machinery. The Court has now opened up a major exception to the principle that the arbitration process in the organized sector of the economy is to be both exclusive and final,[60] though the Court's 1991 *Gilmer* decision held that arbitration provisions in an individual employment context could bar Age Discrimination Act suits.[61] The important point here is that the temptation to avoid the process has been increased, and this will undermine the system of industrial self-government devised by the parties themselves—though it now appears that damage liability in the wrongful discharge cases, as well as those arising under both the Civil Rights Act of 1991 and the Americans with Disabilities Act of 1990, have encouraged the adoption of such procedures outside the collective bargaining relationship. In essence a new ruling undermining finality in both arbitration and litigation in the courts seems to have emerged in the organized sector, but not in its unorganized counterpart.

In a sense this exacerbates a problem that confronted both employee and union in the form of duty of fair representation actions, where a worker alleges that the union, as exclusive representative, has not properly handled or processed his or her claim alleging contractual violation. Unions have felt frustrated and harassed by such proceedings because they were often filed over frivolous matters in which the employees wanted their day in court regardless of the merits. On the other hand, the employee has no contractual or statutory right to proceed to arbitration and can only involve the court in reviewing his or her contract claim if a duty of fair representation violation can be made out. The Court has held that the latter is a prerequisite to contesting the breach of contract claim on its merits, whether it be in arbitration or the courts. In *Clayton v. United Auto Workers*[62] the union conceded that meritorious cases were not taken to arbitration where, for instance, the union lacked financial resources or where the case did not possess sufficient precedential value for the purpose of all employees in the bargaining unit. But now under *Lingle,* workers who sue under a public-policy theory as opposed to a contractual one,[63] may completely bypass grievance-arbitration machinery.

A suitable compromise might be to allow an employee, whose union declines access to the arbitration machinery, to pay his or her own costs with or without union representation. The arbitration process would be final. But this kind of change has not yet emerged through the collective bargaining process, undoubtedly because of employer resistance rooted in the cost that would be imposed upon management. This is especially true given the U.S. Supreme Court's holding in *Bowen v. United Postal Service*[64] that imposes a duty of fair representation and monetary liability upon unions subsequent to the time that a meritorious grievance, declined by the union, should have been processed through arbitration. Given the fact that the duty of fair representation cases, like wrongful discharge actions in the nonunion sector, are a time-consuming, expensive process, most of the time period for which monetary liability exists is subsequent to the time that the matter should have gone to arbitration. Like wrongful discharge actions, without a duty of fair representation component this can mean up to three to four years, the result saddling the union with most of the monetary liability. *Bowen* has resulted in increased management resistance to any kind of compromise that would allow unions to avoid this liability and to, in effect, distribute the liability that exists differently.

Thus, even where privately negotiated machinery exists in the organized sector of the economy that provides for resolution of allegedly unfair dismissals by third-party neutral arbitrators, the effect of the duty of fair representation doctrine is to deny employees their day in court or in some forum. This is not only undesirable from a policy perspective but also inconsistent with international law in the form of the International Labor Organization Termination of Employment Convention which obliges signatory countries—and the United States is one of the few countries to both vote against and not sign this Convention which was promulgated in 1982[65]—to provide for impartial resolution of unfair dismissals. Accordingly this constitutes an additional argument in favor of enactment of wrongful discharge legislation. A wrongful discharge statute must necessarily focus upon both union and nonunion relationships.

In addition a host of factors argue in favor of enactment of wrongful discharge legislation rather than the existing system of common-law litigation. There are considerations that make such reform desirable for both employee and employer. The first is that, notwithstanding *Foley* and its progeny and cases like it in other jurisdictions, the tide of litigation continues to swell—although plaintiff's lawyers now exercise an even greater selective bias in favor of higher-income employees whose contract damage awards are greater than others.[66] Yet institutional and practical obstacles on both sides have thus far created a wall against such change in all states except Montana.

Employees have improved their position considerably under a regime of common-law litigation, and in part it is exceptions to the terminable at-will principle in the courts—and, more important, arrangements through which plaintiffs' lawyers have received handsome recompense—that has diminished advocacy of reform on the employees' side. The financial pursuits of the plaintiffs' bar notwithstanding, the emergence of wrongful discharge litigation in the United States has ushered in a far more civilized environment than that which preceded it.

As noted earlier, employers have become more due process oriented in devising personnel guidelines. Some companies have initiated procedures that provide for peer review of employee dismissals by fellow employees who are not immediately involved and presumably independent in some sense of the word. Indeed some employers have begun to devise arbitration procedures to relate to dismissals—a phenomenon, except in major corporations like Northrup,[67] that was unheard of a decade ago. Admittedly selection of the arbitrator by the employer or payment for fees and expenses by management raises questions of propriety for both the parties and the arbitrator. Still, despite the many problems with the existing system, legal governance of the employment relationship in the 1990s is considerably more fair than it was in the late 1970s.

Yet not the least of the problems posed for employees through the existing state of the law is the cost of litigation in the courts. It is no accident that a disproportionate number of the actions brought appear to be maintained by management or middle-management employees, many of whom have suffered dislocation as a result of corporate merger mania. Notwithstanding contingency prearrangements that postpone the payment of counsel fees until the plaintiff is a prevailing party, the costs of litigation are considerable. Nine years ago the California State Bar Committee Report[68] (as cochairman of the committee, I authored the report) estimated that it would cost between $7,000 and $8,000 just to get to trial, a period of time that might be three to four years in duration. The average employee below the managerial ranks simply cannot afford such a process. Indeed the same may be said for many managers themselves, particularly during the period of economic and psychological stress that flows from termination.

A second factor is that the law in none of the jurisdictions that have carved out exceptions to the principle of the contract of employment as terminable at will have established a just cause standard comparable to that which exists in the unionized sector of the economy where collective bargaining agreements are applicable—or indeed a general concept of fairness at all. Although the California State Bar Committee found that jury instructions "compound and confuse" the applicable standard, juries charged with legal instructions devised by judges appear to operate on a basis of understanding of just cause or community notions of fairness.

From the perspective of the employee, uncertainty and inferior standards are undesirable. From the perspective of the employer, standards other than those established by the courts create a large element of unpredictability. It seems quite clear that juries react intuitively on the basis of justice, or the lack of justice, regardless of instructions relating to relevant standards of law to be applied. In some respects it must be admitted that this approach provides for a refreshing reexamination of sometimes inflexible and archaic arbitral reviews of employee misconduct. This has improved the position of employees. But the fact is that juries do seem to take into account the deep pockets of the employer from time to time, and this is cause for concern.

A problem with the existing system is that judges and juries have less expertise than administrative agencies or labor arbitrators who specialize in the employment relationship. The principal difficulties with this forum are that it lends itself to unpredictability and volatility. Thus, though the Supreme Court of California's *Foley* decision disallowing court damages on a covenant of good faith and fair hearing theory may have eased this problem somewhat, the fact of the matter is that the committee noted in 1984 "[j]uries impose punitive and compensatory damages in what is frequently an erratic fashion."[69] In California damage awards have frequently exceeded the plaintiff's lawyer's demands for settlement.

The public-policy theory is of little use to the average employee. Frequently the employee is claiming that he or she may have information about unsafe practices or drugs that should not be approved by the Food and Drug Administration or, as was the situation in a leading California Supreme Court decision, price fixing.[70] But the average employee simply is not in a situation where he or she will be blowing the whistle on the employer or revealing this kind of information. Penultimately there are at least 150,000 dismissal claims that go unredressed because of the absence of a good cause standard in any form. My judgment is that this state of affairs warrants reform.

Finally, as noted above, employers have used at-will disclaimers to induce employee applicants to waive their rights to sue or to agree that the standard does not apply to their dismissal should such a consequence arise. Some employers have required incumbent employees, as a condition of employment, to execute such agreements. This also seems to be an undesirable state of affairs and one that argues for a statutory approach, even if the courts' disregard such disclaimers in a goodly number of instances. If the disclaimer is conspicuous enough, it will be honored. But even if it is not, employees may be inhibited or intimidated.

On balance therefore it seems as though a statute would be appropriate, given the flaws in the existing wrongful discharge process. But what should be the statute's form and substance? It is to this issue that we now turn.

The Proposed Statutory Framework Coverage

One coverage issue that has frustrated litigants relates to the eligibility of employees. The issue has diminished in importance somewhat in California in the wake of the California Supreme Court's decision in *Foley* with the decline of the covenant of good faith and fair dealing. Still the period of employment is a significant issue in contractual theories of which the covenant now constitutes one branch. Only the legislative arm of government can answer this problem in a definitive fashion. As with so many other issues, including the standard relating to the propriety of the dismissal itself, the courts are ill-equipped in the common-law context to fashion answers.

Collective bargaining agreements negotiated between labor and management address this issue by providing that most, if not all, of the contractual provisions protecting employees against dismissal for cause do not become applicable until the employee has served for a probationary period, generally about three to six months. The California State Bar Report provided for six months. The National Conference of Commissioners on Uniform State Laws have established a one-year period. The National Conference Report would also exempt employees covered by contracts for a fixed period. Under the California State Bar approach individuals who enter into written contracts of a year's duration and have a four-month notice provision in their contract should be exempted from statutory coverage.

This is similar to the approach taken in Britain, Germany, and Canada[71] where exemptions have been provided. In Britain, Germany, and Canada this is by virtue of explicit contracts for a fixed period of time entered into between employee and employer. In 1985 Germany, in response to the argument that employment protection legislation was deterring job creation, allowed employers to enter into contracts for temporary employment, although the statute explicitly states that such contracts may be renewed.

An equally important issue is the kind of employee to be covered. Most labor relations statutes exclude managerial and supervisory individuals from coverage, but that is done because of the presumed conflict of interest between serving both management and labor and the need to build walls that would promote loyalty to one side or the other in what has been an adversarial relationship. There is no similar need in the area of wrongful discharge legislation because industrial relations between labor and management are not involved here.

Yet there must be some demarcation line. The California State Bar proposed that wrongful discharge legislation mirror the provisions of the antidiscrimination laws. The position of the committee was that those excluded be employed as a "bona fide executive" or in a "high policy-making position" for at least two years and were entitled to a pension of at least $27,000 a year. This is the standard of the Age Discrimination Act. However, such individuals, though they were presumed to be able to protect themselves without resorting to the law, could make out a breach of contract action and recover damages comparable to the breach. The National Conference Report did not make any exclusions, although presumably higher-echelon employees would be party to a disproportionate number of agreements of a fixed duration.

One of the more interesting and perplexing issues involving the kind of employee to be covered, is whether public-sector employees, or those covered by civil service, and unionized employees affected by just cause provisions in collective bargaining are to be part of the wrongful discharge statute. The California State Bar Committee recommended that these groups be excluded because they already have protection. However, the National Conference Report has included employees covered by collective bargaining agreements. My own sense is that the National Conference Report has exhibited more perspicacity than the California State Bar Report in this respect. There are a number of factors that have impelled me to come to this conclusion.

The unspoken scandal in American labor law is that in contrast to Europe and Japan, the employee represented by a union and covered by a collective bargaining agreement has no right to take his or her case before an impartial tribunal. This state of affairs is attributable to the principle of exclusivity contained in American labor law and policy considerations first articulated by the Supreme Court in a series of arbitration decisions in the 1960s,[72] both of which have been read to give the unions broad discretion in determining what case will be processed to arbitration.

Because the system of grievance-arbitration in the United States is privately financed, employers and labor have consented to reduce the number of grievances and arbitrations and therefore the costs of the process, a goal that is hardly unworthy in the context of contemporary industrial relations and the litigious characteristics of American society generally. The difficulty here is that despite the desirability of an employee being able to pursue his or her claim, it is possible for the union to deny or refuse to process a worker's grievance on the ground that it is not sufficiently precedential or perhaps even because the union lacks the financial resources to pursue the matter to arbitration.[73]

This system has spawned litigation where informal procedures of arbitration are intended to govern. There are a host of decided cases at the federal and state level where employees are suing both the union and the employer on duty of fair representation and contract violation theories. The effect is to displace the preferred forum designated by the parties to the collective bargaining agreement, or arbitration. This is why, it seems to me, the National Conference draft report is correct in including unionized employees under the statute. The 1988 unanimous United States Supreme Court decision, *Lingle v. Norge Div. of Magic Chef, Inc.*,[74] discussed above, issued subsequent to the California State Bar Report is an additional reason for this position.

The statute would thus provide a minimum standard for machinery through which the employee could protest an allegedly unfair dismissal. In this way the United States could comply with the Termination of Employment Convention of the International Labor Organization, which obliges signatory countries to afford all employees access to such machinery regardless of their collective bargaining status. Even though the United States is not a signatory country, my judgment is that compliance with the convention is good public policy.

There is yet another problem with a wrongful discharge statute and the role of the unions in the United States. The conventional wisdom in America is that job security protection for employees outside the negotiated collective bargaining agreements created by labor and management is at odds with union interests and indeed would undercut union appeals to workers in organizational campaigns. The idea is that unions would not be able to advance in organizational efforts if protection was more widespread. This viewpoint has been held by many segments of the labor movement for some period of time.

But in 1987 the AFL-CIO Executive Council staked out a new position when it advocated wrongful discharge legislation as the "hallmark of a decent society." This is a position that now places the AFL-CIO on the side of legislative support as it is in areas that are also the subject of collective bargaining, such as social security benefits, aid to education, and comprehensive medical care. The council's statement, *The Employment at Will Doctrine*, notes that the public policy exception to the at-will rule is of ". . . a very limited scope and hence, even in theory, of benefit only to a small number of discharged employees."

The idea is that unions can bargain up beyond the floor established by law. The Federation, like others,[75] notes that employers can circumvent contractual obligations imposed upon them by virtue of personnel manuals simply by redrafting them. Although employers in the past expressed unease about taking such a route and concluding a provision to the effect that the employee can be dismissed with or without cause because of the potential invitation for union organizational campaigns, apparently the 1980s have convinced them that the prospects for that eventuality are much less a problem than litigation initiated by individual employees. And the court in *Foley*, while for the first time providing protection for employees under implied contractual theories, has provided employers with encouragement:

. . . the fundamental principles of freedom of contract: employer and employee are free to agree to a contract terminable at will or subject to limitations. Their agreement will be enforced so long as it does not violate legal strictures external to the contract, such as laws affecting union membership and activity, prohibitions on indentured servitude, or the many other legal restrictions which place certain restraints on the employment arrangement.[76]

In my view, the position that organized labor should support uniform protection fits neatly with ideas already propounded by the Federation a bit earlier in its report, *The Changing Situation of Unions* issued by the Executive Council in February 1985. In this landmark document the AFL-CIO, while properly excoriating the administration of national labor law, looked within itself to determine whether its institutional approach to organizational efforts was in need of reform. The Federation answered the question affirmatively.

The formula in *The Changing Situation of Unions* is a concept characterized as associate membership status. The idea is that there are services that the union can provide to employees that do not depend upon collective bargaining with an employer. This idea springs from both a growing percentage of NLRB elections in which unions are losing and the fact that a considerable minority of employees have an interest in unionization where, for instance, 20, 30, or 40 percent have voted for the union or signed a union authorization card. The 1985 report states the following:

> There are hundreds of thousands . . . non-union workers who voted for a union in an unsuccessful organizing campaign or who are supporting or have supported efforts to establish a union in their workplace. These individuals might well be willing to affiliate with a union with which they have had contact or with which they have some logical relationship provided that the costs were not prohibitive; this would be especially true to the extent unions offered services or benefits outside of the collective bargaining context . . .[77]

As the report further notes, ". . . polling data indicate that approximately 28% of all non-union employees—27,000,000 workers in all—are former union members; most of these individuals left their union not only because they left their unionized jobs."[78]

As of late 1991 the AFL-CIO had recruited 270,000 associate members. At this stage, however, the idea of union associate member status may be one of those good in theory and yet at least not sufficiently adapted to practice. This is so in the current circumstance for at least two reasons.

The first is the idea of membership itself. Unions are naturally wary about the admission of a new, potentially unwieldy, and unpredictable political block into its membership fold. The proposition of associate membership status will be acceptable only if the new group is distinguishable from regular membership and made politically subordinate, or indeed impotent. Assuming that membership is attractive to workers on this basis, the history of second-class citizenship in the modern democratic era is, in any event, not a particularly promising one. Internal discord is a real possibility here. Special membership classes with varying rights and obligations will prompt litigation under the Landrum-Griffin Act of 1959, which protects union members' democratic rights vis-à-vis the union. This is not the only reason that eight years after the widely hailed and praised report, the idea has difficulty in its implementation.

A second problem relates to the services provided. The best example articulated by the AFL-CIO is the credit card idea. That is to say, associate members would be attracted by this benefit by virtue of the competitive discount offered by banks on a group basis.

Good, so far—but the assumption behind the attractiveness is that employees must still be creditworthy. If used as an organizing vehicle, the technique could backfire on the union that sees its recruits rebuffed by the credit institution involved. What would be the reaction of such workers whose allegiances are sought and whose union instituted benefit applications are simultaneously and perhaps summarily denied? The idea is particularly troublesome given the fact that many workers involved in union organizational campaigns may have financial problems. That is frequently the attraction of unions. Yet their economic difficulties could serve to make them unworthy credit applicants and thus create more, not less, problems for the unions involved.

Nevertheless, the fact is that the 1985 report's idea contains the genesis of some constructive thinking. American unions traditionally offered the unorganized workers some prospect on improved employment conditions or income. My own judgment is that whatever the merits of the associate status idea, it is a valid one—but perhaps without the trappings of formal status as a sine qua non for realization of the concept.

In the first place the report is correct in advocating the utilization of a benefit of more obvious appeal, such as legal services. Equally important, this benefit is something about which the labor movement has considerable experience. It is a benefit frequently negotiated in collective bargaining agreements. This ought to be the key in terms of assessing the particular conditions or benefits that are made available to employees in the so-called associate membership status, or something akin to it.

A related possibility that might attract nonunion employees would link legal services with job security. This is why the ideas involved in the 1985 report are inherently bound up with consideration of unions and the wrongful discharge issue. Why not offer nonunion workers who are involved in wrongful discharge cases, for instance, legal representation. Quite obviously, this could be done selectively, namely where union organizational prospects hold some promise. Some kind of screening process to evaluate the claims would be required.

But the central point is this. The most propitious circumstances for union entry into the field will take place in the context of wrongful or unfair dismissal legislation of the kind advocated in this chapter. There are at least three good reasons for this position.

The first is that it permits unions to seize the high ground of public opinion and to take a position because it is right. This is the essential thrust of the February 17, 1987, AFL-CIO report on wrongful discharge legislation. This position should serve labor well in building much needed bridges to the outside world which are necessary to construct.

The second reason is that unions are in an infinitely better position to intervene in an organized establishment where arbitration or some other extrajudicial dispute resolution mechanism is brought into play. Clearly their own staff members are involved in the representation of employees in arbitration proceedings where the union is already the exclusive bargaining representative. It is the labor movement that possesses a near monopoly on this kind of experience. Although such a move will involve a diversion of the staff time, a cost that most unions are not willing to undertake, it is an expenditure that unions may make more readily than in the case of litigation. For their part, nonunion employees may be more willing to proceed where the process invoked is less cumbersome and fearsome.

A third factor that could promote union resurgence is that state legislation promoting the arbitration of wrongful dismissal claims, like labor-management arbitration, can protect employees from discharge or discrimination because of union membership. The question of whether the states may enact legislation regulating and prohibiting the antiunion discharge cases is by no means free from constitutional doubt given the doctrine of preemption that frequently holds that the National Labor Relations Board occupies the subject matter field where Congress has legislated pervasively in a detailed fashion.[79] But a plurality of the Supreme Court seems to have accepted the view that states may legislate generally, even though, in doing so, such laws impinge upon areas covered by federal labor law.[80] The matter has hardly been resolved at the Supreme Court level in any definitive fashion.

Assuming its constitutionality, informal arbitration mandated by law for nonunion workers involved in organizational campaigns or other forms of concerted activity is a forum more attractive in many respects than that of the NLRB. Access should be more expeditious and inexpensive than the Board, even one reformed along the lines advocated in chapter 5. Of course the failure of the antiunion discrimination claims will not resolve the just cause issue. The dismissed employee remains free, unlike his or her position in cases arising under the National Labor Relations Act, to pursue a just cause theory that is based upon an allegation of arbitrary treatment unrelated to union membership.

But the wrongful discharge issue sounds a broader theme. Unions can assist unorganized workers and foster their own growth through utilization of the new basket of individual rights that has become a part of the employment relationship in the 1970s and 1980s. Wrongful discharge or unjust dismissal simply happens to be one of the prominent issues today.

Occupational Safety and Health Act violations present another problem confronting workers with considerable frequency. As Clyde Summers has noted, a complaint of a violation of the Act may be filed with OSHA by any "employee or representative of employees," the complaint triggering an inspection.[81] A compliance officer of OSHA may select a member of the safety committee that is a "representative of employees," for the purpose of accompanying the inspecting compliance officer and discussing claims of violations, to participate in the opening conference. Other representation rights are granted. Essentially the same functions engaged in by a majority union may be utilized under OSHA.

Legislation introduced by Senator Edward Kennedy in 1992 would amend the Occupational Safety and Health Act and mandate employee committees charged with responsibility in the health and safety arena. If this legislation is enacted in the future, another institutional basis for representing worker interests relating to employment conditions independent of union majority rule would exist.

Other opportunities exist by virtue of ERISA cases in which many union labor law firms maintain specialized departments. Union specialists at national headquarters and, in some instances, the resources of local union health and safety committees could be brought to bear. The same holds true for assistance aimed at the problems of alien workers.

The United Food and Commercial Workers Union has provided yet another illustration of union initiatives focused upon employment problems of the unorganized. The union has assisted workers at Iowa Beef and Packing Company in connection with violations of the Fair

Labor Standards Act of 1938, the minimum wage and maximum hour legislation. The investigation appears to have yielded valid claims, and this effort may provide a model for other union initiatives.[82]

The point is that the labor movement, without necessarily tying itself to a banner of formal associate membership concepts, can play a role in both self-help as well as addressing and, in some instances, processing the complaints emanating from the nonunion work force where the statute or common law or some other procedure allow them to do so (see table 3.1).[83]

This, it seems to me, is no substitute for full-fledged union representation. Indeed, in the case of employer-initiated wrongful discharge procedures, unions may demonstrate the imperfections inherent in them. If the unions are able and willing to undertake this initiative—and it must be admitted that most of labor has been lethargic in attempting to regain lost ground—they can build upon the nonunion world of wrongful discharge (just as it seems to me that they can utilize the nonunion world of works councils described in chapter 2).

If the conduct of unions is vigorous and effective, employee interest in the collective bargaining process may be sparked. But what is involved here is rather fundamental and far-reaching. It is that unions must assume a role beyond that of the traditional collective bargaining representative. In a sense this is a reemergence of the role of unions before the modern collective bargaining era when they frequently acted as providers of benefits for workers in need.

It is of course more than that. It is a program that is designed to promote the unions in obtaining the goal of a unionized relationship. But the way station of union activity proposed here requires new thinking and expertise, and certainly a commitment to union activism.

Employees and Subject Matter

Finally, the California State Bar Committee Report advocated that employers who employ fifty or more employees should be covered by the statute. The practical effect of this would be that employees who are able to maintain wrongful discharge actions now who are employed by smaller employers would not be able to do so unless they utilize a theory not covered by the statute—in the case of the California report, libel, slander, defamation, loss of consortium, and assault, theories that are not directly related to the propriety of the dismissal itself. The National Commission special conference draft would cover em-

Table 3.1
A sampling of worker associations

Association	Years in existence	Number of members	Union affiliation	Services
Montana Family Union	3	1,400	AFL-CIO	Union credit cards, group-rate health insurance, legal consultation
9 to 5: Association for Working Women (Cleveland)	20	15,000	Service Employees International Union	Toll-free hotline, courses on sexual harassment and VDT injuries, lobbying on workplace issues
National Association for Working Americans (Cincinatti)	2	1,700	AFL-CIO	Hotline, rallies and petitions to support legislation, dislocated-worker support group
California Immigrant Workers Association	3	6,000	AFL-CIO	Help processing immigration papers, legal representation and enforcement of minimum-wage and overtime violations
AIM (Associate ILGWU Members, New York)	5	2,500	International Ladies Garment Workers Union	English classes, graduate-equivalency diploma courses, computer courses, skills training. Legal help with immigration, minimum wage, OSHA, sexual harassment, disability and pensions

Source: *Wall Street Journal*, January 13, 1993.

ployers who employ ten or more employees. Perhaps some kind of intermediate approach would be an appropriate one.

Standard for Dismissal

The standard for dismissal is a major area of dispute, and it plays a central role in legislation efforts. The dissenters in the California report advocated a good-faith standard—but some of the contract cases use just cause or good cause as their standard where contractual obligations are relevant. My own judgment is that the cause standard would be appropriate for wrongful discharge legislation. This is the view adopted by the California State Bar Committee Report.

The California report made it clear that employer dismissals based upon economic considerations were not covered—and the National Conference Report seems to have gone a little further in explicitly defining employers' legitimate economic needs in connection with both disciplinary dismissals and economic layoffs. The National Conference Report also states that good cause means "reasonable basis" for the action taken in light of the employee's responsibilities, conduct, and performance, but that interpretation seems to be almost identical to the standard that has evolved in the arbitral common law under collective bargaining agreements in the organized sector.

Given the possible applicability of such a statute to managerial, professional, and upper-echelon employees, inevitably more deference must be given to the employer's judgment than is the case under collective bargaining agreements, which do not generally apply to such employees. The National Commission, like the California committee, would accord deference and allow employers to change performance standards in this area. Said the California committee:

. . . although [such] . . . employees would be protected by the just cause standard, we subscribe to the view that more substantive deference must be given the managerial decision making process with regard to such employees because of the subjective nature of their work.[84]

Forum and Remedy

In a sense the issues of forum and remedy are deeply intertwined. Many observers believe, erroneously in my view, that particular remedies must flow from a particular choice of forum. The classic assumption in the wrongful discharge arena is that reinstatement must be an automatically presumed remedy if arbitration is the forum rather than the courts.

A related issue is the question of cost and whether the preferred institution under a statute should be privately financed or whether costs should be assumed by the government as is true under the National Labor Relations Act and the administrative portions of title VII of the Civil Rights Act of 1964.

In one of the more thoughtful discussions of this problem, Janice Bellace has proposed that the question of a dismissal's propriety can be heard before an administrative law judge of the unemployment compensation insurance system.[85] Since such judges, Janice Bellace reasons, hear a similar issue every time a worker makes a claim for unemployment compensation assistance—namely is the worker dismissed "through no fault of his or her own"—their consideration of the wrongful discharge statute would simply replicate the function that they would perform in any event. Tied to Bellace's proposal is the idea that any institutional stress would be minimal given the remedy—namely a separation severance allotment that would take the place of reinstatement. This approach proceeds upon the assumption that such a remedy represents the only practical avenue to pursue and that reinstatement, without the presence of unionized representative who can police employer conduct aimed at dissuading the worker from pursuing reemployment, is ineffective.

The same analysis is behind the proposal of the National Conference which would allow either express written agreements providing for good cause or, more important, the waiver of good cause and the provision of severance pay in an amount equal to "at least one month's pay for each period of employment totaling one year, up to a maximum total payment to 30 month's pay at the employee's rate of pay in effect immediately before the termination."[86] The idea of a severance pay arrangement is probably close to what happens in Europe and Japan as well as the way in which litigation is resolved today. The severance pay approach, adopted by the National Conference, would encourage rational problem solving. On this matter the California committee was silent and thus did not provide comparable incentive for settlement.

In a sense the recent Rand report on wrongful termination[87] can support part of the analysis for both of these two proposals. In a very careful examination of wrongful discharge actions before judges and juries, the report concludes:

... despite the high frequency of success and large average rewards, half the plaintiffs actually take home a very modest compensation. After discounting this sum [a median payment of $30,000] (assuming a 9% nominal interest rate over this period and a five-year delay from the date of termination to final payment) one is left with the conclusion that the typical plaintiff received the equivalent of one-half year's severance pay. By inducing terminated employees to accept such a severance, employers could save $84,000 in defense fees.[88]

In part, however, this approach proceeds upon an assumption that not only is reinstatement impractical,[89] but also unemployment compensation administrative law judges would have credibility that would be comparable to either the courts or arbitration. My own judgment is that regardless of other aspects of the remedy argument, this view is erroneous. Resistance to wrongful discharge legislation, particularly by employers, would grow considerably if the jurisdiction were placed in the hands of an existing agency such as the unemployment compensation board and their administrative law judges. Bellace's proposal is logically unassailable, but as Justice Holmes has told us, history assumes considerably more importance than logic. It understates the matter to say that employers do not have confidence in this process.

It is possible that other administrative agencies, such as the National Labor Relations Board at the federal level, would be appropriate. But the difficulty here is that there is always resistance to expanding the Board's jurisdiction—and the same considerations would come into play at the state level if state labor agencies were involved. If legislation contained provisions that would provide for a new agency, it seems unlikely that this would garner support in an age of budget austerity. Accordingly, the choices are essentially between arbitration and the courts. These are not necessarily the best routes to be taken, but given the alternatives, they seem to me to be the best ones available.

Arbitration seems to me—and the California State Bar Committee contained this recommendation in its report—to be the best forum for wrongful discharge complaints. The arbitration would be privately financed. It is interesting to note that again the recommendation of the National Conference appears to mirror this proposal, though its report is deliberately flexible, allowing for a variety of fora and answers to the question of finance.

It will be said that a sharing of the costs between an individual employee and the corporation is unfair to the worker who has less resources. But the limitations identified are even worse in the case of the courts. Recall the inordinate costs that workers as plaintiffs must endure just to have the opportunity to get to trial. Since the union is not present in most of these cases to sift out the less meritorious claims, there must be some financial incentive not to take the case to arbitration in every instance. The National Adjustment Board, operating under the Railway Labor Act, is currently bogged down with cases involving the railroads and the airlines because of the fact that the machinery is without cost to all the parties.

Arbitration would seem to be the best approach for the very same reason that it has won favor in the organized sector of the economy. Informality, expertise, speed, and less expense are all factors that ought to lend themselves to all the parties. Of course there are a host of objections to arbitration. The first is that given its relative inexpensive quality, there will be an avalanche of cases. But in some measure, private financing is a response to this point. In Canada arbitration exists for wrongful discharge cases, and problems of this kind have not materialized.

A second related issue is whether there would be enough arbitrators to hear the cases. In part this relates directly to the avalanche idea identified previously—but to the extent that new third parties are needed, it would seem as though entities like the American Arbitration Association or the Federal Mediation and Conciliation Service could engage in training programs that would recruit new arbitrators. If, God forbid, the entire membership of the National Academy of Arbitrators—the elite professional arbitral body in the United States and Canada—were to perish in an air crash tomorrow, the process would not die with them. New recruits and replacements would be found.

But even if the arbitrators are available, it is said that such a process will be basically unfair to the individual employee. This is so, runs the argument, because in contrast to unions, which maintain lists of arbitrators who can be trusted, there will be no institutional body that will serve the same purpose for nonunion employees. The arbitrator will not see the employee again. But he or she will have contact with the employer, and, the argument runs, there will be an institutional bias therefore in favor of the employer and against the employee.

There is no satisfactory answer to this matter. It cannot but raise doubts about primary or exclusive reliance upon arbitration as a forum. Yet the problem does not seem to have materialized in Canada where arbitrators have jurisdiction over wrongful discharge cases.

Again, given the alternatives, I would think that it would be preferable to take some chances with arbitration despite its imperfections.

A problem that may prove to be political in jurisdictions such as California lies in the constitutional argument that an individual employee or employer is entitled to a judge and jury and that to repose jurisdiction in the hands of the arbitrator is to unconstitutionally abdicate judicial authority. The California Supreme Court has held that only full judicial review can satisfy the state constitution where an administrative entity is authorized to award monetary or damage relief.[90] Of course wrongful discharge litigation provides punitive and compensatory damages, and, as discussed below, some form of damages beyond back pay seems to be appropriate here. The problem with full judicial review under the circumstances is that just as in the cases involving finality of arbitration awards under collective bargaining agreements,[91] review would be unsatisfactory because it would erode the benefits of expertise and invite litigation where the intention of such a statute would be to discourage it.

Nonetheless, given all the doubts expressed and the adamant opposition of both employers and lawyers (who perceive any movement away from judge and jury and punitive and compensatory damages as harmful to their interest in contingent fees), interested parties must think about some kind of compromise that would permit arbitrators and judges to coexist under one statutory scheme. Essentially this would track the Montana statute, which attempts to induce, but will not require, the parties to go to arbitration. In Montana, the party that refuses to go to arbitration must pay the other side's attorneys' fees and costs if it does not prevail. That approach would seem to be a sound one, although, in my view, attorneys' fees would not be an adequate inducement to arbitration.

If the parties agree to arbitration, traditional labor law remedies, alongside of an abbreviated discovery with emphasis upon mediation of the hearings,[92] ought to be applicable. That is to say, if the worker prevails, he or she should be awarded back pay with interest and reinstatement where appropriate. Reinstatement is not presumed to be appropriate where there is an absence of a union, and particularly where the employee is a higher-echelon or professional type whose work is difficult to review because of its subjective nature—with front pay or damages for losses for at least two years (probably the figure advocated by the California State Bar Committee is too small, although the National Conference has recommended less) subsequent to the time at which reinstatement would have taken place. Front pay would be particularly appropriate in the absence of reinstatement.

Reinstatement would be desirable if it is provided expeditiously, and there is a real opportunity to restore the employment relationship. Reinstatement is not available now as a matter of common law because of the law's traditional reluctance to compel relationships where personal services are involved—a reticence that is in sharp contrast to the development of modern statutory labor law in the United States, particularly the National Labor Relations Act and title VII of the Civil Rights Act of 1964. Finally, if the employee prevails, attorneys' fees would be provided, but attorneys' fees would be awarded if the employer prevails and there was evidence of bad faith on the employees' part in pursuing the claim—a policy similar to the standard now employed under title VII.[93]

Perhaps, if the matter goes to court rather than arbitration under a statute that would permit both options, reinstatement should not be available, but the whole of punitive and compensatory damages would be present. If the employee refused to accede to a request for arbitration by the employer, then it would be liable to the employer for attorneys' fees and costs without a showing of bad faith if the employer prevails. The difficulty with this idea is that in California where extended discussions have taken place about a statute that could replace the common law, the respective parties have come nowhere near agreeing upon the amount of damages or a cap as it has been fashioned by the Civil Rights Act of 1991. It might be possible to provide traditional labor law remedies where the employee refused to go to arbitration but to cap it when the employee was willing to do so and the employer resisted.

Reasonable men and women can differ about the details of the wrongful discharge statute. If there is a lid on damages in arbitration or in the courts, perhaps it should take into account the size of the employer as the provisions about the Civil Rights Act of 1991 seem to assume. Conceding that the present state of the law is infinitely preferable to that of a decade ago when employees had virtually no protection against arbitrary dismissals, the law of wrongful discharge nevertheless contains a major deficiency that is harmful to employees, employers, and labor organizations. Employers have been reluctant to support wrongful discharge legislation because they would prefer to trade off unlimited liability for a relatively few workers as against limited liability for the masses of employees. Trial lawyers have been the most hostile of all players because they see limited liability interfering with their present economic status.

Although labor unions organize employees by intervening in the nonunion sector and could use wrongful discharge legislation as a forum in which to protest the dismissal of workers in a more expeditious manner than presently exists before the Labor Board, they have not seen wrongful discharge legislation as a priority on their agenda. But the Court's decision in *Lingle*, which will tempt employees to pursue public-policy claims rather than to resort to grievance-arbitration machinery, as well as the declining status of the unions and their interest in representing workers outside the traditional collective bargaining framework, may change the posture at both the state and federal level in the years to come. The idea of legislation protecting employees against arbitrary dismissals or dismissals without cause is an idea whose time has come. What remains is to implement the idea effectively.

The Collective Bargaining Process

Most of the wrongful discharge litigation law, and certainly all of it that has applicability to the unionized sector, applies only to disciplinary dismissals. Yet inevitably—particularly in those cases where middle management emerges and job and corporate mergers have been instituted by management and protested by employees—the principles have had some applicability to economic dismissals as well. But traditionally under collective bargaining agreements, there has been little protection beyond seniority (last hired, first fired) and compensation arrangements, like those first negotiated by the United Auto Workers thirty-eight years ago—the 1990 agreement between the UAW and the Big Three fashioning some of the most innovative and expansive income guarantees—for workers in connection with economic dismissals.

Except for the Age Discrimination Act and the Employee Retirement Income Security Act of 1974, the federal labor law has been of little help to workers. The Supreme Court held that employers are not obliged to bargain with unions before partially closing operations and dismissing workers in the process.[94] The Court has also declined to protect workers in mergers, acquisitions,[95] and bankruptcies.[96] Although unions possess the potential for blocking business rearrangements where they have negotiated a provision obliging the seller to condition a sale upon assumption of the contract by the purchaser, many of these actions have not in fact succeeded. Once the status quo permits the seller to move ahead with the sale without passing on the contract to the purchaser as a condition of the sale, the dynamics shift the balance of power in favor of management given the union's reliance upon a time-consuming arbitration proceeding where the result is more likely to be limited damages rather than the acquisition of jobs and the other contractual provisions.

Japanese investment in the unionized sector of the United States—the Japanese themselves having established job security for some workers through the permanent employment system in their own country—seems to have served as an impetus for new provisions at this time in the United States, particularly at the General Motors–Toyota joint venture in Fremont, California, and the new General Motors division, Saturn, which has established a plant in Tennessee to compete with Japanese imports, Mazda and National Steel. The agreement between the New United Motors Manufacturing, Inc. (the GM–Toyota joint venture in Fremont, California) and the UAW reads as follows:

> The employer obliges itself not to . . . lay off employees unless compelled to do so by severe economic conditions that threaten the long term financial viability of the Company.
>
> The Company will take affirmative measures before laying off any employees, including such measures as the reduction of salaries of its officers and management, assigning previously subcontracted work to bargaining unit employees capable of performing this work, seeking voluntary layoffs and other cost-saving measures.[97]

Similarly the memorandum between Saturn and the UAW states that employees who are among the 80 percent with the longest service of employment possess "permanent job security eligibility." This means that such workers will not be laid off ". . . except in situations which the SAC determines are due to unforeseen or catastrophic events or severe economic conditions."[98]

Firmer prohibitions against layoffs have been obtained in the major farm equipment manufacturer, J.I. Case. Xerox Corporation and the Amalgamated Clothing Workers have negotiated collective bargaining agreements in which the employer promises not to lay off under any circumstances. This appears to go beyond new arrangements that derive their inspiration from the Japanese industrial relations system.

Such agreements are thought to be the product of partnership and jointness between labor and management, a substitute for the old adversarial system and more of a mirror of new cooperative labor management relations such as those that have been in existence in Japan for some time.[99] At the same time most firms—union and non-union—retain near complete discretion to engage in economic dismissals. This is where unions will have to be active in order not to lose ground, particularly considering the advent of wrongful discharge litigation and the potential for being outflanked by another system that provides for more regulation.

Plant-Closing Legislation

Japan and all the western European countries have some form of statutory protection against unfair or socially unwarranted dismissals and access for employee challenges against employer decisions in industrial tribunals. In the most debated problem area of employee rights in the United States—plant closures—Europe has provided for notification and consultation and relocation rights for employees; only a small number of states have enacted similar laws in this country. The Supreme Court has held that state plant closure legislation providing for severance pay is constitutional, notwithstanding the existence of both the National Labor Relations Act and the Employment Retirement and Income Security Act of 1974 and the argument that the existence of federal law preempts the field avoiding state legislation.[100] At least with regard to state law providing for severance pay, such contentions have been unsuccessful.

A 1988 statute, the Worker Adjustment and Retraining Notification Act (WARN), provides for sixty-day notice to workers or their representatives in a plant closing or mass layoffs that constitute 33 percent of the work force. Given the substantial debate about the 1988 Act and the view of some members of the Republican party that the statute provided for an assault upon employer property rights, the limited scope of the statute as finally enacted is not entirely surprising.

In the first place the Act only covers employers with 100 or more employees, excluding thereby 98 percent of the business community from statutory coverage. Although a sixty-day notice is imposed, the statute contains numerous loopholes. For instance, where an employer was "actively" seeking capital or business that, if obtained, would have enabled the employer to avoid or postpone the shutdown and the employer reasonably in good faith believed that giving the notice would have precluded the employer from obtaining the needed capital or business, the full sixty-day notice requirement does not apply.

Another problem area sure to appear in the federal courts that have jurisdiction over this statute—not for the purposes of imposing injunctions but rather for assessment of monetary damages—relates to a similar reduction of the notice where the dislocation is "caused by business circumstances that were not reasonably foreseeable at the time when notice would have been required." (A third but seemingly less vexatious exception provides for no notice in the event of a natural disaster.)

The Conference Report agreed upon by the House and the Senate provides that "not reasonably foreseeable business circumstances" are present where an employer must suddenly and unexpectedly terminate a major contract or experiences a sudden unexpected or traumatic change in business conditions such as price, cost, or declines in customer orders. With regard to the proviso that reduces notice where the employer is actively seeking capital or business, the report indicates that the burden is upon the employer to demonstrate that it was a realistic opportunity to obtain such financing or business and that success would have enabled the employer to keep the plant or facility open for a reasonable period of time.

Some of these provisions could be grist for the litigation mill. Yet the enactment of federal law in this arena is important and noteworthy. In five years since the 1988 law was enacted in the teeth of President Reagan's threatened veto of it—he ultimately let the Act become law without signing it—litigation about its meaning has been relatively sparse.

Meanwhile the states have been active in providing protection in the employment relationship. Thirteen states have laws regulating plant closings or relocations: Connecticut, Hawaii, Kansas, Maine, Maryland, Mississippi, Michigan, Minnesota, Montana, Oregon, South Carolina, Tennessee, and Wisconsin. An examination of some of these statutes reveals a broad spectrum of legislative responses to the problems caused by plant closings and relocations.[101]

Aside from plant-closing legislation, states have attempted to legislate more effectively or to supplement federal protection. Some jurisdictions, addressing more effectively the protection afforded women denied jobs because of hazards posed to their reproductive capabilities, have protected the right of women to sue their employers for damage suffered by the fetus as a result of unsafe employment conditions.[102] As noted above, some states have gone further than the Civil Rights Act of 1964 in protecting women against dismissal because of pregnancy.[103] More recently the states have intervened to provide wages, hours, and conditions of employment and, as in the pregnancy cases, have encouraged employers to challenge such statutes on the ground that they are preempted by federal labor law. The irony here is that twenty years ago state regulation was pushed to one side in the name of preemption doctrine by proponents of employee rights because of the perceived harm to union organizational activities through such measures as the licensing of union business agents[104] and punitive and compensatory damages fashioned against strikes and picketing.[105] Now one hears the call for a new jurisprudence of preemption that will provide the states with more latitude, particularly in connection with governmental efforts to protect individual rights. The circle seems to be closing.

Not surprisingly the Supreme Court, now populated by a solid Nixon-Reagan-Bush majority, has become supportive of the doctrine of preemption when states attempt to protect the welfare of their employees in a manner that is more ambitious than that provided for by the federal government. In *Gade v. National Solid Waste Management Association* a divided Supreme Court, in an opinion authored by Justice Sandra Day O'Connor, held that state regulation of occupational safety and health issues that have not been approved by the secretary of labor, and for which a federal standard is in effect, is preempted as in conflict with the Occupational Safety and Health Act. The Court came to this conclusion notwithstanding the fact that the state law was aimed at protecting both workers and the public and thus had a "dual impact." Said the Court:

A state law requirement that directly, substantially, and specifically regulates occupational health and safety is an occupational safety and health standard within the meaning of the Act. That such a law may also have a nonoccupational impact does not render it any less of an occupational standard for purposes of preemption analysis. If the State wishes to enact a dual impact law that regulates an occupational safety or health issue for which a federal standard is in effect, §18 of the Act requires that the State submit a plan for the approval of the Secretary.[106]

Conclusion

In all of these legislative efforts there is something of a vague historical parallel in the Norris-LaGuardia Act of 1932 itself.[107] This statute, which represented a kind of apogee for a labor movement led by

Samuel Gompers who sought to keep the courts out of the affairs of unions, was inadequate in addressing employer self-help such as the use of spies, and retaliatory measures against workers involving discrimination in employment conditions, violence, and other measures. Yet the fact that the public policy of the statute promoted freedom of association was of value when the National Labor Relations Act, which contained a similar preamble, was enacted three years later.

It is quite possible that WARN, whatever its limitations,[108] has set the stage for more ambitious initiatives at both the federal and state level in the coming years. In the unfair dismissal arena, involving the individual discharge of a worker, a number of states have enacted so-called whistle-blower statutes. But only Montana and the territories of the Virgin Islands and Puerto Rico have passed more general legislation circumscribing so-called unfair dismissals that are nonetheless limited in both scope and impact. Puerto Rico and the Virgin Islands, however, simply provide for severance pay and not monetary damages or reinstatement. Again the collective and individual employee interests do not exist in vacuo. It may be that these statutes will not affect unionization. Contrary to the widely accepted view, the only impact can be helpful in promoting the process.

The 1980s have transformed this rule of law fundamentally, notwithstanding the defeat of numerous legislative proposals designed to more effectively guarantee worker rights in a number of the state legislatures throughout the country. It is the courts fashioning common law and, more important, the juries administering their own form of both due process and justice that have changed legal developments in recent years. By virtue of the Supreme Court's *Gilmer* decision, which held that arbitration procedures can bar wrongful discharge actions, nonunion employers confronted with the prospect of such litigation will be more likely to opt for company-initiated arbitration that limits their liability as well as provides possible finality against attacks in the courts. But the question of whether such mechanisms are fair to the workers on issues of employee representation, control of the procedures, financing of the process, as well as selection of the arbitrators has not yet been definitely resolved by either the legislative or judicial branches of government. Protection for nonunion employees must not await comprehensive wrongful discharge legislation. All of these changes must affect ideas about the employment relationship as it relates to individual and collective interests in both the organized and unorganized sectors of the economy.

4

The Variety and Vagaries of Workers' Participation: Labor-Management Cooperation or Co-optation

I say to people on the Continent: "Stop talking about worker participation in business management. You are back in the Marxist Era!"
—Former Prime Minister
Margaret Thatcher of Great Britain[1]

Partnerships between labor and management are possible only when both groups possess real freedom and power to influence decisions. This means that unions ought to continue to play an important role in moving toward greater economic participation within firms and industries. Workers rightly reject calls for less adversarial relations when they are a smokescreen for demand that labor make all the concessions. For a partnership to be genuine it must be a two way street, with creative initiative and a willingness to cooperate on all sides . . .

The purpose of unions is not simply to defend the existing wages and prerogatives of the fraction of workers who belong to them, but also to enable workers to make positive and creative contributions to the firm, the community, and the large of society in an organized and cooperative way. Such contributions call for experiments with new directions in the U.S. labor movement.

—"Economic Justice for All: Pastoral Letter on Catholic Social Teaching and the U.S. Economy"[2]

A number of major developments promise to reshape industrial relations between labor and management in this country. One of them, the rising expectations of workers in wrongful discharge actions, was described in chapter 3. None, however, assumes the significance and potential for long-lasting institutional reform in industrial relations as do initiatives toward workers' or employee participation.

Just as the wrongful discharge aspect of the employment relationship has had its first and principal impact in the nonunion sector, so also the engine driving employee participation has its origins outside the established labor-management relationships. Indeed union unease about the matter is fundamentally attributable to managerial reliance upon a variety of employee participation mechanisms that are frequently designed to keep unions out of the establishment altogether—to maintain a "union-free" environment or to diminish union influence where unions exist. Prior to the 1970s employers demonstrated little interest in employee involvement and institutions through which it could be effectuated. During the past twenty years as the union decline has accelerated, employer interest in such systems has grown geometrically. To make matters worse from the perspective of easing union concerns, the roots of trade union distrust are to be found in the development of scientific management in the early part of this century, a mechanism through which job autonomy and the position of skilled workers were eroded through a regimen of dehumanizing time study to speed up a carefully scrutinized work force.

Whatever the merits of that debate past or present, it has spilled over into established and even mature relationships where labor is recognized by management on the contemporary scene. The concern by some elements in the labor movement—the "New Directions" caucus in the United Auto Workers is one of the most outspoken opponents of cooperative relationships with employers—is that they serve as a device to co-opt, subordinate, and ultimately supplant free-trade unionism. Thus the challenge for labor, which emanates from nonunion employers in particular, is one that presents itself in two different forums.

For the past two hundred years there has been a considerable lag between our society's willingness (to a lesser extent this has been true of the West in general) to accept political democracy, conceded in substantial part in the nineteenth century, and a similar view of economic democracy in the corporation and the workplace. Workers' participatory initiatives are a response to this. But they are much more, consisting of an assault on the adversarial "them-us" labor-management mentality which promotes or accedes to conflict by both sides of the table, as well as an employer focus upon efficiency and competition generated by both the Japanese and the deregulation of previously regulated industries.[3]

The most profound impact of all of this in recent years has been changes in the relationship between employee and employer at the shop floor level, a prominent example of which is the team method of work assignments and responsibilities that has found acceptance in much of basic manufacturing. As John Hoerr has written: "the goal is for workers to learn all tasks performed by their team, rotate job to job, and assume most of the management functions of the old foreman. Critics say the gain in power for workers is illusory, and in some cases it is. But by no means always. At an LTV Steel Co. plant in Cleveland, for example, teams of highly trained technicians manage a huge electrogalvanizing line practically by themselves and participate in decisions on hiring, scheduling of work and hours, and operations planning."[4]

As Hoerr said later: ". . . employee involvement or worker participation or labor-management 'jointness,' as it is now known in the auto industry . . . gives managers a powerful tool to improve productivity and quality but could undermine their control . . . [i]t promises workers autonomy over their job, but also threatens their old ways of working."[5]

The backdrop for this relationship between the United Auto Workers and the auto companies—institutionalized through Quality of Work Life agreements beginning in 1973—was declining American competitiveness coupled with the phenomenon of archaic work rules and a plethora of unnecessary job classifications circumscribing managerial flexibility in work assignments. Meanwhile the stifling and frustration of such expression has been presumed to be responsible for the phenomenon of employee alienation, the so-called "Lordstown syndrome" of wildcat stoppages and absenteeism prevalent in the 1960s and early 1970s.[6] Lack of employee involvement exacerbated distrust between employee and employer and deterred employee interest in and loyalty to the firm and its product. This in turn made the prospect for a long-term employment relationship and some form of job security more tenuous, given the erosion of competitiveness and product quality engendered by distrust. The circle was completed in catch-22 form, as the prospects for cooperation between the parties—in- or outside of a unionized situation—declined as stability in the employment relationship diminished.

The response to these phenomena has been a wide variety of employee or workers participation schemes. Some of the more prominent illustrations of this phenomenon are the appointment of worker directors on the board, whether union leaders, representatives, or employees of the firm itself; quality work circles and other forms of shop floor employee involvement; and employee-owned companies.[7] Generally such reforms are instituted in severe economic crises through employee-buyout discussions. They were ultimately unsuccessful at the relatively well-functioning, if not mildly profitable, United Airlines when that company was hardly at death's door. But this has been an exception to the rule.

The most obvious reason for limited acceptance of worker directors or worker representatives on the board, as well as employee ownership, is the obduracy of employers and their unwillingness to share either power or responsibility with union or worker representatives. But a second factor is the trade union leadership itself through much of the past decade. This is hardly surprising. Aside from the rigidity of employers and their resistance to seating union or worker representatives on the board or in other positions of management responsibility, the trade union leadership has been critical of such ideas—particularly the worker director variation—in an outspoken and derisive fashion. This idea, as well as other forms of codetermination between organized labor and management, had been dismissed out of hand by some American labor leaders as alien to our soil, peculiarly European in nature, and fostered in an environment in which the North American system of collective bargaining had not taken root. The assumption is that such processes are inconsistent with the idea of trade union autonomy that has taken root on this continent.

The major areas for debate in the United States about employee participation as a general matter have been the internal political processes of the United Automobile Workers, the United Steelworkers, and the International Association of Machinists. In the UAW this debate has precipitated the formation of the "New Directions Caucus." Union support for the team concept and cooperative undertakings have been articulated by UAW President Owen Bieber and, with more enthusiasm and emphasis, by former President Douglas Fraser. On the other hand, in a White Paper issued in 1991, the leadership of the International Association of Machinists has taken a decidedly hostile posture. The IAM has expressed a policy that is aimed at resisting the team concept program. States the IAM:

By their very nature, these programs [team concept programs] interfere with the union's obligations, (1) to represent each and every member of the bargaining unit, (2) to enter into collective bargaining over wages, hours and working conditions, (3) to abide by and enforce the terms and conditions of any collective bargaining agreement already in affect, and (4) to preserve the integrity of the union as an autonomous, democratic organization free from employer domination according to the laws of the land and the IAM's own Constitution and By-laws.[8]

Taking note of a thesis of Edwards Deming which has been accepted for so long in Japan and now is the object of attention in this country, the IAM maintains that such policies are easy to "sell" to workers because they are "actually a top-down, executive-directed, communication, command and control system intent on achieving efficiency and cost cutting by eliminating rework, scrap, waste and inspection, and it has very little to do with meaningful worker participation."[9] No such programs, maintain the IAM, involve the unions in employer unilateral decision making and therefore make union acceptance of such policies problematic. If there is no alternative to a team policy, the IAM recommends that a "truly joint" system of representation be devised.

Nonetheless, a number of arrangements that include worker director features, have emerged during the past decade, particularly in the unionized sector of the economy. The threat of bankruptcy at RATH Meatpacking in 1978 produced an employee buyout and employee stock ownership plan (ESOP) in which workers obtained ten of the sixteen seats on the board of directors. As part of a broader agreement between Chrysler Corporation and the United Auto Workers in 1979—where the federal government participated in what has been described as a "bailout" of Chrysler, the union providing concessions estimated at $202 million and a one-year deferral of $200 million payment to the pension fund—the UAW President Douglas Fraser was given a seat on Chrysler's eighteen-member board of directors. Chrysler emphasized the fact that Fraser's appointment was due to his own outstanding qualifications and credentials, that his selection did not represent an institutional arrangement with the UAW, and that the appointment was not part of the collective bargaining agreement.

While Fraser's appointment lasted beyond his retirement as president of the UAW in 1983, the UAW eventually talked about inserting the representation on the board principle in the labor contract itself. Ultimately both the union and the company relented in their respective hardline positions. Chrysler acceded to President Owen Bieber's appointment to the board, and the UAW did not seriously bargain for or insist upon incorporation of the concept of the agreement. In 1991, however, Chrysler eliminated the union board seat. The UAW did not take the matter seriously enough to make Bieber's removal a significant issue in their relationship with Chrysler. Yet Fraser, subsequent to his retirement from both union leadership and the Chrysler board, wrote of his successful efforts at convincing the board to take into account the impact upon workers and the community in plant closings.[10]

This was not the UAW's only experience with representation on the board. In 1980 an American Motors Corporation agreement with the United Auto Workers failed when the U.S. Department of Justice took the position that the agreement was unlawful under the antiinterlocking directorate provisions of antitrust law[11] because the union would have had seats on the board of directors of two competitors. Accordingly the union did not have representation on the board at any of the auto companies, even though it once spoke of spreading the Chrysler concept to both General Motors and Ford. Unions also obtained seats on the board of directors at Western Airlines in exchange for a two-tier wage plan as well as other concessions. The early 1980s brought unions seats on the Board in Republic Airlines and Eastern Airlines. These were essentially stock or wage and benefit trades, in which the union accepted the former while acceding to employer insistence upon concessions in the latter areas.

The same kind of arrangement was negotiated by both the United Steelworkers and the United Food and Commercial Workers Unions with Kaiser Aluminum and Chemical Corporation, and Wilson Foods Corporation, respectively. Weirtlin Steel has made a similar deal with the United Steelworkers. Seymour Specialty Wire Company and the United Rubber Workers Union, again in response to concessions negotiated in the context of the decline of American manufacturing in the early 1980s, agreed to the suspension of cost-of-living adjustments, with wage and benefit improvements, obliging itself to open financial records to the union, to establish a profit-sharing program, to establish a joint council to discuss mutual problems, and to permit the president of the UAW to make annual presentations to the company's board of directors.

Kochan, Katz, and McKersie may have made a general characterization of such experiments in commenting upon the results of the RATH Meatpacking deal when they said:

> The primary reason this experiment failed is because the company was not able to identify and pursue a viable business strategy. The pay and work-rule concessions workers granted helped to give Rath some breathing space to search for an economically viable strategy, but these concessions could not substitute for such a strategy. In the end, the firm needed more than just concessions from its work force.

At Rath the parties also confronted another problem typical of firms that put union representatives on the board of directors as part of a concession package negotiated during a financial crisis: placement of union representatives on the board alone did not lead to an abrupt change in worker trust in management, nor did it produce a major alteration in worker-manager relations. Workers change their deep-seated attitudes toward management slowly, and only if other forums for worker and union involvement in decision making that supplement formal board representation are introduced. Workers often rightfully view a seat on the board of directors as a cosmetic change. To be successful, formal union representation on a company board must be supported by other changes at the workplace, in collective bargaining and in day-to-day management decision making. But Rath was either unwilling to make or incapable of making these supporting changes. So, in the end, union formal representation on the board served as an important quid pro quo for the negotiation of concessionary changes but did not fundamentally alter either labor-management relations or the firm's economic performance.[12]

Of course there is the problem of co-optation previously alluded to, a problem that seems to be particularly prominent in discussions about worker director arrangements in Europe. In the investigations of the continental experience which preceded the Bullock Report in Britain, the British noted the German and Swedish preference for employee worker directors rather than outside or external union representatives. The dilemma here—exaggerated in the American context by the antitrust problems experienced at American Motors—is the competing tensions imposed upon union representatives to safeguard their members in the firm, on the one hand, and members throughout the industry or competing industries, on the other.[13]

A European Addendum

Most of what follows focuses upon Germany which has led the way in the area of codetermination. The most important element of European codetermination is the works council system, which involves worker participation at the plant and which has its origins in the previous century. The creation of shop committees in Germany has its origins in the mid nineteenth century. The development continued in the early part of this century and culminated in the Works Council Act of 1920, which provided a legal basis for works councils at plant level as independent entities with some role in employer decision making. Then, as in the previous century, the works councils were not part of the trade unions. Indeed German employers accepted them willingly so as to discourage unions. As for the unions Summers has noted the following:

The unions were willing to accept factory councils only on the condition that the councils not encroach on the functions of unions or act in conflict with union's collective agreements. The result was that the Works Councils Act of 1920, which legally established works councils at the plant level with a limited role in plant decisions and substantial independence of the employer. As with earlier workers' committees, they were constitutional organs of the plant, not branches of the trade unions. They could not strike, and the negotiation of wages, hours and other economic terms was left up to the trade unions. The unions were willing to accept this statutory plant organization only because they lacked effective organization of their own at plant level. The Works Council Act provided an immediate structure of worker representation which unions were not ready to provide.[14]

The Works Council Act of 1952, amended in 1972, covers the private sector and is the contemporary version of the 1920 statute. Every industrial concern that has at least five employees is required to establish a works council. Although in many firms no initiative has been undertaken to implement this statute, approximately 80 percent of all employees have works councils.

Under the law the works council has a right to obtain information regarding economic affairs and planning of a corporation. However, on employer decisions that affect job security, such as corporate rearrangement and mergers, partial or total closure of the plant, the employer must first inform the works council of any change it wishes to make, and in the event that they are unable to agree about a social plan, the matter proceeds to arbitration or Labor Court. The works councils, while substantially influenced by the German trade unions in some industries, are institutionally independent of them and accepted by the employer as a portion of the enterprise. Eighty percent of all works council members elected are union members, generally included on a union list which is devised as the result of meetings between works councils members and union militants.

Thus, from both a legal and practical perspective, Germany possesses a two-tier system in which a works councils, the equivalent of the American local union at plant and corporate level, operate in tandem with the unions. The works council's role is more ambitious in its impact upon management functions than is that of the American trade union. On the other hand, the German unions, which negotiate minimum standards in industrywide agreements at a regional level, play a more limited role than their American counterparts.

Workers participation is part of the German system at the level of the supervisory board as well. At this level there are three forms of participation. The first exists in coal, iron, and steel, where worker representatives have parity with those of the shareholders in the sense that the chair is reserved for a so-called "neutral party" elected by both worker and shareholder representatives. One member of the management board must be a so-called works director, or *Arbeitsdirector*. Such an individual is elected by a majority of the worker representatives on the supervisory board and has responsibility for personnel matters. Because the system provides for parity, it acquired the label "codetermination."

The second is really minority representation. The Works Constitution Act of 1972 applies to all companies, outside of industries covered by the 1951 statute that employ more than 500 employees. Such companies are obliged to include one-third of the supervisory board members as employee representatives.

The Co-determination Act of 1976 which was the product of both considerable and prolonged debate throughout the early 1970s about the extension of parity from coal and steel to the rest of the private sector is yet a third variant. The 1976 statute applies to all business organizations regularly employing more than 2,000 employees, exempting mutual insurance companies, partnerships, the press, television, radio, churches, and educational and charitable institutions. Employee representatives are elected directly by the work force where its size consists of 8,000 employees or less. There is no neutral chairman, and in the event of deadlock, the law provides that the shareholders' representative is to elect the chairman.

The supervisory boards covered by all three of these statutes are involved in such issues as selection of managers, declaration of dividends, issuance of new shares, and capital investment decisions. All of these matters are beyond the realm of collective bargaining in the United States, at least insofar as it can be legally compelled.[15] And at the more significant plant level of workers' participation, where the works councils are a kind of surrogate for a local union, it is obvious that the concept of majority rule makes the introduction of the system into the United States a fundamental, radical reform that would require a basic restructuring of American labor laws.

The European Community

A trilogy of three proposals relating to workers' participation have been introduced at the European commission level during the past twenty years. The Fifth Directive on Company Law provides for minority representation at the supervisory board level on a European-wide basis. The European Company statute, first proposed in 1975, would impose a European-wide works council for each firm that incorporates at the EC level in order to avoid or obtain tax benefits. And in the area of employee involvement and consultations, the Vredling directive (an EC commission proposed legal instrument) proposed information and consultation rights.

In a sense the groundwork has been laid for European-wide labor legislation by the emergence of negotiated European works councils. Prior to 1991 four such councils, crossing European national boundaries, existed in Europe—three of them involving French companies and one in Germany, Volkswagen. Still, despite new discussions taking place between workers' representatives of eleven countries and corporate officials of St. Gobain, the phenomenon is quite peripheral to most labor-management relations in Europe.

The Single European Act of 1986 and the provision in EC law—which now requires merely a "qualified majority" in the Council instead of unanimity, a provision that has allowed the Thatcher government to block the Vredling initiative, for instance—has inhibited the development of labor law on a EC basis, again principally because of British obduracy. The European Company statutes provides for worker participation in one of three manners: (1) worker representation on the supervisory board as in Germany, (2) worker participation through a separate body representing company employees such as works committees in France and works councils in Germany, and (3) worker participation through procedures predicated upon the collective bargaining agreement as in Sweden. The third possibility would allow for Britain, for instance, which has no tradition of works councils along the lines of the continent, to handle matters to which works councils address themselves through traditional collective bargaining. Countries such as France and Italy which are concerned with the possibility of co-optation through such procedures either at supervisory boards or at plant level can accept an alternate system.

As the result of the 1991 European Community meeting in Maastricht, The Netherlands, all of the Community, except Britain, agreed to be bound by European labor legislation in a variety of areas, possibly including a directive establishing European works councils. All EC companies with at least 1,000 employees or a minimum of two facilities in different member states employing at least one hundred people would be covered if present proposals become law. There would be at least three worker representatives and no more than thirty, with meetings at least once a year to discuss ongoing issues that have an impact on employment conditions and workers.

It remains to be seen whether European works council legislation will be adopted pursuant to Maastricht, in which case it would be done by majority vote, or whether something will emerge outside the treaty structure where unanimity would be required. A third possibility that is seemingly forever omnipresent is that of no legislation at all. After all the idea of a European-wide works council legislation is one that has been at the center of discussion and debate in Europe for at least twenty years! Business opposition on the continent has taken the form of the argument that unions would have too much power through such legislation and would destabilize national collective bargaining systems through an attempt to move to European-wide collective bargaining, an admitted goal of the European Trade Union Congress, the European-wide federation. The British government has taken the position that such legislation is inconsistent with its voluntarist system through which law does not compel representation and consultation procedures.

Proponents of a European directive on works councils have been dissatisfied with existing proposals because they neither provide for a mandated system of consultation between management and works councils nor address the role that "external" trade union organizations, national or European-wide, are to play in such a system. Admitting that any attempt to devise a European-wide procedure for a specific role for trade union involvement in a works council directive would have been "highly controversial," Hall has said: "This intersection between the appropriate *external* trade union organization and *internal* company employee representation arrangements in respective nominations to the European-level body would appear to offer a valuable mechanism for ensuring its acceptability to both organs of employee representation . . . ."[16]

Japan

Japan has developed its own unique procedures for workers, providing for employee involvement or workers participation entirely independent of legal compulsion or any legal process. The system of joint consultation *(Roshi Kyogisei)* is linked to the system of employment security, enterprise unions that operate on a companywide basis, and labor-management cooperation.

This informal system of joint consultation—often viewed outside the traditional collective bargaining process—is a vehicle through which workers or their union leaders are advised of information relating to sales, profits, future mergers, acquisitions, plant closures, and the like. The Trilateral Commission's report on the subject stated the following:

> Issues such as the rules concerning large-scale layoffs, transfers to other jobs, and the rules relating to discipline and discharge, if agreement is not readily reached, quickly become the subject of collective bargaining. Questions relating to recruitment methods, selection procedures, education and training, job analysis and job evaluation are usually treated as cases for communication and co-understanding, with a view to obtaining the opinions, understanding and, if possible, approval and support of the union. On production matters involving company plans and schedules relating to investment, equipment, measurement and control of productivity, and quality control, managements are expected to consult with trade unions, although they usually reserve the right to decide. Where executive policies, the financial status of the company and long-range plans for the future are concerned, decisions are often made items for communication, management taking the initiative to report on developments and progress. Where major decisions affect employment and working conditions, such as mergers and plant closures, discussions in consultative committees are treated by unions as prior discussions to collective bargaining.[17]

Thus this system, predicated far more on informal practice than law, contrasts vividly with that of Germany and the procedures under discussion relating to the European Community. But much more than foreign experience is at the heart of current changes in American industrial relations as they relate to employee participation or involvement. To some extent such experience, while instructive, is inevitably limited because of cultural differences between Japan and Germany, in particular where the nature of the trade union movement and the loyalty of the work force and consequent attitudes toward conflict inspire trust on the part of management.

Economics and Adversarial Relationships

A second factor of some consequence is manufacturing's economic ailments manifested in the 1980s. It is quite clear that the modern and industrially developed countries have become increasingly economically interdependent, a factor no doubt substantially responsible for the post–World War II prosperity enjoyed throughout the industrialized world this past half-century. As Brazil, South Korea, and Taiwan have forged their way up the economic ladder, disrupting the previously established hierarchical order in industries such as steel, it has become appropriate to speak of global interdependence and to focus greater attention upon such regions of the world as the Pacific Rim. All of this in turn has meant competition for industries that have been traditionally among the most highly unionized in this country—a competition that accelerated furiously in crescendolike fashion in the late 1970s, producing economic dislocation in its wake.

The economic problems that have been encountered in the unionized sector of the economy in the late 1970s and 1980s, particularly in manufacturing, transportation, and construction—the real union strongholds in this country—have impelled both labor and management to rethink their relationships. The unions, as some of the left-wing critics of industrial democracy never cease to remind us, have not initiated the changes that confront the parties today. As noted earlier, it is the employers who have forged such initiatives, particularly in the nonunion sector. Thus since the early 1980s it has been management that has been formulating the initiatives and making the demands—a phenomenon that, whatever the result, has been the driving force in the 1989 Eastern Airlines dispute as well as in the concessions earlier negotiated in transportation, auto, and steel.

One of management's demands, as in the Eastern Airlines negotiations of 1989, has been for restraint and freezes, or indeed the diminution of wages and fringe benefits. This is the most immediate meaning of concessions. But the negotiations have involved an even more important demand, such as the revision of work rules, the reduction or broad banding of job classification categories, and mechanisms through which employee involvement in and understanding of the job and the company's business will be enhanced.

This has been a significant factor in the promotion of union and employee interest in greater participation and also employer willingness to accede to labor's demands that limit or even abolish management prerogatives, that promote a measure of industrial democracy allowing for employee consultation and a sharing of power through compensation—both areas in which the Japanese have long pioneered.[18]

However, a major obstacle in reshaping relationships in this country has been our adherence to traditional adversarial attitudes, and the fact that labor law has based its assumptions upon the model of conflict. With the exception of industrial relations in Britain and Australia, the American model of adversarial labor-management relations knows no equal throughout the fully industrialized world. It is a philosophy that is well summarized by the Supreme Court, speaking through Justice Brennan, in *Insurance Agents*[19] where the Court said the following of collective bargaining:

> Under a system where the Government does not attempt to control the results of negotiations, [it] cannot be equated with an academic collective search for truth—or even with what might be thought to be the ideal one. The parties—even granting the modification of views that may come from a realization of economic interdependence—still proceed from the contrary and to an extent antagonistic viewpoints and concepts of self-interest. The system has not reached the ideal of the philosophic notion that perfect understanding among people would lead to perfect agreement among them on values.[20]

The law is an important factor here. But more than anything it is the development of industrial unionism and detailed, comprehensive collective bargaining agreements negotiated in the latter 1940s and 1950s that have promoted an adversarial system rooted in a job-control unionism model within which grievance-arbitration machinery is the principal mode of dispute resolution. In some respects the new innovations are designed to strip away the distrust from which the old system emanated. Again Kochan, Katz, and McKersie had this to say:

> The War Labor Board's support for this model served to diffuse and institutionalize this approach. Job-control unionism worked well at this time because it was well suited to the economic environment and to the needs of the parties. It provided management with the stability and labor peace it needed to take advantage of expanding markets, while for the labor the emerging principles of joint contract administration overcame the arbitrariness of prior foreman-driven discipline and workplace administration.
> ... This system of work organization grew out of the principles of supervision, job design, and motivation embedded within scientific management and industrial engineering. Workers were assumed to be motivated primarily by the economic compensation received for job performance, and efficiency was to be maximized by dividing work into simple and narrow tasks. Decisions regarding how work was to be done were to be made by supervisors or engineers, while employees were left to execute their assigned tasks. Job evaluation procedures attached specific wage rates to each job, and seniority became the bedrock principle governing the allocation of scarce job opportunities.[21]

Paradoxically it is the industrial union model that may provide a framework for effective reform. That is to say, given the organization of industrial unions across a large number of job classifications, it is likely that unions like the United Auto Workers or United Steelworkers or United Rubber Workers that have promoted the old adversarial job control system are in the best position to broker the competing interests of employees lodged in a wide variety of classifications. Again reform of job classifications and work rules bound up with them and the enhancement of employer flexibility are an essential part of the employee participation bargain between labor and management. In this respect the United States, because of the prominence of large industrial unions, is better positioned than countries like Britain and Australia where craft unions play a more considerable role in the employment relationship and are likely to possess even greater institutional insecurity when confronted with the employee participation phenomenon.

The Experience Thus Far

It is important to focus upon the relationships that have evolved in both a micro and macro setting and to determine how they have worked in practice and whether they have succeeded in reforming or displacing the systems described in the preceding section. At the micro level particular attention is given to two innovative agreements entered into between the United Automobile Workers and New United Motors Manufacturing, Inc., or NUMMI, the new General Motors–Toyota joint venture, as well as a memorandum of agreement entered into between the same union and the Saturn Corporation, a wholly owned subsidiary of General Motors Corporation.

The collective bargaining agreements and experiences at NUMMI and the memorandum of agreement with Saturn (at this writing there is relatively little experience at that plant) illustrate these and other points. A key theme in most of the agreements is flexibility, and this generally manifests itself through the substantial reduction of job classifications and the discretion of management to assign workers to a variety of tasks. A maintenance mechanic classification has been created that merges a number of the previously separable skilled trades classifications so that the parties maintain four job classifications as opposed to nearly two hundred in other auto plants. Essentially there are three skilled classifications, "tool and die," "try out," and the "general maintenance" classification mentioned previously.

The Saturn agreement anticipates the approximate same number of job classifications with one classification structure for unskilled employees and ". . . three to five additional classifications to which all skilled tradesmembers will be assigned."[22] There is a considerably higher ratio of skilled tradesmen to production workers in the NUMMI plant which has been in operation since 1984 as compared to the old General Motors Fremont facility which it replaced, (i.e., 240 of the 2,200 employees at NUMMI are skilled tradesmen as opposed to 380 out of 6,000 at Saturn).

The team concept is used on the production system, teams consisting of five to eight members who are led by a team leader, a member of the bargaining unit who performs quality control-type functions. The team members are selected by a joint labor-management committee, composed of an equal number of representatives from each side. The team leaders serve under a group leader who performs supervisory functions and has the authority to discipline, discharge, and make management decisions with regard to other changes in the employment relationship. The teams can meet as frequently as once a week or as infrequently as once a month.

The teams are involved in both work standardization and *Kaizen* (Japanese for "continuous improvement"). Work standardization is a process through which employees define each task that is to be performed within a sixty-second period. As Paul Adler has said, ". . . team members themselves hold the stopwatch. They learn the techniques of work analysis, description, and improvement."[23] Another element of the team system is that the workers are rotated from assignments rather than simply performing the same one—although the amount of rotation depends upon the hardships involved in the job. That is to say, the more physically demanding the job is, the more likely it is that a worker will be permitted to rotate to other tasks.

Three major objections to the teamwork concept as adopted by the United Auto Workers and NUMMI have been advanced by dissidents inside the union. The first is that the concept, especially the work standardization idea, is a managerial speed-up in modern clothing. Parker and Slaughter,[24] for instance, state that the system is inequitable because it assumes that the employee is to be continually busy and does not allow the workers to time themselves so that they can schedule certain periods of the day when tasks will be less demanding. The argument is that the standardization system has made the job anything but autonomous and imposes special burdens upon older workers who have difficulty keeping up with the ever-increasing demands of the workplace.

Although NUMMI has not yet reached Japanese levels of production, it is clear that the procedures employed in Fremont, which include the more efficient "just-in-time" method of inventory which does not use plant facilities for storage, have made NUMMI, and presumably others that have emulated the corporation, substantially more productive. A considerable number of the grievances which have been filed by workers at the plant involve allegations of "overloading." The dissidents complain that there is no right to strike over production standards at NUMMI, whereas in the Big Three disputes about production standards are exempted from the no-strike clause. But the fact is that workers may stop the line any time that they see something wrong with the operation as it passes them. Although the Dissident People's Caucus alleged that workers are reticent in exercising such rights, the line appears to be stopped with considerable frequency. As Adler has said, NUMMI shows that hierarchy and standardization need not be predicated upon the "logic of coercion."

A more noteworthy issue relates to what it is that workers are involved with at Fremont. That is to say, is employee involvement meaningful or only a delusion, providing form but not substance? Again the point made by the critics is that employees are not involved in the design of the product. This is a valid and an accurate critique of NUMMI and one that applies to the entire automobile industry in the United States and most of the world. It is anticipated that the Saturn-UAW relationship will be innovative in this respect inasmuch as it establishes a Strategic Advisory Committee, the composition of which will be ". . . determined with appropriate input from Saturn and the Union."[25] The Committee will ". . . undertake the strategic business planning necessary to assure the long-term viability of the enterprise, and will be responsive to the needs of the marketplace relative to quality, cost and timing. Moreover, the employer obliges itself to provide for 'full participation' of the Union; use of the consensus decision making process; placement of authority in decision making in the most appropriate part of the organization, with emphasis on the Work Unit; and, free flow of information and clear definition of the decision making process."[26]

The UAW-NUMMI relationship also possesses limitations in its use of the work standardization process in that there is no real incentive for the employee to devise a more efficient process given the fact that there is no system of revenue or profit sharing, let alone control at the decision-making level in place. This is a deficiency in the existing system and one that the parties have discussed revising. In 1991 union elections virtually swept out the incumbent slate because of substantial dissatisfaction with the status quo.

Yet, despite internal union turmoil, it appears that there is some acceptance of the system if not a failure to provide an effective alternative. Why then has the relationship proved to be acceptable to the parties? Absenteeism has dropped dramatically, productivity has improved, and the consensus among workers, while somewhat unwieldy in the sense that the People's Caucus holds a number of leadership positions, seems to be that the new system is better than the old. The first reason is that wages are the best in the industry. No economic concessions have been extracted in this new industrial relations environment.

Second, the long-term employment relationship is maintained to an extent unknown in the rest of the industry. As David Levine has said: "When participation relies upon work group cooperation and employees monitoring one another, long-term employment relationships are essential. The longer an employee expects to be in a work group the more effective are group-based rewards and sanctions as motivations."[27] At NUMMI the employer obliges itself not to

> ... lay off employees unless compelled to do so by severe economic conditions that threaten the long term financial viability of the Company.
> The Company will take affirmative measures before laying off any employees, including such measures as, the reduction of salaries of its officers and management, assigning previously subcontracted work to bargaining unit employees capable of performing this work, seeking voluntary layoffs and other cost-saving measures.[28]

Similarly the memorandum between Saturn and the UAW states that employees who are among the 80 percent with the longest service of employment possess "permanent job security eligibility." This means that such workers will not be laid off ". . . except in situations which the SAC determines are due to unforeseen or catastrophic events or severe economic conditions."[29] Curiously this agreement has drawn the attacks of UAW dissidents who maintain that the agreement is discriminatory with regard to the 20 percent who are not protected—even though no one enjoys such protection under other collective agreements. Moreover the NUMMI agreement has been criticized on the grounds that it is not sufficiently precise with regard to the circumstances under which management, for instance, must reduce its own compensation. This agreement contrasts vividly with the rest of the automobile industry where union members have thrice risen up in protest over the award of bonuses to management officials at a time in which the union has been required to negotiate concessions in its collective agreement. While the UAW has negotiated income guarantee provisions with the Big Three,[30] that contractual provision does not provide the job security possessed by its members at either Saturn or NUMMI.

Finally, a third attractive feature of both the relationships is the reduction of status differentials. Workers eat in the same cafeteria as management and have the same access to parking facilities. As in Japan, at NUMMI workers and management wear the same uniform, although they are not required to do so.

Like the UAW-NUMMI relationship the new General Motors–Saturn project has been the result of discussions with the union and the employer prior to both construction of the facility in Spring Hill, Tennessee, and the commencement of the car manufacturing process in 1990. At NUMMI recognition was granted to the UAW prior to bargaining about a full-fledged bargaining agreement, and preference was given to workers who had been previously employed at the General Motors Fremont plant upon which NUMMI was constructed and expanded. While Saturn and the UAW were careful to emphasize the voluntary nature of preference for the General Motors work force so as to ensure a retention of a "committed" group of employees, the parties stipulated that because "the best source of . . . training automotive workers is found in the existing GM-UAW work force . . . to insure a fully qualified workforce, a majority of the full initial complement of the operating and skilled technicians in Saturn will come from GM-UAW units throughout the United States." This provision has spawned litigation, initiated by the National Right to Work Committee, which was dismissed by the General Counsel of the Board alleging unlawful discrimination in favor of unionized employees.[31]

The Saturn relationship with the United Auto Workers is probably the best and boldest experiment in devising an effective cooperative model for American industrial relations. In major respects the relationship between company and union is fundamentally different from the traditional arrangements. It resembles NUMMI in some respects, and yet institutionally it appears to be different in a number of areas.

The best illustration of this point is the contrast between Saturn and the rest of General Motors as it relates to management prerogatives. The management prerogatives issue, namely the attempt by the corporation to reserve particular subject matter as its own prerogative and therefore place it beyond the realm of union influence or the collective bargaining process, is very much alive and well in paragraph 8 of the national agreement between General Motors and the UAW. But is absent from the Saturn agreement, a document that repudiates the GM agreement as precedent. Indeed the Saturn agreement recognizes the UAW as a "full partner," in contrast not only to the GM agreement itself but also to federal labor law policy articulated by the Supreme Court in *First National Maintenance,* where the Court held that Congress had intended that unions *not* be partners with management. This approach is implemented in a variety of ways.

The most significant element of implementation is the parties' adherence to the concept of jointness through which all business decisions are apparently disclosed to and discussed with union representatives. The mechanism through which this happens is the Strategic Action Council and Manufacturing Acting Council which is composed of representatives from both sides. Both the company and the United Auto Workers maintain that union representatives participate in decisions relating to the design of the product, the advertising to be done on its behalf—the Union figures prominently in television advertisements that have appeared in 1991—and the union has selected suppliers as well.

The parties in their memorandum of agreement specifically speak of "consensus decision making [that] will be utilized with a strong focus on both current and near term decisions." This feature is absent from the relationship between the Auto Workers and NUMMI, where the joint venture really acts as sort of contractor for two major corporations, General Motors and Toyota.

Like NUMMI the number of classifications at Saturn have been reduced significantly. The approximate number of skilled trades classifications, beyond the classification of "Operating Technicians" for nonskilled tradesmembers, is four. Moreover, while "length of service will be used as a tie-breaker in those unusual situations where competing members are equal in all respects," it is clear that seniority is to be regarded as less important than it is in most American automobile plants. Assignments to Saturn's two shifts will not be made on the basis of seniority. There is periodic rotation between the shifts, regardless of the amount of seniority accumulated because of the inefficiencies associated with transfers from one shift to another when vacancies are filled on the basis of seniority.

The Saturn job security guarantees, alluded to in the discussion about NUMMI, to some extent are directly tied to the job classification provisions and seniority in the traditional sense of job security, namely the more defined the skill, the more difficult for the employer to rely upon substitute labor that would jeopardize job security. Because the corporation assumes the burden of establishing stringent circumstances, "unforseen or catastrophic events or severe economic conditions" are present. (And in the event that Saturn employees are laid off, their recall rights to General Motors under its GM agreement will be revived.)

Another nexus between contractual provisions that exist are those between job security and wages. All bargaining unit employees, blue collar or otherwise, are viewed as salaried employees. Indeed the memorandum of agreement provides that base compensation is to be established on an annual salary basis and that the employees are to be paid semimonthly, on the 15th of the month and the last day of the month. The concept is reinforced with the absence of time clocks which is also part of the NUMMI relationship. The content of the wage bargain itself reflects the general approach. During the so-called bridging period employees are to be paid 80 percent of the "competitive base rate of Saturn's represented domestic U.S. automobile manufacturing competitors including, at least, GM, Ford, Chrysler, Mazda, and NUMMI." In addition to a base rate the objective is to fashion a reward system for employees that is based upon performance, productivity, and profits.

As with NUMMI the teamwork concept is critical to the way in which production goals are achieved. The teamwork concept is implemented through work units. These units consist of approximately between six to fifteen employees. Each worker is within a work unit module that interviews applicants to determine whether they would fit in the teamwork process in which the employees determine assignments and related matters. At NUMMI the team leader is part of the bargaining unit and is selected from among and promoted ". . . from those qualified who are most capable for the team leader position. Where two or more candidates are considered more capable, the employee with the most seniority would be selected." The group leader who organizes the various teams is a management position selected by management outside the bargaining unit.

The equivalent to the group leader in Saturn is the work unit module adviser (WUMA). Reflecting again the parties' predilection to jointness, one union and one employer representative work together as unit module advisers. The problems relating to discipline, production, and the like, go to these two individuals who operate without the shop rules that exist in most automobile plants, including NUMMI. The difference here is that in Saturn union representatives have responsibilities that are more akin to those enjoyed by supervisors than is the case at NUMMI. Those representatives are involved in disciplinary disputes in a nontraditional manner.

The ground rules of course are different. In both NUMMI and Saturn the employee takes responsibility for quality control, and spot checks are the sole basis for review. In both NUMMI and Saturn nonbargaining unit employees are permitted to perform bargaining unit work with the understanding that they are not designed to displace bargaining unit workers. Throughout most of labor-management relations the involvement of nonbargaining unit workers in the performance of bargaining unit work produces the immediate filing of a grievance that can lead to further confrontation in an arbitration proceeding. Job security provisions undoubtedly play a role in making this ground rule more palatable than in traditional relationships.

A broader no-strike clause is in place at both Saturn and NUMMI. In the agreements with the Big Three there are exceptions to the no-strike clause's prohibitions, principally in production standards and health and safety disputes. At both Saturn and NUMMI production standards are jointly hammered out between parties. This is the product of consensus building. In both establishments, where a worker determines that there is a defect with the product, he or she may pull a line, thus bringing the assembly line to a halt.

Arbitration of grievances remains the final step of the dispute resolution procedure, just as it does in the Big Three and most unionized relationships in American industry. But it has been used infrequently in both NUMMI and Saturn. Moreover in Saturn the internal processes of the UAW are involved by virtue of the memorandum of agreement, thus placing stress upon the need to diminish or limit the number of cases in which the parties resort to a third-party neutral to resolve their differences. (In Britain, Japanese companies have pioneered with no-strike clauses and "final offer" arbitration under which the arbitrator must select either the labor or management position from both grievance and interest disputes.) Because of the scaled-down number of full-time representatives investigating grievances in both establishments, particularly at Saturn, there is less of a potential to resolve in the formal, sometimes time-consuming, and expensive manner that arbitration has become in recent years in this country.

A final respect in which the relationship differs from a typical American one is that it provides for a form of perpetual bargaining similar to the "Living Agreement" theory which Walter Reuther espoused in the late 1940s and early 1950s. If a party seeks modification of the agreement, he or she has to use principles of conflict resolution and if this proves unsuccessful after thirty days from the date of the request and the two parties are "unable to reach consensus," a written notice of intent to engage in the lockout or strike may be served on the other party. No formal expiration date is provided. The parties would thus modify the agreement on any issue subsequent to filing their request and only resort to the weapons of economic pressure subsequent to the exhaustion of the conflict resolution process.

The perpetual bargaining approach contrasts vividly with the traditional assumption, which provides for a specific contract expiration date at the end of a given period of time, generally three years. Then the parties try to resolve all or most of their differences within an artificially limited period of time and are almost encouraged to use economic pressure under an eleventh-hour deadline approach to contract expiration which some unions have encouraged through a "no-contract, no-work" policy. The Saturn agreement modifies the strict delineation between the so-called rights and interest disputes, economic pressure having been prohibited or discouraged in the former area but encouraged in the latter.

The systems contain numerous imperfections. Yet they seem to compare well to that which they have replaced or the alternatives that have been thus far referred to as available. Indeed Parker and Slaughter and like-minded others do not appear to have any clear-cut alternatives through which employee and employer could function.

Still, as the Court's language in *Insurance Agents* indicates, there are legal problems with the new relationships. It is not a question of replacing adversarial relationships with new cooperative ones. The more appropriate analysis recognizes that a measure of the autonomous system—the right to strike and lock out and a relatively adversarial grievance-arbitration process—will remain as part of the system. There are of course legal problems involved in introducing the new cooperative elements. It is to these that we turn next, subsequent to an examination of one other aspect of workers' participation.

Workers' Participation with Parallel Arrangements

Compensation, whether or not in the form of a wage, will undoubtedly be more flexible as the workers' participation initiatives take hold. The

Japanese system suggests that a bonus is an important part of involvement of the employee in the company's fortunes as well as a way to protect against unemployment. As Peter Drucker has said:

> . . . a large part of the 'wage' needs to be flexible instead of being fixed. It needs to be geared to performance, to profitability and productivity, with cash wages being lower, perhaps even much lower, in poor ones. This is perhaps the sharpest break with tradition—and one that management may resist as much as union leaders. Middle managers and supervisors, in particular, will be opposed; there is nothing they resent as much as a subordinate making more than they do. But labor has also traditionally accepted pay for productivity and profitability only as a "bonus" on top of a fixed wage, and has altogether rejected the idea of cutting the fixed wage in bad times. "It is unfair to penalize workers for the lack of performance of their employers" has been a stock argument. But what is needed now—and what is now in the interest of the workers themselves—is adjustment to economic fluctuations through flexible wage costs rather than through unemployment . . .[32]

Are employees under various forms of workers' participation arrangements or agreements likely to be more productive? Are they truly more involved in the firm and its product in the sense of being committed to the well-being of the enterprise, thereby presumably enhancing its competitiveness? What follows is an attempt to summarize the existing literature, particularly through a paper written by Levine and Tyson, and to focus upon the above referenced relationships. What difference, if any, does the form of workers' participation make—namely consultation as opposed to decision making, sharing in the firm's profits or revenues such as employee stock ownership plans (ESOPs) which do not take into account profits, quality control circles, team production techniques, and worker representatives on company boards?

The idea behind profit sharing is that employees who have a share in their company's profits will have an incentive to be more productive.[33] Conventional wage systems pay only for time on the job. Employers want more from employees than time; they also want high productivity, loyalty, cooperation, and teamwork. Theoretically employees under a profit-sharing plan will seek to be more productive by working harder, working smarter, taking initiative, and taking advantage of unforeseen opportunities because they will be rewarded with higher pay.

A criticism of profit sharing noted by Mitchell, Lewin, and Lawler in their study of alternative pay systems is that company profits may be too removed from workers to provide them with a meaningful incentive to be more productive. Profits vary for reasons other than employees' efforts. Particularly in large organizations the relationship between individual performance and corporate profits may be minuscule.

Even if profit sharing plans have a minimal effect on worker incentive and on productivity, Mitchell, Lewin, and Lawler asserted that such plans may provide other benefits. Profit-sharing plans keep employees informed about the financial condition of the business. They have symbolic value in that they make employees feel as though they are part of an organization where cooperative effort is needed and rewarded. They also make labor costs variable. With a profit-sharing plan an employer can adjust wages as the financial condition of the company changes instead of altering the size of the work force.

Weitzman and Kruse found in their study of profit sharing and productivity that there was weak support for the proposition that profit sharing increases productivity. Their consideration of the theoretical benefits of profit sharing led them to conclude that there was more of a positive than a negative effect of profit sharing on productivity. In their examination of thirty-three case studies from literature to surveys by the industrial relations community, they found a positive link between group incentives and increased productivity, improved quality, and better labor-management relations.

Conte and Svejnar concluded in their study of employee ownership plans for the Brookings Institution that the effects of ESOPs on company performance, like profit-sharing plans, are not certain.[34] ESOPs are defined in the Internal Revenue Code Sections 401(A) and 4975 (E)(7) and in the Employee Retirement and Income Security Act (ERISA) Section 407 (D)(6). ESOPs provide employer securities to employees as part of a compensation package. An ESOP includes the creation of a trust, with individual accounts for employees to which the employer contributes cash or company stock. Both the original contributions and the appreciation of the trust are tax exempt until the accounts are distributed to the employees.

Approximately 10,000 companies have plans in which ESOP's provide for stock ownership. Perhaps 1,000 or so are those in which employees hold a majority of the firm's stock. There are both advantages and disadvantages to worker ownership. Where capital is relatively firm specific, borrowing to raise more capital may be more feasible in capital-intensive industries such as transportation. Employee ownership makes it more likely that workers will effectively monitor one another and thus provide for enhanced effort collectively as well as individually.

The primary obstacle to worker-owned firms is that of risk bearing. It is assumed that workers do not want to subject themselves to "vagaries" of the market and expose themselves to economic difficulties. Yet, as Hansmann has noted, workers in unionized firms may be laid off for economic reasons even though they are protected by collective bargaining agreements.[35] It is the attempt by workers to extricate themselves from the position of vulnerability that has made worker ownership and other alternative forms of employee involvement more attractive than they once appeared.

One obvious problem from the worker's perspective in such firms, however, is that they do not provide for employee or worker control or involvement in decision making. As of 1986 a survey found that only 4 percent of the firms with ESOPs had any nonmanagerial employee representatives on their board of directors.[36] No firm with ESOPs had a majority of employee representatives on the board of directors. States Hansmann:

> Whatever the motivation for adopting ESOPs, however, one of the most striking facts about them is that they generally provide for participation only in earnings and not in control. Only rarely are they structured to give the workers a significant voice in the governance of the firm.
>
> To begin with, a substantial fraction of the stock held by ESOPs is non-voting stock. Further, the power to vote the voting stock held by an ESOP is commonly not exercised by the workers who are the beneficiaries of the plan. In the latter regard, the tax plays a significant role. For a privately-held corporation to obtain the tax benefits provided for ESOPs, the power to vote stock held by the corporation's ESOP need not be passed through to the workers, but rather can be voted by the plan's trustee. The trustee, in turn, can be appointed by the firm's management without consultation with the workers who are the plan's beneficiaries. In publicly-held corporations, in contrast, voting power must be passed through to the workers on all ESOP stock actually allocated to the workers—which is to say, not purchased through borrowing, as in the popular "leveraged" ESOP.[37]

Closely related to this argument—and one that ignores the fact that members of the board of directors from banks, for instance, have their own self-interest in the corporation's decisions—is that union representatives on the board are confronted with a conflict of interest that inevitably would require them to betray their fiduciary duty. But creditors, like banks, have similar problems.

The lack of any provisions for employee involvement in decision making is troubling. Conte and Svejnar noted that ESOPs are treated in these codes as employee benefits plans, but the 1976 Annual Report of the Joint Economic Committee characterized the purposes of an ESOP as follows:

> ... to provide a realistic opportunity for more U.S. citizens to become owners of capital, and to provide an expanded source of equity financing for corporations.[38]

A problem they identified with employee ownership plans such as ESOPs, stock bonus plans, and deferred profit-sharing plans is that ownership may raise workers' desires for information and participation in decision making. If these desires are frustrated, employee turnover may increase, and work effort could be reduced.

The Experience with Participation and Productivity

Levine and Tyson have concluded that effective participation in productivity is contingent upon the form and content of participation and other aspects of the relationship between labor and management. Their evidence indicates that a positive contribution to productivity is more likely to occur where the plan relates directly to the shop floor environment and when it "... involves substantive decision-making rights rather than pure consultative arrangements, such as quality control circles, and when it occurs in an industrial relations environment that creates employee commitment and the legitimacy of managerial authority."[39] The four characteristics that they have found to be important are profit sharing, long-term employment relationships, measures designed to build group cohesiveness, and guaranteed individual rights. Presumably participatory arrangements, which increase morale and satisfaction, are likely to promote the loyalty that is the sine que non for productivity improvements.

Levine and Tyson show that the effects of substantive shop floor participation on productivity are mainly positive. The problem with teamwork-type participation programs, they note, is often to be found in worker fear that increased productivity will threaten their jobs, in resistance by supervisors or middle- and top-level management because of a concern with sharing authority, and in insistence by employees that successful experiments be rewarded with some sort of increased pay.

For the last of these points the authors note that participation and profit sharing often go together effectively. They state:

... sustained, effective participation requires that employees be rewarded for the extra effort which such participation entails, and that they receive a share of any increased productivity or profits. Workers feel that it is unfair if they do not share in the benefits generated by their cost-saving ideas. Group-based gain sharing gives workers incentives to maintain norms of high effort, to monitor each other, and to sanction workers who are shirking. More positively, group-based pay also gives workers incentives to cooperate, and not to try to advance at the expense of their colleagues.

Just as participation can lead to demand for profit sharing, profit sharing can lead to demand for participation. When there is profit sharing, workers' incomes depend on these decisions of the firm, and workers want to have a say in decisions.

Moreover, there is growing evidence that profit sharing and participation interact positively, implying that the combination is more potent than the sum of its parts.[40]

The Law

Company Assistance to Unions

A focal point for labor lawyers concerned with law and policy is section 8(a)(2) of the National Labor Relations Act, the anticompany union unfair labor practice prohibition that disallows both financial assistance to (other than time off with pay for negotiation during working hours) and employer domination of the labor organization. Much of America's history of industrial relations—especially the portion of it leading directly to the adoption of the NLRA—witnessed the use of employee representation committees or company unions to suppress authentic and autonomous labor unions and thus free collective bargaining. Free collective bargaining was thwarted through such mechanisms, a kind of crude extension of scientific management.[41] Senator Robert Wagner viewed the provision as a cardinal element of the Act,[42] indeed its most important provision.

Today the company union concept is virtually unknown. True, nonunion employers have frequently instituted employee representation committees, quality of work life groups and circles, and the like, which are designed in some instances to ward off the threat of trade unionism. Indeed, as noted earlier, the nonunion sector has been the driving force in such changes.[43] But frequently these committees and programs seem to be different from the company unions that were instituted in the 1920s and that were the object of the anticompany union prohibitions in section 8(a)(2). To be sure, employers seek to supplant an arm's-length relationship with such measures.

Once again employers are attempting to deter genuine trade unionism. But in the nonunion environment they are hardly likely to characterize the new entities as unions for the practical reason that the union is the last thing that the employer wants the worker to believe that he or she needs, let alone the fact that such a strategy works at cross purposes with the law. To the extent that the new entities are characterized as "labor organizations," any financial assistance not authorized by section 8(a)(2) (i.e., payment for time spent negotiating during working hours) is prohibited by the literal language of the statute.[44] This is so because section 8(a)(2) prohibits assistance in connection with so-called labor organizations as broadly defined by the Act. One real concern that involves parties such as the UAW, NUMMI, and Saturn under the NLRA is that new initiatives undertaken in established bargaining relationships can implicate the prohibitions contained in section 8(a)(2) relating to financial assistance.

Yet beginning with the quality of work life programs sponsored by some of the UAW leadership and some elements within GM and Ford, it has been seen that employee involvement is frequently necessary. For instance, employees are provided time off with pay at Fremont's NUMMI joint venture to learn about how the product is marketed. Both NUMMI and Saturn union representatives attend a variety of committee meetings where their time is paid by management, and the purpose is not collective negotiations as such. UAW officials and represented employees have been provided with financial assistance to travel, for instance, to Japan to learn the work processes of Toyota. The NUMMI experiment has been chronicled by the U.S. Department of Labor in its report on "U.S. Labor Law and the Future of Labor-Management Cooperation."[45] Moreover, if in fact employees who are represented by the union within the bargaining unit are performing what can be characterized as supervisory responsibilities, this also can be equated with an unlawful infusion of supervisory employees into the unit, and it theoretically undermines the unit's autonomy.

It would seem as though the financing of union representatives' airfares to Japan and other expenses is unlawful under the NLRA and other federal statutes as well. But some of the courts of appeals have adopted the view that communications between employees and employers, even if fostered by financial assistance, are appropriate as long as they do not result in a paternalistic system that erodes the union as bargaining representative.

There are really two parts to the legal issues involved in company-union litigation. Both involve the tension between a statutory philosophy that promotes adversarial labor relations—an environment that was a basic part of the employment relationship in the 1930s, on the one hand, and modern attempts to achieve more cooperative relationships between labor and management, on the other.

The first of the issues is whether the entity is a "labor organization" within the meaning of the Act. Here a number of component statutory parts are to be considered. If employees within the meaning of the Act participate, can the committee be deemed to "deal with" the employer? Proposals from the committee, which the employer can accept or reject, would meet this standard.[46] On the other hand, the committee that operates without the need to deal directly with the employer may not be a "labor organization" because it can implement matters on its own without the requisite dealing.[47] Here there is an intent to distinguish between entities that are merely involved in communication and those that may be characterized as involved in negotiations. However, if the employee group is simply a knowledgeable segment of the employees with whom the employer is gathering ideas and information or if actual changes do not result from proposals in the workplace, it may be that a labor organization will not be found to exist.[48]

Sometimes the organization or entity will be regarded as a labor organization if the discussions are about what can be traditionally characterized as wages, hours, and employment conditions. The Supreme Court has relied upon the existence of "grievances" to find a labor organization. On the other hand, if the focus is upon traditionally managerial issues, such as sales and quality standards, it will be viewed as an organization that is not a "labor organization" within the meaning of the Act. The practical and legal significance of this is that the financial assistance prohibitions relating to section 8(a)(2) are triggered only in the case of a labor organization. That is to say, if the entity is not a labor organization because it engages in mere communication or is involved in discussions about matters that are not properly characterized as wages, hours, and employment conditions, the employer may provide any kind of assistance, financial or otherwise, without violating the NLRA.

But the distinctions that the Board and courts have made seem to be synthetic and unrealistic. In my judgment, it is a mistake to carry over the demarcation lines established in connection with duty-to-bargain litigation to this arena and to make financial assistance turn on the precise functions involved. Subject matter that includes sales and finance as well as wages, hours, and conditions of employment ought to be viewed the same way, for any demarcation line between the two is artificial.

Given the language of the statute as it relates to the labor organizations, it would seem as though any party that deals with an employer—and the employer itself—could have potential difficulty as a matter of law. This seems undesirable and fashions an obstacle to communication between employer and employee, impeding employee knowledge and involvement in corporate affairs. It seems foolish to distinguish between considerations of wages, hours, and conditions of employment, on one hand, and efficiency or quality, on the other. The demarcation line between them seems synthetic. The quality of the product and promotion of productivity in connection with it inevitably affect employment conditions. Congress should revise the statute so as to allow employee committees to function without adverse consequences regardless of what their relationship with the employer is in terms of communications, negotiations, and the like, and the subject matter with which it concerns itself.

Under current law, for a labor organization to create illegality, there must be a finding of either domination of the organization by the employer or assistance to it. If the employer is found to have put the leadership of the organization together, or created the organization itself, it is likely that unlawful domination will be found. It is difficult to determine whether the employer involvement promotes cooperation or subordinates autonomy under such circumstances.

This was the problem that the Board confronted in the widely discussed *Electromation, Inc.*[49] decision. The Board noted that it could ". . . appropriately take into account changing industrial reality . . ." but not in the teeth of congressional intent, no matter how long ago expressed, or of Supreme Court precedent which has not been reversed by Congress. The Board said: ". . . Congress brought within its definition of 'labor organization' a broad range of employee groups, and it sought to ensure that such groups were free to act independently of employers in representing employee interests."[50] That goal of independence ought to remain under any revisions to this aspect of labor law promulgated by Congress.

The Board in *Electromation* said that there were three forms of conduct prescribed by section 8(a)(2). In this case Action Committees (and that they were labor organizations) were challenged by the Teamsters because of its organizational campaign and its assertion that these committees constituted unlawful employer assistance. The Board found that there was unlawful "domination" in the formation and administration of the committees because they dealt with the employer over such matters as employee absenteeism and remuneration in the form of bonuses and other monetary incentives and employees acted in a "representational capacity." Reasoned the Board, it was the employer's "idea to create the Action Committees." The employer had drafted the purposes and goals of the committees, defined the subject matter, and determined the committee's composition, appointing management representatives so as to facilitate discussions. The Board also found unlawful support because the committee operated on paid time within the structure that the employer had created.

Accordingly the decision was a narrow one. The law properly precludes the kind of domination involved in *Electromation*. But even outside of established relationships, the test should be whether employer assistance is designed to thwart unionism. The inference that this is the employer's intent should be established where such policies are instituted when management becomes aware of a union organizational campaign. The modern cases, which begin with the Seventh Circuit's *Chicago Rawhide* decision,[51] seem to me to be an appropriate view of the relationship between labor and management in a cooperative environment. To cut against the grain of such authority establishes what Judge John Wisdom characterized as an "iron curtain" between employer and employee.[52]

The question of unlawful domination or assistance ought not to be determined by such factors as whether it is the employer that has scheduled meetings, whether the meetings take place on company facilities, and whether facilities such as copying machines are utilized. Absent findings of conduct designed to thwart legitimate trade unions or to deprive employees of free choice in the selection of representatives, all such practices are intrinsically benign. Likewise the question of whether there are employer representatives, including supervisors, involved with employee committees should not be dispositive. Inevitably, in the nonunion situation management will lead even if they are statutory works councils. This reality should be accepted, and with it recognition of more arm's-length autonomous labor-management relationships that may emerge from it.

Yet the NLRA's strict prohibitions against financial assistance and other forms of assistance, as well as domination, make repeal of section 8(a)(2) a desirable objective. In truth, some of the scenarios arising in new cooperative relationships will not survive that provision. An agenda for labor law reform should include a new section 8(a)(2) that allows for discussions with employee committees over a wide variety of subject matter and financial assistance to such organizations unless an inference of antiunion intent can be evidenced in the formation or administration of these committees.

Even if employee committees are fostered by the employer, the committees should be allowed so long as the representatives are chosen by employees and their day-to-day administration is not inhibited by employer involvement, and employer assistance should be permitted. Such committees promote communication between employees and employers and the sharing of information. Additionally the Act should be amended so as to allow nonmajority organizations to represent employees and to be consulted and share information about employer decision making that affect employment conditions where 20 or 30 percent of the employees have petitioned the Board to this effect. Under such circumstances consulation and communication should be mandated. Revision of section 8(a)(2) would simply allow employers and employees, without mandate of law, to communicate effectively with one another so long as the employer does not devise the entity so as to rid itself of a union that is organizing the employees or to thwart employee free choice through top-down institutions.

The team concept used by the UAW and NUMMI seems to me not to be affected by the Board's *Electromation* decision. The UAW and NUMMI teams are autonomous and function without "dealing" with the employer. To the extent that a more bilateral relationship is impelled by the team framework—which is curiously condemned by the Act—the statute should be amended so as to allow it to flourish.

As written, the statute prohibits financial assistance, which includes use of office space and copying machines. This must be amended as well unless domination or subordination is in evidence. Of course the statute should not permit employee committees or any other grouping of workers to bargain or negotiate with the employer over wages, hours, and working conditions—unless the union provides its authorization. It is the union that is the exclusive bargaining representative and that has responsibility for representing the workers. Any attempt to disparage the union's status is unlawful under the statute, and it should remain unlawful in any labor law reform initiative.

To some extent section 8(a)(2) intersects with the question of how one defines an "employee" within the meaning of the Act. The model presented by the NLRA is that employees subject to supervisory discipline are to be protected by labor organizations where employees express such a desire in the collective bargaining process. Although most teamwork examples in American manufacturing do not involve bargaining unit employees in the actual design of the job, the idea of responsibility and autonomy for the workers in shaping their own responsibilities and tasks is sometimes said to be integral to the exercise.

Although team leaders are technically in charge, they follow the Japanese model of obtaining consensus. Where discipline, promotion, and other problems, are placed in their hands, they could be regarded as supervisors or nonbargaining unit employees within the meaning of the Act, even though they are members of the union and sometimes regarded as part of the bargaining unit. (Indeed group leaders are supervisors in the eyes of NUMMI management.) Thus for an administrative agency there could be questions about the union's autonomy and the presence of supervisors within the union, which makes it a subordinate entity with a kind of fifth column within its ranks—*opposite the concern of corporate law* where it is feared that union representatives will not possess a sufficiently fiduciary relationship with the shareholders to make them loyal and effective board members.[53]

In teamwork in its purest form, the leaders are not supervisors but employees. They do not make any "independent" judgments[54] about critical employment matters pertaining to discharge or discipline but rather rely upon consensus building. But in reality, under modern labor law, the team concept does present strains on the traditional dichotomy between supervisors and employees. As with the financial assistance prohibitions in sections 8(a)(2), American labor law, like the Japanese trade union law,[55] may need to be more flexible in establishing demarcation lines, and this can be done best through legislative reform.

Employee Defined and Worker and Union Representatives as Directors of the Board

Other labor law questions are posed by the new managerial work structures. For instance, the Supreme Court in the landmark *Yeshiva*[56] decision concluded, by a 5–4 vote, that the more autonomy and freedom that university professors possess, the more likely that they would be characterized as "managerial" employees under the statute. This holding placed many professors beyond the statute's coverage. The *Yeshiva* decision, while not necessarily applicable to other job categories, does not bode well for reform of the workplace and the way in which workers' functions are to be performed.

The teamwork experiment in automobile manufacturing was designed to enhance flexibility, erode archaic work rules, and to increase employee interest in the job and its relation to the product line. Most employees are not as far up the corporate ladder as the Court imagined university professors to be, but the logic in *Yeshiva* characterizes such employees as managerial and as likely to undercut the bargaining process, so they are beyond the protection and coverage of the Act.

I have long thought that Justice Brennan's dissent on behalf of three other justices in *Yeshiva* was the better view in that case.[57] But, absent a reversal of the Court's 5–4 decision, the holding ought to be limited to the facts of the case. The teamwork approach, with its modification of job classifications and work rules and more flexible work assignments is one of the most successful manufacturing features that we can import from Japan. Although it proceeds from a fundamentally different cultural perspective, teamwork as practiced at NUMMI and Saturn establishes its relevance for manufacturing in the United States.

Yet the tradition of American collective bargaining requires certain safeguards. Among them is the continued use of seniority to limit (but not eliminate) management's discretion in assignments. This is an important response to the criticism aimed at shop floor workers' participation and the allegation that seniority allows management to play favorites, a charge that has been made both in the United States and Great Britain. (The problem is exacerbated in Britain where, by virtue of the "beauty contest" through which union recognition is accorded by the employer based upon which union and its policies are most acceptable—a practice that originates with the Japanese multinationals which have located in Britain—no impartial mechanism exists to correct managerial whimsy!)[58]

In *First National Maintenance v. NLRB*,[59] the Supreme Court, by a 7–2 vote, held that decisions to institute partial plant closures (and presumably complete plant closures) are not mandatory subjects of bargaining under the Act and therefore not issues over which employers are obliged to bargain with the unions to the point of impasse. The Court viewed certain subjects that could be properly characterized as "management prerogatives" as beyond the Act's duty to bargain obligation, and it seems reasonably clear that unions would be precluded from insisting upon negotiating worker director provisions in a collective bargaining agreement or separate agreements inasmuch as this would be characterized as an internal management matter. True, the parties might be free to bargain such provisions. But even if unions view this issue as an important one, it seems unlikely that most employers would bargain on this matter voluntarily.

There are other problems aplenty under section 8(a)(2) of the Act because of the argument that union involvement in management affairs is inconsistent with an arm's-length collective bargaining relationship. Yet the General Counsel has refused to issue a complaint regarding former United Auto Workers Union President Douglas Fraser's appointment to the board at Chrysler. Said the General Counsel:

> There is no immediate danger of a conflict of interest based on the role of a union agent in management affairs. Indeed, such a conflict is far less likely than in [NLRB precedents] . . . where seven of 15 board members were union representatives and several other board members were representatives of employer-union trust funds. . . . There are no union loans to the employer and . . . Fraser himself owns no stock and has indicated that he will not personally accept any payments for his duties as a director. The union has no financial interest in the affairs of Chrysler, except to the extent that it, like any responsible union, has a vital interest in keeping the representative employers [sic] financially healthy in order to preserve and promote jobs and job benefits. Further, Fraser has stressed publicly and in his proxy statement that his prime interest in being on the board of directors is to represent the interest of the employees he represents, particularly with respect to matters which affect terms and conditions of employment, e.g. plant closings. There is nothing in Fraser's conduct which suggests that he has behaved inconsistently with this prime interest in representing employees. Nor is there anything in the reputation of Fraser or of the union which would suggest that Fraser would use his position on the employer's board to compromise the interest of unit employees.
>
> Further, there is nothing to suggest that Fraser would utilize his twin roles to injure competitors of Chrysler and thereby injure the employees of such competitors. Although it is conceivable that the union would take "harsh" positions in bargaining with other auto manufacturers for the purpose of injuring them and benefitting Chrysler, there is no evidence to indicate that the union or Fraser has done that or plans to do that. Further, since the employees of such other manufacturers are also union-represented, and since an injury to those manufacturers would harm these employees, it is unlikely that the union or Fraser would pursue such a course. Finally, the whole relationship between the employer and the union has been free from infirmity. For many years, the employer and the union have been parties to "arm's-length" bona fide collective bargaining relationship.[60]

In one respect, the Board's position seems to be legally appropriate, and yet in another, it contains deficiencies. Union representation on the board does not present an inherent conflict. So far, so good. Yet there is the implicit assumption that the minority representation feature makes the anticonflict of interest case a more persuasive one. My judgment is that the Bullock Commission was correct in its Committee of Inquiry Report on Industrial Democracy in noting that the conflict of interest problems of union representatives are not fundamentally dissimilar from those of other representatives, such as creditors like banks who have their representatives on the board. Said Bullock:

> . . . the argument that employee representatives on the board, regardless of particular circumstances, will tend to push the company toward the high wages and high employment policy rests on the assumption that short term benefits to their constituents—higher wages and more jobs now—will seem more important than the long term benefits to the same constituents represented by profitable growth, i.e., secure or expanding employment in the future. The reasonableness of making such an assumption has received strong criticism in a number of submissions.
>
> . . . We do not see why a board comprising employee as well as shareholder representatives should be unable to strike an adequate balance between short term and long term interests. A board consisting of shareholder representatives is said to be able to strike the correct balance between the short and long term interests of equity investors in determining, for example, the size of dividends. If employee representatives are unable to strike a similar balance on wage and employment policies, it must either be because they or their constituents are more shortsighted than the shareholders and their representatives, or because the real economic interests of employees lie, relatively speaking, in the short term and those of shareholders in the long term. Neither proposition is self-evident, let alone proved. To put it no higher, there does not seem any reason to believe that employee representatives will not have as clear a perception of where their constituents' best interests lie, or that the stake held by employees in the long term health of the company is less than that of the share holders.[61]

Yet there are areas which present genuine conflicts of interest for the unions. For instance, although the matter was addressed within the anti-interlocking directorate provisions of the Sherman Antitrust Act, the problem arose when the United Auto Workers were about to negotiate with American Motors. A union representative was placed on the board of the company following Fraser's election to the board at Chrysler. Under the circumstances there would be a genuine conflict of interest for a union leader under the conflict of interest themes sounded by the NLRB under section 8(a)(2).

One illustrative scenario is that the union will gang up against competitors—even those that are organized—and have a less than arm's-length relationship with the employer where it has a representative on the board of directors. Another possibility is that employers in companies that are competitors of those on whose boards union representatives sit can bring pressure upon the representatives so as to compromise them. One can very easily imagine rank and file reactions in such companies. If they see wages, fringe benefits, and job security lagging behind the worker director companies, they will pressure for information that provides them with a basis for restoring parity. Parity—one can discern from the UAW's pressure to bring Chrysler back to the same range of wages and benefits as those enjoyed by those at General Motors and Ford—remains critical for American unions in so-called pattern bargaining. In contrast to works council leaders who sit on the boards in Germany and company union leaders in Japan, American trade union representatives can override corporate lines, since they have political responsibility to all union members.

One way of protecting codetermination programs might be to enact legislation that would apply with uniformity so that no employees would be in a worker directorless company and the potential for unions ganging up with employers in worker director companies would be diminished or eliminated. But a difficulty with this proposal is that it is politically impractical given the relatively low position assigned the issue by unions as well as employer resistance to the idea. Legislation that does not take into account the peculiarities of the American culture of industrial relations, would hardly be effective and good legislation.

Electing employees to the boards who are not union representatives would not be very different from the practices of Germany which has pioneered in the codetermination area and where representatives of works councils or union activists who may not hold top positions inside the union are frequently those who are promoted by labor for positions not specifically allocated to the union. Thus unions play a role in this connection. The absence of a works council tradition makes this approach difficult to enact in the United States.

Still, it must be acknowledged that the tradition of an adversarial relationship coupled with the philosophy of trade unions creates substantial problems for the new era of worker participation advocated here. American unions have been traditionally decentralized. True, information that relates to investment decisions and rearrangements, such as mergers, closures, and relocations of plants, will come from corporate headquarters. But there is no reason why that information cannot be transmitted to the local level, and perhaps the law (as advocated in chapter 5) should mandate this. The presence of worker or union directors is not the only means through which this can be accomplished. In any event what is required is a change in the preoccupation of industrial unionism with the grand or commanding heights of the corporate world and a greater focus upon the individual financial circumstances of the firm or plant.

Another problem is one that made the British unions balk at the Bullock Report on Industrial Democracy and the codetermination idea, namely the representative role of employees who are not union members. This has been a sticky point for the German unions. They have taken the position that management employees should not be counted as labor representatives on the board but rather more properly identified with management itself. Similarly the British unions wanted union representation on the board that would cover nonunion employees as well. American unions with a tradition of exclusivity and a shrinking base that exaggerates feelings of insecurity would be similarly disposed.

Conclusion

Four factors make it likely that employee involvement and worker participation will grow in importance. The first is that competition will intensify, particularly from Japan. America needs to eliminate inefficient practices.

The second is that the nonunion sector in the United States is expanding. This means that employers will become even more interested in finding some mechanism or institution through which employee interests can be represented. It is improbable that works councils will be dictated by legislation as in Europe. But the absence of representation will mean that employers will cast about for mechanisms, sometimes as a substitute for unions and sometimes with a view toward defeating a union. Of course the law should remain hostile to employers' attempts to defeat unionism. But as a general matter the law should facilitate employee representation mechanisms.

Inevitably job security is linked up with discussion of future institutions outside of collective bargaining. Particularly in large firms, employees must have some collective voice about matters of job security and wrongful discharge. These are the kinds of jurisdictions exercised by committees and work circles. To the extent that the law facilitates such mechanisms, it facilitates the realization of new employee rights.

Foreign experience cannot be dismissed. Japan may be culturally dissimilar to the United States, and its labor management relations are predicated upon a framework that does not involve autonomy and arm's-length relationship but facilitates dialogue between employee and employer. The labor law protections enshrined at Maastricht in December 1991 impliedly favor works councils. American unions, which in the 1970s saw these practices as inherently alien, have already begun to mute the xenophobia of their recent past. The swing will be toward such imaginative codetermination mechanisms. The European experience, unlike the Japanese, will be more readily accepted here as an example for future employment practices.

Clearly the Supreme Court's *Gilmer* decision (discussed in chapter 3) has prepared the way for more dialogue between employers and employees about waivers, arbitration, and other conditions, and there have been new job protection laws, particularly the Civil Rights Act of 1991 and wrongful discharge litigation. Where there are no unions, employee groups, whether employer sponsored or not, have proved to be more effective watchdogs than the individual employee acting on his or her own.

Finally, amendments to the Occupational Safety and Health Act of 1970 introduced by Senator Edward Kennedy make dismissal of health and safety issues impossible. Senator Kennedy's bill will mandate the establishment of employee committees that address these issues. The goal of the legislation is to provide for "joint participation of employers and employees" through the method of establishing a committee at each work site. The committees are to be given time off during working hours to pursue these matters. The secretary of labor would promulgate regulations relating to the "establishing and functioning" of such committees at work sites where there are at least eleven employed. Where no union is present, the committee members are to be elected.

It is easy to see that this legislation will simply provide another step toward facilitating much needed communication between workers and their bosses. Obviously employee committees will not be regarded as illegal company unions. There is no reason why the principle involved in this legislation cannot be extended to other aspects of the employment relationship, albeit on a voluntary basis to which section 8(a)(2), as presently written, should not be applicable.

Unions, perhaps because they have been so seriously weakened, may well be more receptive to such programs than they have been previously. This, of course, assumes that other reforms, such as those advocated in chapters 5 and 6, become part of any new amendments to the National Labor Relations Act. Support for reform by unions like the United Auto Workers and the United Steelworkers[62] is not immutable. There may now be a window of opportunity for union support of new cooperative relationships in both union and nonunion establishments. The new law must reflect the emerging social realities. Industrial democracy can be translated into change at all levels of the employment relationship.

5
The National Labor Relations Act: The Reform of Labor Law

If repeal of the National Labor Relations Act is not in order—a misguided argument now made by some labor lawyers—then reform surely is warranted. The Act has not been working effectively during much of the past twenty years. In the first place, as others have noted,[1] the increased resort to unfair labor practice litigation indicates that the remedies for statutory violations are not an effective deterrent. Second, the collective bargaining process is not being facilitated by the Act. Third, the unions are having more difficulty with the electoral process established by the Act. While this matter is hardly dispositive of any judgment about the statute—the amount of union effort as well as market forces are obviously factors here—some of the rules of the Act make the establishment of collective bargaining more arduous than should be with a law that favors freedom of association and the resolution of differences through the collective bargaining process.

Considerable debate has broken out between LaLonde and Meltzer, on one side, and Weiler, on the other, about the use to which a variety of statistics compiled by the Board can be put and, specifically, the extent to which it can be said that its statutory deficiencies and frailties can be ascribed to lawless employer resistance to the unions.[2] Weiler's view has been that the National Labor Relations Act is a major factor in the decline of private sector unionism.[3]

My view has always been that the causes of union decline are far more complicated and that, as LaLonde and Meltzer show, there has never been any evidence for the volume of unfair labor practice litigation and union organizational activity or statistical data developed by Weiler relating to back-pay orders that establishes a causal connection between the failures of the Act and the failure of organizational activity. As LaLonde and Meltzer persuasively point out, a variety of employer conduct unrelated to the problems of union organizational campaigns has been regulated by Board and Supreme Court doctrine over the past two decades.[4] It may be that more precise Board data will allow for judgments to be made about these issues in the future. But, for the time being, my proposals are based upon more modest assumptions. The evidence that we have thus far is inconclusive about the impact of the regulation of organizational campaigns upon voting behavior.[5] It is unclear that the votes of workers will be cast differently if the law intervenes to provide an environment for employee free choice that is free of intimidation or, as has been expressed, constitutes "laboratory conditions."[6]

Whatever the resolution of this debate, my view is that the Board engages in excessive regulation of representation proceedings by creating full employment for labor lawyers through detailed rules regarding what constitutes coercive and noncoercive speech. The Board should get out of this area and establish relatively mechanistic rules through which both labor and management can reach employees to gain their allegiance.

As Table 5.1 makes clear, the union rate of success in NLRB conducted elections has declined considerably. The union win rate has dropped from 72 percent between 1950 and 1954 to 46 percent between 1980 and 1984, rebounding a bit to 48 percent between 1985 and 1988. Even in the traditional union strongholds of mining, construction, manufacturing, transportation, communications, and public utilities, the decline has been dramatic, comparable to half of the representation of the Canadian unions north of the border. The win–loss ratio may be attributable to factors that have nothing to do with what ails the law. Even if the inability of the Act to function effectively is responsible for the unions being less successful in the certification process, this does not show that the law is a major factor in union decline in the United States. The fact is that the law is not working, and it is not performing the functions envisioned for it by its framers. This in itself is cause for alarm.

In major respects the law is producing results and practices that are antithetical to those of the statute. An across-the-board reexamination of the law is also imperative because of the passage of time since the law was amended previously. The law ought not to be tinkered with for change's sake alone, although the fact that the most recent set of amendments is indiscriminately one-sided in its regulation of unions may have something to do with our contemporary problems.

Table 5.1
Declining union success in NLRB elections (annual averages)

Years	Newly represented employees	Share of work force	Number of elections	Size of unit	Union win rate
1950–54	554,100	1.3%	5,906	121	72%
1955–59	277,100	0.6	4,731	94	64
1960–64	274,800	0.6	6,854	73	58
1965–69	315,800	0.6	7,776	73	59
1970–74	254,400	0.4	8,298	67	54
1975–79	185,000	0.3	7,884	63	49
1980–84	115,500	0.2	5,048	60	46
1985–88	80,300	0.1	3,558	60	48

Sources: 15–53 NLRB Annual Reports (1950–88); Economic Report of the President 1990, 342–43, Table C-43 (GPO, 1989).

The Ideal of Repeal

Frustration with the efficacy of the NLRA has led AFL-CIO President Lane Kirkland to opine about the desirability of repealing the statute on a number of occasions.[7] This position has not been adopted as formal policy by the Federation nor any other union. But, because of Kirkland's widely quoted comments about this issue, it is a matter that must be considered on its merits before examination of the issue of labor reform. The preliminary question is whether reform is inherently misguided because of the flawed nature of the statute.

The argument is that the benefits of the statute are so limited and the burdens, particularly in the form of the Taft-Hartley unfair labor practice prohibitions aimed at unions, are so considerable, that a return to the Norris-LaGuardia period of collective laissez-faire in which neither party can intervene before government to obtain substantive advantage would be the best policy. Unions would be able to engage in secondary picketing and boycott (by which pressure is placed upon a third party that does business with a primary employer with whom the union has a dispute in order to get union demands), as well as primary picketing for organizational and other purposes. Restrictions upon all organizational picketing contained in section 8(b)(7) of the Landrum-Griffin 1959 amendments to the Act would be eliminated. Common law, as it was defined at the time of Norris-LaGuardia, would govern relationships between unions and employers and thus all forms of self-help. Workers could no longer be protected by law against discharge or discipline, and employers could not be restrained by the courts or an administrative agency.

But arguments in favor of repeal fail. In the first place, while some unions, like those in the construction industry, frequently do not need the Board's electoral and certification processes to obtain recognition, most industrial and service unions find the Board useful. True, some unions, like the United Food and Commercial Workers, have boycotted the Board from time to time during the past decade because of its antiunion positions. The paradox is that the labor would be the first to say that prior to the Court's reversal of this doctrine, the *Jean Country* decision (which gave unions organizational access to private property, particularly in shopping malls) was helpful to unions in asserting self-help organizational rights and that a prerequisite for utilization of the doctrine would be to invoke the Board's procedures. But one of the ironies and contradictions in the repeal argument is that though decisions like *Jean Country* were hailed by the unions as a signal victory, they would not protect the unions' use of self-help activities if the Act were to be repealed.

The gains that would flow to the unions by virtue of repeal in terms of the elimination of the Taft-Hartley prohibitions against both primary and secondary organizational activity are not clear-cut. Unions are able to evade the Taft-Hartley prohibitions against organizational picketing if the picket signs speak of an area wage standards objective[8] and if union organizers do not contradict this message by formally demanding recognition. As for the secondary boycott prohibitions, most of the industrial and service unions do not use the secondary boycott and did not do so prior to the Taft-Hartley amendments. The United Auto Workers and the United Steelworkers, for instance, have rarely invoked this weapon prior or subsequent to Taft-Hartley. The union that has resorted to it most effectively is the International Brotherhood of Teamsters, which has used it ever since the Great Depression.[9] But even the Teamsters' ability, should they choose the secondary boycott, is limited. This is not only because of decline in union representation in critical Teamsters' sectors like trucking and the rise of nonunion carriers in a deregulated environment but also because of the presence of independent contractors who are self-employed and beyond the reach of the Act and who are unresponsive to picket signs and other union weapons.

There is another problem with the repeal argument that rarely surfaces in the debate. The Taft-Hartley Act prohibits state jurisdiction over strikes and picketing, the use of criminal prosecution, tort actions for punitive and compensatory damages, and administrative regulation over strikes and picketing. The preemption doctrine, rooted in the Constitution, proceeds upon the assumption that Congress has regulated the subject matter in detail and has thereby manifested an intent, inferred from the regulation, to oust the states because of the potential for conflict between federal and state jurisdiction. The argument with regard to other entities, whether they be federal or state, is that the board possesses expertise that is superior to that possessed by comparable authorities at either the state or federal level.[10]

The preemption doctrine has diminished state regulation and thus has not suppressed union activities, despite the decline in the Supreme Court's protection—the most prominent example was the protection of picketing as free speech.[11] A statute that placed limitations upon organized labor's use of both primary and secondary economic pressures (e.g., mass picketing and secondary boycotts) has displaced the states, many of which used tort, administrative, and antitrust regulation in a more repressive fashion than Taft-Hartley. If the Act were repealed, state regulation would no longer be preempted by federal authority. Indeed the omnipresent antitrust law could easily be revived to a far greater extent than it has been already.[12]

Although repeal of the statute has not been debated, supporters of repeal would presumably attempt to preclude the assertion of state jurisdiction. Though some doubt was voiced about the matter at one time,[13] Congress could implement this objective notwithstanding the Tenth Amendment to the Constitution, as interpreted by a Supreme Court decision of eight years ago.[14] This amendment gives to the states that which is not taken from them by the Constitution and would not inhibit federal law that is designed to deprive the states of jurisdiction otherwise possessed.

Even if Congress had the desire to repeal the statute—after all many employers advocate this, given traditional employer antipathy toward a statute that triggers more unfair labor practice charges against employers than unions—and to keep the states out of what had previously been the federal domain, it seems unlikely that Congress could implement both effectively. Congress would hardly be able to restrain the states because employer opponents of the Act would hardly be supportive of the elimination of state regulation. No restraint imposed upon the states would preclude state and local government from retaining law and order jurisdiction and prohibiting, for instance, picketing if it becomes violent. Mass picketing that interferes with ingress and egress of workers or customers from facilities can always be regulated by the states, even with an anti-state's-rights rider to a federal repeal of state statutes.

Inevitably states and localities would be called upon to define what is mass picketing and what is not conducive to law and order. This point contradicts some of the reasoning in Massachusetts Supreme Judicial Court Justice Holmes' dissenting opinions of the previous century[15] which argued persuasively that picketing was not inherently violent. Picketing often presents questions about how intimidation is to be defined.

Where picketing is aimed at other employees and sometimes even customers in a consumer boycott, it takes on characteristics that are far beyond those associated with free speech.[16] That is why the United States Supreme Court has permitted regulation of the tactic. That is why it is and would be always difficult to rein in state regulation. Undoubtedly the temptation to intervene at the state and local level will become more considerable with the decline of federal authority.

As superficially appealing as the repeal idea may be, it would be better to reform the statute. While this subject does not abound with panaceas, the fact is that reform is a more profitable idea than is repeal. It is to the former subject that we now turn.

It seems both logical and important to begin at the beginning, that is to say, with the process through which unions are certified as collective bargaining representatives to represent workers. In Board-ordered elections most of the dispute under the law relates to the tactics and propaganda that each side may use. The Board attempts to regulate the propaganda and determine whether it constitutes coercion, threats, misrepresentations, and unlawful inducements or benefits aimed at workers designed to get them not to vote for the union. A considerable debate has broken out about the actual impact that such campaigning methods, lawful or unlawful, have upon the way in which workers vote or the extent to which they change their mind as a result of the campaign. Much of the argument relates to the use of statistics, methodology, and the time period by scholars to determine the impact of both union and employer campaigns. But a strong case exists for eliminating this regulatory effort regardless of the impact that the campaign has upon the minds and actions of workers. As Archibald Cox has noted,[17] a speech found to be coercive when made by an employer to a South Carolina mill hand may have nothing resembling that impact on a Detroit or Chicago Teamster-affiliated truck driver—indeed the speech may engender militancy rather than produce intimidation.

The same problem occurs in attempts to regulate benefits. The law prohibits the award of benefits designed to interfere with employee selection of a union. Surely the bestowal of wage or fringe benefits increases makes workers less interested in the union—indeed many workers have filed for representation with the view to obtain benefits rather than union representation (which after all is only a means to an end). Some workers may react to the benefits with militancy or greater appetite, proceeding on the assumption that more determined or calculated pressure can produce more substantial concessions. But the problem with legal regulation of this arena is that it is simply impossible to determine the impact of propaganda on workers. The major benefits that flow from this aspect of the law is, as is so frequently said of much of Taft-Hartley, to provide for full employment for lawyers. It has become a kind of cottage industry to examine the hundreds of Labor Board decisions dealing with phrases, statements, and speeches to determine which side of the line of legality the conduct will fall. Involvement in this area by the Board is at best a wasting asset, at worst, fundamentally counterproductive because of the litigation and consequent delay to the electoral process spawned by it.

Solicitation and Access to Company Property

While employees have the right to solicit others and to distribute literature, as well as to wear union insignia on plant property, their right to have nonemployee union organizational assistance is carefully circumscribed by the Supreme Court's decision in both *NLRB v. Babcock & Wilcox*[18] and especially *Lechmere v. NLRB*.[19] It is fair to say that *Babcock & Wilcox* creates something of a presumption against nonemployee union organizational access,[20] an approach substantially rigidified by the Court in *Lechmere*. But in many recruitment drives workers may be badly in need of outside more professional assistance. While it may be fair to assume that some kind of balance between statutory rights and private property are presumed under the Act, it seems reasonable that the balance ought to be weighted on the side of the freedom of association rights protected by the statute itself and not private property, because of the statute's explicit protection of the former and not the latter. This is particularly true where by definition the presence of union organizers during nonworking time ought to have a minimal impact on the employers' legitimate business interest in production and discipline. *Lechmere* is completely out of step with these themes, and Congress should reverse the decision as part of labor law reform—and provide for periodic nonemployee union-organizer access to company property open to the public—and on private property closed off to the public once a representation petition has been filed.

Yet, despite the need for promoting communication to workers on choices relating to union representation, the fact is that the contest will often be unequal. Even where unions have access to company property for putting forth their view, the employer, by virtue of the control over the employment relationship and the potential for confusing its ideas about union representation with its orders about job assignments,[21] will have a distinct advantage.

The Problems of Delay

A substantial benefit in holding the election expeditiously is to diminish the propaganda advantage for either side and to permit employees to exercise their right to free choice in a prompt fashion and a noncoercive atmosphere. This means that labor law reform must assure workers of an expedited election to take place within a specific period of time. In Nova Scotia the Provincial statute mandates that an election shall take place within five days of filing.[22] In California the Agricultural Labor Relations Act of 1975 establishes the same general principle. This means that disputes about the unit and the eligibility of voters in the election—which is really all that there is to fight about in these cases—must be put over and resolved subsequent to the time that recognition and bargaining takes place, assuming that the union prevails.

The problem with delay at the Board has a direct relationship to the ability of unions to keep employees' interest in unionization and ultimately to the effectiveness of the remedies available under the statute. If out of the campaign there arises substantial delay in either the handling of representation petitions or the unfair labor practice litigation, employees will simply lose interest and draw the conclusion—sometimes with the subtle assistance of employer communications—that they can more effectively address employment concerns in a nonunion environment.

Although the problem appears to have diminished somewhat in the last couple of years, the past decade has seen an enormous increase in the time that it takes to decide unfair labor practice cases. The median time in fiscal 1989 according to the United States General Accounting Office[23] was 300 days as compared to 133 days for it at the start of the decade, 1980. In the fiscal year 1988 the median between filing of charges and Board adjudication was 762 days, and an additional 430 days between the Board order and judicial enforcement. This meant that the median interval between filing a charge and judicial enforcement was over three years. Between 1984 and 1989 the median time for processing unfair labor practice cases ranged from a low of 273 days to a high of 395—two to three times higher than the medians of the 1970s. For representation cases, where petitions have been filed, medians ranged from 190 to 256 days—also considerably in excess of the medians established during the 1970s. A substantial number of these cases are of course appealed to the courts, adding to the delay incurred.

In "major" cases, according to statistics prepared by the Board (see table 5.2), in the fiscal years 1989 and 1990, it took 736 and 691 days, respectively, from the time that the charge was filed until the Board's decision was issued in unfair labor practice proceedings. In representation cases the figures for these years for the time between the filing of the representation petition and the decision by the Board in Washington was 258 and 309 days, respectively.

A number of factors appear to be responsible for delay. One is the view propounded by the General Accounting Office that the Board fails to establish binding internal time limits within which cases are to be processed. In some measure the same problem of delay afflicts Board-conducted elections—though an equally formidable difficulty lies in the Board's failure to provide the ill and laid-off workers, as well as employees with leaves of absence, with a postal ballot that would encourage full participation. Ironically the political process seems to be moving in the opposite direction, with more absentee voting availability and easier access to the ballot generally. A second factor responsible for delay is the frequency of Board member turnover and, more important, the existence of vacancies which Presidents Reagan and Bush have been slow to fill. This problem was most prominent between 1980 and 1984 and may have led to a backlog of cases between 1984 and 1989.

The decline in union win rates in representation elections may be, in part connected to the changing median in processing unfair labor practice cases. As we have noted, the union win rate in elections has declined dramatically. Reduced union resources and energy for organ-

Table 5.2
Time elapsed for major case processing stages completed (fiscal year 1990, age of cases pending)

Stage	Median	Days
Unfair labor practice cases	FY89	FY90
Major stages to complete		
1. Filing to complaint	45	48
2. Complaint to close of hearing	133	154
3. Close of hearing to ALJ	153	149
4. ALJ decision to board decision	259	315
5. Filing to board decision	736	691
Age of cases pending ALJ decision, September 30, 1990	339	732
Age of cases pending board decision, September 30, 1990	738	783
Representation cases		
Major stages complete		
1. Filing to notice of hearing	8	8
2. Notice of hearing to close of hearing	13	13
3. Close of hearing to		
a. Board decision issued	256	234
b. Regional director decision issued	23	23
4. Filing of petition to		
a. Board decision issued	268	309
b. Regional director decision issued	45	45

izational campaigns as well as increased employer resistance may have something to do with this phenomenon. But the considerable delays that unions encounter in the Board's administrative process surely have a bearing.

True, the Board's administrative backlog has now diminished. The case backlog at the Board in 1983 and 1984 was 1,059 and 1,054, respectively. In 1991 the backlog for unfair labor practice cases was 272 cases, declining from 342 and 369 in 1989 and 1990, respectively. Yet the problem of delay persists.

Section 10(j) of the Act authorizes the Board, in its discretion, to seek temporary injunctive relief where unfair labor practices are in particular need of an expeditious remedy. But the total cases submitted to Washington appears to be declining from the early 1980s, as does the number of Board authorizations and General Counsel's requests for such relief (see table 5.3).

The decline of section 10(j) requests and authorizations is puzzling, given the fact that they attack the basic problem of delay by bypassing

Table 5.3
Section 10(j) statistics (fiscal years 1982–90)

Fiscal year requests	Total 10(j) cases submitted to Washington	GC 10(j) requests	Board 10(j) authorizations	Percentage of total GC requests
1982	255	58	53	23%
1983	309	71	51	23
1984	195	40	30	21
1985	168	42	38	25
1986	163	45	43	28
1987	155	37	37	24
1988	166	44	43	27
1989	163	62	62	38
1990	157	41	39	26
1991	142	36	38	25

Source: NLRB executive secretary.
Notes: (1) Two GC 10(j) recommendations were pending before the Board at the close of fiscal 1986. (2) The Injunction Litigation Branch excluded 86 drug-testing cases from this total. (3) One GC 10(j) recommendation was pending before the Board at the close of fiscal 1987. (4) Two GC 10(j) recommendations were pending before the Board at the close of fiscal 1988. (5) One GC request was pending before the Board at the close of fiscal 1989. (6) Two Board authorizations were in cases which were requested by the GC and were pending before the Board at the close of fiscal 1988. (7) Of the 30 Board 10(j) authorizations in FY 1990, one was in a case pending before the Board at the close of Fiscal 1989. The remaining 38 authorizations secured from the Board in FY 1990 were in cases in which the General Counsel requested authorization in the fiscal year. Three requests for authorization were pending before the Board on September 30, 1990. (8) Three GC requests were pending before the Board at the close of FY 1990. All three cases were authorized by the Board.

the tortuous unfair labor practice process. It may be that more recent General Counsels simply do not have the interest that is comparable to that in evidence a decade ago. Moreover union boycott and criticism of the Board may make the unions less interested in utilizing such procedures. This may simply reflect the decline in union organization. To repeat, the decline of reliance upon this provision is profoundly puzzling. It warrants attention, perhaps, in the form of more rigorous guidelines that exhort the Board to seek injunctive relief in a new labor law environment.

One answer to the delay problem is adherence to firm timetables for both representation and unfair labor practice proceedings by the Board. A second response is to extend the Board's rule-making approach to the appropriate unit issue—a technique already approved in hospitals by the Supreme Court in *American Hospital Association*—to other industries. This would eliminate much of the delay in such proceedings because the major issue prompting litigation would no longer exist. The same impact will be made if elections are held prior to litigating the unit issue.

But the issue of injunctive relief still warrants attention, perhaps in the form of more rigorous guidelines that exhort the Board to seek injunctive relief in a new labor law reform environment. Since 1947 the Board is *mandated*, through its regional attorney, to seek injunctive relief in connection with *union* unfair labor practices involving some forms of unlawful economic pressure. The same principle cannot apply to all employer unfair labor practices, for that would frequently bypass and thus gut the Board's own administrative processes. But if discretion is given to the regional attorney in such cases—it is the regional attorney who is mandated to initiate proceedings in union unfair labor practices—the process could be expedited considerably because the lawyers who are on the ground, and who have conducted the investigation, could move into court without delay. The statute should instruct the regional attorney to both provide investigative priority and seek relief where, in the regional attorney's view, a pattern of unlawful conduct exists. Notwithstanding this delegation of responsibility, failure by the regional attorney to seek relief could still be reviewed by the General Counsel and the Board in Washington as it is today.

Authorization Cards

Prior to the Taft-Hartley amendments in 1947, the Board could and did certify unions as majority representatives on the basis of authorization cards rather than secret ballot-box elections. This practice is followed in Canada today where 55 percent or more of workers in an appropriate unit have signed cards. The objection to the use of authorization cards lies in the fact that the signing of the card may result from peer pressure or may not reflect the employee's intent. In large part the latter situation exists because many unions in this country have so-called dual authorization cards, which state that the signing of the card is for the purpose of membership, assumption of union obligations, or employee interest in conducting an NLRB election.[24] Of course, if the law were changed so as to allow unions to obtain recognition on the basis of authorization cards—by virtue of the Supreme Court holding in *NLRB v. Gissel*, cards can be used as an obligation to bargain where the employer is guilty of unfair labor practices that may impede the electoral process—unions would be less likely to use such cards and could clarify their meaning.

Peer pressure can serve as a basis for inducing the employee to sign, but in some measure, those fears can be assuaged by establishing the prerequisite for a certification or recognition obligation above the 50 percent level. Since the Boards' experiences on both sides of the Canadian border leaves one to conclude that authorization cards are unreliable where more than one union is involved in the campaign, they should never be used under such circumstances. But it seems difficult to resist the idea of reliance upon authorization cards when one notes the difficulties that the Board and the courts are having with cases in which a majority of workers have not provided their allegiance to the union because of the success of the employer's unlawful campaign. That is to say, where the employer's unlawful conduct begins at a very early stage in the campaign, all that one can do is to speculate that workers would have expressed an interest in collective bargaining but for the employer's conduct. The fact of the matter is that this judgment is always speculative and the difficulties with determining what would have happened have made the Board and the courts reluctant to remedy such unfair labor practices through *Gissel* bargaining orders.

The use of authorization cards as a basis for certification would avoid the considerable litigation that has been spawned by the *Gissel* principle. The Board's use of cards as a basis for certification might not only promote collective bargaining but also diminish the lengthy and unfair labor practice litigation that is especially difficult where the union has not crossed the 50 percent line with its cards. In the absence of an amendment to the statute that would permit recognition on the basis of authorization cards, the Board should provide for minority union bargaining orders where the organizational activity has been squelched prior to obtaining the majority because of egregious employer unfair labor practice conduct.[25] In this connection it is interesting to note that under new legislation in Ontario where an employer commits an unfair labor practice during an organizational campaign, a *Gissel* bargaining order can be imposed without any showing of employee support for the union. A sensible intermediate position might be to impose a bargaining obligation where egregious employer conduct is present and when the union has reached a threshold of 40 or 45 percent support based upon authorization cards or other evidence.

Whatever rules are established relating to the basis upon which representation will be accorded, whether it be through union authorization cards or elections, reforms will all go to naught if judicial review is allowed to both lengthen the process and second guess the Board's judgment of the recognition issue. The availability of judicial review related to recognition or certification disputes is, as noted elsewhere, one of the principal contrasts between labor law of the United States and Canada.

A curious anomaly exists today in American labor law regarding this matter. On the one hand, the Act states that a Board certification is not a "final order" within the meaning of the statute, thus making the appellate process inapplicable to such cases.[26] The idea is to provide for the expeditious resolution of such matters. But an escape hatch in the law exists by virtue of the employer's ability to raise (generally without the prospect of obtaining consideration) objections to the unit, and legitimacy of the way in which the election has been conducted. The Act ought to explicitly preclude an employer from raising disputes relating to representation matters in unfair labor practice proceedings that have already been handled in the representation election arena. Moreover, where the employer is ordered to bargain with the union as the result of an unfair labor practice charge, bargaining ought to commence immediately unless the employer is able to obtain judicial review and a temporary reversal of the Board's order. That is to say, in the ordinary course of events, collective bargaining should proceed while the employer's appeals are winding their way through the courts. But there are necessary additional reforms beyond both minority bargaining orders and the need for some form of expedited judicial review.

Where 20 to 30 percent of the workers, for instance, have expressed interest in collective bargaining, either through an authorization card or an election, it seems perfectly appropriate to compel some form of relationship between the employer and the union for those employees if they are not already covered by collective bargaining machinery. The genius of the AFL-CIO associate membership status concept is that it proceeds upon the assumption that representation need not only be available where the traditional collective bargaining model has been established. The law now permits "members-only" bargaining for employees without regard to majority rule or an appropriate unit and without regard to exclusivity. But collective bargaining could be mandated, as it is in Japan, for instance,[27] where a minority of workers in a firm seek collective bargaining—without of course exclusivity for the union or the concept of an appropriate bargaining unit.

Against this it might be argued that the evolution of such processes would be untidy. Again it must be remembered that members-only bargaining is lawful today. This proposal would simply compel bargaining for members only where 20 to 30 percent of the workers desire it and on a members-only basis. But members-only relationships ought not to be compelled where a unit has already been certified and where Board procedures indicate that employees want representation under the traditional model. This would be disruptive and a distraction from the basic attempt to provide some form of representation where none exists.

A second objection is that an employer would seek the lowest common denominator; namely the employer would opt for a members-only arrangement as opposed to exclusivity. That is always a danger, and yet it seems that it would be difficult to increase the amount of employer vigor devoted to resisting union organizing. It is likely that resistance would be maintained in this country against both models.

But the minority representation approach was the one used by public-sector unions in the federal government prior to President Kennedy's 1962 executive order, relating to such workers, which provided for NLRB-type exclusivity. Full-fledged bargaining of the kind engaged in by a majority status union was not required. Consultation and the provision of information to the union was sufficient. This was then a kind of mandated version of employee committee representation.

Monetary Relief for Workers

Another answer to egregious employer conduct is to provide more effective remedies for discriminatory discharges as the Labor Reform Bill of 1978 advocated. (This statutory proposal, passed by the House of Representatives and endorsed by the Carter administration,[28] was the first major labor law reform to be seriously considered subsequent to the Landrum-Griffin Act amendments of 1959.) The 1978 bill would have overruled current Board law so as to provide workers with income lost during the period of time that an employer refused to bargain with a certified collective bargaining representative. The secretary of labor would have also been required to bar those guilty of recidivist behavior and unfair labor practice violations from bidding for future government contracts. The bill would have dealt with the problem of administrative delays so as to permit decisions of the administrative law judge, the fact-finder, and trial court below the Board to be summarily affirmed by the NLRB where, in the ALJ's judgment, the issues presented did not involve an unresolved question of law. The overwhelming number of cases coming before the Board involve factual disputes that put to test the credibility of competing witnesses about disciplinary or dismissal disputes. Expedited procedures providing for judicial enforcement were contained as well. But the bill was filibustered to death in the Senate.

Double or triple back-pay awards would reduce the incentive for employers to engage in unlawful discriminatory dismissals. Interim earnings that could have been obtained with reasonable diligence should not be deducted from the back-pay award, as provided for in the Supreme Court's *Phelps Dodge*[29] decision. The Court's ruling a half-century ago comports with the Anglo-American tradition supporting mitigation of damages incurred. But Congress should reverse this aspect of *Phelps Dodge* because intrinsically the decision and others like it[30] assume the existence of a demarcation line between that which is punitive, as opposed to remedial, and therefore appropriate under American labor law. The former is regarded as *verboten.* The idea of a distinction between that which is punitive and remedial is, in my view, synthetic and makes no sense as a matter of logic and industrial relations practice. Disputes about the calculation of interim earnings and the question of whether reasonable diligence was utilized are themselves time-consuming procedures that create new layers of delay in labor law.

In contrast, Japanese labor law does not provide for automatic deduction of interim earnings or that which could have been obtained with reasonable diligence.[31] The reasoning is that nothing can be an adequate substitute for the employment relationship that has been lost by virtue of unlawful conduct. This difference between the two systems is ascribed by the Japanese courts to the system of permanent employment in that country. Like so much of Japanese labor law, the approach to the *Phelps Dodge* issue proceeds upon the assumption that the relationship must be preserved and its disruption repaired effectively.

Finally, though the Supreme Court held in the *Sure-Tan*[32] decision that illegal aliens are employees within the meaning of the Act, it invalidated the Board's back-pay remedy for such workers because those involved in the instant case had been deported and were not available for work. It is not clear whether the deportation of the workers in question was critical to the Court's reasoning.[33] But labor law reform should make back pay available to all workers, whether they are present in the country legally or not.

The fact is that lack of protection for illegal aliens is harmful to all workers, a point recognized by Justice O'Connor in her majority opinion in *Sure-Tan*. Denial of monetary remedies such as back pay as well as reinstatement has the same deleterious effect as complete exclusion of such workers from statutory coverage. Protection for illegal aliens reflects the employment relationship reality more than it countenances unlawful activity. The Internal Revenue Service, for instance, does not report filings on income derived from unlawful activity such as gambling, drugs, and prostitution to criminal prosecutors. The Board need not report its remedies to the Immigration and Naturalization Service. Admittedly, in labor law, availability for work is a critical factor in connection with a back-pay remedy—and if the worker has been deported, this should be taken into account when the remedy is devised. But the Board should be authorized to provide all remedies to all workers without cooperating with or reporting to the federal authorities.

The Duty to Bargain Cases Subsequent to Recognition

Our focus thus far in this chapter has been the law relating to recognition and certification. This is appropriate because that issue is a central ailment of the American labor law system today. But even if these shoals are traversed, the relationship between labor and management is still fragile, in part because of the way in which the law works once bargaining commences subsequent to recognition or certification. The best evidence for this proposition is that in a majority of instances unions and employers are unable to conclude a collective bargaining agreement. It is easy to see how the bargaining process is impeded when there is an unlawful refusal to bargain in good faith. Refusal to bargain in good faith is prohibited by the National Labor Relations Act. Neither labor nor management can engage in such illegalities. Of course, in practice, unlawful intent or conduct from which the intent may be inferred is difficult to prove.

The fundamental problem with or without a duty to bargain in good faith is that the players are not required to enter into a collective bargaining agreement. Paradoxically an intent to consummate such an agreement is required. As we have seen, in those cases where a violation is made out, the matter can take three or four years if it is appealed through the courts, and all too frequently no agreement is ever negotiated.

General Electric Co. v. NLRB,[34] which involved the company's now abandoned tactic of so-called Boulwarism in which the employer announced its last offer at the beginning of negotiations and stated its unwillingness to depart from its position unless changed economic circumstances dictated, illustrates some of the problems well. Precluded from inferring bad faith from the refusal of the employer to accede to a substantive contractual proposal, the court relied upon a "totality of conduct" as a basis for finding a violation.[35]

The Board's examination of so-called surface-bargaining cases highlights another aspect of the difficulties with the refusal-to-bargain cases. The Supreme Court has made matters more complex by concluding that the unwillingness of employers to accede to the most minimal of well accepted collective bargaining contractual provisions accepted by most or all parties elsewhere is not a basis upon which the Board of the courts can infer a bad faith intent not to consummate a collective bargaining agreement.[36] The Board has stated that it does not examine a particular proposal to determine whether it is "acceptable" or "unacceptable" but rather whether the demand is designed to frustrate an agreement or a contract.[37] If the Board finds that the employer is attempting to remove the union's ability to represent the employees—for instance, through contract clauses under which management would unilaterally determine wages; manning; scheduling and hours; layoffs, recall, and the granting and denial of leave; promotion, demotion, and discipline; the assignment of work outside the unit; and changes of past practice—it will infer a bad faith intent not to consummate a contract with the union. Said the Board in another case:

> In determining whether a party has bargained in good faith, making a genuine effort to reach agreement, we will seldom find direct evidence of a party's intent to frustrate the bargaining process. Rather, we must look at all of its conduct, both away from the bargaining table and at the table, including the substance of the proposals on which the party has insisted . . . such an examination is not intended to measure the intrinsic worth of the proposals, but instead to determine whether, in combination and by the manner in which they are urged, they evince a mindset open to agreement or one that is opposed to true give-and-take.[38]

Yet, even where there is no unfair practice, the parties may simply not be able to bargain effectively—because of union or employer obduracy—and the relationship will soon dissipate, given the inability of the union to produce anything for the rank and file for whom it is obliged to bargain.

If the union cannot negotiate an agreement, the result is virtually the same as decertification or lack of certification during the organizational campaign. The delay in unfair labor practice litigation, even if unsuccessful from the employer's perspective, erodes support. The remedy in the Boulwarism context is simply an admonition to employers to "go thou and sin no more." Many of the Canadian provinces, as noted in chapter 7, have adopted some form of first-contract arbitration as a remedy for this problem under circumstances considerably less pressing. Provinces such as British Columbia, Ontario, Quebec, Newfoundland, and Manitoba have accepted first-contract arbitration in some form. The fact is that in Canada, most collective bargaining agreements, subsequent to certification, are concluded successfully.

Indeed 1992 legislative proposals debated in the Senate (discussed in chapter 6) involved the concept of arbitration over "interest" disputes about the new terms of a negotiated collective agreement and were linked to the rules relating to the right to strike and employer responses to that tactic. The principal problem with this idea in any context has been the fear that the collective bargaining process would be eliminated altogether given the propensity for parties, anticipating the entry of an impartial third party, to rigidly preserve their position so that a compromise of it will not be harmful to them. One answer to this problem is to follow the so-called final offer system of arbitration or some variation on that theme—its use in baseball salary disputes over the past two decades has gained national attention. The idea here is to keep the parties in a state of uncertainty by precluding any arbitral compromise and then require the arbitrator to accept one side or the other's last position. This presumably would induce both sides to be more flexible and reasonable as they approach the bargaining table.

This final-offer idea might be suitable to disputes involving the negotiation and ultimate arbitration, if necessary, of the first collective bargaining agreement between the parties. Although the genesis of first-contract arbitration lies in the inability of new unions to obtain secure and ongoing collective bargaining relationships, it would seem that a statute should provide for employer as well as union access to the machinery, an idea to which we return in chapter 6. This would permit an over confident union to be caught up short without resort to industrial strife if it makes extraordinary proposals—the strike becoming unlawful if the union sought an award that was inconsistent with that rendered by the arbitrator.

Unlawful behavior ought not to be a prerequisite for triggering the machinery. It should not be necessary to make, for instance, egregious behavior involving dismissals of union adherents a prerequisite to arbitration's invocation. For instance, antiunion discharges are likely to be relatively infrequent and insistence upon their presence as a prerequisite for invoking the machinery would make it unimportant. Refusal to bargain violations ought not to be a prerequisite either. This is so not only because of the fact that litigation is necessarily lengthy, and therefore would undercut an effective arbitration remedy, but also because unfair labor practice liability as a prerequisite for arbitration is counterproductive. That is to say, the idea of a process where one finds fault or blame or liability is not compatible with the idea of promoting a binding or permanent institutional relationship. In a sense the United States has been fairly tardy in making this discovery in connection with unfair labor practice litigation generally. Japan, which like Canada and the United States also has undertaken an unfair labor practice approach to portions of labor policy, has been singularly successful in using that process to promote relationships that are ongoing.[39]

One objection to the first contract arbitration idea lies in the fact that it is not only the first contract that is likely to give rise to the problems described above and the consequent employer refusal to accept the bargaining representative. Subsequent to the negotiation of the first contract, specifically at the time of the negotiation of ensuing contracts, there will be problems as well. As we will see, Canada has not been able to provide completely satisfactory answers to the problem of second- and third-contract disputes. The answer, if there is one, would seem to lie in providing the Board with discretion to intervene, albeit in a more limited fashion, in circumstances even outside of the first-contract dispute.

Mandatory Subjects of Bargaining and Job Security

Another feature in the statute that is in need of reform relates to the concept of mandatory bargaining and impasse established by the Supreme Court's 1958 *Borg Warner* decision.[40] As the law stands now, unions and employers are obliged to bargain with one another over so-called mandatory subjects that affect wages, hours, or conditions of employment. This has allowed the Board, and ultimately the Supreme Court, to indirectly control the substance of bargaining by determining which issues are more directly important to conditions of employment. For instance, the Supreme Court has said, in *First National Maintenance v. NLRB*,[41] that a management decision to engage in a partial closure of an establishment did not involve a condition of employment and therefore trigger mandatory bargaining but was rather a "management prerogative."

The practical consequence of these decisions is to make it impossible for serious bargaining to take place because insistence on that which is *not* mandatory to the point of impasse is unlawful. On the other hand, the refusal to discuss a mandatory subject to the point of impasse is also unlawful. In part it is the unsatisfactory way in which the statute works on such critical issues as job security in *First National Maintenance* and elsewhere that necessitated the enactment of plant-closing legislation at the federal level in 1988 and in the state legislatures both prior and subsequent to the enactment of WARN. *First National Maintenance* found that the partial closure was not a condition of employment within the meaning of the Act, which states that the focus of bargaining is to be on wages, hours, and other conditions of employment, and therefore not a mandatory subject of bargaining.

The assumption of both labor and management appears to be that because certain employer decisions are management prerogatives—the closure of plants, partial closures, and the like—the union is not entitled to information about employer conduct or intentions in this regard. This seems to be a terribly shortsighted approach and one that is not dictated by existing Supreme Court authority. Information about the economic facts of life is critical for a union engaged in the collective bargaining process. The Act should mandate disclosure of employer intentions regarding both plant closures and future investment decisions.

A framework for bargaining is established by the *Borg Warner* line of cases. Aside from the policy-making scope that is given to the Board and the courts on a regular basis, a rather artificial framework for bargaining is established. As Justice John Harlan pointed out in his dissenting opinion in *Borg Warner*,[42] in which the entire concept of mandatory bargaining was first established, it is frequently difficult for the parties to know precisely when the moment of impasse has been reached, particularly, as the Board has sensibly noted, deadlock need not be reached on all issues for impasse to be realized.[43] Indeed, as the Supreme Court has said in *Charles Bonnano v. NLRB*,[44] frequently bargaining revives subsequent to impasse.

Finally, inasmuch as there is no provision for declaratory judgments or advisory opinions under the Act permitting the parties to know in advance what the status of the item on the table is (i.e., whether mandatory or nonmandatory), the parties must guess as best they can and attempt to bargain intelligently in light of this. The remedy for a violation is imposed long after the fact and, again, only involves an admonition to "go thou and sin no more." This is a fairly ineffectual exercise of handwringing. But if there is a strike and it is deemed to be caused, in part or whole, by the unfair labor practice violation, the strikers are unfair labor practice strikers and have the right to reinstatement and, where they have made it an unconditional offer to return to work, back pay with interest as well. Without such a finding the workers are economic strikers who may be permanently replaced (more about this in chapter 6). But it is frequently difficult to know whether the strike is of the unfair labor practice or economic variety. This is a problem that can be only corrected through a statutory amendment, which would provide for advisory opinions on such issues by the Board.

While *Borg Warner* is an attempt to regulate the bargaining table so that bad faith can be inferred from both the refusal to discuss issues as well as the insistence upon discussing those that can be characterized frivolous ones, it seems far better to compel bargaining on all subjects. True, the potential for obstructing the bargaining process is ever present. Yet the potential problems with which *Borg Warner* is concerned seem minor when one considers (1) the unsatisfactory nature of policy-making decisions involved in cases like *First National Maintenance*, (2) the difficulties involved with determining when the abstract state of impasse is actually present and the potential for negotiations thereafter in any event, (3) the unsatisfactory way in which such cases are resolved after violations are established, namely through relatively insignificant remedies or the uncertain status of strikers where a strike is engaged in as well.

The problems with *First National Maintenance*, however, are more profound. That decision declaims against the proposition that labor is to be an "equal partner" with management in the United States, setting federal labor policy at odds with the codetermination philosophy that has taken root in northern Europe, particularly Germany. Perhaps it is inappropriate to require an equal partnership under a statute that promotes collective bargaining. But surely the idea of a partnership, as a general proposition, is consistent with attempts to promote cooperation, the policy that should be promoted in the section 8(a)(2) cases and the revision of that portion of the statute. This is truly the sine qua non for some kind of accommodation between the adversarial approach to collective bargaining promoted by the Supreme Court in *Insurance Agents* and the attempt to take into account new industrial relations realities.

Equally troubling, in my view, is the Court's statement in *First National Maintenance* that such matters as advertising and product design are peculiarly within the province of management prerogatives and therefore always nonmandatory subjects of bargaining beyond the purview of the Act. Throughout much of the 1950s, Walter Reuther, then president of the United Auto Workers, criticized the car firms' failure to produce small fuel-efficient cars, warning against the likelihood of oil scarcity and the consequent need for the consuming public to purchase something different than what the Big Three was providing. The failure of the employers to heed these statements assisted in causing considerable loss of employment for the UAW membership. Surely, not only should the partial closings at issue in *First National Maintenance* be bargainable within the meaning of the Act but also any employer decision that has even, in the Court's *First National Maintenance* language, an "attenuated" impact upon employment conditions.

The automobile example indicates that decision making in the managerial prerogative arena has a more than attenuated impact on employment. The Court's decision—as it affects job security, management prerogatives, and the idea of a partnership—would make it impossible for unions to bargain seriously for representation on the board of directors, notwithstanding the fact that both Doug Fraser and Owen Bieber, presidents of the UAW, have served on the Chrysler board and that union representation has been obtained in other industries such as the airlines. Accordingly labor law reform should provide for a reversal of *First National Maintenance* on both the job security issue and its attempt to categorize managerial decisions as nonmandatory.

Successorship Cases

Equally vexatious is a doctrine of law that has emerged from a trilogy of Supreme Court decisions.[45] The Court has made it difficult for unions to continue their representative status with employers who are engaged in takeovers or mergers and acquisitions of predecessors, and equally important, unless a union is able to get specific language in a collective bargaining agreement obliging a successor to assume the contract,[46] the Court has made it even more difficult for the collective bargaining agreement to apply to a new employer. This line of cases has assisted the union decline, particularly in industries like the restaurants, where management turnover is substantial. Exceptions to this exist where the unions have some kind of leverage with the employer involved in a joint venture, such as that which existed in auto and steel firms, with which the unions have a solid relationship, and other companies. The UAW's ability to negotiate a collective bargaining agreement with NUMMI, the product of a merger between General Motors and Toyota Corporation, is illustrative of this pattern.

The cases create an incentive for the purchaser to dismiss the predecessor's workers because the decisions make continued representation and contractual rights dependent upon the retention of such employees by the successor employer. The statute should be amended so that there is a presumption of continued representation and collective bargaining obligations that will apply to the successor employer.

Disclosure of Information

In the 1950s, the Supreme Court, in an opinion authored by Justice Hugo Black, *NLRB v. Truitt Manufacturing*,[47] held that an employer that resisted union economic demands on the ground that it possessed an inability to provide them was required to "open its books" and to disclose the basis for its position. A decade earlier the United Auto Workers, then under the leadership of Walter Reuther, had fought a lengthy strike against General Motors on the same issue. But sophisticated employers, recognizing that *Truitt* only applied in the event of a claim that it had an inability to pay, frequently phrased their position differently so as to avoid any interference with this management prerogative. Their position might be that they could not provide the wage claims as demanded by the union because they were different from the ongoing rate in the industry or in the particular geographic area. This would be a legitimate position to take but, where the real reason was inability to pay, a dishonest one taken (frequently, I fear, on the advice of counsel) to avoid legal obligations under the statute.

The assertion that an employer cannot pay demands because of declining market conditions attributable to competition from other businesses[48] or competition directly is not a basis on which a union may oblige the employer to disclose.[49] An unwillingness to pay because of competition, unless put forward as a basis for imminent corporate collapse, reflects an unwillingness as opposed to an inability to pay in the view of the Board and the courts. The idea is that the unwillingness to pay because of competition simply would place the employer in a disadvantageous position. Here the Board can compel disclosure without statutory amendments[50]—and it should do so in the interest of honest and genuine bargaining.

There are two major problems with this line of cases. The first is the one previously already alluded to, namely the potential for sophisticated obfuscation or just plain old-fashioned dishonesty. The second is that some of the cases that have allowed employer management prerogatives in the job security arena involving relocations, for instance, have turned on the question of what the employer's motives really are.[51] Any incentive to give the legally correct (though often factually erroneous) answer—the one that will remove any burden of bargaining with the union to the point of impasse over a mandatory subject—is enhanced by the fact that disclosure requirements under *Truitt* are so limited. Though publically traded companies must disclose relevant information to the Securities and Exchange Commission, it may not be particularly revealing regarding costs and profitability at the plant level, where most collective bargaining in America takes place. The profitability of the firm is not dispositive of the viability of a particular work site. Moreover, generally SEC data are inadequate for the union's purpose.

Labor law reform should reverse the *Truitt* approach entirely. Disclosure of the true basis for the true employer's position should not only be required—periodic disclosure without a union request, should be obliged and all decision making that could conceivably have an impact upon employment conditions, namely investment closures, advertising, and basic product decisions such as the manufacturing of small cars that are not as dependent upon oil as the gas guzzlers.

Where the Union Is a Problem

Thus far most of the proposals in this chapter are designed to provide unions and employees with rights that they do not presently possess. The ideas propounded here proceed upon the assumption that the balance has been tilted in favor of management and against labor through a variety of factors, not the least of which is the tilt provided by both Taft-Hartley and Landrum-Griffin in 1947 and 1959 and in subsequent Labor Board and Supreme Court decisions interpreting the statutes.

Yet there are areas in which union practices need to be circumscribed by law. One example of this relates to the violation of no-strike clauses in collective bargaining agreements and the ability of employers to obtain injunctions against such. While the Supreme Court in *Boys Market v. Retail Clerks, Local 770*[52] held that employers may obtain injunctions against such contractual violations, notwithstanding the broad prohibitions against injunctions in labor disputes contained in the Norris-LaGuardia Act, part of the holding was predicated upon the view that the no-strike clause is the quid pro quo for the arbitration clause that may be enforced through a motion to compel arbitration in the courts. Accordingly the same result has not been obtained where so-called sympathy strikes are involved, and there is not an underlying issue that can be arbitrated by a third-party neutral. Where employees refuse to cross picket lines established by other unions, the Court has held, by 5–4 vote,[51] that an injunction may not be obtained.[53] This decision ought to be reversed by Congress on the ground that the no-strike pledge, part of the enforceable collective bargaining agreement, is a vital part of the labor contract from the employer's perspective. The Court's holdings supportive of arbitration are laudable—although a bit exaggerated in their assessment of arbitral competence. But they are undercut by the unwillingness of the Court to strengthen the integrity of promises made in collective bargaining agreements to limit or prohibit economic pressure such as refusal to cross picket lines.

Similarly another example of union abuses or excesses in need of regulation is the internal union electoral process. The trusteeship which the U.S. Department of Justice placed upon the International Brotherhood of Teamsters in 1988 may have been an indiscriminate and poorly thought out remedy for a problem of corruption at the highest levels of that union. Yet ironically the problem then was worse than when it was first attacked in the 1950s as the result of the McClellan hearings resulting in the Landrum-Griffin Act of 1959. But a major element in the Teamsters difficulties—and indeed a problem in ensuring union democracy generally—relates to the way in which officers are elected, namely through indirect participation provided by delegates at conventions. Delegates, frequently on more than one payroll in the union's internal structure may not reflect the rank-and-file sentiment. It is interesting to note that the most vibrant and competitive electoral campaigns inside unions have been maintained where members have the opportunity, through one form or another, to cast a direct vote for their leadership.

The trusteeship specifically addressed this issue by providing for direct vote for the rank and file for national officers. The result was that the outsider, Ron Carey, was elected president, and it is widely assumed that a new leadership will provide for both reform and an attack upon corruption. Labor law reform ought to include expanded and direct voting rights for the rank and file in connection with national as well as local officials. Responsiveness appears to be facilitated under such circumstances, and there is no reason why what works for the Teamsters in this regard should not have general applicability to the labor movement and its rank and file. All workers ought to have a direct involvement in their union just as all workers, along the lines advocated in chapter 3, should have their day in some kind of court or arbitration proceedings so as to be able to protest an unlawful dismissal.

Conclusion

To sum up, labor law reform requires the amendment of the Act to eliminate reliance upon propaganda to determine the lawfulness of company and union speech during organizational campaigns but should promote widespread access for nonemployee union organizers to distribute their message to employees during nonworking time on company property where employees can be effectively reached. A modified form of bargaining should be available to employees where no union is in the establishment and where a minority of employees, about 20 to 30 percent, want the representation for themselves only without exclusivity. Recognition on the basis of authorization cards should be obligatory where a union has, for instance, 60 percent support in a bargaining unit predicated upon employee evidence such as cards or petitions. Where the employer engages in egregious unfair labor practices, bargaining should be compelled under the authority of *Gissel*, even though the union's authorization card support falls short of a majority. My view is that this kind of minority bargaining order can be properly obtained under the Act as it is presently written. But in light of Board and circuit court authority to the contrary, the statute should also be amended in this area to clarify any ambiguities.

Once the relationship has been established, if the parties are unable to agree upon the provisions of a collective bargaining agreement, third-party arbitration should impose a contract upon them, especially the first time in their first exposure to the collective bargaining process and in some circumstances even afterward. The erosion of the collective bargaining process could be protected by providing for a form of final arbitration (a matter discussed in chapter 6 at more length). The Act should be amended so as to provide for advisory opinions on the lawfulness of a refusal to bargain, but more basically the demarcation line between mandatory and nonmandatory subject matter should be eliminated, and the right to bargain on all issues should be made available to both sides. Collective bargaining agreements and representation rights should be imposed upon successor employers. The obligation to assume the old collective bargaining agreement should be imposed upon any purchaser as a condition of purchase.

Unions should be obliged to adhere to no-strike provisions. The injunction should be made available in violations of no-strike clauses even where only a sympathy strike—when the bargaining unit members do not have an underlying grievance that can proceed to arbitration—is involved. The rank and file should be guaranteed the right to vote directly for national as well as regional offices in secret ballot-box elections. It should not be necessary for the government to take the extraordinary initiatives that it did in the Teamsters litigation in order for the rank and file to possess this elemental right.

Additionally the remedies advanced in the Labor Reform Act of 1978, filibustered to death in the Senate in that year, should be adopted at least where employer conduct is egregious. It seems inappropriate to deduct interim earnings from back pay. Contrarily, double or triple damages would be appropriate under such circumstances as well as providing authority to the secretary of labor to debar or to cancel contracts. The administrative process before the Labor Board should be expedited in line with the proposals of the bill. Under some circumstances, where certification subsequent to the union's recognition or certification of exclusive bargaining representative, contract terms may have to be imposed through arbitration.

The *Borg Warner* and *First National Maintenance* decisions should be reversed by Congress insofar as they establish a demarcation line between mandatory and nonmandatory subjects of bargaining. Both parties should be able to bargain to the point of impasse with the other on anything that is important from its perspective, be it the ballot clause (under which the employees would be required to vote on the question of whether they would strike during the term of the agreement) which the employer insisted upon in *Borg Warner*, the decision to partially close an operation in *First National Maintenance,* or representation on the board of directors in codetermination or some other modified union or worker participation in managerial decisions. Reversal of these decisions is in line with attempts, either through Board law or new amendments to the statute, to achieve effective cooperation between labor and management. Cooperative relationships can be enhanced if unions are entitled to employer disclosure about subject matter that relates to employment conditions—a disclosure that is not dependent upon union request but rather provided periodically, such as three or four times a year. Workers ought to have the facts of life about the viability and prospects of their firm. This would require statutory amendment in order to be completely effective.

Other needed reforms are to be found in the areas of cooperation (explored in chapter 4), the right to strike in the private sector, and the increasingly difficult problem of replacements of economic strikers. It is to these matters that we turn in chapter 6.

6

The Strike Weapon and Other Forms of Economic Pressure: Self-help for the Workers in a Democratic Society

Global competition, coupled with a rising nonunion sector fostered by deregulation in the transportation and communication industries, has weakened the strike and other forms of economic pressure by unions, caused a general decline in the use of the strike, and ultimately argues for a reassessment of its importance in industrial relations systems. By account of both the Federal Mediation and Conciliation Service, charged by Taft-Hartley amendments with responsibility for assisting in the resolution of disputes in the private sector (a party seeking modification of collective bargaining agreements must notify the Service as well as state agencies of its intention to do so) and the U.S. Department of Labor, Bureau of Labor Statistics, strikes have plummeted dramatically (see table 6.1 and figure 6.1). According to the Services Statistics, based upon the reports given by both labor and management, there were about 1,250 work stoppages a year in the 1980s as opposed to 2,660 a year during the 1970s, a decline of approximately 53 percent. According to BLS calculations of strikes involving 1,000 or more workers, in the 1960s there were an average of 300 or more a year of such stoppages, compared to 40 in 1991. As noted in *The New York Times* about 1992 bargaining between the Communications Workers of America and AT&T:

Despite nearly three months of sometimes bitter bargaining, the tentative labor agreement announced this week between AT&T and its two principle unions disclosed a remarkable degree of common purpose. Each side really feared not the other, but a noncompetitive AT&T in a global market.[1]

Where there is not comparable cooperation, bitter conflict over such issues as pattern bargaining, as in the five-month 1992 dispute between the United Auto Workers and Caterpillar[2] has resulted in employer use of permanent replacements, a tactic that quickly devastated the UAW,

Table 6.1
National estimates of the number of workers on strike and permanently replaced (1985, 1989)

	1985		1989	
	Estimate	Sampling error (±)[a]	Estimate	Sampling error (±)
Number of workers on strike				
Total	393,000	30,000	458,000	14,000
Small[c]	136,000	30,000	86,000	14,000
Large[d]	257,000	[b]	372,000	[b]
Number of workers permanently replaced				
Total	14,000	6,000	14,000	3,000
Small	11,000	6,000	5,000	3,000
Large	3,000	[b]	10,000	[b]
Percent of striking workers replaced				
Total	4	2	3	1
Small	8	5	6	4
Large	1	[b]	3	[b]

a. Sampling errors are calculated at the 95 percent confidence level.
b. No sampling errors were computed because these results are based on the universe of strikes.
c. Strikes with 0 to 999 workers in bargaining unit.
d. Strikes with 1,000 or more workers in bargaining unit.

inducing its leadership to urge its members to return to work without any settlement. The decline in the effectiveness of the strike is undoubtedly assisting employers in their attempt to erode pattern bargaining, which does not take into account the individual firm's ability to pay, and is moving relationships toward a more decentralized form.

Meanwhile the decline in the strike as a tactic has occurred simultaneously with more pressure for regulation of strikes, which the public regards as intolerable in some sense. Certainly this is the lesson of congressional legislation which provided for arbitration in nationwide railway disputes in 1991 and 1992 and the fact that Congress intervened eighteen times in such disputes between 1963 and 1992. As Congress seems to have recognized in the 1992 debate about strike replacement legislation (a matter to which I return to below), there is a direct relationship between equitable and rational rules relating to the use of industrial conflict and methods of dispute resolution in lieu of strikes.

Number of work stoppages

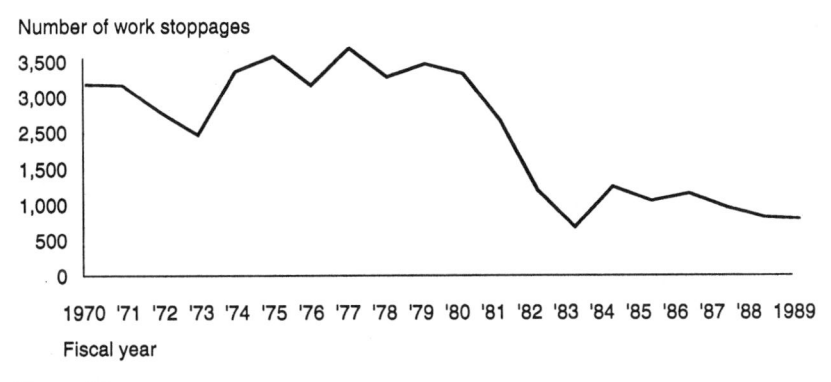

```
3,500
3,000
2,500
1,500
1,000
 500
   0
     1970 '71 '72 '73 '74 '75 '76 '77 '78 '79 '80 '81 '82 '83 '84 '85 '86 '87 '88 1989
     Fiscal year
```

Figure 6.1

The assumptions in chapter 3 and 4 have been that various forms of participatory arrangements will enhance both job security and productivity, although not necessarily in that order. Another assumption bound up with such proposals is that just as was true of the widely heralded American experience with grievance-arbitration machinery which was so dominant in this country's industrial relations landscape during this past half-century, such initiatives will serve as a kind of substitute for industrial strife and for the strike weapon itself. Indeed creative and innovative third-party intervention beyond that provided for by the Federal Mediation and Conciliation Service and by comparable state agencies ought to provide a more rational surrogate for confrontational and potentially harmful industrial conflict. Unfortunately in a democratic society the objective of avoiding conflict cannot always be realized. A variety of methods of third-party intervention must exist in tandem with the strike.

The United States is not a signatory to International Labor Organization conventions which guarantee workers the right to exercise freedom of association and collective bargaining rights that include within them a limited right to strike. The assumption in this country has been that at least in the private sector (a seemingly ceaseless debate that is only now subsiding has raged for decades about the right to strike in the public sector) the right to strike is integral to the collective bargaining process, at least under some circumstances.

The assumption is best articulated by Justice Brennan in the landmark U.S. Supreme Court *Insurance Agents*[3] opinion. It brings to mind a point first articulated by Dr. Samuel Johnson: It is the prospect of hanging that concentrates men's minds marvelously. Sometimes the collective bargaining process receives more attention when the threat of economic pain becomes more imminent. The idea in the *Insurance Agents* opinion is that resort to economic strife and the presupposed infliction of pain—and especially the *threat* of such conduct—will induce parties to reassess their positions and to compromise despite the unassailability of the proposition that the strike or other economic pressure is more often an irritant and harmful to the company's economic posture and thus job security of the workers, rather than a lubricant for dialogue.

Congress, when it enacted the Wagner Act in 1935, protected workers' rights to engage in concerted activities. The Labor Board designated conduct as protected to immunize workers from retaliatory discipline or discharge. In section 13 Congress stated that nothing in the Act was designed to limit the right to strike, the proviso contained in the Taft-Hartley amendments being that strikes and other forms of economic pressure that constituted secondary boycotts, jurisdictional strikes, and disputes in violation of no-strike pledges in collective bargaining agreements became *verboten*.[4]

In contrast to other countries such as France, Sweden, and Japan, the right to strike has not been an issue in constitutional litigation in the United States. The high water mark was Justice Louis Brandeis' declaration that the right to strike is not protected under the Constitution in an "absolute" fashion[5] in that the Constitution does not refer to the right to strike—the Bill of Rights was written well before the arrival of unions, let alone a modern and mature labor movement. But the regulation of the strike in both the private and public sector has been tolerated in the teeth of continual constitutional challenges unlike cases that characterize picketing as free speech or symbolic speech.[6] The strike has not enjoyed the same degree of protection as picketing has.

The strike thus remains somewhat protected by statute if not by the Constitution itself. Yet its protection under the National Labor Relations Act is curiously limited. In the first place, economic action that involves slowdowns,[7] work to rule,[8] refusals to work overtime under certain circumstances,[9] and unannounced or intermittent stoppages[10] is unprotected, thus exposing workers to retaliatory employer self-help measures such as discipline and discharge. (Strikes undertaken in violation of collective bargaining agreements, as well as unauthorized stoppages that do not have the *imprimatur* of the exclusive bargaining agent placed upon them, are similarly unprotected.) But two of the most perplexing and puzzling limitations upon the strike weapon are to be found in Supreme Court's authority dealing with the right of employers to permanently replace economic strikers[11] and the authority of unions to discipline strike-breakers who cross the picket line in defiance of an authorized stoppage.[12]

The first line of authority emerges from a Supreme Court decision written three years after the passage of the Act in 1938, *NLRB v. Mackay*.[13] In *Mackay* the Court held that despite the protected status accorded strikers, the employer had a management prerogative to replace them permanently in the interest of implementing its legitimate business interest in continued production. My sense is that the *Mackay* decision is both badly flawed and inconsistent with a number of labor policies frequently reflected in Supreme Court decisions in the federal labor law arena. The issue has become increasingly important, not only by virtue of the labor movement's need to maintain an independent and arm's-length relationship with management where cooperative relationships are unable to substitute completely for more adversarial confrontations but also because the permanent replacement tactic has been used with greater frequency in the decade of the 1980s.

Some of the Causes of Permanent Replacement Tactics

President Reagan's dismissal of 12,000 striking air traffic controllers in the summer of 1981 is thought by many people to have started the permanent replacement trend. That dispute, however, arose out of an unlawful strike against the federal government, and not a private sector lawful economic strike like the kind involved in *Mackay*. Two obvious causes of increased employer willingness to replace strikers are growing foreign competition in manufacturing and deregulation in transportation industries like airlines, trucking, and rail—all at the core of the unionized sector of the economy.

A second and not unrelated factor is the imperviousness of the new work force—particularly part-timers, two and more income families who may have family responsibilities—to the clarion call not to cross the picket line. Major employers with established labor relationships like Greyhound, Phelps Dodge, International Paper, United Airlines, Trans World Airlines, Eastern Air Lines, the New York Daily News, and Caterpillar Tractor have either threatened to use or have implemented this weapon in the 1980s and 1990s. As Senator Edward Kennedy has noted on the Senate floor, 30,000 machinists, pilots, and flight attendants were permanently replaced at Eastern Air Lines; 9,000 Greyhound workers replaced in a matter of weeks; 2,300 longtime employees at International Paper Co. were suddenly jobless in Jay, Maine; and 1,200 permanently replaced at Magic Chef in Cleveland.[14] The 1992 Caterpillar dispute is in some respects the most remarkable incident in this trend because of the unwillingness of major manufacturers bargaining with the United Auto Workers to use the permanent replacement tactic as of early 1993.

According to testimony provided to the Subcommittee on Labor-Management Relations of the House Committee on Education and Labor in 1990 by the U.S. General Accounting Office, both employer and union representatives believe that permanent strike replacements were hired in proportionately fewer strikes in the United States from 1975 to 1980 than in strikes from 1985 to 1990. In 1991 the GAO estimated that employers had announced that they would hire permanent strike replacements in 31 percent of the strikes that occurred in 1985 and 35 percent of those in 1989. The GAO estimated that employers hired permanent strike replacements in about 17 percent of the strikes in 1985 and 1989. It also estimated that about 45 percent of the employers believe that permanent replacements were used less often between 1975 and 1980 and that about 77 percent of union representatives have the same view. Of the employers that announced that they would hire permanent replacements, about 56 percent actually did so in 1985 and 46 percent in 1989. These figures did not differ for small strikes with up to 199 workers in the bargaining unit, and large strikes with 1,000 or more workers.[15]

Limitations on the Mackay Doctrine

The Court itself has undercut some of the impact of *Mackay* and its harsh qualities by holding that the permanently replaced economic striker remains an employee within the meaning of the Act,[16] entitled to preferential hiring as vacancies occur for apparently an indefinite period of time.[17] Indeed in 1990 the Court held, albeit by 5–4 vote, that it would not apply any presumption regarding striker replacements as a function of antiunion sentiments—and thus allow employers to refuse to bargain with unions on the basis of such replacements—but would determine their views on a case-by-case basis.[18] However, only the year before the Court, within the context of the Railway Labor Act, reaf- firmed the validity of *Mackay* and extended it to new frontiers.

The Railway Labor Act

In *Trans World Airlines Inc. v. Independent Federation of Flight Attendants*,[19] Justice Sandra Day O'Connor, writing for a 6–3 majority, held that employers are not required to displace nonstriking employees in order to reinstate striking employees with greater seniority. Noting that the Court has in the past often utilized "carefully drawn analogies from the federal common labor law developed under the NLRA" as "helpful" under the Railway Labor Act,[20] the Court looked for "guidance" to precedent under the former statute. The issue in *Flight Attendants* was the question of whether nonstrikers with less seniority could hold jobs that they had taken from striking employees. The union sought to use the National Labor Relations Act precedent, *Erie Resistor*,[21] under which the offer and award of superseniority for nonstriking employees had been condemned. The Court distinguished that decision on the ground that in contrast to *Flight Attendants*, it presented the ". . . prospect of a continuing diminution of seniority upon reinstatement at the end of the strike . . . ."[22] Said Justice O'Connor:

> It is clear that reinstated full-time strikers lost no seniority either in absolute or relative terms. Thus, unlike the situation in *Erie Resistor*, any future reductions in force at TWA will permit reinstated full-term strikers to displace junior flight attendants exactly as would have been the case in the absence of any strike. Similarly, should any vacancies develop in desirable job assignments or domiciles, reinstated full-term strikers who have bid on those vacancies will maintain their priority over junior flight attendants, whether they are new hires, cross overs, or full-term strikers. In the same vein, periodic bids on job scheduling will find senior reinstated full-term strikers maintaining their priority over all their junior colleagues. In short, once reinstated, the seniority of full-term strikers is in no way affected by their decision to strike.[23]

Moreover the Court was able to deny the strikers their right to utilize their seniority by characterizing the right to strike as a "gamble" rather than a right:

> Because permanent replacements need not be discharged at the conclusion of the strike in which the union has been unsuccessful, a certain number of strike employees will find themselves without work. We see no reason why those employees who choose not to gamble on the success of the strike should suffer the consequences when the gamble proves unsuccessful. Requiring junior crossovers, who cannot themselves displace the newly hired permanent replacements, "who rank lowest in seniority," . . . to be displaced by more senior full-term strikers is precisely to visit the consequences of the lost gamble on those who refused to take the risk.[24]

But as Justice Brennan said in a dissenting opinion, joined in by Justice Marshall,[25] in words that could be applicable to *Mackay:* "What is unarticulated is the Court's basis for choosing one position over the other. If indeed one group or the other is to be 'penalized', what basis does the Court have for determining that it should be those who remained on strike rather than those who returned to work? I see none, unless it is perhaps an unarticulated hostility towards strikes."[26]

The Union Discipline Cases

A second line of authority that has created difficulties for the unions involves union disciplinary authority over strikebreakers who cross authorized picket lines. In 1967 the Warren Court in a 5–4 vote held, in *NLRB v. Allis-Chalmers,* that the contractual relationship between member and union provided a basis for union disciplinary fines to be imposed upon strikebreakers.[27] Justice Brennan's reasoning was that the trade unions' inability to wield such weaponry on behalf of the strike would undermine the union's status as exclusive bargaining representative for all employees in the unit and cripple its ability to effectively implement stoppages. However, the fact is that industrial unions—craft unions after all have traditionally used expulsion of so-called scabs and blacklegs in this country—did not begin to impose fines upon strikebreakers until the early 1960s, and the matter remained controversial for years among major unions like the United Auto Workers. From the vantage point of morality and public image, unions were reticent to impose sanctions upon workers—even those workers who lacked allegiance to trade union principles—that were financially injurious to them. In a sense increased reliance upon this union tactic, as well as the frequency with which the *Mackay* doctrine is invoked by employers, has been a mirror image of labor's decline.

In the 1970s and 1980s an increasingly beleaguered trade union movement found the tactic of disciplinary fines to be a more tempting one. When the Court dramatically reversed course, albeit following the logical implications of the contract theory adumbrated in *Allis-Chalmers,* and held that unions violate federal law where they impose fines upon workers who have resigned, consternation in the ranks of organized labor was the most immediate result. In *Patternmakers' League of North America, AFL-CIO v. NLRB,*[28] Justice Lewis Powell, writing for the Court, said that unions could not place constitutional restrictions upon the right to resign in light of the ". . . inconsistency between union restrictions on the right to resign and the policy of voluntary unionism . . ."[29] enshrined in Taft-Hartley's prohibition of the closed shop. The fact that the Act did not address the so-called right-to-resign issue and that the absence of explicit statutory language or legislative history suggested an accommodation between the competing principles of the right to engage in concerted activities and the right to refrain from such did not dissuade the Court's majority.[30]

Yet it is *Mackay* and not *Patternmakers* that is the most pernicious aspect of federal labor law's treatment of the strike. The Court's decision in that case is contrary to a number of Supreme Court rulings in related areas and seems increasingly to be a remnant of another era when entrepreneurial and property rights were viewed as constitutionally impregnable[31]—one in which the due process clause reigned supreme as a barrier against economic and social welfare legislative regulation at both the state and federal level. On the other hand, the *Mackay* ruling is incongruous when juxtaposed with other Supreme Court decisions interpreting the NLRA on the use of economic pressure.

An obvious conflict between *Mackay* and subsequently decided case law emerges through the landmark *Insurance Agents* opinion, which stresses the strike weapon and its credibility as integral to the collective bargaining process. *Mackay* deters the strike and thus erodes the collective bargaining process.

A second inconsistency is present in the cases that address the employers' use of the lockout as a bargaining tactic. The "lockout," going back to the Pullman dispute of the previous century, was once a dirty word in the lexicon of American industrial relations. But the Court in the 1950s and the 1960s accepted the proposition that lockouts *per se* were not inappropriate weapons in the rough and tumble of the collective bargaining process. Like the Court in the lockout cases,[32] I accept the view that when the collective bargaining process commences, the law ought not to recognize good guys and bad guys as a general proposition. The bad guys only become apparent on this canvas when the practices in question substantially erode or eliminate the collective bargaining process altogether.

Granted, it is frequently difficult to distinguish between successful management tactics that make the union and its constituents weary and interested in new negotiation positions or new leadership as opposed to those pressures that promote the elimination of the collective bargaining process. I think that the Court, in the *Brown Food Stores*[33] decision, where the legal propriety of temporary replacements for employees locked out in a multi-employer association was at issue, adopted the appropriate reasoning in resolving the matter.

The Court held that the use of temporary replacements during the lockout was lawful, and in supporting its position, the Court stated that the union and the collective bargaining process had clearly continued to function and flourish despite the employers' lockout tactic. This was evident, the Court reasoned, given the fact that the union was still able to negotiate a union security clause, to process grievances, and to strike the relevant employers subsequent to the lockout itself.

In other words, although many decisions of the Supreme Court speak of motive as the critical test in determining whether employer and union behavior is illegal under the Act, it is the actual impact and what can be assumed about the impact in certain circumstances that is critical in determining whether employer conduct is "inherently destructive."[34] The Court's focus upon the viability of the union's procedures in *Brown Food Stores* illustrates the use of that test. But the impact of employer permanent replacement of strikers—a factor that was not even considered by the Court in *Mackay* or *TWA*—is clearly different from that of temporary replacement in *Brown Food Stores*.

Permanent strike replacements mean the loss of jobs for the strikers for the foreseeable future despite the employee's right to be reinstated at some point in the future when vacancies become available. It is difficult to imagine a prospect more likely to dissuade employees from exercising their statutorily protected rights than the loss of jobs and the benefits bound up with them. In the wake of the Taft-Hartley amendments which created section 9(c)(1)(B)[35] and its decertification procedures, where there are large-scale permanent replacements, employees may lose the right to collective bargaining altogether. Although Congress, in enacting the 1959 Landrum-Griffin amendments, tacked on the so-called sweetener that gave strikers who had been permanently replaced the right to vote in Board-conducted elections for up to a year,[36] this is a relatively slight limitation upon the permanent replacement tactics inasmuch as management can always petition for decertification after the year has elapsed.

The same commentary must be made about the Court's holding in *Curtin-Matheson Scientific*[37] that an employer cannot refuse to bargain with an incumbent union based upon the presumed antiunion hostility of the replacements. Independent evidence of replacement dissatisfaction, frequently prompted sub rosa by antiunion employers, will make any presumption unimportant. Chief Justice William Rehnquist, who supplied the fifth vote for the *Curtin-Matheson* 5–4 majority, would enhance this potential by allowing employers to poll strikebreakers about their support for or antipathy against the union.

The flaws in the reasoning contained in *Mackay* become even more obvious when one looks at the Court's *Erie Resistor*[38] decision involving awards of superseniority to nonstrikers. The Court concluded that this practice constitutes an unfair labor practice under the NLRA for striking workers. In *Flight Attendants*[39] the Court balked at the slightest extension of the *Erie Resistor* holding. Yet, if the award of superseniority is inherently destructive of the section 7 right to engage in concerted activities and to strike, why is it that the elimination of jobs altogether is not so destructive?

In *Erie Resistor* the Court, hard put to distinguish *Mackay*, nevertheless did so on the following grounds: that superseniority affects the tenure of all strikers, whereas replacements only affect those workers who are actually replaced; that superseniority necessarily operates to the detriment of those who engage in the strike as opposed to nonstrikers; that superseniority is an offer of an individual benefit to induce employees to abandon the strike, and promises of benefits by an employer are generally viewed as unlawful; that the use of new replacements with superseniority would deal a crippling blow to the strike effort; and that future bargaining would become extremely difficult for the union because of the built-in tension between those employees who had superseniority and those who did not.

Once again we are looking through the Emperor's Clothes when we see how ephemeral is the difference between these two cases comparable to the artificial demarcation line between discharge and permanent replacements, a point that I develop below. The Court in *Erie Resistor* seemed to assume that even the presence of a substantial or valid business justification for the practice could not override the unlawful impact upon strikers. What substantial interest or business justifications does the employer then have in permanent replacements?

As noted elsewhere, the business interest of the employer is to keep production operating. This is the management prerogative of business justification in the striker replacement context. Sometimes where an employer must make a substantial training investment, such as in a bus drivers' dispute as at Greyhound, where licenses must be obtained, the burden for the employer and the case for permanent replacements may be substantial. But in many circumstances employers can operate production without relying upon permanent replacements to cross the picket lines of strikers. This is particularly true where there is a surplus of labor or where the jobs in question are unskilled or semiskilled. If one assumes, as the Court seems to do in *Erie Resistor*, that in a substantial number of circumstances the permanent replacement tactic will not result in the ouster of all strikers, then the potential for divisiveness between strikers and nonstrikers, once the workers go back to the job, is just as great as it was in *Erie Resistor*. It is really very difficult for the Court to have it both ways in *Mackay* and *Erie Resistor*, two decisions completely at odds with one another.

Either permanent replacements do have distinctive and separate effects between strikers and nonstrikers as in *Erie Resistor* and thus make union elimination more probable, or if they do not, at least they obstruct an effective collective bargaining process because of the potential for conflict between workers found in *Erie Resistor*.

The Significance of Protected Activity

I am again reminded of the Emperor's Clothes when I reflect upon the significance of protected activity. Every year, when I teach my students about the rules relating to the strike weapon in Labor Law I, I explain the practical significance of engaging in protected activity. I point out to them that this is to be found in employee immunization from employer self-help instituted against the worker in the form of discipline or discharge for engaging in the conduct in question. Then I tell them that despite the fact that workers cannot be discharged or disciplined for engaging in a strike, they can be permanently replaced. This produces nervous laughter or expressions of puzzlement, or both—and well it should!

Even though the employer's right to engage in production is nowhere mentioned in the statute, in contrast to the right to engage in the strike itself, the protection of the employer's business interest is both appropriate and necessary. I am not in accord, for instance, with the approach taken in Quebec (a position now emulated in Ontario) that prohibits employers from operating during a strike. The employer should be in a position to conduct its business in a free entrepreneurial and capitalistic system, and it should not be precluded from so doing simply because workers withdraw their labor through their duly designated representative. But I think that the notion that employees lose their right to reinstatement because they engage in protected activity confounds the statutory scheme and the promotion of freedom of association and collective bargaining, which the preamble of the Act reminds us is still a basic purpose of the statute.

My judgment is that Congress should overrule *Mackay* altogether. But at a minimum there ought to be a presumption that temporary replacements are sufficient to protect the employer's interest.[40] While the approach in *Erie Resistor* would mean that there is no business justification for permanent replacements, the burden ought to be placed upon the employer to show that it is unlikely that it could recruit workers, an approach advocated by Justice Harry Blackmun in *TWA v. Flight Attendants*. True, this would create complicated litigation—the best argument for a more radical reversal of *Mackay* by Congress—but certainly no more complicated than the kind involved in *Brown Food Stores*, where one takes a snapshot, so to speak, of the relationship between labor and management after the practices are engaged in. The optimal solution would provide economic strikers with the right to reinstatement and thus accommodate considerations of both equity and balance to the competing interest of labor and management.

The Relationship between Strike Replacements and the Terminable-at-Will Principle

In 1983 the Court had occasion to consider the relationship between wrongful discharge actions and the rules established in *Mackay* in *Hale v. Belknap*.[41] The Court held that employees who were promised permanent employment in order to replace strikers can sue for damages under one of the wrongful discharge action theories accepted by the courts, even though they may be dismissed pursuant to an NLRB settlement. The question in *Belknap* was whether the ability of the employees to sue was preempted by the Act, a question that the Court answered negatively.

In so doing, the Court seemed to assume that employers could recruit workers and condition their right to permanent employment upon the outcome of litigation arising under the National Labor Relations Act before the Board and the courts. The effect is to stiffen employer resistance against the reinstatement of strikers in many instances and thus to create both litigation and conflict.

Belknap has created a whole new litigation arena, with the Board struggling with the question of whether the communication of permanent employment status of strikebreakers has been sufficiently clear to deprive returning strikers of their right to reinstatement.[42] In *Hansen Brothers* the Board indicated that where the employer simply says to the strike replacement that he or she "may" have to give up his or her job as a result of litigation, the employee is only a temporary replacement. Yet both the majority and dissenting opinions in *Belknap* seem to support the proposition that employers could recruit permanent replacements, and yet condition their permanency upon the outcome of litigation—in other words, to have their cake and eat it too! *Belknap* has simply created more confusion in litigation.

The Workplace Fairness Act of 1992

Members of Congress have attempted to reverse *Mackay* on numerous occasions. In 1991 when George Bush was still in the White House, the House of Representatives passed, by less than veto-proof margins, a reversal. But in the 1990s and before, two objections, which contain some degree of validity, have been raised. The first is that removal of the employer's ability to permanently replace strikers can create more conflict because a sanction that can be used against the weapon would be removed. Loss of income, the relatively low level of strike benefits, and the problems that flow from this seem to make this a relatively unlikely prospect. Yet the argument is that a policy designed to encourage a true maturation of industrial relations ought to encourage peaceful resolutions of dispute rather than conflict.

A second and somewhat related point is that unions will not be encouraged to strike, but they will be more likely to take positions that are unreasonable. For instance, it is said that if the employers did not have the ability to permanently replace strikers in the Caterpillar dispute, the union would have been able to prevail through a rigid insistence upon pattern bargaining, which would not take into account the individual firm's ability to pay or differences from their competitors.

These ideas have come together in the form of the Packwood-Metzenbaum amendment to the Workplace Fairness Act, which was designed to diminish opposition to the reversal of *Mackay*. The Packwood-Metzenbaum amendment would allow unions to seek mediation and fact-finding, providing for recommendations about unresolved interest disputes concerning the content of a new collective bargaining agreement. If the union did not seek the process or rejected the findings of the fact-finder, the employer would have the right to respond to a strike by using permanent replacements. Conversely, if the union invoked the process and abided by the recommendations—and they were resisted by the employer—permanent strike replacements could not be used. (Though the statute did not so provide, certainly the idea that union strikes designed to implement positions inconsistent with the award or recommendations itself should be unlawful.) Traditionally, because of the concern that compulsory arbitration or compulsory third-party intervention would undermine an incentive to engage in collective bargaining, a mandatory procedure has been anathema to both labor and management. The virtue of the Packwood-Metzenbaum amendment is that it would make the system voluntary and not prohibit the strike in the process. Thus an alternative system that promotes rationality and peace would diminish the prospects for industrial strife.

The difficulty is that labor, which saw the Packwood-Metzenbaum amendment as a concession, does not pursue the idea enthusiastically, and management does not see the issue as a concession because it involves the potential for interference or intervention in the collective bargaining process as well as the potential loss of the permanent replacement weapon. The system is not mandated, and unions do not relinquish the strike. The strengths of the system contain the obvious political pitfalls.

Emergency Disputes

Some of the debate bound up in the Packwood-Metzenbaum amendment has already taken place in connection with both Taft-Hartley emergency strike provisions and those contained in the Railway Labor Act. Where a strike or lockout would affect the nation's health and safety, the president may appoint a board of inquiry to investigate the dispute but with no authority to make recommendations. Subsequent to the board of inquiry's submission of a report to the president, the attorney general is authorized to seek an eighty-day injunction in federal district court and, fifteen days prior to the expiration of the eighty-day period, the workers vote on the employer's last offer. Here (we return to this theme below) the idea seems to have been that the workers would accept offers that their militant and unreasonable leaders would be unwilling or unable to accept—a theory that has proved to be remarkably incorrect, inasmuch as every single last offer has been voted down! Under the Railway Labor Act there is no such provision, and subsequent to the submission of a so-called president's emergency board report, the parties are free to engage in the strike or lockout. But the railroads have found that Congress will simply not tolerate a national dispute—in 1991 and 1992 the employers locked out the workers nationwide in response to a strike against one particular employer. In both instances Congress intervened to prohibit the strike and mandate arbitration in the event that the parties were unable to settle their differences.

The 1992 legislation in the railroads and much of the public sector legislation providing for arbitration in the event of a dispute in police and fire in the public sector, provide for so-called final-offer arbitration. Eight of California's cities provide for interest arbitration—Alameda, Gilroy, Hayward, Oakland, Palo Alto, Redwood City, San Jose, and Vallejo. (Only Vallejo provides for arbitration outside the police and fire departments.)

The virtue of the approach is that the parties have an incentive to compromise because they wish to posture in a reasonable fashion before the arbitrator who is precluded from doing anything other than selecting one of the other side's final or best offer. The example of baseball is often cited, although the owners have been fairly unhappy with this procedure in baseball given the fact that the players have been relatively successful. But there is another problem that makes use of final- or best-offer arbitration different in these emergency areas than it is in baseball. The experience in Michigan, which has had legislation relating to police and fire now for the past two decades, indicates that the process can be very long. In 1990 and 1991 the firefighters in the city of Detroit had seventy-two issues on the bargaining table and dozens of days of hearings extending for almost two years. The problem is that, in contrast to baseball where only the player's salary is involved, most disputes involve a wide variety of issues and unions, in particular, will attempt to hold on to a large number of demands so that they can trade their weak ones away.

This approach provides the union with an opportunity for issue-by-issue resolution of the impasse and thus creates, at least theoretically, an incentive for unions to place more issues on the bargaining table so that the arbitrator would feel impelled to come to its side on the issues that really count. As Richard Lester has noted: ". . . unions are prone to present for arbitration some demands with the low likelihood of panel selection."[43] The more issues that are on the table, the more matters there are where one side, usually the union because it is making more demands than the employers, can sacrifice or concede on. But this obviously cuts against the incentives to compromise and creates long proceedings.

There are two ways to deal with this matter. One is to eliminate issue-by-issue resolution and to provide for resolution through one package. This is, for instance, what Wisconsin has done, apparently with considerable success. The difficulty with this approach is that the package lends itself to mistakes and misjudgments and unsuitable awards, since one side's offer on a variety of issues will frequently include some proposals that are unsuitable or impractical.

One other approach to this matter is to control the number of subjects that can be on the table or to provide, as Michigan has, that only wage disputes are subject to the last-offer machinery through which the arbitrator is supposed to induce the system of autonomous collective bargaining to function and to rob the parties of their incentive to engage in obdurate behavior in anticipation of a third-party award. But this approach can prove troublesome in most industries where disputes about work rules or seniority may well be a major problem.

Another approach is to attempt to promote settlements with a kind of med-arb technique. The final-offer approach can be self-defeating where, as in Michigan, the parties are not required to reveal their position until the hearing is completed. They may not know what the other side would be likely to do, and thus the prospect for voluntary negotiation may be eroded. The trick would be to devise a system that provides a kind of discovery, understanding, and more important from the point of view of partisanship, a sense of what the arbitrator is likely to do and how he or she is likely to react to the positions of the parties. Perhaps the parties should be required to reveal their positions at an earlier stage in the process, giving the arbitrator the authority to require the parties to provide a kind of penultimate position either in a prehearing or in the course of the hearing so that mediation can take place in light of each party's "final" position.

James Stern has described in laudatory terms the process employed by Wisconsin, which uses med-arb in conjunction with a full package. Says Stern:

> The arbitrator is sent the final offers of the parties and then initiates part of the process that he or she controls. After a "public hearing [at which the parties may explain their positions], if there is one, the arbitrator who is identified in

the statute as the mediator-arbitrator" is mandated by statute to "endeavor to mediate the dispute and encourage a voluntary settlement by the parties" during this mediation session, final offers may be modified if the other side consents. Typically offers are modified during the mediation session, but if agreement is not reached, an arbitration ensues; it is final offer package arbitration in which the arbitrator chooses in its entirety one of the two final offers submitted initially.

. . . During the mediation phase, mediator-arbitrators ignore the usual restraints on arbitrators. They meet privately with either party, and encourage the parties to resume negotiations and act as mediators normally would without regard to the fact that they eventually may have to arbitrate the dispute.[44]

Wisconsin's one-package approach is designed to minimize the potential for unyielding or rigid positions in collective bargaining and allows for what Stern characterizes as "mediation with clout" because the parties know that in the final analysis the arbitrator can impose a settlement upon them. While the finality of this approach should not apply to industry generally—and the Packwood-Metzenbaum amendment ensures that this is not the case—it should apply to emergency disputes in the public or private sector. Accordingly the mediation mechanisms contained here could be applied to all disputes, but the process would culminate in recommendations for nonemergency sectors.

Reflections on Foreign Experience on the Replacement Issue

The International Labor Organization, through Conventions 87 and 98, protects the right to strike. As a result an employee's employment status cannot be affected for engaging in the strike. As noted earlier, Japan, Sweden, and France provide strikers constitutional protection in some measure. There are two features that are fairly uniform for Japan and western Europe, excluding in some measure Britain and in North America, Canada. The first is that strikers denied reemployment may contest the employer through labor courts that have jurisdiction over unfair dismissals. Britain has recently joined Germany, France, and Sweden in establishing industrial tribunals that have jurisdiction over such matters. Accordingly in these countries, except for special statutory provisions that affect Britain (to be discussed below), workers on strike may protest the refusal to reinstate through a statutory mechanism. In Japan these issues are heard in the civil court that has jurisdiction over them; no labor courts are involved.

The other feature that is common to all countries except Canada, where it is usually litigated through labor relations boards and arbitration, is that reinstatement cannot be compelled where a dismissal has been instituted. (It should be noted that Sweden constitutes a major exception because of statutory provisions that oblige the employer to employ the worker while the unfair dismissal complaint is pending.) In sharp contrast to this, modern labor legislation in the United States accords a presumption to reinstatement as a remedy for dismissal under the National Labor Relations Act, other modern employment legislation such as the Civil Rights Act of 1964, and in arbitration proceedings pursuant to collective bargaining agreements.

What is instructive about other industrialized countries is the different status provided to the strike and reinstatement and the limitations that such countries place upon the strike weapon itself. In Germany a peace obligation is thrust upon the parties during the term of a negotiated collective bargaining agreement. The same is true in Canada where in most provinces a statutory no-strike obligation exists for both sides. In the United States, except for the Railway Labor Act's jurisdiction over airlines and railways and some segments of the public sector, any peace obligation is voluntarily negotiated in the form of a no-strike clause in the collective bargaining agreement. Accordingly the right to strike is generally waived during the agreement period.

Since the *Mackay* issue generally arises subsequent to the expiration of the agreement, legislative restraints contained in other countries' labor laws are more analogous. For instance, in many Canadian jurisdictions a ballot must precede the strike, an approach that often tests the support for the collective bargaining representative.[45] The Trade Union Act of 1984 in Britain makes immunity from court actions dependent upon a properly conducted ballot by the union. That country's Employment Act of 1990 has linked the ballot procedure with authorization of the stoppage by the union.

To understand the British statutory scheme, it is important to recognize what the Donovan Royal Commission characterized in 1968 as a system of two-tier unionism. The Donovan commission had noted that the British pattern of industrial relations failed to involve national union officials in local plant bargaining, as it frequently does in the United States. A weaker dues structure than that which exists in most other industrialized countries, except Australia, made it impossible to finance such national union involvement and relatively detailed collective bargaining agreements. Out of this vacuum emerged unorganized work groups and shop stewards, shop steward committees composed of full-time employees that assumed a de facto influence without the responsibility to any of the unions authorized to bargain. Donovan had recommended plant collective bargaining and had properly seen that unofficial stoppages, then and now, are the principal manifestation of industrial warfare in Britain, as a direct outgrowth of this two-tier system.

Although Donovan recommended that the law not be used to remedy this matter by imposing dispute resolution procedures or making collective bargaining agreements enforceable, ultimately legal regulation has played a substantial role, most recently through the Employment Act of 1990.[46] Again the approach to regulation is through unfair dismissal legislation as it is on the continent and in Japan. The Employment Act of 1982 brought the selective dismissal of strikers within the jurisdiction of the industrial tribunals. While the selective dismissal of strikers was within the jurisdiction of industrial tribunals, not only was the dismissal of the entire work force beyond it, but also hiring could commence on a discriminatory basis if there was a gap of three months between the dismissal of the striking workers and any rehiring. But the 1990 Act has given the unions a choice that is designed to either bridge the gap between national and local leadership (the view of the statute's proponents) or to widen it (the view of the critics).

To avoid tort liability for a strike, the principal executive committee, the president, or general secretaries must repudiate it as soon as practicable. If repudiation is not accomplished, the union must conduct a ballot among its members to authorize the stoppage, an obligation that has existed since the Trade Union Act of 1984. If repudiation is accomplished, the stoppage becomes unofficial, and no strikers can protest their dismissal through the industrial tribunal.

Thus the union must take responsibility for determining the identity of its principal officers who have authority in this area to either authorize the strike through the secret ballot box, failure to do so rendering them liable in damages. This makes British and American labor law regarding the strike comparable—inasmuch as unauthorized stoppages are unprotected under the National Labor Relations Act in America. But in the United States if a collective bargaining agreement is in effect with an arbitration provision, the dismissal issue may be heard by the arbitrator, although the prospects for success for the wildcat striker are not good.[47] The difference between the two countries is that the right to permanently replace may be instituted against economic strikers in the United States when the strike is completely lawful. In

Britain and in all other countries, sanctions come into play when the stoppage is viewed as unlawful or with some disfavor by the law.

But it is of some note that the 1982 statute has already run afoul of the freedom of association principles contained in the ILO conventions. In 1991 the governing body of the International Labor Office held in Case No. 1540 that "[r]espect for the principles of freedom of association requires that workers should not be dismissed or *refused re-employment* on account of their having participated in a strike or other industrial action." A subsequent offer of reemployment on less favorable terms, said the ILO, was in violation of the standards of international labor law. Accordingly the ILO took the position that British labor law was in need of amendment ". . . to give effective protection to workers who have been dismissed for having participated in a strike and in particular to enable workers who are dismissed in the course of, or at the conclusion of, a strike or other industrial action to challenge their dismissal before a judicial authority."[48]

The *Mackay* rule would clearly fail under the relevant ILO conventions. Of course the difficulty is that the United States has not ratified those conventions, and thus their precepts have relatively little impact upon American labor law. The American labor movement has not manifested much enthusiasm for ratification of such ILO conventions, and when it was in a position to do so during the Carter administration, its main mission was to withdraw from the ILO because of the organization's perceived unfair treatment of Israel. Thus, notwithstanding the incompatibility between *Mackay* and international labor law, the former cannot be challenged because of international labor law's lack of applicability.[49]

The requirement of authorization or a strike ballot might nonetheless suggest a compromise on the replacement issue. The opponents of labor law reform in the United States argue that unions or strikers will be more likely to take the "gamble," as Justice O'Connor characterized it, if they have the right to reinstatement, thus promoting more conflict. A requirement that a strike ballot, such as is required both in Britain and Canada, be a prerequisite to this reinstatement does not seem unreasonable under the circumstances. It might induce workers to deliberate more carefully—and the vote might guide unions in resisting challenges to their majority status, particularly in the negotiations of the first or second contract.

Another approach that would enhance the strike's effectiveness and enable reinstatement for strikers is that tried by Ontario prior to 1992, when the rights of strikers were expanded. In Ontario economic strikers had a right to reinstatement until six months after the commencement of the strike.[50] Congressman Joseph Brennan of Maine[51] has proposed such a compromise. The fact is that a strike of substantial duration often is lost—the 1990–91 *New York Daily News* dispute seems to be something of an exception—and if strikers do not seek reinstatement until after six months, the chances are that they have found alternate employment. Such an accommodation would provide the employer with a chance to recruit a new work force with some permanency.

All of these proposals in some measure deny employers the right to treat strikers as at-will employees who can be immediately dismissed. An argument against these proposals might be that a change in the legal rules will incite workers to strike because the "gamble" is gone. Yet there is a serious deterrent. The strike generally is a weapon of last resort. There is the obvious loss of income and unavailability of unemployment compensation in all states except for New York and Rhode Island.[52] The factor of lost income makes workers particularly reluctant to utilize the right to strike.

Employers have alleged that strikes are often unreasonable uses of power by unions that thrust anticompetitive conditions upon industries and dissuade them from using technological innovation. The law ought not to protect obdurate unions against taking their lumps. But the answer is not to deprive labor of the one weapon that it possesses. Employers have the right to lockout and, subsequent to bargaining to the point of impasse, to unilaterally institute their own position on wages, hours, and terms and conditions of employment. The right to permanently replace, without appropriate safeguards such as those contained in the Packwood-Metzenbaum amendment, is the right to use nuclear weaponry in the arsenal of industrial warfare.

Conclusion

Mackay and *Patternmakers* are truly products of another era. They ring a bell of a distant past—an era in which the Court was just emerging from the frequent and indiscriminate use of the due process clause of the Constitution so as to strike down economic and social legislation of the New Deal. The Court and Congress should not be bound by half-century-old opinion. As we move toward the twenty-first century, we should attempt to establish more civilized standards in labor-management relations, a more competitive and cooperative environment inextricably tied to such standards, and an order in which we can compete effectively with Germany, Japan, and other countries.

One of the ironies of World War II is that the defeated powers have not only revived economically, and thus won a different form of war, but have also fashioned societies and standards that promote both mature labor-management relations and a civilized treatment of employees alongside independent unions that have arm's-length bargaining relationships—practices from which we in the United States have a good deal to learn.

The lawfulness of the permanent replacement tactic is a factor in the erosion of the strike and the labor movement itself. The industrial relations climate of the past decade ought to make us reassess the compatibility of job loss as a price for the strike's exercise and the ideal of a civilized and democratic society.

7

Canada and the United States: A Tale of Two Contiguous Countries

Canada and the United States share a common border, a common language, notwithstanding the dominance of French in Quebec, many multinational corporations, and unions that have the same dual nationality. Indeed the origin of the term "international union," which is a part of so many union names in the United States, is attributable to the fact that their affiliates are in both the United States and Canada.

The trade union movement in Canada developed in a different manner. In the 1930s and 1940s, as the American trade union movement was developing into its contemporary form, the Canadian unions, whose membership growth in the 1920s had exceeded that of its American counterpart's, trailed the Americans considerably. (Even in 1941, in the wake of the first impact of the National Labor Relations Act upon American unions' organizational activity, Canadian unions still represented 18 percent of the work force as opposed to their American counterpart's 26 percent.) Leading Canadian politicians openly opposed the organization for workers into the Congress of Industrial Organizations (CIO) because of its presumed dominance by the Communist party.

The emergence of Canadian trade unionism, even by American standards, is essentially attributable to terrain which Phelps Brown of Britain has characterized as its denial of an "agglomeration to the Canadian labour force," a division promoted by the large distances between population centers.[1] It is after all the contact between workers and the fact that workers traveled from one locality to another and could experience the working conditions in other areas that was a major factor in the growth of trade unionism[2] in the United States, and in Britain as well. This simply was not possible in Canada.

True, Canadian unions, like those in most of the other industrializing countries of that time, had become active in the 1880s, the Knights of

Labor playing a more influential and lasting role than was the case inside the American labor movement. But, unlike the Australians who were pushed into defensiveness by major strikes during that period, Canadian labor thrived, tentatively attracted to the arbitration system that was enshrined during the next twenty years in both New Zealand and Australia. That the attraction was so tentative and temporary can only be explained by examining a number of factors.

In the first place, the Canadian government foresaw a number of pitfalls in the arbitration process in the dispute involving the Boot and Shoe Workers in Quebec City which was arbitrated by Archbishop Begin of Quebec during the winter of 1900–1901. The Archbishop's award required the unions to reform their internal constitutional procedures, a ruling that stunned union leaders and prompted them not to comply on the grounds that the archbishop had exceeded his authority. The government quickly perceived that pressure for arbitration could involve it directly, as it was confronted with pleas for relief in the wake of the Quebec award.

Richard Mitchell has written that the fundamental reason for the rejection of arbitration in Canada was that there was so little association between the dispute settlement and union recognition issues, unlike Australia and New Zealand prior to and at the turn of the century. Support for compulsory arbitration in Canada was limited to industries that were viewed as within the "public domain." Says Mitchell:

Australian colonial parliaments seemed to have had a far greater proportion of their members from the ranks of unions and union supporters both through the emergent Labor Party and independently. There was therefore a critical connection in Australia between union policy and parliamentary policy which was largely absent in Canada.[3]

Ultimately the Canadians, partially as the result of prompting by American delegates at their 1902 convention, took the same road as the Americans and avoided a process that Gompers and others south of the border viewed as anathema to the collective bargaining process. Yet Mitchell contends that the factors that led to the rejection of compulsory arbitration were more fundamental: ". . . in the late 1890's and early 1900's [Canada was] experiencing a period of rapid growth and unprecedented industrial activity, particularly in the craft and skilled industries centered in the Eastern provinces. It is possible that this period of upsurge and confidence was less likely to encourage unions into compulsory arbitration as a defensive measure."[4]

The comparative lack of political representation in the trade union movement vis-à-vis Australia and New Zealand, as well as the absence of a group of individuals in the Canadian parliament and provincial legislatures who possessed the same zeal for compulsory arbitration as did those who were prominent in Australia, buttressed this further. Again the inability to couple union recognition and dispute resolution matters was important. Concludes Mitchell:

> The Canadian government was prepared for a system of dispute settlement, but not to concede or enforce trade union recognition through such a measure. Thus the union side of the equation was missing in the Canadian debate, and the Canadian union movement had no institutional reasons to support such a scheme.[5]

The 1896 Conciliation Act, borrowed from British law of the same period, promoted a process that precluded interference through binding awards but authorized strikes and lockouts after the conciliation machinery had been exhausted. In 1907 the Industrial Disputes Investigation Act, sponsored by MacKenzie King, later to become prime minister of the country, established the basic legal framework.[6]

Yet despite deliverance from employer counterattacks of the kind experienced in Australia and the United States, at the turn of the century Canada was at a different stage of development. In 1901 three-fifths of the country was completely rural, and two-fifths of the labor force was in agriculture. The two major cities, Montreal and Toronto, had populations of 300,000 and 200,000, respectively. At the same time in Australia, the other major English-speaking colony, Sydney and Melbourne had populations of 400,000 and 473,000. The contrast was obvious. Canada did not possess a sufficient congregation of workers to promote awareness of their common plight throughout the nation. Again, as Phelps Brown has said:

> It was indeed the need to provide for the travelling brother of the craft that knit local clubs into national unions both in Great Britain and the U.S. But in Canada distances were vast, and even in Eastern Canada communications long remained difficult.[7]

Moreover membership was hard to maintain because of the constant immigration southward into the United States for better jobs. This meant that the mobility did not promote national unity and, in part, helps explain the dominance of the American Federation of Labor and Gompers in some of the early years of the Canadian movement.

A third characteristic of Canada—and again one that contrasts with the United States—is that the employers with whom the unions dealt were price-takers and not price-makers. They were disproportionately situated in the mining industry, the sector to which the trade union movement in Canada owes its origins. Since the turn of the century, employees in Canadian mining have been subject to the wild fluctuations of basic commodities in other countries. This was a system in which the presence of the middle class was not as considerable as in either the United States or Britain. Despite the wide expanse of the country, it could not contain a frontier in which permanent workers were likely to "work up" their own "holding" and thus develop the individualistic ethic so prominent in this country. The frontier in Canada frequently existed in the form of mining and lumber employers, that hired large numbers of manual workers, more frustrated and disappointed than hopeful like Horatio Alger.

As Phelps Brown has noted, in Britain, the sheer concentration of wage earners in industrial towns and closely packed industrial areas produced an entirely different environment. In Canada there was no doctrine that inculcated an abhorrence of collectivism such as prevailed south of the border.[8] The lack of a frontier sense of individualism produced a collectivism that provided for common ground between hierarchical Toryism, on the one hand, and socialism, as well as worker solidarity, on the other. It was one in which ". . . the strong tradition of Toryism in Canada laid its stress on solidarity, and against individualism and the fissiparous impact of market forces."[9]

Yet, as noted above, Canadian unions took considerable time to gain momentum in this century. While table 7.1 demonstrates that the Canadian trade union movement maintained an advantage over the Americans from 1924 until 1936, with the advent of the National Labor Relations Act and the second New Deal, American trade unions spurted ahead in the late 1930s. They maintained a steady lead over Canada until the late 1950s. The decline in the United States began to become apparent between 1956 and the early 1960s,[10] and the gap clearly emerged between the two movements from the mid 1960s onward.

Neither the Canadian nor American unions have had much success with organizing white-collar employees in the private sector. Canadian unions, however, have been more successful than American unions in stimulating public employee unionism, though the American unions were also on the move in the public sector during the 1960s, with the

American Federation of State, County and Municipal Employees Union (AFSCME) acting as a particularly prominent recruiting force. But the larger public sector in Canada, as well as a superior record in penetrating white-collar professional employees north of the border, accounts for much of the difference between Canadian and American unions.

Indeed, as Leo Troy has pointed out,[11] the differences between the public sector in the United States and Canada help explain some of the differences between those two countries and indeed the rest of the world. Twenty-nine percent of American trade union membership is in the public sector, whereas 56.4 percent of the Canadian membership are public employees. Moreover the gap between public and private sector membership is widening, the comparable figures for 1975 showing 42.1 percent of the Canadian members in the public sector and 26.2 percent of Americans similarly situated.

These figures are made more dramatic by the way in which Troy has defined the public sector so as to include education, health, and welfare services funded predominantly by public monies. Not only is there a growing gap in trade union membership in the two countries between public and private sectors but also in total employment. As Troy has pointed out: "In the public service sector the Canadian lead over the U.S. increased to 1.6 times by 1985, compared to a ratio of 1.3 in 1975. On the other hand, private services in the U.S. exceeded the Canadian by 1.17 times (17 percent) in 1975 and increased the margin to 1.22 (22 percent) by 1985."[12] Table 7.2 provides a fuller picture.

The gap is increasing, albeit on a somewhat lesser scale, among public goods as well. The United States continues to be the leading service economy, ahead of not only Canada but also all of the industrialized countries. This is the sector of the economy that is most labor intensive and therefore one in which market forces resistant to unionization will flourish most.

Given the disparity between trade union membership density in both Canada and the United States, the figures provided by Troy distinguishing between the public and private sector in goods and services are particularly intriguing when one looks at the general trend between 1975 and 1985. During that period public sector density increased from 47.8 to 66.2 percent. But private sector density declined from 25.7 to 20.7 percent. This suggests a number of things. The first is that not only are the overall comparative figures for trade union membership in Canada and the United States somewhat camouflaged

Table 7.1
Union membership in Canada and the United States, 1921–90 (percent of nonagricultural workers)

Year	Canada	United States
1921	16.0	18.3
1924	12.2	11.9
1927	12.1	11.3
1930	13.1	11.6
1933	16.7	11.3
1936	16.2	13.7
1939	17.3	28.6
1942	20.6	25.9
1945	24.2	30.4
1946	27.9	31.1
1947	29.1	32.1
1948	30.3	31.8
1949	30.2	31.9
1950	—	31.6
1951	28.4	31.7
1952	30.2	32.0
1953	32.6	32.5
1954	33.6	32.3
1955	33.7	31.8
1956	33.3	31.4
1957	32.4	31.2
1958	34.2	30.3
1959	33.3	29.0
1960	32.3	28.6
1961	31.6	28.5
1962	30.2	30.4
1963	29.8	30.2
1964	29.4	30.2
1965	29.7	30.1
1966	30.7	29.6
1967	32.3	29.9
1968	33.1	29.5
1969	32.5	28.7
1970	33.6	29.6
1971	33.6	29.1
1972	34.6	28.8
1973	36.1	28.5
1974	35.8	28.3
1975	36.9	28.9

Table 7.1 (continued)

Year	Canada	United States
1976	37.3	27.9
1977	38.2	26.2
1978	39.0	25.1
1979	—	24.5
1980	37.6	23.2
1981	37.4	22.6
1982	39.0	21.9
1983a	40.0	20.7
1983b	40.0	20.4
1984	39.6	19.1
1985	39.0	18.3
1986	37.7	17.8
1987	37.6	17.0
1988	36.6	17.0
1989	36.2	16.4
1990	36.2	16.1

Sources: *1921–45:* Canada: G. Chaison in *Union-Management Relations in Canada*, Anderson and Gunderson, eds. (1982), p. 149, from Labour Canada Statistics. U.S.: Bain and Price, *Profiles of Union Growth* (1981) pp. 88–89. *1946–90:* P. Kumar, "Industrial Relations in Canada and the United States: From Uniformity to Divergence" (1991). Canada: Labour Canada, *Directory of Labour Organizations in Canda* (annual). Because of change in reference dates, no figure is reported in 1950. Survey not conducted in 1979. U.S.: *1945–83a:* L. Troy and N. Sheflin, *Union Sourcebook: Membership, Finances, Structure, Directory* (Industrial Relations Data and Information Services, 1985); *1983b–90:* U.S. Bureau of Labor Statistics, *Employment and Earnings*, (monthly).

by the public-private and goods-service disparity, but also the Canadians have been and are more vulnerable in the sector in which trade union membership in the United States has been decimated due to both foreign competition and deregulation. Accordingly, although Troy does not place much credence in the idea that law can have an impact upon trade union density, he states the following: "The Canadian lag in the descent of private sector density, about 22 years (the U.S. peaked in 1953), is explained by the earlier and much more rapid growth of private services in the U.S., pro-union public policy and higher tariffs in Canada."[13]

Indeed Troy has noted that more recent statistics appear to confirm this trend. Unions in manufacturing and construction have continued to lose their market share, manufacturing density declining from 37.9

Table 7.2
Labor market structure in Canada and the United States, 1975–85

	Canada		United States	
1985				
Total employment	10,159.1	100.0%	100,698	100.0%
Services	6,481.7	63.8	67,422	67.0
Goods	3,677.4	36.2	33,276	33.0
Service employment	6,481.7	100.0	67,422	100.0
Public services	2,474.4	38.2	16,394	24.3
Private services	4,007.3	61.8	51,028	75.7
Goods employment	3,667.4	100.0	33,276	100.0
Public goods	558.6	15.2	1,767	5.3
Private goods	3,118.8	84.8	31,509	94.7
Total employment	10,159.1	100.0	100,698	100.0
Public	3,032.9	29.9	16,394	16.3
Private	7,126.2	70.1	84,304	83.7
1975				
Total employment	8,375.0	100.0	80,353	100.0
Services	4,889.0	58.4	49,803	62.0
Goods	3,486.0	41.6	30,550	38.0
Service employment	4,889.0	100.0	49,803	100.0
Public services	1,938.8	39.7	14,685	29.5
Private services	2,950.2	60.3	35,118	70.5
Goods employment	3,486.0	100.0	30,550	100.0
Public goods	557.9	16.0	1,556	5.1
Private goods	2,928.1	84.0	28,994	94.9
Total employment	8,375.0	100.0	80,353	100.0
Public	2.496.7	29.8	14,685	18.3
Private	5,878.3	70.2	65,668	81.7

Sources: Canada, Corporations and Labour Unions Returns Act (CALURA). U.S. Bureau of Labor Statistics.

percent in 1985 to 36.8 percent in 1988.[14] States Troy: "This is the lowest density for manufacturing since the Canadian government began publishing data by industrial sector in 1966."[15] Construction unions, accounting for 63.1 percent of the labor market in 1983, declined to 52.8 percent in 1988. The average density of both the private and public sectors has declined since 1980, with more recent figures in 1990 bringing them back to their 1975–76 level. Again, says Troy: "equally telling has been the loss in the number of local organizations among private-sector unions in Canada . . . are these signs of vibrancy or decline?"[16]

A final point emphasized by Troy is that the inclusion of Quebec in these data, just like indiscriminate merging of private- and public-sector statistics, tends to distort a comparison with the United States.

Of course, as of this writing, Quebec is a part of Canada. Quebec has always exceeded national density statistics for Ontario and the national average altogether.

The Law

Just as Troy has dramatized the fact that the economies of the United States and Canada are not truly comparable but fundamentally dissimilar in a number of respects in the public–private sector story, so also is this the case with labor law. For instance, in contrast to America, where the doctrine of preemption has made the National Labor Relations Act virtually the exclusive statutory instrument in the private sector,[17] Canadian labor law is in the most part provincial law. Only the industries that are perceived to have a national impact, such as airlines, railways and banks, are covered by federal legislation and subject to the Canadian Labour Relations Board's jurisdiction.

Since 1944 Canadian labor law has emulated America in the sense that it contains key characteristics found in this country: the creation of labor relations boards both at the federal and provincial level, the certification of unions as exclusive representatives when they represent a majority of employees within an appropriate unit, and the use of a system of unfair labor practices as a check on improper conduct. Canada and Japan are the only industrialized countries that share the labor relations board and unfair labor practice concepts with the United States. Canada, unlike Japan, however, shares the other central characteristics with the American system: exclusivity and certification of the majority representative.

But there are a number of differences between American and Canadian law, and they start with the administrative process. The American board is split into two parts, the General Counsel or prosecutor and the Board or judicial branch. The 1947 Taft-Hartley amendments that created this formal split have two immediate consequences that cut in opposite directions.

The first is that under the American system the General Counsel has discretion not to issue a complaint subsequent to the filing of an unfair labor practice charge by a private party. As the U.S. Supreme Court said in *NLRB v. Food and Commercial Workers, Local 23*,[18] speaking through Justice Brennan:

> ... The General Counsel ... [has] ... concededly unreviewable discretion to file a complaint.... The General Counsel's unreviewable discretion to file and

withdraw a complaint, in turn, logically supports a reading that she must also have final authority to dismiss a complaint in favor of an informal settlement, at least before a hearing begins.[19]

In Canada the board solicitors play no such role. Like Japan, which also has an unfair labor practice system,[20] it is the private party that prosecutes the case before the Board. The Canadian boards, both at a provincial and federal level, typically have no responsibility for conducting an investigation and issuing a complaint subsequent to it. One consequence is that the board solicitors cannot abort a hearing of a charge on the merits independent of a formal labor board disposition as in the United States. The Canadian system thus avoids complaints about a lack of due process resulting from General Counsel's decisions not to issue a complaint based upon investigations conducted without a hearing. On the other hand, the virtue of the American system, from the workers' perspective, is that the employee has free counsel in the form of representation by the General Counsel in hearings that commence subsequent to the issuance of the complaint.

Another issue, which bears upon the efficacy of the respective systems, is the adequacy of the investigation that takes place through the Board's own initiative. Although Peter Bruce has criticized the American Board for an inadequacy of investigative resources, his critique is based upon the infrequency with which the Board utilizes subpoenas.[21] The difficulty with this critique is that, in the first place, there are no available statistics on the instances of frequency with which the Board does use subpoenas and thus his case is impossible to prove or, for that matter, to completely disprove.

Second, the utilization of subpoenas does not necessarily correlate with the thoroughness of an investigation. This is so for two reasons: The subpoenas may not be used where the charged party or respondent makes information available voluntarily, and, more important, the Board's *Wright Line* doctrine, confirmed by the Supreme Court,[22] facilitates investigations in which subpoenas are not invoked by allowing the Board to establish a prima facie case where, for instance, union and nonunion employees have been treated differently. The burden is upon the employer to rebut the General Counsel's prima facie case, either in the investigation or in the hearing, by showing that the employee would have received the same treatment in any event. The Board will frequently resolve doubts against an obdurate employer who is not forthcoming with information. Thus, while it is difficult to determine with precision the comparative virtues and deficiencies of the two countries' investigative systems in this respect, it would not seem that there is evidence to support the idea that a clear advantage lies with either one.

Canadian and American law regarding certification and unfair labor practices are different in a number of important ways. In the first place, the federal sector and most of the provincial systems permit—as did the American system prior to the 1947 Taft-Hartley amendments—certification on the basis of authorization cards. In some instances certification is provided on the basis of 55 percent[23] of employees within the unit and in some circumstances 60 percent. The only provinces that do not provide for certification on the basis of cards and require a vote in all circumstances are Newfoundland, Saskatchewan, Nova Scotia, and, more recently, Alberta.

British Columbia, one of the more important Canadian jurisdictions, as a result of amendments to the Industrial Relations Act in 1987, presently requires a certification vote in the majority of certification applications filed by unions. However, British Columbia, like Ontario, has recently elected a new provincial government sympathetic to the labor movement (the New Democratic party). After relatively comprehensive consultation, a bill was introduced in the BC legislature on October 27, 1992, that will, when enacted, repeal and replace the current Industrial Relations Act. Bill 84, as it is called, significantly amends the statutory scheme in that province. Although the bill will undoubtedly receive many revisions before becoming law, one of the sections that will likely pass through the legislature relatively unscathed is the provision reverting back to certification based on recognized membership support through the use of authorization cards. The amendments proposed by Bill 84 will also address other trade union concerns with the current legislation, which permits a vote on an employer's final offer, prohibits secondary picketing not previously precluded, and bans strikes and lockouts for a forty-day cooling-off period where services are essential and where an industrial dispute "poses a threat to the economy of the Province or the health, safety or welfare of its residents or the provision of educational services."[24]

In those jurisdictions that do use cards, where a union is unable to demonstrate clear majority support in the bargaining unit through the use of authorization cards, the labor board will conduct a secret ballot-box election. In Ontario, for example, under recently enacted legislation, an election will be ordered by the Board only if the union is capable of showing 40 to 55 percent bargaining unit support through cards. If the union demonstrates less than 40 percent support, the certification application will be rejected without a vote. When more than 55 percent support is shown, automatic certification without resort to an election will result.

Nova Scotia provides for prehearing secret ballot-box elections[25] within five days of the petition's filing. This compares quite favorably with the speed with which American certification petitions are heard, and the presumption that the secret ballot box will be the only method of determining which, if any, union is the exclusive bargaining representative in the absence of unfair labor charges substantial enough to warrant the imposition of a bargaining order.

Alberta, on the other hand, has changed the law of representation to require secret ballots along the lines provided for in the United States by the National Labor Relations Act rather than certification on the basis of authorization cards. The position in that province is that the ballot box more effectively protects employer opportunities to campaign against unionization and that the cards are not sufficiently reliable to test employee sentiment about the representation issue. This line of reasoning of course is similar to that employed in the United States, where it is thought that peer pressure produces employee execution of cards in all too many instances. The labor movement in Alberta has strenuously opposed the province's adoption of this approach.

As is true in many jurisdictions throughout the country, the current BC legislation requires unions to take a vote for the purpose of strike ratification. Thereafter the union must give a seventy-two-hour notice before commencing a strike. In addition the legislation employs a tight definition of employee successorship that imposes no successorship obligation where a "key man" from the predecessor employer is present in the new enterprise.

Alberta now shares a common feature with the current British Columbia legislation in the sense that it has shifted to secret ballot-box elections. In neither province was there apparently any abuse or indeed concerted pressure from the business community to obtain this legislative objective. In both provinces one of the evils associated with the electoral process in America does not seem to have materialized—delay which provides the employer with an opportunity for an extended antiunion campaign. On average, where a mail ballot is not required, it takes sixteen days for the certification process to be completed in Alberta. In British Columbia the unions initially refused to recognize the 1987 amendments but now have created an exception for ballot-box elections. In Alberta the caseload has increased, perhaps as much as anything, because of the economic recovery in that province, and the unions appear to be winning even more elections than they were under the old authorization card procedure.

There are many who believe that the secret ballot-box election in the two provinces has proved to be as expeditious under the new system as it was under the old, although Alberta does not maintain statistics that can resolve this debate one way or another. In Alberta an additional factor that makes comparisons especially troublesome is the fact that the province experienced such an economic trough prior to the new law. One of the principal areas of dispute related to an Alberta labor board decision, the *Stewart Olson* case,[26] in which the board allowed employers in the construction industry to engage in "double breasting" (i.e., the substituting of new nonunion companies for operations that have been previously organized) with mere impunity.

Again, however, Alberta and British Columbia are against the grain on the issue of union recognition. The majority position in Canada, and the position soon to be reinstated in British Columbia, is well articulated by the British Columbia Labour Relations Board in *Plateau Mills, Ltd.*,[27] where that agency concluded that cards are "normally a good index" of employee "true feelings about union representation,"[28] that the alternative is frequently "messy campaigns" in which retaliation is instituted and where the future union-employer relationship is "thoroughly poisoned," and that doubts about the union's representative status can always be sorted out at the time of a secret strike vote mandated by the statute. Said the Board:

The union must maintain its support among the employees during months of certification proceedings and collective bargaining so that it can win that vote. As a practical matter, it must win the vote by a solid rather than by a bare majority. If it does not, it will not obtain a first contract. The real life experience is that a great many certifications are effectively abandoned by unions, who see that the employee unit has new members or new sentiments, and realize that a continued expenditure of union resources in trying to represent these employees is useless and unwarranted.[29]

But one of the legal features that contrasts Canada vividly with the United States is the standard employed in connection with the allegiance of employees through authorization cards. As the British Columbia Board said:

The union must show the Board that individual employees have signed an application for union membership and have paid a minimum initiation fee. The law's assumption is that when a group of employees takes this action as the result of a union's organization drive, they do want the trade union to be their exclusive bargaining representative.[30]

The Supreme Court of Canada, in *Central Broadcasting Co., Ltd. v. Canada Labour Relations Board,* in considering the Canada Labour Code, has said that the Board ". . . is not limited to a strict and technical interpretation of union constitution and bylaws . . . [It] . . . may take a broader approach."[31] Thus, the Canadian position contrasts sharply with that of the United States, where the authorization card that was relied upon prior to the Taft-Hartley amendments is now used for obliging employers to accord recognition pursuant to a *Gissel*[32] bargaining order. Recall that in *Gissel*, the Court ruled that the employer engaged in independent unfair labor practices that made it unlikely that the secret ballot-box election preferred by the statute would constitute a true test of employee sentiment.

Critical to any understanding of the differences between American and Canadian law regarding proof of majority status is the more searching scrutiny of authorization cards required in Canada. In the United States all that is required is that the employee intend to support or designate the union as exclusive bargaining representative. Indeed, for the purpose of establishing a "showing of interest" (i.e., the 30 percent prerequisite to conduct a secret ballot-box election), employee support can be manifested through petitions as well as authorization cards, and in support of an election as well as the union itself. But in Canada, in order to suffice for establishing the necessary 55 or 60 percent for certification, the worker must undertake an obligation to pay dues on a monthly basis which would signify full membership in the union. Presumably employees who obligate themselves financially will have given more thought to the question of support for the union as an exclusive bargaining representative than would have been the case under the American system where less meaningful evidence is all that is required.

But an even more important factor demonstrating the contrasting features of the Canadian and American systems relates to judicial review and, in turn, the question of how expeditiously the Boards' orders on certification of recognition can be implemented. Two points are important in this connection. The first is that sometimes certification will be accorded, as in Ontario, on an "interim" basis—through the use of a so-called interim certificate—while challenges to matters such as eligibility for voting and the scope of the appropriate unit are being undertaken. In America, where the employer disagrees with the Board's determination on these issues, it cannot challenge the representation election in court because certifications are not "final orders" within the meaning of the Act and thus are not reviewable by the courts.[33] But the avenue all too frequently taken by the employer is simply to refuse to bargain. This triggers an unfair labor practice proceeding that permits review of the representation issues in the unfair labor practice context and delays collective bargaining, and thus wages and benefits that would flow to workers ordinarily. In a sense, under the American system, workers who choose representation when dealing with an obdurate employer may be worse off than those who choose not to be represented by a union in a Board-conducted election, a message that will be not lost upon all workers who have contact with such proceedings. Interim certifications pending dispute resolution and an approach to judicial review of certification orders that is more deferential to the Board than in America circumvent that problem in Canada. An even more critical difference, however, is that the employer's duty to bargain is not suspended by an application for judicial review of the Board's certification order. To obtain relief from its bargaining obligation, an employer must apply to either the Board or the courts for a stay of the certification order pending judicial review. Such an application generally meets with significant resistance in both forums. The Ontario Labour Relations Board's view of this situation is reflective of the general Canadian approach to this issue:

As the Court of Appeal has noted . . . the law which has grown up around labour relations recognizes the principle that "labour relations delayed is labour relations denied." In our view the effect of any delay in the commencement of collective bargaining after a trade union has been certified is particularly acute. Employees join a trade union to secure the benefits of collective bargaining. Where such bargaining does not even begin for a protracted period of time because of a refusal of an employer to meet with the trade union, a likely result is that the trade union will become discredited in the eyes of the employees, causing support among the employees to erode. Even if collective bargaining does get underway subsequently, the union may well find itself unable to fully reclaim the lost ground.[34]

Sanctions and Remedies

A very different picture exists in the area of sanctions and remedies that are utilized by the Board. In Ontario, for instance, the Court of

Appeal imposed a fine of $100,000 in lieu of imprisonment upon an employer who had engaged the services of security firms in thwarting unionization and attempted to deceive the Board through false evidence. The court's view was that the fine was necessary to deter the sophisticated conspiracy involved here so that it would not be ". . . tantamount to a license fee to commit illegal activity," but would rather serve as a deterrent to ". . . warn others that such illegal activity will not be tolerated."[35] In contrast, as noted by Bartosic,[36] the American experience relating to sanctions has not been nearly as significant. In part, this is because contempt penalties are fashioned by circuit courts of appeals—the reviewing tribunals in most unfair labor practice proceedings—which are not accustomed to this role normally played by trial courts in both United States and Canada. It is not without significance that trial courts impose penalties in Canada.

Another important distinction between the two countries in this regard is that the American cases, which pose the potential for civil or criminal penalties, involve contempt. In Canada contempt does not appear to be a prerequisite for the imposition of fines, the sanctions being dependent upon the nature of the conduct engaged in by the defendant.

But even in the area of remedies itself, there are a number of vivid contrasts. For instance, the U.S. Supreme Court in *H.K. Porter*[37] has held that a bad-faith failure to bargain by an employer may not be remedied through the imposition of a contract clause that might promote a measure of institutional security for the union and the growth of the collective bargaining process. The Court theorized that such a remedy would be inconsistent with the constraints imposed upon the Board by the Taft-Hartley amendments so as to avoid the finding that a refusal to bargain violation has been made out on the ground that the employer or union has not agreed to a particular contract clause. The refusal to bargain prohibitions in Taft-Hartley did not speak to the question of remedies, but the Court concluded that the philosophy contained in the statutory admonition against contract imposition as a basis for determining unfair labor practice violations was equally applicable to the fashioning of the kind of remedies that the Board might fashion. On the other hand, in Canada, the Ontario High Court of Justice in *Tandy Electronics, Ltd. (Radio Shack)*[38] concluded that where an employer was resisting demands for a union security provision with the purpose of undermining the union, even though the Board should ". . . strive to avoid the imposition of terms of a collective agreement upon the parties,"[39] the company would be directed to ". . . cease and desist in its position on union security that we have found to be part of a continuing scheme to divide the loyalties of its employees . . . ."[40]

The American Board has held that rigid insistence on a wide variety of issues that would remove any institutional role for the union could constitute bad-faith bargaining where the tactic was viewed as an attempt to thwart an agreement altogether.[41] On the other hand, the Board has taken the position that its position cannot be based upon its views about what would be desirable or acceptable as the terms of a collective bargaining agreement.

Similarly, where the collective bargaining process has been delayed by virtue of unfair labor practices, the American Board has refused to fashion "make-whole" damage relief that deprives workers of wages and benefits that would otherwise be negotiated in a collective bargaining agreement. In the landmark *Ex-Cell-o*[42] case the Board took the position that such a remedy would be inappropriate under the Act, in part because it would indirectly necessitate the same kind of contract imposition that the Court had found to be inconsistent with the statutory policy in *H.K. Porter*. The Supreme Court stated in *H.K. Porter* that the NLRB's powers are broad, "but they are limited to carrying out the policies of the Act itself."[43] The Board cannot impose an agreement on the parties that they would not have reached themselves: ". . . [T]o do so would violate the fundamental premise on which the Act was based—private bargaining under governmental supervision of the procedure alone, without any official compulsion over the actual terms of the contract."[44]

The Ontario Board, while noting that it "cannot get too far ahead of the expectations of the parties [it] regulates . . . ," held such damages to be appropriate.[45] Said the Board:

Employees join the trade union with, in their minds at least, the reasonable prospect of obtaining improvement in their working conditions. . . . When an employer responds with flagrant unfair labour practices, he wrongly prevents his employees from realizing their expectations or delays having to deal with any of their demands. For example, an employer may be able to escape with no contract at all if the initial organizing strength of the union can be so eroded by unfair labour practices that a strike can be outlasted. Moreover, the employer receives an unfair competitive advantage over those employers who do bargain in good faith, making the unlawful conduct attractive to other employers. In labour relations terms these employee losses are real; the potential employer gains unjust; and both are accomplished by the violation of a fundamental duty imposed by the legislation–bargaining agent recognition. The failure to consider any monetary relief seems to encourage these consequences.[46]

However, the fact is that even when the kind of limited imposition of contract terms authorized in *Tandy Electronics* or "make whole" is at the Board's disposal, tough and hard bargaining—and indeed bargaining that is subsequently condemned by the Board and the courts to be unlawful on the grounds that it is in bad faith—will not provide workers with assurance or even the likelihood that the union will be able to negotiate a collective bargaining agreement for them and thus realize some of their expectations. As the British Columbia Board properly noted, the certification of a union as exclusive bargaining representative does not provide it with the "keys to the vault."

First-Contract Negotiations and Arbitration

In the United States in an increasing number of instances there has been an inability of the parties to conclude a collective bargaining agreement in first-contract negotiations. According to an AFL-CIO study,[47] in the early 1980s, only 63 percent of newly certified bargaining units of one hundred employees or more successfully negotiated first collective agreements. This figure decreases by 10 percent when employers already engaged with another union in respect of other of its employees are excluded. As table 7.3 clearly demonstrates, the problems faced by Canadian unions in this regard are mild by American standards. Nonetheless, the problem is one that has been recognized by Canadian legislators in a number of jurisdictions.

In addition, and particularly in Ontario, there have been an increasing number of celebrated cases involving employers that have engaged in hard bargaining, or what the unions characterized unsuccessfully as "surface" bargaining, a process designed not to consummate an agreement and thus to erode collective bargaining. This kind of behavior led to first-contract arbitration in British Columbia beginning in 1973, then in the federal sector governed by the Canadian Labour Relations Board, and eventually in Quebec, Manitoba, Newfoundland, and Ontario. The provinces and the federal sector have taken different statutory approaches to a number of key issues.

The most important of these issues relates to the triggering mechanism for access to arbitration. The traditional concern with arbitration—whether first-contract or not—of interest disputes, or an inability to resolve the terms of a new collective bargaining agreement, has been

Table 7.3
Union success rates in negotiating first contracts after Ontario Labour Relations Board certification, 1970–71 to 1990–91 (nonconstruction industry certifications)

Years	Total board certifications	Collective agreements reached successfully	Success rate
1970–71	478	393	82.2%
1971–72	373	313	83.9
1972–73	483	405	83.9
1973–74	577	494	85.6
1974–75	590	515	87.3
1975–76	492	432	87.8
1976–77	454	402	88.5
1977–78	429	363	84.6
1978–79	492	425	86.4
1979–80	594	509	85.7
1980–81	636	553	86.9
1981–82	517	459	88.8
1982–83	364	311	85.4
1983–84	402	349	86.8
1984–85	517	452	87.4
1985–86	574	501	87.3
1986–87	496	420	84.7
1987–88	493	415	84.2
1988–89	444	372	83.8
1989–90	390	324	83.1
1990–91	376	316	84.0

Source: Len Haywood, Office of Collective Bargaining Information, Ontario Ministry of Labour. (Statistics provided by Mr. Haywood from an as yet unpublished and untitled study.)

that it is narcotic. Disputing parties come to increasingly rely upon it to the exclusion of collective bargaining. Because both sides know that arbitration is available to resolve the dispute, they will remain rigid at the bargaining table and thus the inability to resolve differences will be exacerbated. Likewise in first-contract arbitration, where the remedy is necessary because the balance of power is in the hands of an employer that can eliminate trade unionism altogether, the concern is that the union would inevitably use arbitration as a crutch and refuse to compromise, knowing that it can always be bailed out by a third-party neutral. Although the cause is far from clear, it is interesting to note that the statistics in table 7.3 demonstrate the success rate for unions newly certified in Ontario reaching first collective agreements dropped by approximately four tenths of a percent in the years subsequent to 1986, the year that first-contract legislation was enacted in that province.

Two issues arise in connection with this aspect of first-contract arbitration: (1) Should the minister of labor act as a "screen" to determine what cases will go before an administrative agency, which then will resolve the question of whether arbitration should be available and either remand the case to an arbitrator or resolve the issues in dispute between the parties itself? (2) Should there be a requirement that bad-faith bargaining—or something akin to it engaged in by the employer—trigger the statutory mechanism? In the federal sector, the Canadian Board possesses the "screen" of ministerial discretion and requires either illegal conduct or something more than hard bargaining to trigger the statutory mechanism. As in British Columbia the remedy has been an exceptional one, the fear expressed by both boards being that anything other than a sparing approach would interfere with the collective bargaining process.

There are obvious difficulties, however. Both the ministerial action and an investigation by the Board mean delay. In essence, the investigation approach, while arguably suitable to the resolution of an immediate dispute, does not serve to promote a lasting bargaining relationship. The reason is that it is designed to find fault with one side and thus is not conducive to promoting the bargaining process. One of the vivid contrasts between Japan and the United States (as noted above, both countries possess an unfair labor practice system) is that the Japanese have used their procedures to mediate and to promote a relationship that will bring the parties together. In British Columbia, prior to the legislation introduced at the end of 1992, a trade union boycott of most of the provisions of the 1987 amendments to the Industrial Relations Act has made first-contract arbitration irrelevant, simply because no party invokes it. While no similar union boycott toward the Federal Board exists, the process is used so infrequently as to be relatively unimportant in the federal sector, notwithstanding substantial unionization problems in industries such as banking and insurance.

At the other end of the continuum are Quebec and Manitoba. Initially Quebec legislation resembled that which is in place in British Columbia and federally—the initiating party was required to demonstrate that the respondent had engaged in bad-faith bargaining. However, the Quebec Labour Code was amended in 1978–79 and the arbitrator was given the authority to ". . . determine the content of the first collective agreement where he is of opinion that it is unlikely that the parties will be able to reach a collective agreement within a reasonable time."[48] The arbitrator then advises the minister of labor and the parties of this matter, and the parties are able to request the intervention of the minister or an arbitrator.

Quebec maintains two screens. The minister of labor has discretion to defer a request for first-contract arbitration to an arbitrator. The arbitrator may refuse to impose a first contract where the parties are reasonably close to resolving their differences through collective bargaining. But, in contrast to British Columbia and the federal sector, first-contract arbitration has not been viewed as an exceptional process or an aberration that can be rarely tolerated.

Manitoba has also initiated changes. Until 1984 that province modeled its first-contract statutory procedures along the lines of British Columbia. However, the 1984 amendments provide that a first-contract dispute may go directly to the Manitoba Board subsequent to issuance of a "no board" report by a conciliation officer or where the minister considers it inappropriate to appoint a conciliation board. The ministerial screen enacted in 1982 no longer exists. It was removed in 1984 so that the parties could make application directly to the Board where (1) certification has been granted, (2) notice to bargain has been given, (3) a conciliation officer has been appointed, (4) ninety days has expired from the date of certification of the union, and (5) a collective bargaining agreement has not been concluded.

What is unusual about Manitoba is the adoption of a statutory timetable within which the first-contract arbitration process is to be concluded. If the parties do not settle the outstanding issues within fifty days of the original application, the Board will impose a first contract within an additional thirty-day period or, alternatively, notify the parties that they have the capability to resolve their differences within another thirty-day period. If the parties are not able to resolve their differences, the Board must either settle the matter or impose a first contract within thirty days.

Accordingly in Manitoba there is no attempt to identify bad-faith, egregious, or inappropriate behavior on the part of the employer as a vehicle to invoke the process. Moreover there is no ministerial screen. And given the strict statutory timetable that is imposed, delay seems to be far less of a problem. The parties are assured that a first contract will be imposed or that their differences will be resolved through the mediatory efforts of the Board during an additional time period. However, Manitoba too has embarked on a process that will significantly amend its Labour Relations Act. Bill 85, among other changes, will amend the first-contract legislation to require, as a precondition to an application to the Board, that the conciliation officer first report to the Board on the efforts of the parties to reach settlement. The stated purpose of such a step is to ensure that the parties have reached impasse prior to the commencement of first-contract proceedings. Whether this form of ministerial screen will simply delay the imposition of first-contract relief is yet to be seen.

From 1982 to 1988 thirty-six applications were received by the Manitoba Labour Board for first agreements, or 9.9 percent of the certifications granted. The Board imposed thirteen agreements, 3.4 percent of the certifications granted.[49] Seventeen of the 36 cases were resolved voluntarily, presumably through the mediatory efforts of the Board. It is possible that Manitoba has been the most successful of all the Canadian jurisdictions in this venture. However, the most sophisticated undertaking to date appears to be the approach adopted by Ontario.

Bill 65, amending the Ontario Labour Relations Act, came into effect in 1986 and, like Manitoba, does not provide the minister of labor with a screen or discretionary power to refuse to refer the case to arbitration. Rather the Board itself must make a determination whether first-contract arbitration is appropriate, taking into account a number of considerations. The Board must conclude, in order to trigger first-contract arbitration, that collective bargaining has been "frustrated" because of (1) the refusal of an employer to recognize the bargaining authority of the union, (2) the uncompromising nature of bargaining positions adopted without "reasonable justification," (3) the failure of the respondent to make "reasonable efforts" to conclude a collective bargaining agreement, or (4) any other reason that the Board deems relevant.

In 1986 the Board, in *Nepean Roof Truss, Ltd.*,[50] attempted to provide some guidance in interpreting these statutory terms. In this case the Board took the position that since the statute directs it to impose a settlement through first-contract arbitration where it appears that the "process of collective bargaining has been unsuccessful,"[51] the focus must be upon the conduct of both parties. Recognizing the "considerable range of bargaining positions and tactics"[52] and the fact that the process is a "dynamic exchange," the Board stated the following:

It is the totality of the process that is under scrutiny and the Board must be cautious not to examine the complaint in a factual vacuum. The conduct of both parties is therefore relevant, not only for understanding why the process has been unsuccessful, but also for assessing whether it has been unsuccessful for any of the enumerated reasons. This does not intend to suggest that the applicant's conduct will be a bar to the imposed settlement of a first contract, but rather that its conduct is relevant in assessing the reason for the process.[53]

Once the process has been found to be unsuccessful, the statute, in the Board's words ". . . contemplates a cause and effect oriented assessment,"[54] namely whether the failure has been attributable to any of the reasons enumerated by the statute. The Board emphasized that a duty-to-bargain violation was not a prerequisite for triggering first contract arbitration. Noting that the Board had held that hard bargaining is not necessarily bargaining in bad faith, the Board said, ". . . one is left with the inescapable conclusion that the statute has intended a different standard to apply in the determination of first contract disputes, a standard peculiar to . . . [such] . . . adjudications"[55] notwithstanding the possible relevance of duty to bargain considerations. Thus, the Board stated, rigid bargaining proposals, while not a violation of the duty to bargain in good-faith provisions of the statute, could well violate the first-contract arbitration provisions, thus triggering such a mechanism. In the same decision the Board stated that while one could frequently identify an uncompromising position in collective bargaining, the question of whether that posture was "without reasonable justification"[56] is a more difficult one. The Board indicated that evidence in the proceeding was necessary to provide justification for an individual bargaining position on an individual item and that ". . . [in] . . . today's labour relations climate . . . the significance to the labour movement of . . . [a] . . . basic principle . . ." would be relevant.[57]

In 1992 the Ontario ministry of labor has proposed a change in the law that would eliminate the criteria noted above and what the ministry characterized as the "extensive litigation" involved with it. Said the ministry in its proposal:

This [the existing system] may result in extensive delays, expensive hearings before the Board and lingering animosity at the beginning of the collective bargaining relationship.

The government's proposal would prevent lengthy first contract disputes as well as the need for extensive OLRB litigation. The proposal is intended, however, to support the integrity of free collective bargaining by requiring a pre-application period in which the parties would be required to engage in negotiations and mandatory third party conciliation. The thirty day period required to trigger access to arbitration would only begin to run following the report from the conciliator that the parties had been unable to reach an agreement and the subsequent two week waiting period had elapsed. The proposal is not intended as an avenue for either party seeking to avoid the requirement to bargain. Indeed, in order to obtain access to first agreement arbitration both parties would have to face the possibility of a legal strike or lockout occurring and lasting for at least thirty days.[58]

It may be that in the United States some comparable waiting period concept would be appropriate as part of the Packwood-Metzenbaum amendment to the Workplace Fairness Act of 1992. Of course the Canadian legislation involves binding arbitration. But even in connection with fact-finding recommendations such as those contained in the Packwood-Metzenbaum amendment, some preliminary hurdle might be required, that is, a waiting or notice period during which there would be a pause and a prohibition on strikes or lockouts, similar to that which now exists in American law during the sixty-day period prior to the expiration of a collective bargaining agreement. On the one hand, criteria such as those that have existed in Ontario between 1986 and 1992 involve multiple considerations that may inspire litigation. On the other hand, some kind of screen or pause could discourage frequent use of third-party intervention.

In another important decision in Ontario,[59] the Board addressed the standards to be applied in the arbitration proceeding. Adhering to a position previously taken by the British Columbia Board, the Ontario Board said that first-contract arbitration should not be used, "to achieve major breakthroughs in collective bargaining" but rather should be "in accord with a fairly generous consensus on the issues in dispute to the extent that employees would give serious consideration before deciding to terminate the bargaining rights of the applicant . . . [union]."[60] Commenting on the positions of the parties in this case, the Board said:

Firstly, the Board does not agree that the process envisaged under a determination of a first contract by this Board . . . is to be based upon the concept of a final offer selection. In attempting to set forth a collective agreement which is in the Board's view, fair to both sides, it is not sufficient for the Board to simply look at the most attractive or the least unattractive proposal of either side. Secondly, the Board also rejects the argument of the respondent that the collective agreement which the Board determines . . . ought to reflect the relative strengths of the bargaining position of the parties. In this case, it was the position of the respondent that it was in the stronger bargaining position and that, therefore, the determination of the Board should wholly or substantially reflect the proposals advanced by the respondent. The Board rejects this notion because the imbalance of the bargaining position of the parties was certainly a factor in the inability of the parties to conclude a collective agreement which was satisfactory and acceptable to both sides. If the Board were to accept the argument of the respondent that the collective agreement determined by the Board ought to reflect the relative bargaining positions of the parties then there would be little point in having an application made for a first collective agreement . . . since the parties would know in advance the collective agreement which would be determined by the Board. Moreover, an endorsement of the concept of the relative bargaining positions of the parties would encourage extreme positions by the parties which would perceive themselves to be the stronger position.[61]

Just as most of the disputes in Manitoba have been resolved without the need for arbitration, so have most cases been settled in Ontario without the need to carry the procedure through to its conclusion. This pattern may be attributable to the fact that some unions file requests for first-contract arbitration without a serious intention of proceeding to conclusion, simply using it as a bargaining tactic to pressure the employer. Moreover it would appear that such statutory procedures shift the balance of power from management to labor in some measure. Yet the experience in the provinces—particularly in these two provinces—indicates that the collective bargaining process has not been eroded.

But are the objectives being implemented? That is to say, are lasting relationship being produced? It is too early to say to any authoritative degree, but aside from what has been said above about the counterproductive effect of unfair labor practice litigation upon first-contract settlement or arbitration, the duration of the contract imposed may have some bearing upon this. British Columbia, the federal sector, Manitoba, Newfoundland, and Ontario, all provide for arbitration of a contract for a duration of one year, while Quebec provides two years. On the one hand, commitment to the collective bargaining process made the framers of such legislation reticent about prolonged interference. On the other hand, contracts of such limited duration, even in Manitoba which has fast-moving procedures, make it unlikely that lasting relationships can be promoted and that new contracts can be negotiated. At this state it is too early to judge the success or lack of success of the statutory approach to this problem. Given its significance, policy considerations ought to weigh on the side of collective agreements that have a duration of two or even three years. That would be the kind of trial period that might lead to the negotiation of a second contract, and it would make a further request for intervention less likely.

Of course another, albeit not mutually exclusive, approach to this matter would be to provide the Board with the authority to resolve second- or third-contract disputes. This ought to be more compatible with the Canadian tradition than that in the United States, given the Australian–New Zealand approach alluded to earlier. If employee sentiment remains in favor of unionization and yet hard bargaining will not permit the collective bargaining process to function, the philosophy of the first-contract arbitration statutes in all of the provinces would not preclude arbitration farther on down the road. The problem throughout such an exercise is to weigh employee sentiment, the likelihood that the collective bargaining process will be able to revive, against the costs of governmental interference. But there ought not to be anything sacrosanct about limiting intervention to the first contract. Indeed such limitations may well invite conduct designed to stifle the collective bargaining process in its incipient stages, with the knowledge that the parties will be left to their own devices the second or third time around, thus exposing the weaker party to the same behavior that prompted first-contract arbitration. The point here is that while there are risks involved with intervention in collective bargaining and the desirability of promoting autonomy for the parties, the conundrum of the law is that legal intervention is sometimes necessary to save the bargaining process. In principle the balance of power between labor and management is something for the parties to shape themselves in a free market. But where the collective bargaining process is just beginning, it may be too vulnerable to withstand pressures that are hostile to genuine relationships between organized labor and management.

The Collective Bargaining Process

The law relating to the collective bargaining process operates in different ways in Canada. For instance, in the United States, an employer may permanently replace economic strikers under the so-called *Mackay* doctrine.[62] In much of Canada, the law is quite different. For instance, in Quebec employers are precluded from operating during a strike. And although the managerial work force may be retained to perform the function of the workers, frequent disputes arise out of the question of what is managerial work and what is that of the strikers within the bargaining unit. In Ontario the law provides that strikers have the right to return until six months after the commencement of the strike. As the Ontario Board rules in *The Becker Milk Co., Ltd.*,[63] the employee must meet three conditions in order to invoke the right to return within the six-month period: (1) the employee must be returning to work after engaging in a lawful strike, (2) he or she must make an unconditional written application to return to work, and (3) the application must be made within six months after the beginning of the strike. Said the Board: "The striker who returns to work under the protection of section 64 [the six-month provision] of the Act, therefore, has the unequivocal right to bump a replacement if that is what must be done to reinstate him in his job."[64] The theory of course is that the balance between the strikers and nonstrikers must be fashioned to take into account, on the one hand, the right of workers to engage in economic pressure without the fear of retaliation and, on the other hand, the assumption that at a certain point the strikers may not be returning and that the employer will want to be able to assure nonstrikers of job security in the interest of maintaining its production and discipline. Accordingly the view of the Ontario legislature was that a balance must be struck and that six months was a reasonable period of time.

Again the 1992 ministry of labor reforms are designed to change the state of the law in Ontario and to make it comparable to Quebec's. The reforms limit the employer's ability to operate during a strike by decreeing which employees may continue to work and what work may be performed. Indeed in some ways the Ontario proposals go at least as far as their Quebec counterparts. A prime example is found in what some have called the "legislated solidarity" provision of the Ontario bill. The proposed legislation includes the following prohibition:

The employer shall not use the services of an employee in the bargaining unit that is on strike or is locked out.[65]

During a strike or lockout this provision makes it illegal for an employer to use the services of a strike or lockout employee, even if that employee has lost faith in the trade union and no longer wishes to participate in the collective action.

The Ontario proposal is vulnerable on two grounds. The first is its one-sided nature, its refusal to allow the employer to operate effectively during a strike as opposed to protecting the jobs of workers who are on strike. The Ontario government's position is that the use of replacement workers as scabs has been "disruptive to affected communities." But what is the experience with the Quebec legislation? States the ministry of labor report:

> While it was difficult to assess the precise effect of the Quebec legislation, it seems clear that from the outset, there has been a decline in picket line violence and hostility, as well as a marked improvement in the collective bargaining climate. There is mixed evidence as to whether, in its initial years, the legislation reduced the incidents and duration of strikes, particularly because in a number of disputes the new law was violated. The Quebec Ministry of Labour reports, however, that more recently, (including the period of time following the 1983 amendments) there has been a decline in both the number and length of disputes which is at least in part attributable to the legislation itself.[66]

But the reliance upon Quebec has been roundly condemned by business groups such as the More Jobs Coalition. In its February 1992 report, it said:

> . . . there is no evidence to suggest that Quebec legislation has resulted in an improvement in the collective bargaining climate in that province . . . in the fourteen years in which the legislation has been in effect, Quebec has suffered a higher number of strikes than Ontario involving a significantly greater number of workers and producing more person-days lost. Moreover, statistics indicate that the number and ratio of strikes in the province of Quebec increased over the three year period following the introduction of the legislation from the three year period immediately before the legislation.[67]

The More Jobs Coalition also states that such a proposal would produce a greater employer interest in seeking alternate sources of production—indeed the proposal would allow the employer to carry out its production at another site—the argument being that this is the way employers have reacted to similar legislation in Quebec. But the decline of business in Quebec may be attributable to a wide variety of considerations other than those involving strike legislation. Still Ontario has tilted the balance too far in labor's direction.

Other Areas of Canadian Labor Law

In two other important aspects of labor law, Canada is different from the United States. One of them relates to the so-called successorship doctrine where, if the employer that purchases or merges with a predecessor does not hire a majority of the employees, no bargaining obligation, let alone a contractual obligation, exists. In Canada the question is essentially whether there has been a sale of the business or a "part" of the business. This is true even in British Columbia where the law has been amended so as to narrow the successorship obligations.

Another area of difference is the so-called free-speech right of employers. The position of the Taft-Hartley amendments is that employers have the explicit statutory and constitutional right to engage in free speech unless coercion or threats or promises are contained in it. But the fact is that the skillful employer is able to walk the line of illegality successfully by advertising the negative impact that a union might have upon employment opportunities as the result of excessive demands or strikes. The Ontario Labour Relations Board has taken the position in *Viceroy Construction*[68] that, while the employer has the right of free speech in Canada, factors other than coercion will constitute a basis for making the speech unlawful. Said the Board: "While he is of course free to express his view of representation by a trade union he may not use that freedom of expression to make *overt or subtle threats or promises motivated by anti-union sentiment which go to the sensitive area of changes in conditions of employment or job security*."[69] Similarly the British Columbia Board, interpreting a statute that precludes "intimidation, coercion or threats," has said that such language evokes,

... images of compulsion with its accompanying fear and insecurity. Undue influence, on the other hand, appears to contemplate a less blunt form of acting upon the natural vulnerability of employees.

Undue influence is a species of intimidation. It may be distinguished from the more direct form of equally coercive pressure by a certain subtlety of application. Its effectiveness is perhaps enhanced by this characteristic. The Legislators [in British Columbia] have clearly stated that the use of such a weapon by an employer has no place in the industrial relations arena.[70]

In the United States the problem with taking this approach is that not only can speech be interfered with on a broad basis at the peril of violating the First Amendment but, as noted in chapter 5, regulation of this tactic seems to be something of a wasting asset. The better approach would be to establish rules that provide for equal opportunity for communication between labor and management so that both parties may more effectively reach workers.

Conclusion

The United States has much to learn from Canada in the labor law arena. Contrary to what some writers assume, the differences between the United States and Canada cannot be simply dismissed as differences between legal approaches; much more is involved than that. To begin with, there is Canada's history and culture; it has a tradition that shares more characteristics with Britain than the United States. Even more profound differences lie in its occupational industrial distribution. These differences may now change as the free-trade treaty between the United States and Canada, and more recently NAFTA, expose Canada to some of the competitive whims that have long been in place in this country.

8

The Civil Rights Act of 1991: The Law and Politics of Race

Beyond wrongful discharge litigation the most important rules in the American workplace relate to employment discrimination legislation. But almost thirty years after the Civil Rights Act of 1964, Congress found it necessary to adopt new legislation—the Civil Rights Act of 1991—as an amendment to the earlier law. In part the Congress meant to address remedial deficiencies contained in title VII of the 1964 Act. The immediate trigger for the new statute, however, was rooted in a conflict between the Supreme Court and Congress that emerged in the 1970s and reached new heights in 1989, when the new conservative Court majority, appointed by Presidents Richard Nixon and Ronald Reagan, issued a series of decisions emasculating important provisions of modern antidiscrimination law. Justice Anthony Kennedy, whose ride through the Senate approval process was relatively painless in the wake of the celebrated hearings involving Judge Robert Bork, provided the margin of victory.

Congress responded to the 1989 decisions by drafting the Civil Rights Act of 1990. President Bush vetoed the bill, quite simply because he approved most of the new case law that had been articulated in 1989. As the debate raged onward, it became clear that the White House saw a splendid opportunity to renew the politics of racial divisiveness that it had so skillfully employed in the 1988 election, particularly through use of the celebrated Willie Horton advertisement which subtlety equated crime with blacks. Bush promoted the view that rigorous enforcement of antidiscrimination law was tantamount to the imposition of quotas—a buzz word in the American political process—notwithstanding Congress' undeviating refusal to address affirmative action in the bill and reverse a recent antiaffirmative action ruling of the Court.

A new bill was introduced the following year. After considerable debate, an October 24 "final compromise" between Congress and the White House was negotiated. But on the key issues in dispute—the standards relating to "unintentional" discrimination remedies, "mixed motive" discrimination, seniority questions, and other issues—civil rights proponents in Congress prevailed over President Bush in the Civil Rights Act of 1991.

The Civil Rights Act of 1991 reverses or modifies most of the 1989 employment discrimination holdings, as well as another decision of the Court in 1991. It promises to restore some of the protections that Congress had placed in the law almost thirty years ago and to provide effective remedies in cases involving sexual or religious discrimination. True, it does not address the basic social and economic inequities that spawned the 1992 riots in Los Angeles and the worsening economic condition that confronts young black males in particular. Nonetheless, the statute revives some sense of balance and equity that many thought was in the 1964 statute. To the extent that it provides new remedies in the form of compensatory and punitive damages, which were deemed to be available to job applicants or workers only under the Civil Rights Act of 1866, it will catalyze the reform of discriminatory practices in the workplace.

Historical Background

In a sense the struggle over the Civil Rights Act of 1991, which was signed into law by President Bush on November 21, 1991, began in the late 1960s in the wake of the enactment of title VII of the Civil Rights Act of 1964. President Bush, along with the 1964 Republican presidential candidate, Barry Goldwater, opposed the Nation's first comprehensive antidiscrimination law, which prohibited discrimination on the basis of race, sex, religion, and national origin and established the Equal Employment Opportunity Commission (EEOC) as an expert administrative agency with the authority of both investigate and conciliate claims of discrimination. The politics of race, they found, played particularly well in the South and, as Governor George Wallace of Alabama was to discover thereafter, in the industrial states of the North as well.

The very focus upon blacks and the attempt to remedy centuries of racial injustice immediately produced resentment and outcries against so-called preferences (this is before affirmative action was even at issue), creating waters in which unprincipled politicians were only too happy to fish. For a quarter of a century, the "backlash"—as it was first characterized by President Lyndon Johnson—provided the essential ingredients for racial acrimony that would serve to elect three presidents, Richard Nixon, Ronald Reagan, and George Bush. As Andrew Hacker has said:

> One of the two major parties—the Republicans—has all but explicitly stated that it is willing to have itself regarded as a white party, prepared to represent white Americans and defend their interests. Of course, Republican administrations make sure that they appoint a few black officials, either vocal conservatives or taciturn moderates willing to remain in the background. (And they were especially adroit at finding apt candidates for the Supreme Court and Chairman of the Joint Chiefs of Staff.) An unwritten plank in the party's strategy is that it can win the offices if it wants without black votes. More than that, by sending a message that neither wants nor needs ballots cast by blacks, it feels that it can attract even more votes from a much larger pool of white Americans who want a party willing to represent their racial identity.
> —By the close of 1992, twenty of the preceding twenty-four years will have been an era of Republican hegemony . . . a politics purposely permeated by race has consolidated enough white Americans as a self-conscious racial majority.[1]

The Court's Erratic Path toward the Protection of Civil Rights

Two decades of Republican hegemony resulted in appointments to the Court that were to give it an increasingly conservative cast, but as is so often true of the judiciary, the proposition was not always a clear and glaring one. This has been particularly true in the area of employment discrimination law, like much of the Court's work on racial equality. In 1971 a unanimous Supreme Court held in *Griggs v. Duke Power*,[2] an opinion authored by President Nixon's first appointee, Chief Justice Warren Burger, that discrimination violated the 1964 Act even where the discrimination was not overt or intentional. This far-sweeping decision would become a powerful force for the principle of fairness and nonarbitrary conduct in the workplace and ultimately radiate into other sectors of the employment relationship.[3] In 1975 the Court held that, notwithstanding title VII's relatively narrow monetary remedial focus (i.e., back pay, front pay,[4] costs, and attorney's fees), punitive and compensatory damages could be obtained under Reconstruction legislation that had been dramatically revived by the Warren Court.[5] But the ride downhill gained momentum soon thereafter.

Griggs, the disparate impact line of authority that followed it, and remedies that were available in racial discrimination cases were at the heart of fair employment practice reform in the United States. *Griggs* placed a substantial burden upon the employer through its obligation to rebut a prima facie case. Though the Supreme Court did not address the issue definitively until *Wards Cove Packing Company v. Atonio*[6]—the first of its 1989 employment discrimination decisions—the view of a number of circuits was that the employer could only approve a practice producing disparate impact if it was central to the safety of the enterprise. The 1989 Supreme Court decisions that led to the Civil Rights Act of 1991 modified the doctrines previously established in both the *Griggs* doctrine and the area of punitive and compensatory damages applicable only in race cases. By raising the issue of remedy, the basic inadequacies of title VII as applied to sex and religious discrimination cases became all the more dramatic.

This was not the first time that the Court and Congress had clashed in the employment discrimination arena. In 1976 the Court narrowed the application of the *Griggs* holding,[7] made it difficult for pregnant women to come within the ambit of title VII's protection,[8] and, notwithstanding the unanimity of circuit courts of appeals,[9] resisted interference with discriminatory seniority provisions in collective bargaining agreements.[10]

In the seniority cases the Court disregarded Congress' approval of decisions of the circuit courts through the enactment of 1972 amendments to the 1964 Act ("1972 Amendments").[11] Although the amendments did not explicitly address the seniority issue, they allowed the EEOC to sue in federal district court and extended jurisdiction of the 1964 Act to governmental employees. The legislative reports that led to their enactment specifically approved the then prevailing view of the circuit courts regarding seniority.

The Congress found it necessary to intervene and reverse the pregnancy decisions through the Pregnancy and Disability Act of 1978.[12] It also reversed the Court's holdings in other civil rights arenas outside the employment relationship[13] and did not act on the seniority issue until 1991.

The Court seemed to shift gear when it dramatically rebuffed the Reagan administration's attempts to emasculate affirmative action policies that had been tentatively undertaken in the 1970s.[14] Echoing a maxim first articulated by Justice Powell in the *Bakke* case,[15] the Court held that under some circumstances race- and sex-conscious policies relating to the employment relationship were compatible with both civil rights legislation and the Constitution,[16] though there was much dispute about the precise circumstances under which this proposition could be appropriately realized.

This setback for the Reagan administration would lead to later efforts by the Bush administration to amend the 1990 Civil Rights Bill by preying upon unease with both affirmative action and quotas. The administration's idea was that by creating the impression that the new legislation mandated preferential treatment for minority employees, efforts by the Democratic party legislators to retain precedent that had approved quotas, as well as more flexible goals for hiring and promotion on the basis of race or sex, would be difficult to explain. The Bush administration's view was that, notwithstanding that the Supreme Court had already ruled on the quotas and that nothing in the legislation addressed this issue, the Democrats would be pressed to back away from the rulings in the new legislation. If they did not, they could be attacked as supporting quotas.

The Court Rolls Back Title VII Rights

In 1989 the Court shifted gear once again in a series of holdings involving employment discrimination.[17] The Court gave surprisingly narrow statutory interpretations to civil rights legislation, which in some instances were disruptive if not entirely unexpected. The two most prominent examples involved the application of the disparate impact language standards in *Griggs* and Reconstruction legislation, which had been the focus of the Court's earliest and most important employment discrimination holdings.

In *Wards Cove v. Atonio*[18] a 5–4 majority of the Court, its conservative wing now bolstered by the appointment of Justice Kennedy, overturned or limited three key portions of the *Griggs* holding. The Court's opinion, authored by Justice White, purported not to overrule *Griggs*. On the first of its significant holdings, this was literally true.

Wards Cove held that a plaintiff could properly make out a prima facie case of discrimination only by a showing that the statistically significant exclusion of racial minorities could be attributable to a particular employment practice. In *Griggs* only high school education and written examination, both objective criteria, were at issue. In the years since *Griggs* employers had frequently relied upon a wide variety of criteria,[19] as did the employer in *Wards Cove*. But in *Wards Cove*—a case involving old-fashioned de jure segregation of housing and dining facilities—much more was involved, such as nepotism and rehiring preferences, lack of objective hiring criteria, separate hiring channels, and a practice of not promoting from within. Thus the Court held that disparate impact was not in evidence simply because there was a racial imbalance in the work force produced by a number of practices and procedures utilized by the employer.

Said Justice White:

> ... as a general matter, a plaintiff must demonstrate that it is the application of a specific or particular employment practice that has created the disparate impact under attack. Such a showing is an integral part of the plaintiff's *prima facie* suit in the disparate impact case under Title VII.[20]

To the argument that such a requirement was unduly burdensome for plaintiffs, particularly since the knowledge of a particular set of practices and their impact would more likely be available to the defendant rather than the plaintiff, the Court responded that "liberal discovery rules give plaintiffs broad access to employers' records in an effort to document their claims."[21]

In its second important departure from *Griggs*, the Court held that the standard the court should use to evaluate whether a prima facie case constituted a conclusive violation or the standard relating to a rebuttal was one of "business justification" and not "necessity," as the *Griggs* Court had held. The idea that the practice must be essential or indispensable to the employer's business was rejected. Said Justice White, "... the dispositive issue is whether a challenged practice serves, in a significant way, the legitimate employment goals of the employer."[22]

In a finally and equally troublesome departure from *Griggs*, the Court concluded that the employer's rebuttal to a charge of disparate impact discrimination simply required a burden of producing "evidence" of its business justification, and not a burden of persuasion. The burden of proof remained with the plaintiff, though *Griggs* had established the contrary point.

In *Patterson v. McLean Credit Union*,[23] rendered only ten days later, the Court held that the Civil Rights Act of 1866, which it had approved in the 1970s, did not protect a black woman employee from racial harassment. Justice Kennedy, writing for the majority in yet another 5–4 vote, stated that the statute only applies to racial discrimination in hiring.[24]

The effect of the *Patterson* ruling was to cut back upon remedies that were available to black plaintiffs. Now, not only did title VII not provide for punitive and compensatory damages, but its Reconstruction antecedents did so as well inasmuch as no liability could be established in connection with the bulk of bias cases outside the hiring process. Experience with more than a half-century of case law under the National Labor Relations Act, where only back pay is available, had demonstrated conclusively the ineffectiveness of monetary relief, which was designed to merely make applicants and workers "whole" for employment losses incurred. The catalyst for reform was removed in most of the racial cases and not available at all in cases involving religious and sex bias, predicated as they are on title VII alone.

Neither of these decisions could be regarded as completely unexpected. The holding in *Patterson* was fashioned in a case in which the Court had invited briefs on the question of whether changes or development in the law had undermined the application of Reconstruction legislation to private contracts. With one hand, the Court adhered to stare decisis, but with the other, it reinterpreted the statute so as to give it what the dissenters called a "cramped" application.[25]

Wards Cove itself was foreshadowed by a 1988 plurality opinion authored by Justice O'Connor, in *Watson v. Fort Worth Bank and Trust*.[26] In *Watson*, albeit within the context of subjective criteria,[27] a plurality had concluded that the plaintiff's burden was to identify particular employment practices, that the standard of rebuttal was legitimate business purposes, and that the "ultimate burden" was not to be shifted to the defendant.

The approach espoused in *Watson* was transformed into a majority opinion in *Wards Cove*, which was remarkably similar to the burden of production that the Court had thrust upon employers in disparate treatment cases.[28] But the disparate treatment cases were different from the *Griggs* disparate impact situation because a relatively light burden for the employer in the former group of cases was regarded as appropriate, given the similarly light burden thrust upon the plaintiff. The plaintiff's burden in establishing a prima facie case in *Griggs* was more burdensome—it involved considerable collection of statistical evidence, multiple regression analyses, and an examination of personnel records—and it became even more so with *Wards Cove*. The employer's relatively light burden, while applicable to disparate treatment cases where one or a small number of employees was attempting to prove intent to discriminate in a contest about that particular individual's qualifications and those of the person obtained, was hardly suitable to disparate impact disputes where the plaintiffs carried a considerable prima facie burden themselves.

A third decision in 1989, *Price Waterhouse v. Hopkins*,[29] was authored by Justice Brennan and considered by some elements in the women's movement and the business community as a victory for the plaintiff's bar. This view stems from one of the Court's conclusions in that case that inferences of sexual discrimination can be drawn from comments that reflect sexual stereotypes.[30] But another conclusion of the Court was hardly as favorable to victims of discrimination. All of the justices accepted the view that even where discrimination was a motivating factor or substantial motivating factor in a dismissal, no liability could be imposed upon the employer if the employee would have been nonetheless dismissed because of a valid nondiscriminatory reason for dismissal. While the Court had previously accepted this mixed motive test in the context of both the National Labor Relations Act[31] and the First Amendment,[32] unqualified acceptance of racial or sexual discrimination that went completely unremedied seemed particularly wrong. Moreover the decision failed to take into account the reality of the workplace and the fact that it is a rare employee who has an unblemished record and whose personnel record does not maintain a valid nondiscriminatory reason for some form of discipline or action, perhaps even dismissal.

A fourth 1989 decision, this one handed down a week after *Wards Cove*, was *Lorance v. AT&T Technologies, Inc.*[33] In this case (a 6–3 majority of the Court, in an opinion authored by Justice Antonin Scalia) women workers who were demoted as a result of their low seniority under collective bargaining agreement complained that their position was attributable to an earlier alteration of the rules that was a conspiracy designed to protect incumbent male workers in their job classification and to discourage women from being promoted into this traditionally all male arena. A 6–3 majority of the Court rejected the claim because it was not filed within the applicable limitations period, concluding that the limitations period runs from the date that the seniority system was changed, and not the date of actual harm suffered as a result of it. Justice Scalia, who authored the majority opinion, stated that ". . . allowing a facially neutral system to be challenged, and entitlements under it to be altered, many years after its adoption would disrupt those valid reliance interests [male incumbent employees] that §703(h) [the bona fide seniority proviso] was meant to protect."[34]

Ironically on the very same day as *Lorance*, the Court, in a 5–4 decision, came to a conclusion that appeared to be at odds with its reasoning in the seniority case. In *Martin v. Wilks*[35] Chief Justice Rehnquist authored an opinion in which the Court allowed employees to challenge a consent decree which they claimed had harmed their employment, even though they had been aware of the decree at the time that it was entered and had not protested at that time. Thus such workers could come forward at any time regardless of the period of time that has elapsed subsequent to the entering of the decree. One concern with the holding, aside from its basic unfairness, was that the parties would be discouraged to enter into consent decrees and encouraged to litigate if decrees could be challenged by the disgruntled at any time under any circumstance.

Congress Reacts: Introduction of Civil Rights Legislation

In 1991, after this raft of restrictive civil rights holdings, the Court, in *EEOC v. Arabian American Oil Co.*,[36] held that title VII does not apply extraterritorially to regulate employment practices of U.S. employers who employ American citizens abroad. This decision, along with the 1989 holdings, became a matter of great concern to the public and the Congress. Although the Court, in a continuation of the trend established in the 1989 rulings, declared unconstitutional an affirmative action program involving minority contractors in Richmond, Virginia,[37] both because of the unpopularity of race-conscious affirmative action and the difficulties involved in altering a constitutional decision through amendment, Congress gave the affirmative action issue a wide berth and steered away from this subject.

The relevant legislation was introduced in early 1990.[38] From the beginning it sought to reverse the Supreme Court's 1989 decisions, though undoubtedly there was dissatisfaction with the Court's Richmond, Virginia, ruling. A calculated decision was made to steer clear of the affirmative action issue because of its political explosiveness and debate about the congressional authority to rely on the Constitution to reverse the Court.

Two-Year Deadlock over the "Quota Bill"

Ironically President Bush, eventually conceding the need for legislation in this area though reluctant to confront the holdings directly,[39] responded to congressional initiatives by claiming that they would result in quotas—the very issue that the Congress had made a determination to circumvent. But the president's reaction set the stage for a two-year confrontation between the executive and legislative branches of government. The view that the Civil Rights Act of 1991 would create quotas had its origins in Justice O'Connor's opinion in *Watson*, where she had warned against ". . . the inevitable focus on statistics in disparate impact cases [which] could put undue pressure on employers to adopt inappropriate prophylactic measures."[40] Said Justice O'Connor for a plurality in *Watson*:

> . . . respondent and the United States are thus correct when they argue that extending disparate impact analysis to subjective employment practices has the potential to create a Hobson's choice for employers and thus to read and practice to perverse results. If quotas and preferential treatment become the only cost-effective means of avoiding expensive litigation and potentially catastrophic liability, such measures will be widely adopted. The prudent employer will be careful to insure that its programs are discussed in euphemistic terms, but will be equally careful to insure that quotas are met. Allowing the evolution of disparate impact analysis to lead to this result would be contrary to Congress' clearly expressed intent and it should not be the effect of our decision today.[41]

This theme was woven into the fabric of *Wards Cove*, although not with the extensive emphasis provided by the plurality opinion for Court in *Watson*. It was to shape much of the debate about disparate impact, with President Bush continually referring to congressional legislation as a "quota bill," notwithstanding the many compromises that were put forward particularly by Senator Danforth of Missouri during the summer of 1991.

In truth, both sides were somewhat disingenuous with their arguments. First, as critics continuously pointed out,[42] President Bush simply argued for the conclusion that legislation would provide for quotas without articulating clearly the way in which they would do so. Second, as Justice O'Connor herself had noted, preferential treatment and the use of quotas "can violate the Constitution,"[43] conceding a fact of which all employment lawyers were aware, namely that the Court had approved both quotas and preferential treatment in certain circumstances. But one could not find this concession in President Bush's many letters and policy statements. This raised the very strong suspicion that he sought reversal of the Supreme Court's affirmative action decisions, particularly when the Democrats offered amendments that would outlaw quotas, except as provided for by the Supreme Court's decisions.[44] The White House rejected this proposal on much the same grounds, stating that the proposal put forward by the Democrats as a compromise would still provide for quotas, notwithstanding the language of the amendment. Since the amendment would have preserved the Supreme Court's rulings, one must assume that the Democrats' disclaimer against quotas was only objectionable because it simultaneously sought to preserve the Supreme Court's existing decisions in the affirmative action arena.

Bush's congressional opponents had their own set of problems. The basic conundrum of antidiscrimination law—a matter to which they were unable or unwilling to admit—is that prohibitions against discrimination necessarily make employers more race or sex conscious in their hiring or promotion policies. The obvious response to potential liability is to find qualified minorities or female workers and thus diminish the potential for litigation based upon statistics. But the point is that this phenomenon has nothing to do necessarily with quotas or preferences. Race or sex consciousness is promoted by virtue of antidiscrimination law itself and the consequent potential of liability that flows from it. The more formidable the remedies and other consequences of liability, the more race or sex conscious an employer necessarily becomes.

Again another factor was overlooked in this debate altogether. Not only had the Supreme Court already approved of both voluntarily negotiated and judicially imposed preferences (including quotas), but virtually every large company, particularly those that do business or are likely to do business with the federal or state government, have some form of "goals" for both hiring and promotion. This is undoubtedly why there was an effort by the Business Roundtable to find some kind of middle ground for legislation early in 1991.[45] Business seems to have come to terms with the voluntary affirmative action programs—first as a move to defend themselves against disparate impact employment discrimination litigation predicated upon statistics, then by virtue of the judicial approval given to such practices by the Supreme Court's rulings.

Third, some proponents of the legislation specifically disavowed goals and quotas altogether. This position was misleading and, insofar as it sought to characterize the position of civil rights organizations generally, was completely disingenuous.

The Debate over Damage Awards

For the most part, it appears that President Bush lost in this debate with Congress. But in principle he succeeded in imposing a cap for damage awards. Both *Patterson*—with the narrow scope of employment disputes it now made subject to compensatory and punitive damages—and the inadequacy of title VII dramatized the need for damages. Nonetheless, conservatives, led by the White House, insisted that damages be capped because of large damage awards fashioned in tort damage actions, wrongful discharge suits constituting part of this pattern. Bound up with this objection was the argument that big damage awards attract attorneys with contingency fee arrangements, and this phenomena creates excessive litigation, some of it frivolous.

The numbers in the cap for civil rights actions were negotiated upward in the final compromise agreed upon between the White House and Congress. It was the principle of the cap that Bush wanted, and here he prevailed, a tactic that was surely designed to divide black organizations from others, particularly representatives of the women's movement.

A fundamental dilemma confronting the proponents of reform in Congress and outside its halls was their desire to overturn *Patterson* and thus restore punitive and compensatory damages to the bulk of employment discrimination disputes arising under section 1981. But section 1981 did not apply to sex discrimination. This meant that such damages could be obtained for discrimination on the basis of race and not sex, a situation that existed prior to *Patterson* but with a difference that now was exacerbated in the public mind by the debate about the decision. All of this was fueled by an increased focus upon sexual harassment cases and a growing awareness that there was no remedy for harassment where the worker was not dismissed or denied a job opportunity such as a promotion.[46] Women's organizations maintained that it was unacceptable to cap damages for sex discrimination when they were not capped elsewhere. Civil rights proponents were unwilling to cap in the area of race. This was the cause of considerable tension and division which the Bush administration was able to effectively exploit. For instance, in May 1991 the Bush administration took the position that damages beyond back pay should be provided only in connection with sexual harassment cases.[47]

In the final analysis, of course, it appears that the Anita Hill–Clarence Thomas hearings may well have been the element that galvanized the

White House to accede to legislation.[48] The convincing nature of Professor Hill's testimony and Senator Danforth's loyal support of Justice Clarence Thomas may well have provided the basis for the Civil Rights Act of 1991.

There were other factors as well beyond the Hill-Thomas hearings and the 1989 decisions. A legislative review took place at a time when studies, particularly those of testers,[49] made clear the continued pervasive nature of racial discrimination in the United States. True, of all the "white" industrially advanced nations of the world, the United States is far more advanced in terms of a general race relations sophistication, with a changing as well as comprehensive antidiscrimination legislation, than countries such as Britain, Australia, New Zealand, and South Africa. But as the Los Angeles riots of 1992 made clear, occurring a full half-year after the statute's enactment, racism is deeply embedded in our country's fabric. Moreover the lack of substantial damage relief, a contrast that the employment discrimination cases have to the newly "judge-made" law of wrongful discharge, makes it particularly difficult for plaintiffs to obtain legal representation.[50]

This then was the backdrop for the legislation that was enacted. We now turn to the details of the Act itself.

The Civil Rights Act of 1991

The findings and purposes of the 1991 Act do not explicitly overrule *Wards Cove* but rather state that additional remedies are needed to deter both harassment and intentional discrimination, taking note of the fact that *Wards Cove* had "weakened the scope and effectiveness of federal civil rights protections" and that legislation therefore was necessary to provide "additional protections" against unlawful discrimination. The purpose is not only to provide additional remedies but to "codify" the concepts of "business necessity" and "job related" that had been set forth in *Griggs* and in other Supreme Court decisions before *Wards Cove*. The legislation also aims to confirm statutory authority, provide statutory guidelines for the adjudication of disparate impact suits, and to respond to other "recent" decisions of the Court by expanding the scope of relevant civil rights statutes to provide victims of discrimination with adequate protection. Thus for the first time employment discrimination legislation explicitly acknowledges and recognizes the disparate impact concept contained in *Griggs*.

The Scope of Protection

Section 101 of the Act clearly reverses *Patterson* by providing that postcontract formation racial discrimination, (including harassment) that occurs after formation of the employment contract is prohibited. States section 101(2)(b):

The term "make and enforce contracts" includes the making, performance, modification and termination of contracts and the enjoyment of all benefits, privileges, terms, and conditions of the contractual relationship.[51]

A Ceiling on Damages

Damages are provided for in connection with intentional discrimination under title VII of the Civil Rights Act of 1964 as well as under the Civil Rights Act of 1866. They are triggered by the existence of unlawful "intentional" discrimination, and specifically excluded from this definition are disparate impact cases and cases involving reasonable accommodations and good-faith efforts under the Americans with Disabilities Act of 1990 to which the damages provision is also made applicable. Compensatory and punitive damages are provided but only for private employers and not against government. The concept of front pay is somewhat ambiguous, since the statute excludes from the concept of compensatory damages back pay, interest on back pay, or "any other type of relief authorized under" the 1964 statute. Compensatory damages are to include "future pecuniary losses, emotional pain, suffering, inconvenience, mental anguish, loss of enjoyment of life, and other nonpecuniary losses," but to both punitive damages, applicable in intentional cases where defendant has engaged in discriminatory practices "with reckless indifference to the federally protected rights of an aggrieved individual," are subject to a cap. The cap is $50,000 for employers who employ more than 14 and fewer than 101 workers, $100,000 for more than 100 and fewer than 201, $200,000 for more than 200 and fewer than 501, and $300,000 for employers who have more than 500 employees. A jury trial may be obtained where a party seeks such damages. One of the many ironies of the 1991 statute is that in the 1950s and the 1960s the jury trial was thought to be an enemy of plaintiffs' lawyers, but today it is generally assumed that in employment discrimination and wrongful discharge cases, the contrary is true.

As noted above, the cap was enlarged considerably through the October 24 final compromise beyond the administration's earlier offers. Democrats, such as senator Edward Kennedy, have introduced legislation to reverse the cap, but thus far such provisions have not become law, let alone voted upon by Congress.

Burden of Proof: Establishing a Prima facie Case of Discrimination

The Civil Rights Act of 1991 establishes guidelines with regard to burden of proof in disparate impact cases. What is not generally recognized is that Congress, when it first enacted title VII of the Civil Rights Act of 1964, did not speak of disparate impact or disparate treatment cases. Critics of *Griggs* have pointed out correctly that the Court's decision was not based upon explicit congressional intent.[52] The 1972 amendments of course confirmed Congress' favorable view of *Griggs,* and whatever debate existed about the holding has been lost in the language of the 1991 Act, which provides some details about the applicable standards.

A complaining party may demonstrate that a particular employment practice "causes" a disparate impact. The word "cause" was placed in the statute at the insistence of the administration, particularly former Special Assistant John Sununu.[53] Many feared that the administration sought to reverse *Griggs* on the ground that disparate impact was really "caused" by societal conditions, such as poor education rather than the conduct of employers themselves. But legislative history, such as it is, seems to contradict this view or any argument to the effect that some concept of intentional discrimination has been introduced into disparate impact by virtue of such language. As Senator Danforth said in his interpretive memorandum: ". . . a plaintiff would not be required to prove that a disadvantaged background was not an alternative, possible hypothesis for the disparate impact."[54]

Senator Edward Kennedy has persuasively addressed the issue of causation, and none of the other legislators appear to rebut his view on this point, either through their speeches or memoranda. Said Senator Kennedy:

> In requiring that a complaining party demonstrate that a respondent uses an employment practice that "causes" a disparate impact, the substitute [the Danforth-Kennedy substitute] does not require a complaining party to prove that antecedent or underlying causes did not contribute to the disparate impact. Instead, the complaining party must show that the application of the

practice or process in question gave rise to a disparate impact. For example, as the Supreme Court discussed in McDonnell Douglas Corp. versus Green, if a complaining party demonstrates that the application of a written examination results in a disparate impact on blacks, the plaintiff is not required to demonstrate that differences in educational backgrounds or cultural differences did not cause the difference in performance between black and white test takers.[55]

The Employer's Rebuttal

If the complaining party demonstrates that the employment practice causes a disparate impact, the next step for the respondent is to demonstrate that the challenged practice is ". . . job related for the position in question and consistent with business necessity . . .."[56] On the one hand, the test is rigorous in the sense that it is the position "in question" that is at issue—the rigorous test previously employed in the Americans with Disabilities Act of 1990[57]—not the "job family" as Senator Danforth's bill proposed in June 1991.[58] What constitutes "business necessity" is left undefined, however, except that it is to encompass, as the purposes of the Act state, the law as it was prior to *Wards Cove*. Here both Senator Robert Dole and Senator Orin Hatch relied upon two considerations to argue for a narrow view of business necessity. First, while they cannot dispute the fact that the Act explicitly rejects the *Wards Cove* holding on burden of proof,[59] conservative opponents of the Act maintain that very little else has changed. Senator Hatch, for instance, has compared the earlier 1990 legislation, which provided that business necessity means "essential to effective job performance" and later substantial and demonstrable relationship to effective performance, to argue that a more relaxed standard is provided by the 1991 Act.[60] This argument is tied to the view that subsequent Supreme Court authority following *Griggs* is really identical to *Wards Cove*. Thus Senator Hatch refers to the fact that *Washington v. Davis*[61] provided for a "flexible concept" that meant more than actual job performance or job activities. The difficulty is that the language in the 1991 statute—namely the "position in question" and job related—seems to undercut this view. Moreover the preamble to the 1991 Act declares its opposition to the 1989 rulings, including *Wards Cove*.

Relatively more persuasive is Hatch's view about the 1979 *Beazer*[62] decision which upheld an employer exclusion of methadone use, despite its disproportionate impact upon blacks or Hispanics. Clearly, as Senator Hatch contends, *Beazer* applied a more relaxed standard than what the proponents of the 1991 Act wanted. But it may be that *Beazer* is best understood by the employer's very special concern with excluding drug addicts from the workplace, an objective that the 1991 legislation takes into account by protecting any rule "barring the employment of an individual who currently or knowingly possesses a controlled substance . . . ."[63] In other words, the argument that *Beazer* establishes a more relaxed standard is best understood in light of the idiosyncratic issue involved there and the attempts by Congress to take into account the concerns expressed by the Court in that case.

This should argue for the proposition that *Beazer* in no way redefined *Griggs* so as to constitute a separate standard to which the Civil Rights Act of 1991 must adhere. On the contrary, it can be argued effectively that the Act's treatment of drug addicts addresses that problem on its own merits and leaves *Griggs* intact to deal with a wide variety of other employment disputes.

Finally, Senator Hatch notes that Justice O'Connor's opinion in *Watson*, which also preceded *Wards Cove*, contained a similar standard. While this is an accurate conclusion, *Watson* applied only to subjective criteria. Moreover the views propounded in *Watson* were held only by four justices. When the vote of a fifth justice, Justice Kennedy, was obtained in *Wards Cove* (involving objective criteria as well as subjective criteria), Congress reacted by disapproving that decision. In essence *Watson* reflects nothing more than the *Wards Cove* decision, which was disapproved by the 1991 statute.

The 1991 act makes it clear that a complaining party may make out a disparate impact case even if job relatedness or business necessity is in evidence in some sense of the word, provided that the complaining party establishes that "an alternate employment practice will accomplish the same objectives and the respondent refuses to adopt that practice."[64]

Recall that an important part of *Wards Cove* required that a plaintiff establish that a particular practice caused the significantly statistical exclusion of minorities or women. A compromise was embodied in the 1991 Act to the effect that the complaining party continues to carry the burden of demonstrating that "each particular" challenged practice causes a disparate impact, except that if the complaining party can demonstrate to the court that the elements of a respondent's decision-making process "are not capable of separation for analysis, the decisionmaking process may be analyzed as one employment practice."[65]

Senator Kennedy stated that the demonstration that the elements of a decision-making process were not capable of separation could be made in three circumstances. First, a challenge is appropriate where the process constitutes a "black box mush," that is, where the employer subjectively combines several practices so as to make an independent separable evaluation impossible because no particular weight is assigned to any of the factors. Second, a challenge to one decision is appropriate where ". . . new information [is] reasonably available to the complaining party through discovery or otherwise" after diligent effort, from which the complaining party can identify the particular practice or practices that actually caused the disparate impact. For example, if a defendant has destroyed or failed to keep records showing which practices it relied upon and the plaintiff, after diligent effort, is unable to locate other evidence permitting the separation of the decisionmaking process into its component parts, the court should permit the plaintiff to challenge the decisionmaking process as a single process . . . .."[66]

Finally, Senator Kennedy alludes to the language to the final compromise of October 24, which states that where the process involves ". . . particular, functionally-integrated practices which are components of the same criterion, standard, method of administration, or test, such as the height and weight requirements designed to measure strength" in the Supreme Court's important *Dothard*[67] opinion which applied the *Griggs* analysis to height and weight requirements.

This analysis has drawn the fire of Senator Dole, for instance, who noted that Senator Danforth had begun to move away from a direct reversal of *Wards Cove* on this issue, namely that statistics were simply applied to all employment practices. First, Dole believes that the presence of "cause" in the disparate impact provisions are important in this respect in emphasizing that a particular practice must cause the exclusion. Second, language in the previous bill that a practice must cause a "significant part" of the disparate impact has been eliminated. As Senator Dole stated:

> . . . likewise, there is no language exonerating the complaining party of the obligation to demonstrate that a particular employment practice caused the disparity of he or she cannot do so from records or other information reasonably available from the respondent . . . it [be not capable of separation proviso] does not apply when the process of separation is merely difficult of may entail some expense—for example, where a multiple regression analysis might be necessary in order to separate the elements. It also does not apply in situations where records were not kept or have been destroyed. In such circumstances, the elements obviously are separable.[68]

Senator Kennedy's view seems better, notwithstanding the fact that legislative history is solely the two-page final compromise of October

24. The particularity issue, which is specially difficult for the plaintiff because of the employer's knowledge of the information and the financial burden and difficulty of the discovery process, is at the heart of the dispute. While Justice O'Connor articulated the concerns of both Senator Hatch and Senator Dole as well as President Bush in *Watson*, it seems that the hostility to the *Wards Cove* opinion, which propounded what is a practically insurmountable burden for plaintiffs, argues for an expansive and practical interpretation of the relevant language, as Senator Kennedy as argued.

Mixed Motives in Employment Disputes

The rest of the 1991 congressional reversals of the Court are relatively straightforward compared to the complications of *Wards Cove* and *Griggs*. The 1991 Act reverses *Price Waterhouse,* although Senator Danforth, responding to the administration's insistence, had given ground in the area of mixed motive as early as June 1991. The statute created unlawful practice liability where race, color, religion, sex, or national origin was "a motivating factor for any employment practice, even though other factors also motivated that practice." Where the employer would have taken the same action absent the impermissible motivating factor, the Court may still grant declaratory or injunctive relief (not including an order of hiring, admission, reinstatement, promotion, or the payment of damages). Attorney's fees and costs that are "demonstrated to be directly attributable" only to the pursuit of a claim establishing a motivating factor, can be obtained, the qualifying language having been placed in the statute at the insistence of the Bush administration. There is no reason why the same approach should not be adopted for discrimination under the NLRA—except that back pay should be available given the general unavailability of attorneys' fees.

The Civil Rights Act of 1991 also reverses *Martin v. Wilks*.[69] Anyone who has "actual notice" of a proposed judgment or order sufficient to apprise them that they might be adversely affected have an opportunity to present objections, but any person whose interests were adequately represented by another who had previously challenged the judgment or order on the same legal grounds and with a similar fact situation may not challenge such a practice.

Aramco is reversed in the sense that it now becomes unlawful to engage in practices prohibited by the statute ". . . in a workplace, in a foreign country if compliance was such with regard to a United States citizen unless compliance with the statute would cause the respondent to violate the law of the foreign in which the workplace is located." The test for regulation of the employer is whether an employer controls a corporation whose place of incorporation is a foreign country.

The Vexing Problem of Seniority Systems

Section 112 of the 1991 Act reverses *Lorance* by expanding the right to challenge discriminatory seniority systems beyond the time they are adopted[70] to the time ". . . when an individual becomes subject to the seniority system, or when a person aggrieved is injured by the application of the seniority system or provision of the system."[71] This disruption, Justice Scalia warned, was less important to Congress than was protection of the discrimination.

The Unsettled Issue of Affirmative Action

Section 116 states that nothing in the 1991 statute is to be construed to affect "court-ordered remedies, affirmative action, or conciliation agreements, that are in accordance with the law." Nonetheless, some legislators, notably Senator Dole, have mentioned that affirmative action is affected by the amendments made last year. This argument rests upon a novel interpretation of section 107 which, as mentioned earlier, was designed to create liability in mixed motive cases. Since the presence of race as a motivating factor triggers liability, it is said that race-conscious affirmative action plans could in some circumstances run afoul of these provisions. This interpretation seems to be inconsistent with the literal language of section 116, which states that these amendments do not affect affirmative action provided that they are in accordance with the law. It would seem implausible therefore for a statute that deliberately avoided any confrontation with the *Croson* decision to run afoul of this law under review predicted upon the amendments themselves.

The Court will continue to struggle with race preferences and race-conscious affirmative action programs and presumably will take an increasingly narrow view of that which is permissible. But it would be most difficult to read such limitations into the 1991 statute itself.

Alternative Dispute Resolution under the Act

President Bush has emphasized section 118 which provides for alternative means of dispute resolution and encourages them as a matter of statutory policy. The Supreme Court's 1991 ruling in *Gilmer*,[72] which held that an arbitration provision in an employment application bars a suit under the Age Discrimination Act of 1967,[73] has made this provision more significant. The Court appears to be more tolerant than in the past of agreements providing for arbitration that preclude employment discrimination suits. To date, most employers seem reluctant to part with managerial authority in job dismissal cases, even though doing so would protect them against more substantial statutory liability. Nonetheless, it is quite possible that an increasing number of employers will provide form arbitration agreements. The unresolved question is whether the Court in the future will provide safeguards in such arrangements so as to promote fairness and protection for the individual employee.[74]

Retroactivity of the 1991 Act

The most immediate issue of the 1991 Act is that of retroactivity. The Supreme Court's precedent is not clear, and federal appeals courts have been divided on this issue.[75] The question of legislative intent is complex. The statute simply states that its provisions take effect upon its enactment on November 21, 1991. Senators Danforth and Kennedy have split on this issue, while Senators Dole and Hatch, along with the Equal Employment Opportunity Commission appointees of the Bush administration, have predictably taken the view that the 1991 Act does not apply retroactively.

Arguing for some measure of retroactivity is the fact that Congress had taken particular care to make the provision relating to extraterritorial conduct prospective only as was the law with regard to the litigants in *Wards Cove*. Similarly the reversal of *Martin v. Wilks* does not apply to contempt judgments or orders that have already been entered, again providing for prospective application. This would indicate that these provisions are exceptions to the general rule that the statute should be retroactive. On the other hand, it could be contended that a general philosophy in favor of making the statute prospective was reflected in these provisions.

Complicating the debate about prospective application of the 1991 Act is the fact that some of the Supreme Court's decisions, particularly *Patterson* but to a lesser extent *Wards Cove*, provide a kind of window through which it may be said that the Court diminished or limited liability for a relatively brief period of time. Until 1989 it was generally assumed that racial discrimination cases could be maintained under the Civil Rights Act of 1866. *Patterson* represents a hiatus only for the relatively brief period from 1989 to 1991. This kind of argument can be made less persuasively in connection with *Wards Cove* where the *Watson* plurality opinion of Justice O'Connor presaged the majority opinion in *Wards Cove*.

The same cannot be said of most of the other cases where the Court's decision was truly a decision of first impression. The issue is one that has divided the Congress, notably Senator Kennedy and Senator Danforth, and it will surely divide the Supreme Court.

Conclusion

Although title VII of the Civil Rights of 1964 is in some ways settled law, much like *Brown v. Board of Education*[76] which preceded it by only a decade, the implementation of its goals, particularly through remedies, has proved to be vexatious and difficult. Resistance to the 1991 Act mirrors the racial tensions that continue to divide American society. As Andrew Hacker has written, though black access to a variety of jobs has improved considerably in the past twenty years, income and employment inequities have remained the same or worsened. Indeed, it is frequently argued that civil rights legislation cannot address the wide variety of difficult problems confronting black youth.[77]

My own sense is that Congress was correct in avoiding the quota or affirmative action issue. Clearly the political reality is that the matter cannot be addressed in a responsible fashion through the majoritarian political process.

It appears that the fallout of the Hill-Thomas hearings overcame the obduracy of the Bush administration and diminished their long-held fascination with the politics of racial divisiveness. Archivists can only tell us of the basic motivations behind this volte face of the White House.

The 1991 Act will be one of the most important in the workplace. It is for the most part unambitious. It simply restores much of the law to what it was. But it goes beyond the 1964 Act by firmly establishing the position that punitive and compensatory remedies for employment discrimination violations of the law are appropriate and that the unpredictability of large jury awards, particularly against smaller employers, makes it appropriate to cap damages. Thus was a compromise found between traditional labor law remedies and the wide open-ended approach to employment cases that has prevailed, for instance, in litigation about wrongful discharge and privacy disputes.

My judgment is that the Act represents an appropriate compromise. Women's organizations state the obvious in arguing that the same standard for damages must apply to both sex and race cases. One concern, given the problems of unlimited damages in tort actions and some of the evils associated with erratic jury behavior, is that all damages will become capped in the event of uniformity. Depending upon the level of the cap, this may not be an inappropriate response, though one of Congress' first steps in 1993 may be to uncap all damages.

Of course it is a Supreme Court well-populated by the appointees of Presidents Reagan and Bush that will ultimately interpret the Act and its provisions designed to reverse the 1989 Supreme Court ruling.[78] But the Congress has clearly expressed its deep dissatisfaction with the 1989 decisions, and the theories involved with *Griggs* and its progeny are now well and explicitly established in the Act. Justice Felix Frankfurter provided an expansive interpretation to a labor law question in which he had been deeply involved before being appointed for the bench,[79] and one cannot be certain how Justice Thomas would be affected by the debates that both surrounded his appointment and constitute part of the background and content of the Civil Rights Act of 1991. Although one cannot predict what the Court will do, and indeed what its composition will be, it would be difficult for the high tribunal to ignore these realities. Perhaps Justice David Souter, part of the new moderate block of the Court that appears to have emerged in 1992 on other issues such as abortion, will lead the way in accepting reversal of the 1989 rulings—though others of the new moderate block, such as Justices Kennedy and O'Connor are responsible for a number of the key rulings that led to the 1991 statute.

Accordingly the Civil Rights Act of 1991, like the 1972 amendments that preceded it, can take its place as an important piece of workplace regulation. It ratifies *Griggs* and the Court's previous interpretations of Reconstruction legislation and expands the law in the remedies arena. It may play a role in the eradication of workplace inequities— the societally corrosive "psychological pollution"[80] of discrimination— an initiative that is vital to a democratic society. The major effort must now be to utilize some of the remedial approaches in employment discrimination law in attempts to overhaul the National Labor Relations Act.

9 Conclusion

Labor law in the United States has changed considerably. In a sense the shift from the focus on collective labor law, which emerged during the Great Depression, is the antithesis of that which took place in Europe. For both the Continent and Britain, regulation of the individual relationship, most prominently in the job security area, took place in the 1960s. The difference of course was that union movements were more established there, and although a goodly number of them have declined like their American counterparts in the interim, they remain more firmly entrenched.

The National Labor Relations Act, once thought to be a model statute with international significance, is now in complete disarray. Indeed as is the case with much of the civil rights legislation of the 1960s, the statutory scheme seems wide open to abuse through delay, particularly the use of deleterious litigation tactics of delay, and ineffective remedies. The difference is that Supreme Court decisions that exacerbated the difficulties with title VII were reversed by Congress in 1991, in the form of the new Civil Rights Act which has at least provided the protection that existed at the end of the 1980s through more effective remedies. The latter point can be made with the same emphasis in connection with the new and important Americans with Disabilities Act of 1990, the most profound challenge to the employment-at-will doctrine aside from the wrongful discharge litigation itself.

Nothing is more important to the labor or employment law field than the changing nature of employment relationships. The rise of part-time and temporary workers, fueled by the two-income family which in turn is a mirror image of the growing economic inequities in our society of which the obscene executive-employee differential is one of the most important phenomena in the deteriorating status of workers. Part-time employees can be defined as "employees" under labor law,[1] but their recruitment is more difficult for the unions. Since the absence of fringe benefits for such workers provides the incentive to hire them, the Clinton administration's ability to resolve the health care issue could diminish the incentive and assist union organizing.

Similarly independent contractors, who are not employees within the meaning of the Act, make it more difficult for unions like the Teamsters in the trucking industry, once a union stronghold. Illegal aliens have undermined union organizational efforts in the service sector. Employees who are afraid to speak are not likely to become involved in a union campaign that could expose them to much worse than dismissal, the potential difficulty for the average worker who is a citizen or lawful resident alien. While illegal aliens have been regarded as employees within the meaning of the Act, the Court's *Yeshiva* decision provides an unduly cramped view of the employee universe, consigning individuals who are given authority and responsibility to the world of managerial employees who are excluded from labor law's protections.

The rise of wrongful discharge litigation and job security developments on both the legislative and collective bargaining front—providing firmer protection against economic dismissals, notification of plant closings, and severance pay retraining arrangements—are matters that will be important in a buoyant economy. Changes in labor mobility, and an environment in which workers must necessarily be assisted in fashioning their own rearrangements in the market, cannot be done by workers alone, particularly with the decline of their tra- ditional representatives, the unions. At either the federal or state level, comprehensive wrongful discharge legislation must be enacted (at the federal level perhaps as part of the National Labor Relations Act) so as to both provide equity and avoid wasteful litigation. Emerging inadequacies in the federal plant closing law (WARN) must be remedied.[2]

Unions look wobbly and obsolescent at this point. They are able to devise organizational theories at the Federation in Washington that frequently bear little resemblance to programs that are being put into effect at the union or local union level. The United Food and Commercial Workers Union has provided a number of examples of ways in which the movement can make use of the new individual employee legislation, and some that are not so new. Amendments that may be enacted to the Occupational Safety and Health Act of 1970 promise the same kind of openings. Unions must reorganize, perhaps go through a restructuring as fundamental and as dramatic as that of the Great

Depression out of which the industrial unions were born. It is important that unions focus and be organized around the new employers and employees and new industries presently unorganized, for the most part by default. But it is unlikely that unions will disappear.

The new work force affects every aspect of labor-management relations. Strikes are now declining because they are no longer credible weapons. Employers confronted with new competition are increasingly resorting to the permanent replacement tactic because there are so many workers outside the unionized sector who are anxious to avail themselves of the wages, benefits, and conditions of employment being offered to and rejected by the unions. This is why this area of law under the National Labor Relations Act has become so important and why the Workplace Fairness Act of 1992 was so critical to the labor movement. The 1992 strike by the United Auto Workers against Caterpillar Tractor Company failed because the ranks of the new work force are so filled with those impervious to the picket sign's call as a result of their own vulnerable employment situation. Again, unions have felt the effect of the rise in part-time employment.

The Packwood-Metzenbaum amendment, providing for a nonbinding form of arbitration or third-party intervention, has highlighted the need for more rational ways of resolving disputes. As a general proposition the amendment suffices as a step toward removing one of the main employer objections to unions. The strike-happy unions of employer propaganda sheets would be less tempted to strike.

Revision of the right-to-strike law must either lead the way to labor law reform or be made part of a broader labor law reform that encourages employee participation in strikes and other matters. Employee rights thus would be implemented in an industrial democracy.

Some, in the Federation and in scholarly circles, argue for works councils. For the reasons that I have stated, not the least of which is the exclusivity doctrine which makes the works councils poorly fitted to the American system, this would be counterproductive. Either unions would have to give up that which falls in the collective bargaining realm today, and I have argued that the duty to bargain is already too narrowly structured, or works councils would assume relatively unimportant functions. If works councils existed in the nonunion system, they could conceivably become rivals to the trade union movement, an undesirable effect given the problems with national labor policy that I have outlined in this book. On the other hand, if works councils are designed to coexist with the unions, this means a restructuring and further weakening of latter's role.

The best approach—and admittedly an imperfect one—is to permit employers to have greater latitude in devising systems that promote and provide for communication between employees and employers on their own without their condemnation under the anticompany union unfair labor practice provision of the Act. The reforms can be undertaken both through Board and judicial interpretations of the statute as well as congressional amendments to it. Because of the attention given to the Board's relatively unimportant *Electromation* decision, the ruling may facilitate this process.

Employee involvement and worker participation programs can be promoted inside organized relationships, along the lines of what has been done in the automobile industry during these past twenty years, and more recently at Saturn and NUMMI. But such reforms should not be undertaken independent of labor law amendments that give unions access to company property to engage in organizational campaigns and representative status even when majority rule is not provided—as well as other far-reaching reforms advocated in this book. Trust is the sine qua non for reform, and this means respect for one another by both labor and capital.

In a sense developments in the wrongful discharge and workers' participation areas have coalesced around one broad theme. The fallout from both wrongful discharge, accelerated by the passage of the Civil Rights Act of 1991 and the Americans with Disabilities Act of 1990, is that employers will attempt to limit their damage liability through special arrangements, including arbitration. While nonunion employers have been reluctant to concede arbitration, the advent of more legislation outside the wrongful discharge area, coupled with the Supreme Court's *Gilmer* decision which allows arbitration to preclude such litigation, may make employers rethink their approach. The natural instinct will be for the employers to both finance and control the new institutions. To some extent the few instances of wrongful discharge arbitration in the nonunion sector confirms that basic tendency.

What about the unions themselves? Whether unions can take advantage of the new institutions or be undermined by them is difficult to say. At this juncture labor cannot be optimistic about its abilities. A complete verdict cannot be rendered until unions make a greater effort than that which they have in the early 1990s. Whatever develops, some form of employee involvement will be required.

The direct election of new leadership in the International Brotherhood of Teamsters in 1991 is a welcome development for labor. The direct vote and the results obtained through this method inside the

The direct election of new leadership in the International Brotherhood of Teamsters in 1991 is a welcome development for labor. The direct vote and the results obtained through this method inside the Teamsters and other unions suggest that union democracy is more effective under such circumstances. The labor movement should promote this internal process. Indeed the Landrum-Griffin Act should be amended to mandate direct, secret ballot-box procedures at both national and local levels in all unions—just as strike ballots are appropriate as part of strike law reforms. Some unions, noted for their democratic procedures, like the United Auto Workers, will oppose such reforms because they depart from their own tried and trusted mechanisms. But labor should not oppose this change in the law—it is in the leadership's interest as well as in the interests of the rank and file.

Similarly, unions should not oppose labor law reform that reverses the U.S. Supreme Court's holding that employers cannot obtain injunctions against sympathy strike violations of no-strike clauses in collective bargaining agreements.[3] As in the case of the ballot-box measures such as those imposed upon the Teamsters by the U.S. Department of Justice, this reform can only help promote labor and counter antiunion employer propaganda about unsavory and irresponsible unions.

Can unions come back? Only a confluence of factors can bring this about. The first is a friendly administration, like Roosevelt's New Deal in the 1930s which provided help to the unions in the midst of the Great Depression, and legislation designed to promote both collective bargaining and industrial democracy.

The second is the unions themselves. They must rid themselves of their lethargy and radically restructure their organizations along the lines of early industrial unions. This of course is unlikely to happen unless some external force, economic or otherwise, prods them to do so. Economic history in this century suggests that the dramatic ebbs and flows of the economy coincide with the growth and decline of the unions.

A cautionary note is in order. While there is no evidence that unions can come back and reverse their downward movement in this century, it is quite possible that unorganized workers, less well protected than their union counterparts in difficult economic circumstances, may be storing away a resentment that will explode in coming years. This could be helpful to the unions but ultimately harmful to the development of mature relationships. Many years ago Lord Acton noted that unlimited power can produce a potential for overreaching.

A civilized society provides for a voice. The challenge of the 1990s, and into the next century, is to devise policies and laws through which workers and management, with mutual self-respect and civility, can institutionalize their inevitable interdependence.

Notes

Chapter 1

1. Kilborn, "Unions at a Loss to Reverse Failing Fortunes of Workers," *The New York Times*, September 2, 1991, p. 1, col. 1 at 10.

2. Greenhouse, "Attention America! Snap Out of It: The Core Problem Is Lack of Productivity Growth," *The New York Times*, February 9, 1992, Section 3, p. 1.

3. Uchitelle, "The Undercounted Unemployed," *The New York Times*, January 8, 1992 at C1, col. 3.

4. Silk, "Worrying over Weakened Unions," *The New York Times*, December 13, 1991, at C2, col. 1. This article is based upon *Remarks by The Honorable George P. Shultz NPA Gold Medal Award Dinner;* New York, October 9, 1991. In this speech, former Secretary of Labor and Secretary of State Shultz expressed concern over the demise of "checks and balances" in the workplace.

5. See, for example, L. Troy, "Will a More Interventionist N.L.R.A. Revive Organized Labor," 13 Harv. J. Law and Public Policy 583 (1990); Troy, Market Forces and Union Decline: A Response to Paul Weiler," 59 U. Chi. L. Rev. 681 (1992). This point has been made rather dramatically in connection with Troy's comparisons of the United States and Canada, developed in more detail in chapter 7. See L. Troy, "Convergence in International Unionism, etc. The Case of Canada and the U.S.A.," 30 Brit. J. Indus. Rel. 1 (1992).

6. See F. Swoboda, "AFL-CIO Is Shifting: Survey Shows Growing Strength among Government, Service Unions," *The Washington Post*, October 31, 1991, p. 7.

7. R. B. Freeman and R. G. Valletta, "The Effects of Public Sector Labor Laws on Labor Market Institutions and Outcomes," p. 81 in R. B. Freeman and C. Ichiniowski, "Introduction: The Public Sector Look at the American Unionism," pp. 3–4 in *When Public Sector Workers Unionize* (R. B. Freeman and C. Ichiniowski, eds. University of Chicago Press, 1988).

8. Troy, *supra* note 5.

9. M. Reder, "The Rise and Fall of Unions: The Public Sector and the Private," 2 J. Econ. Persp. 89 (1988).

10. See W. B. Gould, "Substitutes for the Strike Weapon: The Arbitration Process in the United States," 28 Arbitration J. 111 (1973).

11. See A. P. St. John, "Comment, Updating Arbitration," 26 Proc. Ann. M. National Academy of Arbitrators 73, 78 (1973); A. Anderson, "Lessons from Interest Arbitration in the Public Sector: The Experience of Four Jurisdictions," 27 Proc. Ann. M. National Academy of Arbitrators 59 (1974). See generally Irving Bernstein, *Arbitration of Wages,* (1950). Several states now mandate arbitration for the resolution of disputes involving public employees.

12. See P. Jacobs, "Old before Its Time: Collective Bargaining" at 28 (Center for the Study of Democratic Institutions, 1963); R. Taylor, "The Crisis of American Labour" (Fabian Research Series 346, 1980).

Chapter 2

1. W. Galenson, *The CIO Challenge to the AFL* (1960).

2. See L. H. Keyserling, "The Wagner Act: Its Origin and Current Significance," 29 Geo. Wash. L. Rev. 199 (1960).

3. See R. J. Barnet and R. E. Muller, *Global Reach: The Power of the Multinational Corporations* (1974).

4. R. Blanpain, *The OECD Guidelines for Multinational Enterprises and Labour Relations, 1976–1979* (1979); W. B. Gould, "Multinational Corporations and Multinational Unions: Myths, Reality and the Law," 10 International Lawyer 655 (1976).

5. See W. Baer, "North American Free Trade Foreign Affairs," p. 132 (1991); R. Flanagan, "NAFTA and Competitive Adjustments in North American Labor Market," (unpublished September 1992); G. C. Hufbauer and J. J. Schott, "North American Free Trade: Issues and Recommendations (Institute for International Economics, 1992). For a Canadian perspective, see M. Gunderson, "Labour Market Impacts of Free Trade" (report to the Fraser Institute), March 1992; M. Gunderson, "Wage and Employment Impacts Related to the North American Free Trade Agreement" (prepared for the Fraser Institute), October 1992.

6. However, see K. Bradsher, "Trade Pact Gains Discounted: Forecasters See Just a Short-Term Rise," *The New York Times,* February 22, 1993, p. C1, col. 5 (suggesting that some experts are now predicting that any net increase in job gains in the short term—estimated by some to be even as high as 175,000 by 1995—will evaporate after fifteen to twenty years).

7. Europe of course has its own difficulties with this issue; some of these are discussed in chapter 4. See "E.C. Attacks Job Transfers as 'Social Dumping,'" 142 L.R.R. 183 (1993); D. Goodhart, "Social Dumping: Hardly an Open and Shut Case," *The Financial Times* (London), February 4, 1993, p. 2.

8. D. G. Blancheflower and R. B. Freeman, "Going Different Ways: Unionism in the U.S. and Other Advanced O.E.C.D. Countries," Working Paper Series No. 3342, National Bureau of Economic Research (1990), p. 9.

9. This reflects the shift toward a service economy in the United States. See W. Serrin, "Unionism Struggles through Middle Age: The Shift to a Service Economy Hurts Organized Labor," *The New York Times*, October 27, 1985, p. 4E, col. 3.

10. S. Fraser, *Labor Will Rule: Sidney Hillman and the Rise of American Labor* (1991).

11. P. Drucker, "The Decline in Unionization," *Wall Street Journal*, October 5, 1977.

12. "AFL-CIO Seeks Ways to Seek Union Membership in U.S., The Bureau of National Affairs, Inc.," *Daily Labor Report*, November 15, 1991, p. 7.

13. L. Wolman, *Ebb and Flow in Trade Unionism*, at 17 (1936).

14. A. Rees, *The Economics of Trade Unions*, p. 13 (1989, 3d ed.)

15. *Id.*

16. "U.S. Living Standards Are Slipping and Were Even before Recession," *Wall Street Journal*, June 17, 1991, at p. A4.

17. I. Bernstein, *The Lean Years: A History of the American Worker 1920–1933*, p. 89.

18. *Id.* at 84.

19. See Miller, "Unions Curtail Organizing in High Tech," *Wall Street Journal*, November 13, 1984, p. 33.

20. See the very interesting discussion of this issue in M. Reder, "The Rise and Fall of Unions: The Public Sector and the Private," 2 J. Econ. Persp. 89 (1988).

21. Whether this pattern can be altered in the 1990s is problematical. Nasar, "Clinton Job Plan in Manufacturing Meets Step Decision," *The New York Times*, December 27, 1992, p. 1, col. 3.

22. R. Marshall, "The Future of Government in Industrial Relations," 31 Indus. Rel. 31 (1992); Uchitelle, "Stanching the Loss of Good Jobs," *The New York Times* (Business) January 31, 1993, p. 1; Kilborn, "Wanted: Those High Tech Jobs for Re-trained Workers," *The New York Times* (Week in Review) February 21, 1993, p. 1.

23. *Supra* note 17 at 87.

24. B. Bluestone and I. Bluestone, Negotiating the Future A Labor-Management Perspective on American Business (1992).

25. *Coppage v. Kansas*, 236 U.S. 1 (1915); *Adair v. U.S.*, 208 U.S. 161 (1908).

26. 254 U.S. 443(1921).

27. 257 U.S. 312(1921).

28. "Has Labor Law Failed?" Joint Hearings before the Subcommittee on Labor-Management Relations and the House Government Operations Committee Subcommittee on Manpower and Housing to Assess the Adequacy of Federal Labor Laws, including the NLRA, and of the NLRB and Federal Court labor enforcement policies, 98th Congress, 2nd Session 77-95(1984).

29. See, for instance, criticisms also made by R. Trumka, *Id.* at 3–27; B. Jolles and R. Pleasure, *Id.* at 128–181.

30. 395 U.S. 575 (1969). The leading case in the dispute about so-called minority union bargaining orders is *Conair Corp. V. NLRB*, 721 F.2d 1355 (D.C. Cir. 1983).

31. *NLRB v. First National Maintenance Corp.* 452 U.S. 666, 667–678, 4772 (1981); *Fibreboard Paper Products Corp. v. NLRB*, 379 U.S. 203 (1964); *Otis Elevator Co. (II)*, 1383–84 CCH NLRB 16, 181, 269 NLRB No 182(1984). See also W. B. Gould, "Fifty Years under the National Labor Relations Act: A Retrospective View, 37 Lab. L. J. 235, 238–239(1986).

32. 465 U.S. 513 (1984).

33. 11 U.S.C. §113. This provision modifies *Bildisco* and requires an employer filing for bankruptcy to "bargain" with the union over necessary modifications of the collective bargaining agreement before filing an application seeking rejection of the agreement. The court can only approve a rejection of the collective bargaining agreement if the union refuses to accept the employer's proposal without good cause and "the balance of the equities" favors rejection. If the court does not rule on the employers application within thirty days, the employer can terminate or alter the collective bargaining agreement.

34. *Pattern Makers League of North America v. NLRB*, 473 U.S. 95 (1985). *Pattern Makers*, which upheld the right of workers to resign from the union at any time, was predicated upon the anticlosed shop philosophy of the Taft-Hartley amendments and distinguished *NLRB v. Allis-Chalmers Mfg. Co.*, 388 U.S. 175 (1967) which has provided that unions have the authority to discipline strikebreakers.

35. W. B. Gould, "Solidarity Forever—or Hardly Ever; Union Discipline, Taft-Hartley, and the Right of Union Members to Resign," 66 Cornell L. Rev. 74–115(1980).

36. A thorough examination of the early history of the various National Labor Relations Boards is contained in J. Gross, *The Making of the National Labor Relations Board: A Study in Economics, Politics, and the Law*, vol. 1 (1933–1937) (1974); J. Gross, *The Reshaping of the National Labor Relations Board: National Labor Policy in Transition 1937–1974*, vol. 2 (1981). See also H. Millis and E. Brown, *From the Wagner Act to Taft-Hartley: A Study of National Labor Policy and Labor Relations* (1950).

37. 282 NLRB 1375 (1987) enforcement granted 843 F.2d 770 (3d Cir. 1988).

38. *Building and Construction Trades Council v. Associated Building and Contractors of Massachusetts/Rhode Island, Inc.* ___U.S.___ (March 8, 1993).

39. 111 S.Ct. 1539 (1991).

40. *Edward J. DeBartolo v. Florida Gulf Coast Bldg.*, 485 U.S. 568 (1988).

41. 291 NLRB No. 4 (1988).

42. 112 S.Ct. 841 (1992).

43. *Pruneyard Shopping Center v. Robins,* 447 U.S. 74 (1980).

44. *H.B. Zachry Co. v. NLRB,* 886 F.2d 70 (4th Cir. 1989). *Sunland Construction Co., Inc.* 309 NLRB No. 180 (1992); *Town & Country Electric, Inc.* 309 NLRB No. 181 (1992).

45. 303 NLRB No. 66 (1991).

46. *Id.* at pp. 17–18.

47. W. B. Gould, "The Burger Court and Labor Law: The Beat Goes On—Marcato," 24 San Diego L. Rev. 51 (1987).

48. See "G.A.O. Finds Greater Use of Contingent Workers, Warns of Strain on Income Protection System." *Daily Labor Report* No. 59 (BNA), March 27, 1991, at A-6.

49. *Sure-Tan v. NLRB,* 467 U.S.883 (1984). (However, the Court notwithstanding its declaration that illegal aliens are employees within the meaning of the Act, made the traditional remedies of reinstatement and back pay difficult, if not impossible, to obtain for unlawfully dismissed workers.

50. See Kilborn, "Law Fails to Stem Abuse of Migrants, U.S. Panel Reports," *The New York Times,* October 22, 1992, p. A10 (describing criticism of the Immigration Reform and Control Act of 1986 which has attempted to impose sanctions upon employers for employing illegal aliens).

51. 29 U.S.C. Sec.1053 (b) (2) (A).

52. Kilborn, "Part-time Hirings Bring Deep Changes in U.S. Workplaces," *The New York Times,* June 17, 1991, p. A1.

53. See Bob Baker, "Unions Try Bilingual Recruiting," *Los Angeles Times,* March 25, 1991, at A1, col. 1.

54. *Zamora v. Local 11, Hotel Employees and Restaurant Employees, International Union (AFL-CIO),* 817 F.2d 566 (9th Cir. 1987).

55. See *NLRB v. Aerospace Co.,* 416 U.S. 267 (1974); *NLRB v. Yeshiva University,* 444 U.S. 627 (1980). These cases stand for the proposition that managerial employees are excluded from the Act, notwithstanding the fact that the statute does not mention them explicitly. *Yeshiva* is particularly troublesome because it proceeds upon the assumption that the more autonomy is given the worker, the more likely it is that he or she will be excluded from any potential for representation because such employees are not "employees" within the meaning of the Act. The roots of this thinking—and the law's assumptions about the adversarial nature of the labor-management relationship—are to be found in Justice William Douglas' dissenting opinion in *Packard Motor Co. v NLRB* 330 U.S. 485, 496 (1947) which challenged the pre–Taft-Hartley view that there was no inherent conflict between supervisors and employees.

56. See, for instance, P. B. Voos, "Union Organizing Expenditures: Determinants and their Implications for Union Growth," 8 J. Lab. Res. 19 (1987). For a broader discussion of the wide variety of factors involved in union decline and the complexity bound up with such a discussion, see, for instance, generally *Employment Outlook*, ch. 4 *Trends and Trade Union Membership*, (Organization for Economic Cooperation and Development, July 1991), pp. 97–129; H. S. Farber "The Decline of Unionization in the United States: What Can Be Learned from Recent Experience?" 8 J. Lab. Econ. S75 (1990).

57. "Union Organizing: Avalanche of Union Petitions in Health Care Industry Has Not Occurred," Bureau of National Affairs, Inc., Daily Labor Report, October 9, 1991, p. 37.

58. See generally W. B. Gould, *Black Workers in White Unions* (1977) at 15, 305, 363, and 430.

59. See W. B. Gould, "The Supreme Court and Employment Discrimination law in 1989: Judicial Retreat and Congressional Response," 64 Tul. L. Rev. 1485–1519(1990); *Jett v. Dallas School District*, 49 U.S. 701(1989); *Independent Flight Attendants v. Zipes*, 491 U.S. 754(1989); *Patterson v. McLean Credit Union*, 491 U.S. 164(1989); *Lorance v. AT&T Technologies, Inc.* 430 U.S. 900(1989); *Martin v. Wilks*, 430 U.S. 755(1989); *Ward's Cove Packing Co. v. Antonio*, 490 U.S. 642 (1989); *Price Waterhouse v. Hopkins*, 430 U.S. 228(1989). (See chapter 9)

60. S. Estrich, "Sex at Work," 43 Stan. L. Rev. 813–861 (1991).

61. Civil Rights Act of 1991, 42 U.S.C. §1981A(b)(3).

62. *Board of Regents v. Roth*, 408 U.S. 564 (1972); *Perry v. Sindermann*, 408 U.S.593(1972); *Arnett v. Kennedy*, 416 U.S. 134(1974); *Goss v. Lopez* 419 U.S. 565(1975); *Bishop v. Wood*, 426 U.S. 341(1976); *Davis v. Scherer*, 468 U.S. 183 (1984); *Cleveland Board of Education v. Loudermill*, 470 U.S. 532 (1985).

63. 401 U.S. 424(1971).

64. *Dothard v. Rawlinson*, 433 U.S. 321 (1977).

65. *Wards Cove v. Antonio*, 490 U.S. 642 (1989).

66. The term "Bill of Rights" was used by Samuel Gompers to refer to section 20 of the Clayton Act, which provided that no restraining order or injunction should be granted by any U.S. court in "any case between an employer and employees, or between employers and employees, or between employees, or between persons employed and persons seeking employment, involving, or growing out of, a dispute concerning terms or conditions of employment" unless a showing of irreparable injury was made, and there was therefore no adequate remedy at law. For further discussion of this provision, see W. B. Gould, *A Primer on American Labor Law* 16–20 (2d ed. 1986).

67. See W. B. Gould, *Black Workers in White Unions: Job Discrimination in the United States* 66–98 (1977) (discussing discrimination and seniority in labor unions); see also W. B. Gould, "Seniority and the Black Worker; Reflections on Quarles (*Quarles v. Phillip Morris*) and Its Implications," 47 Tex. L. Rev.

1039(1969); W. B. Gould, "Employment, Security and Race: The Role of Title VII of the Civil Rights Act of 1964," 13 How. L. J. 1 (1967).

68. O. Kahn-Freund, *Labour and the Law*, pp. 17–18 (1983, 3d ed., Davies and Freedland).

69. *Ford Motor Co. v. EEOC*, 458 U.S. 219 (1982).

70. R. B. Freeman and J. L. Medoff, *What Do Unions Do?* 8–9 (1984).

71. For a discussion of the voice concept generally, see A. O. Hirschman, *Exit, Voice, and Loyalty* (1971).

72. Note 38 *supra*.

73. See D. P. Levin, "Nissan Workers in Tennessee Spurn Union's Bid," *The New York Times*, July 28, 1989, at A1, col. 1

74. *United Steelworkers v. American Manufacturing Co.*, 363 U.S. 564(1960); *United Steelworkers v. Warrior & Gulf Navigation Co.*, 363 U.S. 574 (1960); *United Steelworkers v. Enterprise Wheel and Car Corp.*, 363 U.S.593 (1960).

75. *NLRB v. Exchange Parts Co.*, 375 U.S. 405 (1964). See generally C. C. Jackson and J. S. Heller, "Promises and Grants of Benefits under the National Labor Relations Act," 131 U. Pa. L. Rev. 1 (1982).

76. Cf. L. Ulman, "Why Should Human Resource Managers Pay High Wages," 30 Brit. J. Ind. Rel. 177 (1992).

77. See P. Weiler, "Promises to Keep: Securing Workers' Rights to Self-Organization under the NLRA," 96 Harv. L. Rev. 1769 (1983).

78. R. Flanagan, *Labor Relations and the Litigation Explosion* (1987).

79. R. Flanagan, *Labor Relations and the Litigation Explosion* (1987).

80. D. G. Blancheflower and R. B. Freeman, *Going Different Ways: Unionism in the U.S. and Other Advanced O.E.C.D. Countries* (April 1990).

81. George Meany was asked by *Washington Post* reporters whether he had a "concern about organizing new workers." Meany replied, "To me it doesn't mean a thing . . . I have no real concern about it, because the history of the trade union movement has shown that when organized workers were a very, very tiny percentage of the work force, they still accomplished and did things that were very important for the entire work force." Quoted in W. B. Gould, *Black Workers in White Unions: Job Discrimination in the United States* 17(1977).

82. See generally L. Ulman and *The Rise of the National Trade Union* (2d ed.) (1966).

83. W. E. Forbath, "The Shaping of the American Labor Movement," 102 Harv. L. Rev. 1111 (1989).

84. W. E. Forbath, *Law and the Shaping of the American Labor Movement*, pp. 105–106 (1991). There are a number of important discussions of the historical development of modern trade unionism. See, for example, S. Webb and B.

Webb, *The History of Trade Unionism* (1894); S. Webb and B. Webb, *Industrial Democracy* (1897); S. Perlman, *The Theory of the Labor Movement* (1928); P. Taft, *The AF of L in the Time of Gompers* (1957); P. Taft, *The AF of L from the Death of Gompers to the Merger* (1959); S. Slichter, J. Healy, and E. R. Livernash, *The Impact of Collective Bargaining on Management* (1960); D. Bok and J. Dunlop, *Labor and the American Community* (1970).

85. Forbath, *supra* note 83 at 1113.

86. 45 Mass. (4 Mete.) 111, 38 Am.Dec. 346 (1842).

87. W. B. Gould, *A Primer on American Labor Law*, 3d ed. (1993).

88. *J.I. Case v. NLRB*, 321 U.S.322, 338 (1944).

89. Norris-LaGuardia Act, March 23, 1932, c.90, 47 Stat. 70(1932), 29 U.S.C. 101–15(1970).

90. W. B. Gould, *Black Workers in White Unions*, ch. 2, pp. 39–52.

91. See T. Geoghegan, *Which Side Are You On?: Trying to Be for Labor When It's Flat on Its Back* (1991).

92. See generally M. Goldfield, *The Decline of Organized Labor in the United States* (1987). There is a body of critical legal scholarship about labor law that focuses upon a reconceptualized approach to the union-management relationship and its role within our present system. See, for example, K. E. Klare, "Judicial Deradicalization of the Wagner Act and the Origins of Modern Legal Consciousness, 1837–1941," 62 Minn. L. Rev. 265 (1978); K. E. Klare, "The Labor-Management Cooperation Debate: A Workplace Democracy Perspective," 23 Harv. C.R.–C.L.L. Rev 39 (1988); K. Van Wezel Stone, "The Post-war Paradigm in American Labor Law," 90 Yale L. J. 1509 (1981); K. Van Wezel Stone, "Labor and the Corporate Structure: Changing Conceptions and Emerging Possibilities," 55 U. Chic. L. Rev. 73 (1988); J. Atleson, "Values and Assumptions in American Labor Law (1983); A. Hyde, "Democracy in Collective Bargaining," 93 Yale L. J. 793 (1984). For a more conservative school of thought, one can look to law and economics scholars. See generally "Symposium: The Conceptual Foundations of Labor Law," 51 U. Chic. L. Rev. 945–1230 and the numerous articles contained therein. See also G. Dau-Schmidt, "A Bargaining Analysis of American Labor Law and the Search for Bargaining Equity and Industrial Peace," 91 Mich. L. Rev. 491 (1992).

93. *NLRB v. Drivers, Chauffeurs, Helpers, Local Union No. 639 (Curtis Bros.)*, 362 U.S. 274(1960).

94. *U.S. v. Hutcheson*, 312 U.S. 219 (1941).

95. *Edward J. DeBartolo Corp. v. Florida Gulf Coast Bldg and Construction Trades Council* 485 U.S. 568(1988).

96. Industrial Relations Act 1971, c72.

97. O. Kahn-Freund, *Labour Law* 224.

98. See Weiler, *supra* note 77.

99. H. Phelps Brown, *The Origins of Trade Union Power*, p. 291 (1983).

100. W. B. Gould, "Taft-Hartley Comes to Great Britain: Observation on the Industrial Relations Act of 1971," 81 Yale L.J. 1921–1986(1972). See B. Weekes, M. Mellish, L. Dickens, and J. Lloyd, *Industrial Relations and the Limits of Law* (1975). See generally P. Fosh and C. Littler (eds.) *Industrial Relations and the Law in the 1980's* (1985); R. Lewis (ed.), *Labor Law in Britain* (1986).

101. K. Wedderburn, *The Worker and the Law* (3d ed.)

102. Employment Act of 1980, ch. 42; Employment Act of 1982, ch. 46; Employment Act of 1988, ch. 19; Employment Act of 1990, ch 38.

103. Royal Commission on Trade Unions and Employers Associations Report, Cmnd 3623, British Parliamentary Papers, (1967–68), vol. 32, p. 288.

104. See Gould, *supra* note 35, 67–98.

105. *United Auto Workers v. Johnson*, 111 S.Ct. 1196(1991).

106. See Employee Polygraph Protection Act of 1988, 29 U.S.C. 2001–2009. With certain exceptions, the Act prohibits employers from requesting or requiring that their employees take polygraph examinations. Moreover employers are forbidden by the Act from discharging employees because of their refusal to take such an examination or because of the results of a polygraph. Exempted from the Act are governmental employers and private employers who provide security for state interests.

107. Worker Adjustment and Retraining Notification Act (WARN), 29 U.S.C. §2101–04 (1988).

108. HR770, 101 st. Cong., 1st sess. (1989).

109. The good case for employee participation with union representation is made in B. Bluestone and I. Bluestone, *Negotiating the Future: A Labor Perspective on American Business* (1992).

110. *NLRB v. Cabot Carbon Co.*, 360 U.S. 203 (1958). An employee organization or employee committee that deals with management and has responsibility for handling grievances is a "labor organization" within the meaning of the Act.

111. The relevant section is 29 U.S.C. sec.158(a) (2) (1976). There is considerable debate about how expansively this provision should be interpreted. See *Chicago Rawhide Mfg. Co. v. NLRB*, 221 F.2d 165 (7th Cir. 1955); *NLRB v. Scott & Fetzer*, 691 F.2d 288 (6th Cir. 1982).

Chapter 3

1. 47 Cal 3d 654 (1988).

2. *Brock v. Roadway Express*, 481 U.S. 252, 264 (1987).

3. Rand Report, "Labor Market Responses to Employer Liability," (Rand Corp., 1991).

4. R. Flanagan, "Employment Arrangements in the United States," in J. Hartog and J. Theeuwes (eds.), *Comparative Labour Markets Institutions and Contracts* (Amsterdam: North Holland, 1992).

5. *Id.* at 36.

6. *Board of Regents v. Roth* 408 U.S. 564 (1972); *Perry v. Sindermann*, 408 U.S. 593(1972).

7. *Cleveland Board of Education v. Loudermill* 105 S.Ct. 1487, 1491(1985).

8. *Brock v. Roadway Express, supra* at 259.

9. See generally "Statutory Protection for Whistle Blowers Spreading in Public and Private Sectors," Government Employment Relations Reporter (BNA) No. 1105, at 405 (March 18, 1985). There are currently nineteen states with some form of statutory protection for whistle-blowers: California, Connecticut, Delaware, Illinois, Indiana, Iowa, Kansas, Louisiana, Maine, Maryland, Michigan, New Hampshire, New York, Oklahoma, Oregon, Rhode Island, Texas, Washington, and Wisconsin.

10. California Labor Code §1101.

11. California Labor Code §230 as amended by Ch. 161, L.1978.

12. Mont. Code Ann. 32.2.901 et. seq. (1987). Under the Montana statute, employees may not be discharged (1) without "good cause" (as defined therein), (2) in retaliation for refusing to violate or reporting a violation of public policy, or (3) in violation of the express provisions of an employer's own written personnel policy. Employees who are wrongfully discharged may be awarded lost wages and fringe benefits for up to four years, as well as punitive damages in cases where there is evidence of actual fraud or actual malice by the employer, 9A Lab. Rel. Rep. (BNA) 505: 521 (1989). The Supreme Court of Montana has upheld the constitutionality of this statute in which the 1987 Wrongful Discharge from Employment Act permits an award of punitive damages only in cases involving fraud or malice. Compensatory damages for emotional distress are eliminated all together. *Meech v. Hillhaven West, Inc.* 4 IER Cases 737 (Montana Supreme Court, 1989); *Allmaras v. Yellowstone Basin Properties* 6 IER Cases 939 (Montana Supreme Court, 1991).

13. Puerto Rico provides employees serving under an indefinite term contract who are discharged without good cause (1) any back pay due, (2) one month's salary, and (3) "an additional progressive indemnity equivalent to one full week for each year of service." P.R. Laws Ann. tit. 29, 185a (Supp. 1983). In the Virgin Islands the permissible grounds for discharge are described by a statute which also provides for reinstatement and back-pay remedies under certain circumstances. In addition an employee may bring an action for compensatory and punitive damages. (V.I. Code Ann., tit. 24, ch. 3, 76–79 (1986).

14. See Rand Report, *supra* note 3 at 14 & 17.

15. *Korb v. Raytheon Corporation,* 6 IER Cases 1002 (Mass. 1991).

16. *Foley v. Interactive Data Corp. supra* note 1 at 670.

17. *Id.* at 670 and 671.

18. *Belline v. K-Mart Corp.,* 6 IER Cases 1121 (7th Cir. 1991).

19. *Smith-Pfeffer v. the Superintendent of the Walter E. Fernald State School* 404 Mass. 145(1989).

20. *Smith v. Calgon Carbon Corporation,* 917 F.2d 1338 (3d Cir. 1990).

21. 52 Cal. 3d 65 (1990). See also *Gantt v. Sentry Insurance,* 7 IER Cases 289 (1992).

22. *Id.* at 542–543.

23. *Wagenseller v. Scottsdale Memorial Hospital,* 147 Ariz. 370, 710 P. 2d 1025 (1985).

24. *Slohoda v. United Parcel Service, Inc.,* 475 A.2d 618 (N.J. Super A.D. 1984).

25. *Novosel v. Nationwide Ins. Col* 721 F. 2d 894 (3d. Cir. 1983). However, Court of Appeals in *Smith v. Calgol Carbon Corporation* 5 IER Cases 1542 (3d CIR. 1990) has been cautious in defining what is within public interest for the purpose of the public policy exception doctrine. See generally S. Winterbauer, "Wrongful Discharge in Violation of Public Policy," 13 Indus. Rel. L.J. 306 (1991–92).

26. W. B. Gould, "Stemming the Wrongful Discharge Tide: A Case for Arbitration," 13 *Employee Relations L.J.* 404 at 412.

27. 47 Cal. 3d 654 (1988).

28. *Toussaint v. Blue Cross & Blue Shield,* 408 Mich. 579, 292 N.W. 2d 880 (1980).

29. *Rowe v. Montgomery Ward & Co.,* 6 IER Cases 1185 (Mich. 1991); *Dumas v. Auto Club Insurance Association,* 6 IER Cases 1249 (1991). Cf. *Elsey v. Burger King Corporation,* 5 IER Cases 1458 (6th Cir. 1990).

30. *Fogel v. Trustees of Iowa College,* 446 N.W. 2d 451 (1989).

31. *Arledge v. Stratmar Systems, Inc.,* 6 IER Cases 1593 (2d Cir. 1991).

32. Cf. *Shapiro v. Wells Fargo Realty Advisors,* 152 Cal. App. 3d 467, 199 Cal. Reporter. 613 (1984).

33. *Pagdilao v. Maui Intercontinental Hotel,* 703 F. Supp. 863(1988).

34. In *Courtney v. Canyon Television & Appliance, Inc.,* 5 IER Cases 431 (9th Cir. 1990), the court held a disclaimer to the effect that an employee handbook was not a contract was valid where ". . . the handbook did not reflect contractual terms of employment, and that, at any time, management could make unilateral changes in or exceptions to the policies. In addition Courtney has failed to present any evidence to suggest that Canyon's actions were not consistent with the disclaimer." But see *Seubert v. McKesson Corporation,* 5 IER

Cases 1396, 1398 (California Court of Appeals, First Appellate District Division Four, 1990). See also *Slivinsky v. Watkins-Johnson Company*, 221 Cal. App. 3d 799 (1990); *McLain v. Great American Insurance Companies*, 208 Cal. App. 3d 1476 (1979), two cases seemingly in conflict.

35. *McDonald v. Mobil Coal Producing, Inc.* 789 P.2d 866 (1990).

36. *Shoemaker v. Myers*, 6 IER Cases 1 (Cal. 1990). See also *Livitsanos v. Superior Court*, 7 Cal.Rptr.2d 80 (Cal. 1992).

37. See *Foley v. Interactive Data Corp.* 47 Cal. 3d 654 (1988) at 701 for series of cases pertaining to tort cause of action for bad faith discharge which were rejected by majority opinion.

38. *Koehner v. Superior Court* 181 Cal. App. 3d 1155, 226 Cal. Rptr. 820 (1986).

39. Id at 1169–71, 226 Cal. Rptr. at 828–29 (quoting *Seaman's Direct Buying Serv. v. Standard Oil Co.*, 36 Cal. 3d 752, 769–70, 686 P.2d 1158, 1172, 206 Cal. Rptr. 354, 365 (1984).

40. *Foley v. Interactive Data Corp.* 47 Cal. 3d 654 (1988) at 718.

41. *Livitsanos v. Superior Court of Los Angeles County supra* note 36.

42. See generally, Bierman and Youngblood, "Interpreting Montana's Pathbreaking Wrongful Discharge from Employment Act: Preliminary Analysis," 53 Montana L. Rev. 54 (1992).

43. *Culpepper v. Reynolds Metals Co.*, 421 F.2d 888 (5th Cir. 1970) at 891.

44. *Woolley v. Hoffman-La Roche, Inc.*, 491 A.2d 1257 (N.J. 1985) at 1266; modified, 499 A.2d 515 (N.J. 1985).

45. See the different points of view put forward about the reasons for the absence of explicit provisions in most employment relationships in M. G. Freed and D. D. Polsby, "Just Cause for Termination Rules and Economic Efficiency," 38 Emory L. J. 1097 (1989); Peck, "Penetrating Doctrinal Camouflage: Understanding the Development of the Law of Wrongful Discharge," 66 Washington L. Rev. 719 (1991).

46. *Ozark Trailers Inc.*, 161 NLRB 561 (1966) at 566.

47. See R. Flanagan, "Implicit Contracts, Explicit Contracts and Wages," 74 Am. Econ. Rev. 345, 349 (1984).

48. *Foley v. Interactive Data Corp.*, 47 Cal. 3d 654 (1988) at 701.

49. Books dealing with dismissal in Britain are L. Dickens, M. Jones, B. Weekes, and M. Hart, *Dismissed* (1985); L. Dickens, *A Study of Unfair Dismissal and the Industrial Tribunal System* (1985).

50. See Nova Scotia Reports, Management Reports (6701–6720); discipline and dismissal of employees (6571–6589); and Statutes of Quebec, ch. 27.

51. W. B. Gould, *Japan's Reshaping of American Labor Law* (1984). See also K. Sugeno, *Japanese Labor Law* (1992); Hanami, *Labor Relations in Japan* (1979).

52. Of course, as in Freed and Polsby, *supra,* cultural differences between the countries mean that the same result will not necessarily pertain to the United States. This point has been made in connection with the Industrial Relations Act of 1971 in Britain. Cf. W. B. Gould, "Taft-Hartley Comes to Great Britain: Observations on the Industrial Relations Act of 1971," 81 Yale L. J. 1421 (July 1972).

53. Of course for the affirmative action decisions that involve the Constitution as discussed in chapter 8, it would seek that a constitutional amendment, requiring more than Congress' *imprimatur* might be required.

54. *Pierce v. Ortho Pharmaceuticals, Corp.,* 84 N.J. 58, 66, 417 A.2d 505, 509 (1980).

55. *Gilmer v. Interstate/ Johnson Land Corp.,* 111 S.Ct. 1647 (1991).

56. *Alexander v. Gardner-Denver,* 415 U.S. 36, n. 21 (1974).

57. 415 U.S. 36 (1974).

58. *Murphy v. American Home Products,* 58 NY2d 293 (1983). Cf. *Wieder v. Skala* 8 IER Cases 132 (1992).

59. *Lingle v. Norge Division of Magic Chef, Inc.,* 486 U.S. 399 (1988).

60. The principle was established earlier in the employment discrimination context in *Alexander v. Gardner-Denver,* 415 U.S. 987 (1974).

61. *Gilmer v. Interstate/Johnson Lane Corp.,* 111 S.Ct. 1647 (1991).

62. *Clayton v. International Union, UAW,* 451 U.S. 679 (1981). The Court held by a 5–4 vote that an individual union member does not have an obligation to utilize internal union procedures and remedies prior to filing suit where the union cannot contractually reactivate the grievance in the event that it was in error in not processing it.

63. The Court established guidelines relating to the preemption of wrongful discharge cases involving employees covered by grievance-arbitration machinery in collective bargaining agreements in *Allis-Chalmers v. Lueck,* 471 U.S. 202 (1985).

64. 459 U.S. 212 (1983).

65. ILO Convention #158. See "Employment-at-Will: The French Experience as a Basis for Reform," 9 Comp. Lab. L. J. 294 (1988) (U.S. only nation whose government representative voted against Convention #158).

66. "Employee Relations Special Report: Three Years after Foley Decision, Its Effects Are Still Felt," the Bureau of National Affairs, Inc., January 27, 1992.

67. L. R. Littrell, "Grievance Procedure and Arbitration in a Nonunion Environment: The Northrop Experience," 34 Proc. Ann. M. Nat. Acad. Arbitrators 35 (1981); see also F. Foulkes, *Personnel Policies in Large Nonunion Companies* (1980).

68. California State Bar Committee Report, "To Strike A New Balance," in Labor & Employment Law News, Feb. 8, 1984 (on file at Stanford Law School Library).

69. *Id.* at 5.

70. *Tameny v. Atlantic Richfield Co.*, 27 Cal. 3d 167, 610 P.2d 1330, 164 Cal. Rptr. 839 (1980). In *Tameny*, an employee brought a wrongful discharge suit when he was fired for refusing to participate in an illegal scheme to fix gasoline retail prices.

71. See generally R. Heenan and T. Brady, "Arbitrating Dismissals of Nonunion Employees: A Canadian Perspective," 13 Comp. Lab. L. J. 273 (1992); G. Simmons, "Unjust Dismissal of Unorganized Workers in Canada," 20 Stanford J. Int. L. 473 (1984).

72. The landmark decisions relating to the law of arbitration are *United Steelworkers v. American Manufacturing Co.*, 363 U.S. 546 (1960); *United Steelworkers v. Warrior and Gulf Navigation Co.*, 363 U.S. 547 (1960); *United Steelworkers v. Enterprise Wheel and Car Corp.*, 363 U.S. 593 (1960). See also, William B. Gould IV, "Judicial Review of Labor Arbitration Awards—Thirty Years of the Steelworkers Trilogy: The Aftermath of AT&T and Misco," 64 *Notre Dame L. Rev.* 464 (1989). G. Minda, "Arbitration in the Post–Cold-War Era—Justice Kennedy's View of Postexpiration Arbitrability in *Litton Financial Printing Division v. NLRB*," 22 Stetson L. Rev. 83 (1992).

73. The leading case in processing grievances to arbitration is *Vaca v. Sipes*, 386 U.S. 171 (1967). This decision makes it clear that the union is not obliged to pursue a meritorious grievance to arbitration if it makes a good faith investigation and its decision-making process is not tainted by arbitrary, bad faith or discriminatory behavior.

74. *Supra*, note 59, 486 U.S. 399 (1988).

75. "Only the employee manual or booklet cases through which contracts are implied appear to have a wide sweep to them. The policies behind these manuals are the traditional response to union organizational drives. They are devised to assure workers that they already have everything that a union could promise, let alone deliver. But now the confluence of perceived union lethargy and exposure to wrongful discharge litigation have made numerous companies cast such strategy and discretion to the winds. Many employers, by their insistence that applicants, and sometimes existing employees, sign forms agreeing to be terminated at will or without just cause, are attempting to erode the contractual protection which the courts have extracted from such manuals." W. B. Gould, "The Idea of Jobs as Property in Contemporary America: the Legal and Collective Bargaining Framework," 4. B.Y.U. L. Rev. 885 (1986).

76. *Foley v. Interactive Data Corp.*, 47 Cal. 3d 654 (1988) at 659.

77. AFL-CIO Committee on the Evolution of Work, *The Changing Situation of Workers and Their Unions* (Feb. 1985) at 19.

78. *Id.* at 19.

79. See M. Gottesman, "Rethinking Labor Law Preemption: State Laws Facilitating Unionization, 7 Yale L. J. on Reg 355 (1990).

80. *New York Telephone Co. v. New York State Dept. of Labor* 440 U.S. 519(1979).

81. C. Summers, "Unions without Majority—A Black Hole?" 66 Chicago-Kent L. Rev. 531 (1990).

82. "Battered by hard times, broken strikes and waning support, some unions are using regulatory laws as strategic weapons in their organizing and bargaining battles. By exposing companies to penalties, damaging disclosures and expensive legal wrangles, they aim to win converts and pressure employers without risking strikes." R. Tomsho, "Union Search for Regulatory Violations to Pressure Firms and Win New Members," *Wall Street Journal*, February 28, 1992, p. B1; see also C. Heckscher, *The New Unionism* (1988); R. Edwards, *Contested Terrain: the Transformation of the Workplace in the Twentieth Century* (1979); J. Hoerr, *And the Wolf Finally Came* (1988).

83. Milbank, "Labor Broadens Its Appeal by Setting up Associations to Lobby and Offer Services," *Wall Street Journal*, January 13, 1993, p. B1.

84. *Supra* note 68 California Bar Committee Report, "To Strike a New Balance," in Labor & Employment Law News, Feb. 8, 1984 at 12. See generally, W. B. Gould, "Reflections on Wrongful Discharge Litigation and Legislation," in *Arbitration 1984: Absenteeism, Recent Law, Panels, and Published Decisions*, 32 (W. Gershenfeld, ed.) (Proc. 37th Ann. Mtg, National Academy of Arbitrators); W. B. Gould, "Protection from Wrongful Dismissal," *The New York Times*, October 22, 1984, p. A21, col. 3; J. Steiber and Murray, "Protection Against Unjust Discharge: The Need for a Federal Statute," 16 U. Mich. J. L. Ref. 319 (1983); Miller and Estes, "Recent Judicial Limitation on the Right of Discharge: A California Trilogy," 16 U.C. Davis L. Rev. 651 (1982); Note, "Implied Contract Rights to Job Security," 16 Stan. L. Rev. 335 (1974); C. Summers, "Individual Protection for Unjust Dismissal: Time for a Statute," 62 Va. L. Rev. 481, 485 (1976); Note, "Protecting at Will Employees against Wrongful Discharge: The Duty to Terminate Only in Good Faith," 93 Harv. L. Rev. 1816, 1824–26 (1980); M. Glendon and Lev, "Changes in the Bonding of the Employment Relationship: An Essay on the New Property," 20 B.C.L. Rev. 457 (1979); S. Mendelsohn, "Wrongful Termination Litigation in the United States and Its Effect on the Employment Relationship," (Employment and Social Policy, Occasional Papers, Paris, 1990). For an illustration of a radical attack upon the modern wrongful termination cases, see R. Epstein, "In Defense of The Contract at Will," 51 U. Chi. L. Rev. 947 (1984).

85. J. Bellace, "A Right of Fair Dismissal: Enforcing A Statutory Guarantee," 16 U. Mich. J. L. Reform 207 (1983).

86. National Uniform Law Commissioners Model Employment Termination Act §4(c).

87. *Supra* note 3 Rand Report, "Labor Market Responses to Employer Liability" (Rand Corp., 1991).

88. *Id.* at 46–47.

89. A thorough discussion of this matter is contained in M. West, "The Case against Reinstatement in Wrongful Discharge," 1988 *Illinois L. Rev.* 1.

90. *McHugh v Santa Monica Rent Control Board*, 49 Cal.3d 348 777 P.2d 91 (Cal. Sup. Ct. 1989).

91. See *Steelworkers of America v. Enterprise Wheel & Car Corp.*, 363 U.S. 593 (1960). See also Gould, *supra* note 51.

92. "The arbitral form provides considerably more expertise than does the existing system. Generally arbitrators, whether they are full- or part-time, specialize in labor cases and are expert not simply in fact-finding but also by virtue of an awareness of basic rules which apply to the employer-employee relationship. Judges, and more particularly juries, do not possess comparable expertise." California State Bar Committee Report, *To Strike a New Balance*, in "Labor and Employment Law News," February 8, 1984, at 8–9 (on file with author).

93. See *Christianburg Garment Co. v. EEOC*, 434 U.S. 412 (1978); *Texas State Teachers Association v. Garland Independent School District*, 109 S. Ct. 1486(1989); *Hanrahan v. Hampton*, 446 U.S. 754(1980); *Maher v. Gagne*, 448 U.S. 122(1980); *New York Gaslight Club, Inc. v. Carey*, 447 U.S. 54(1980); *Hewitt v. Helms*, 107 S. Ct. 2672(1987); *Roadway Express, Inc. v. Piper*, 447 U.S. 752(1980); *Blum v. Stenson*, 465 U.S. 886(1984); *Hensley v. Eckerhart*, 461 U.S. 424(1983); *Fitzpatrick v. Bitzer*, 427 U.S. 445 (1976); *Independent Federation of Flight Attendants v. Zipes*, 491 U.S. 754 (1989).

94. *First National Maintenance Corp. v. NLRB*, 452 U.S. 666 (1981). See generally W. B. Gould, "The Supreme Court's Labor and Employment Docket in the October 1980 Term: Justice Brennan's Term," 53 U. Colo. L. Rev. 1, 6–8 (1981).

95. *Howard Johnson Co. v. Detroit Local Joint Executive Board*, 417 U.S. 249 (1974).

96. *NLRB v. Bildisco and Bildisco*, 465 U.S. 513 (1984). Congress subsequently amended but did not repeal the relevant statute.

97. Agreement between New United Motor Manufacturing, Inc. (NUMMI) and the UAW, July 1, 1988, at 4.

98. Saturn Agreement, at 16–17.

99. Cooperation and employment security in Japan require a more complete discussion than is presented here. See generally W. B. Gould, *Japan's Reshaping of American Labor Law*, MIT Press (1984).

100. *Fort Halifax Packing Co., Inc. v. Coyne, Director, Bureau of Labor Standards of Maine* 482 U.S. 1 (1987).

101. "Plant Closings", 9A Indiv. Employ. Rts. Man. (BNA) §§507:101–119 (June 1992).
Connecticut: Connecticut enacted legislation in 1983 covering employers who have employed one hundred or more persons within a twelve-month period preceding a plant closing. The statute regulates both regulations and closings and provides that the existing group health insurance is to be paid for a period of 120 days or until such time as the employee becomes eligible for other group coverage. The statute does not cover employees who choose to be employed at the relocated facility. Any contractual provision that has been "arrived at

through a collective bargaining process that contains provisions requiring the employer to apply for the continuation of existing group health insurance" in a relocation or plant-closing context superseded the requirements of the statute.

Hawaii: In Hawaii employers employing fifty or more persons permanently shutting down all or part of their business at one establishment due to sale, transfer, merger, or takeover must give forty-five-day notices of such closure. In addition employers may be required to supplement unemployment compensation for four weeks for each affected employee to the employee's pretermination average weekly earnings. The statute also requires prompt payment of all outstanding wages, benefits, or other forms of compensation after the closure.

Maine: Enacted in 1980, the Maine legislation regulates both plant relocations and terminations. In a plant employing one hundred or more persons, if there is a removal of operations one hundred or miles from its original location, an employer is required to pay a worker one week's severance pay for each year of employment in that establishment. An employer is not liable for severance pay when the relocation or termination of a covered establishment is "necessitated by physical calamity," when the employee is covered by an "express contract" providing for severance pay, when the employee accepts employment at the new location, or when the employee has been employed less than three years. There is an obligation to notify the state sixty days prior to a relocation and to give comparable notice to employees and the municipality if the business is relocating outside the state.

Maryland: Maryland enacted legislation in 1985 covering employers with at least fifty employees. The statute covers so-called "reductions in operations" which include the "relocation of part of an employer's operation from one workplace to another existing or proposed site" and the "shutting down" of a workplace or portion of a workplace that reduces the number of employees by at least 25 percent or fifteen employees, whichever is greater, over a three-month period. "Whenever possible and appropriate" at least a ninety-day notice of the work force reduction shall be given. The Maryland Secretary of Employment and Training is to develop guidelines governing the "appropriate time" for advance notification. Guidelines are to be established to address the appropriate continuation of benefits such as health insurance, severance pay, and pension plans that an employer should provide for employees who will be terminated due to a "reduction in operations" or a "specific mechanism" that the employer can utilize by seeking assistance from the state's quick response program.

Massachusetts: Enacted in 1985, the Massachusetts legislation, like that of Maryland, provides for voluntary notification and requires the employer to "promptly report a plant closing to the state and it shall determine whether the closing will affect ninety percent of the employees through permanent separation within a six-month period prior to the plant closing." The Massachusetts law also established a reemployment assistance program to provide counseling, placement, training, and other services deemed necessary to employees terminated in plant closings that will lead to reemployment.

Michigan: Michigan enacted legislation in 1985 that addresses both relocation and plant closings. The Michigan Department of Labor is instructed to establish a program to assist in development of employee-owned corporations that "may operate when an establishment is closing or transferring operations resulting in a loss of jobs and when a request for assistance is made by an affected individual or group of individuals." The department is instructed to encourage employers considering a "decision to effect a closing or relocation of operations" to give notice of the decision "as early as possible" to both the department, employees, and any labor organization that represents the employees.

Minnesota: Minnesota enacted plant closure legislation in 1989. The provisions establish a government committee to collect information and to attempt to identify which industries and businesses are likely to experience large employment losses through plant closures or mass layoffs. The commissioner of the committee is directed to encourage employers likely to experience mass layoffs or closures to provide employees with as much advance notice of job loss as possible. Such notice is to be in addition to any notice required by the Workers Adjustment and Retraining Notification Act. The legislation also requires employers to report a substantial amount of information about the closure or layoffs. The legislation applies to permanent and temporary shutdowns and layoffs which affect 50 or more full-time employees (working 20 hours per week or more) or at least 500 employees who in aggregate work at least 20,000 hours per week, exclusive of overtime.

Oregon: Oregon enacted legislation in 1989. It essentially mirrors and incorporates the provisions of the WARN Act requiring additional notification of a closure to a state agency designed to assist workers, employers, and communities in coping with the effects of plant closings and mass layoffs.

South Carolina: The South Carolina statute imposes an obligation upon the employer to provide notice in the event that the employee is required to give notice that he or she will quit. Such employers

> . . . shall give notice to its employees of its proposal to quit work or shutdown by posting in each room of its building not less than two weeks in advance or the same length of time in advance as is required by it of its employees before they may quit work, a printed notice of such purpose, stating the date of the beginning of the shutdown or cessation from work and the approximate length of time the continuous shutdown is to continue.

These obligations are inapplicable where shutdown is cause by an unforeseen accident to machinery, or by "some act of God or the public enemy." An employer that fails to post the notice subjects itself to a fine not to exceed $5,000 and is liable to each of its employees for "such damages" as they may suffer by reason of failure to give the notice.

Tennessee: Tennessee has enacted plant closure legislation that only applies to employers employing 50–99 employees at a workplace. The legislation requires that employers notify the state at the time a closure or permanent work force reduction caused by either modernization or implementation of management policy affecting the employment of fifty or more employees in any three-month period.

Wisconsin: Wisconsin enacted legislation effective September 15, 1989, that requires a private or public employer with fifty or more employees to provide their workers and the local government with sixty-days' notice of a plant closing or layoff of at least 25 percent of their work force. Failure to notify allows affected employees to recover back pay and benefits. "The employee is now permitted . . . to recover pay for the days the employee would have worked during the 'recovery period' if the business closing or mass layoff had not occurred, or the value of any benefit the employee would have received under an employee benefit plan during the recovery period but did not receive because of the closing." The recovery period begins on the day of the layoff or closing. Additionally failure to notify carries a maximum fine of $500 per day. Proceeds from the fines will benefit the state's job retraining and job search program.

102. For example, Connecticut, Act FEPM 453:1225 (BNA); Cf. *United Auto Workers v. Johnson Controls,* 111 S.Ct. 1196 (1991).

103. States that have laws protecting women from pregnancy discrimination are Alaska, California, Colorado, Connecticut, District of Columbia, Florida, Hawaii, Illinois, Iowa, Kansas, Louisiana, Maine, Maryland, Missouri, New Hampshire, New York, Ohio, Oklahoma, Oregon, Pennsylvania, Puerto Rico, Virgin Islands, Washington, and Wisconsin.

104. See *Hill v. Florida Ex. Rel. Watson, Attorney General,* 325 U.S. 538 (1945).

105. See *International Union, United Automobile, Aircraft and Agricultural Implement Workers of America (UAW-CIO) v. Russell,* 356 U.S. 634 (1958); *United Construction Workers v. Laburnum Construction Corp.,* 347 U.S. 656 (1954).

106. 112 S.Ct 2374, 2388 (1992). Justice Anthony Kennedy filed a separate concurring opinion. Justice David Souter, joined by Justices Harry Blackmun, John Paul Stevens, and Clarence Thomas, dissented. Cf. *Martin v. OSHRC,* 111 S.Ct 1171 (1991).

107. W. B. Gould, "Plant-Closing Law May Herald Better Reforms," *San Jose Mercury News,* August 4, 1988.

108. W. B. Gould, "Job Security in the United States: Some Reflections on Unfair Dismissal and Plant Closure Legislation from a Comparative Perspective," 67 Nebraska L. Rev. 28 (1988).

Chapter 4

1. *International Herald Tribune,* April 19, 1989, at 13.

2. "Economic Justice for All: Pastoral Letter on Catholic Social Teaching and U.S. Economy," pp. 150–152 (1986).

3. K. Van Wezel Stone, "Labor Relations on the Airlines: The Railway Labor Act in the Era of Deregulation," 42 Stanford L. Rev. 1485 (1990).

4. J. Hoerr, "Is Teamwork a Management Plot? Mostly Not," *Business Week,* February 20, 1989, at 70.

5. Hoerr, "The Payoff From Teamwork," *Business Week*, July 10, 1989, at 56.

6. "The Spread of GM's Lordstown Syndrome," *Business Week* October 7, 1972, No. 2249 at 27; "Lordstown's Issues Linger at Norwood," *Business Week* July 29, 1972, No. 2238 at 46.

7. See H. Hansmann, "When Does Worker Ownership Work? ESOP's Law Firms, Codetermination, and Economic Democracy," 99 Yale L. J. 8 (1990). "Ten million U.S. workers, about one-fourth of all corporate employees, are enrolled in an ESOP, up from 3 million only a decade ago. By giving workers a stake in the company's success, enthusiasts say, the programs boost morale and productivity." See also "Labor's Voice on Corporate Boards: Good or Bad?" *Business Week*, May 7, 1984, at 151; J. Schwartz, "Giving Workers a Piece of the Action," *Newsweek*, April 17, 1989, at 45; B. Naylor, "Not Just a Capitalist Tool," *The Nation*, January 22, 1990, at 90; *Employee Ownership Report*, July/August 1990, vol. 10, no. 1,3,4.

8. IAM Policy on "Team Concept" Programs (undated and unpublished) at 1.

9. *Id*. at 3.

10. As Fraser commented, "At the second of the board meetings I attended, I advanced the idea that decisions involving the closing of a plant should take into account not only the economic reasons for the closing, but the effect that decision has on the lives of the workers and on the community in which they live. A resolution was passed at the next board meeting which adopted this philosophy, and a committee was established to deal with plant closings and to implement this resolution. I served on that committee, which was structured so that it would receive all information well in advance of any decision to close a plant. As soon as a study was undertaken, our committee had the information that plant closing was a possibility. At that point, we considered the study in terms of its economic factors and the impact the closings would have both on the workers and on the community. In a few situations, but certainly not in all, a further study was undertaken to determine if there was an alternative to closing a specific plant." Excerpt taken from "A Labor Director Looks at the Board." J. Rostow, *Teamwork Joint Labor Management Programs in America* (1986) at 64.

11. See B. Forst, "Labor Union Representation on Boards of Corporate Competitors: An Antitrust Analysis," 7 J. Corp. L. 422 (Spring 1982); D. Olson, "Union Experiences with Stock Plans, Cooperatives, and Board Membership," 5 Wis. L. Rev. 729 (1982).

12. T. Kochan, H. Katz, and R. McKersie, *The Transformation of American Industrial Relations* (1986) at 190 and 191.

13. "... a union may make wage agreements with a multi-employer bargaining unit and may in pursuance of its own union interests seek to obtain the same terms from other employers. No case under the antitrust laws could be made out on evidence limited to such union behavior.... [A] union forfeits its exemption from the antitrust laws when it is clearly shown that it has agreed

with one set of employers to impose a certain wage scale on other bargaining units. One group of employers may not conspire to eliminate competitors from the industry and the union is liable with the employers if it becomes a party to the conspiracy. This is true even though the union's part in the scheme is an undertaking to secure the same wages, hours or other conditions of employment from the remaining employers in the industry. . . . This Court has recognized that a legitimate aim of any national labor organization is to obtain uniformity of labor standards and that a consequence of such union activity may be to eliminate competition based on differences in such standards. *Apex Hosiery Co. v. Leader,* 310 U.S. 469, 503. But there is nothing in the labor policy indicating that the union and the employers in one bargaining unit are free to bargain about the wages, hours, and working conditions of other bargaining units or to attempt to settle these matters for the entire industry. On the contrary, the duty to bargain unit by unit leads to a quite different conclusion. The union's obligation to its members would seem best served if the union retained the ability to respond to each bargaining situation as the individual circumstances might warrant, without being straitjacketed by some prior agreement with the favored employers." Opinion of Justice White in *Mine Workers v Pennington,* 381 U.S. 657 at 665–666. See also *Meat Cutters v. Jewel Tea,* 381 U.S. 676.

14. "Both free trade unions and elected works councils were destroyed by the Nazis, but after 1945, the institutions for worker representation were reconstructed in the general pattern developed during the Weimar Republic. Elected works councils were reestablished as part of the shop constitution, separate from the trade unions which determined wages and hours under regional collective agreements." In C. Summers, *Workers Participation in the U.S. and West Germany: A Comparative Study from an American Perspective,* 28 Am. J. Comp. L. 367 (1980). See also C. Summers, *An American Perspective of the German Model of Worker Participation,* 8 Comp. Lab. L. 333 (Summer 1987).

15. "Section 8(a)(5) of the National Labor Relations Act, as amended, makes it an unfair labor practice for an employer to refuse to bargain collectively with the representatives of his employees. Collective bargaining is defined in 8(d) as the performance of the mutual obligation of the employer and the representative of the employees to meet at reasonable times and confer in good faith with respect to wages, hours, and other terms and conditions of employment. The question posed is whether the particular decision sought to be made unilaterally by the employer in this case is a subject of mandatory collective bargaining within the statutory phrase terms and conditions of employment. That is all the Court decides. The Court most assuredly does not decide that every managerial decision which necessarily terminates an individual's employment is subject to the duty to bargain. Nor does the Court decide that subcontracting decisions are as a general matter subject to that duty. The Court holds no more than that this employer's decision to subcontract this work, involving the replacement of employees in the existing bargaining unit with those of an independent contractor to do the same work under similar conditions of employment, is subject to the duty to bargain collectively. Within the

narrow limitations implicit in specific facts of this case, I agree with the Court's decisions." Concurring opinion of J. Stewart, *Fibreboard Paper Products Corp. v. NLRB*, 379 U.S. 203(1964) at 218. See also *First National Maintenance Corp. v. NLRB*, 452 U.S. 666 (1981), where majority opinion concurred with the opinion of J. Stewart.

16. Hall, "Behind the European Works Councils Directive: The European Commission's Legislative Strategy," 30 Brit. J. Ind. Rel. 547 (1992).

17. W. B Gould, *Japan's Reshaping of American Labor Law* (1984) at 100 and 101.

18. *Id.*

19. *NLRB v. Insurance Agents' International Union*, 361 U.S. 477 (1960).

20. *Id.* at 488–89.

21. T. Kochan, H. Katz, and R. McKersie, *The Transformation of American Industrial Relations* (1986) at 88 and 89.

22. Memorandum of Agreement between Saturn Corporation and General Motors, July 1985, at 16.

23. P. Adler, "Time and Motion Regained," Harv. Bus. Rev., January–February 1993, pp. 97–103.

24. M. Parker and J. Slaughter, *Choosing Sides: Unions and the Team Concept* (1988).

25. Memorandum at Saturn Agreement, at 7.

26. *Id.* at 5.

27. D. Levine, "Public Policy Implications of Imperfections in the Market for Worker Participation," 103 Econ. Indus. Dem. 183, 187 (1992).

28. Agreement between New United Motor Manufacturing, Inc. (NUMMI) and the UAW, July 1, 1988 at 4. Another good discussion of the relationship between UAW and NUMMI is to be found in Paul Adler, "The 'Learning Bureaucracy': New United Motor Manufacturing Inc." in B. Staw and L. Cummings (Edts.) Research in Organizational Behavior (Jai Press, Greenwich, CT, 1992).

29. Saturn Agreement, at 16–17.

30. W. B. Gould, "Watch for a Historic Auto Pact," *The New York Times*, July 27, 1987, at 19, col. 1; D. Levin, "Auto Union to Seek Job Guarantees," *The New York Times*, May 22, 1990, at A8.

31. *General Motors Corp., Saturn Corp. and UAW,* 122 LRRM 1187 (1986) Advice Memorandum of NLRB General Counsel.

32. Peter Drucker, "Where Union Flexibility's Now a Must," *Wall Street Journal*, September 23, 1983, p. 26. Cf. M. Weitzman, *The Share Economy* (1982).

33. M. Weitzman and D. Kruse, *Profit Sharing and Productivity,* (The Brookings Institution, 1989); D. Mitchell, D. Lewin, and E. Lawler, *Alternative Pay Systems, Firm Performance and Productivity,* (Brookings Institution, 1989).

34. M. Conte and J. Svejnar, *The Performance Effects of Employee Ownership Plans,* (Brookings Institution, 1989).

35. H. Hansmann, "When Does Worker Ownership Work? ESOP's, Law Firms, Codetermination, and Economic Democracy," 99 Yale L. J. 8 (1990) at 1773.

36. *Id.* at 1798.

37. *Id.* at 1797 and 1798.

38. M. Conte and J. Svejnar *Annual report of the Joint Economic Committee,* Washington, D.C.: U.S.G.P.O., 1976.

39. D. Levine and L. D'Andrea Tyson, "Participation, Productivity and the Firm's Environment," in A. Blinder (ed.), *Paying for Productivity* (1990) at 189–190.

40. *Id.* at 209–210.

41. See R. Lester, *As Unions Mature—An Analysis of the Evolution of American Unionism,* p. 37 (1958).

42. U.S. NLRB, *Legislative History of the National Labor Relations Act of 1935,* vol 1, p. 15 (Washington, 1949), 78 Cong. Rec. 3443 (March 1, 1934).

43. T. Kochan, H. Katz, and R. McKersie, *The Transformation of American Industrial Relations* (Basic Books, Inc. 1986).

44. Section 8(a)(2) provides that, "[i]t shall be unfair labor practice for an employer . . . to dominate or interfere with the formation or administration of any labor organization or contribute financial or other support to it: *Provided,* That subject to rules and regulations made and published by the Board pursuant to section 156 of this title, an employer shall not be prohibited from permitting employees to confer with him during working hours without loss of time or pay." 29 U.S.C. 158(a)(2) (1976). I have proposed other reforms to the NRLA that should be made in the interest of fostering cooperation between labor and management in the administrative process and remedy areas in W. B. Gould, *Japan's Reshaping of American Labor Law* (1984).

45. U.S. Dept. of Labor, Bureau of Labor-Management Relations and Cooperative Programs, "U.S. Labor Law and the Future of Labor-Management Cooperation," 16–22 (BLMR 104, 1986). That report, and other writings, e.g., Gould, "Fifty Years under the National Labor Relations Act: A Retrospective View," 37 Labor L. J. 235 (1986), discuss the problems posed by such programs for the NLRA. For analysis by the Board and the courts of some of the section 8(a)(2) issues, see generally *Sparks Nugget, Inc.,* 230 NLRB No. 43 (1977) (management created employee-employer grievance council is not violative of section 8(a)(2), since it is not a labor organization within the meaning of section 2(s) because council serves an adjudicatory function and therefore does not deal with employer); *Mercy-Memorial Hospital Corp.,* 231 NLRB No. 182 (1977) (employee-employer grievance committee not a labor organization dealing with employer since committee established to give employees a voice in resolving grievances); *General Foods Corp.,* 231 NLRB No. 122 (1977) (job en-

richment programs which are not established to "head off organizing drives by outside unions or in response to any employee unrest" are not violative of section 8(a)(2)); *NLRB v. Streamway Division of the Scott Fetzer Co.*, 691 F. 2d 288 (6th Cir. 1982) (representation committee created by employer is not a labor organization since it did not deal with employer but was a way to determine employee attitudes regarding working conditions); *Hertzka & Knowles v. NLRB*, 503 F.2d 625 (9th Cir. 1974) (objectivity of NLRA to facilitate employee free choice and self-organization requires balancing of concerns of employer domination with employee desires for employee-employer cooperation).

46. *NLRB v. Cabot Carbon*, 360 U.S. 203 (1959).

47. *General Foods Corp.*, 321 NLRB 1223 (1977).

48. *NLRB v. Streamway Division of Scott and Fetzer*, 691 F.2d 288 (6th Cir. 1982); *Airstream v. NLRB*, 877 F.2d 1291 (6th Cir. 1989).

49. 3030 NLRB No. 163 (1992).

50. *Id.* at p. 9.

51. *Chicago Rawhide Mfg. v. NLRB*, 221 F.2d 165 (7th Cir. 1955).

52. *NLRB v. Walton Mfg. Co.*, 289 F.2d 177, 182 (5th Cir. 1961) (Wisdom, dissenting).

53. The problem and cases are discussed in such articles as Stone, "Labor and the Corporate Structure," 55 Univ. Chi. L. Rev. 73 (1988) and Harper, "Reconciling Collective Bargaining With Employee Supervision of Management," 137 U. Pa. L. Rev. 1 (1988).

54. Note, "The NLRB and Supervisory Status: An Explanation of Inconsistent Results, 94 Harv. L. Rev 1713 (1981).

55. W. B. Gould, *Japan's Reshaping of American Labor Law* (1984).

56. *NLRB v. Yeshiva Univ.*, 444 U.S. 672 (1980).

57. W. B. Gould, "The Supreme Court and Labor Law: The October 1978 Term," 21 Arizona L. Rev. 621 (1979); Rabban, "Distinguishing Excluded Managers from Covered Professionals under the NLRA," 89 Columbia L. Rev. 1775 (1989); Rabban, "Can American Labor Law Accommodate Collective Bargaining by Professional Employees?" 99 Yale L. J. 689 (1990).

58. See P. Bassett, *Strike Free: New Industrial Relations in Britain* (1986).

59. 452 U.S. 666 (1981).

60. Case 7-CB-4815, Advice Memorandum of General Counsel, October 22, 1980. Other cases dealing with issues of this kind are cited in the memorandum. Generally they arise under section 8(a)(2) of the NLRA.

61. Report of the Committee of Inquiry on Industrial Democracy (Dept. of Trade, 1977, HMSO), at 53.

62. See Milbank, "USW Relaxes Its Hard Stance on Labor Pacts," *Wall Street Journal*, January 6, 1993, p. A3.

Chapter 5

1. See P. C. Weiler, *Governing the Workplace: The Future of Labor and Employment Law* (1990).

2. See R. J. LaLonde and B. D. Meltzer, "Hard Times for Unions: Another Look at the Significance of Employer Illegalities," 58 Univ. of Chi. L. Rev. 953 (1991), and P. C. Weiler, "Hard Times for Unions: Challenging Times for Scholars," 58 U. Chi. L. Rev. 1015 (1991).

3. P. C. Weiler, "Promises to Keep: Securing Workers' Rights to Self-Organization under the NLRA," 96 Harv. L. Rev. 1769 (1983) and "Striking a New Balance: Freedom of Contract and the Prospects for Union Representation," 98 Harv. L. Rev. 351 (1984).

4. Lalond and Meltzer, *supra* note 2.

5. Cf. J. G. Getman, S. B. Goldberg, and J. B. Herman, *Union Representation Elections: Law and Reality* (1976).

6. *United Dairy Farmers Cooperative Association v. NLRB*, 633 F.2d 1054, 1067 (3d Cir. 1980).

7. See "AFL-CIO Chief Calls Labor Law a Dead Letter," *Wall Street Journal*, August 16, 1984, at 8, col. 2. See also W. B. Gould, "Mistaken Opposition to the NLRB," *The New York Times*, June 20, 1985, sec. A, p. 27, col. 2.

8. See *Houston Building and Construction Trades Council*, 136 NLRB 321 (1962). See also *Barker Brothers v. NLRB*, 328 F.2d 431 (9th Cir. 1964).

9. R. C. James and E. James, *Hoffa and the Teamsters: A Study of Union Power* (1965).

10. *San Diego Building Trades Council v. Garman*, 359 U.S. 236 (1959).

11. See *Hudgens v. NLRB*, 424 U.S. 507 (1976), *rev'd, Food Employees v. Logan Valley Plaza*, 391 U.S. 308 (1968). See also *Teamsters v. Vogt*, 354 U.S. 284 (1957) (prohibition on picketing directed toward achieving "union shop" in violation of state law).

12. *Local 24, International Brotherhood of Teamsters v. Oliver*, 358 U.S. 283 (1958).

13. See *Maryland v. Wirtz*, 392 U.S. 183 (1968), *overruled, National League of Cities v. Usery*, 426 U.S. 833 (1976).

14. *Garcia v. San Antonio Metropolitan Transit Authority*, 469 U.S. 530 (1985), (overruling *National League of Cities*, *supra* note 13)

15. See *Vegelahn v. Gunter*, 167 Mass. 92, 44 N.E. 1077 (1896).

16. *Bakery Drivers Local v. Wohl*, 315 U.S. 769, 775–777 (1942) (Douglas, J. concurring).

17. A. Cox, *Law and the National Labor Policy* 43–44 (1960).

18. 351 U.S. 105 (1956).

19. *Lechmere v. NLRB*, 112 S.Ct 841 (1992). Contra, D. Bok, "Reflection on the Distinctive Character of American Labor Laws," 84 Harv. L. Rev. 1394 (1971); W. B. Gould, "The Question of Union Activity on Company Property," 18 Vanderbilt L. Rev. 73 (1964); W. B. Gould, "Union Organizational Rights and the Concept of Quasi-public Property," 49 Minn. L. Rev. 505 (1965).

20. *Sears, Roebuck & Co. v. San Diego County District Council of Carpenters*, 436 U.S. 180, 204–208 (1978).

21. See *Livingston Shirt*, 107 NLRB 400 (1953). In his dissent Board Member Abe Murdock wrote: "In contrast to the means open to the organizing employees, the employer speech on company time and property has the tremendous advantage of securing the individual attention of all employees— interested, passive, and antagonistic. A carefully planned, extensive and well-organized speech, under these circumstances, is hardly on a par with the limited time, argument, and opportunity open to the union." *Id.* at 407.

22. See Trade Union Act, RSNS 1989 c. 475, section 25(3).

23. "National Labor Relations Board: Action Needed to Improve Case-Processing Time at Headquarters," United States General Accounting Office, Report to Congressional Headquarters (January 1991).

24. Employees are presumed to have designated the union as their bargaining agent where the authorization card so states unless oral misrepresentations clearly cancel the language on the card. A single-purpose authorization card remains valid for bargaining order purposes even if the solicitor orally represents that the purpose of the card is to obtain an election. The Board has taken the position that ambiguous cards that state that the union will represent the signer in "collective bargaining" and that the "purpose" of the card is to obtain an election will not establish a basis for a *Gissel* bargaining order. *Nissan Research and Development, Inc.*, 296 NLRB NO. 80 (1989), Member Craycroft dissenting at slip op. p. 9. But some of the circuits have accepted dual purpose cards in support of a bargaining order. See *NLRB v. Fosdal Electric*, 367 F.2d 784 (7th Cir. 1966); *Auto Workers v. NLRB*, 366 F.2d 702 (D.C. Cir. 1966); *NLRB v. C.J. Glasgow Co.*, 356 F.2d 476 (7th Cir. 1966); *Sahara Datsun v. NRLB*, 811 F.2d 317 (9th Cir. 1987), cert. denied 454 U.S. 835 (1987); *NLRB v. Anchorage Times Publishing Co.*, 637 F.2d 1359 (9th Cir. 1981).

25. Although the issue has not been decided by the Supreme Court, two courts of appeals have held that recognition may be imposed upon an employer where the union convincingly alleges that but for the employer's unfair labor practices, it would have obtained a majority of cards or that there is a reasonable likelihood that the union would have obtained majority status. See *United Dairy Farmers Cooperative Ass'n v. NLRB*, 633 F.2d 1054 (3d Cir. 1980) and *J.P. Stevens & Co., Gulutan Div. v. NLRB*, 441 F.2d 514 (5th Cir. 1971).

26. See *American Federation of Labor v. NLRB*, 308 U.S. 401 (1940).

27. W. B. Gould, *Japan's Reshaping of American Labor Law* (1984).

28. *Phelps Dodge Corp. v. NLRB*, 313 U.S. 177 (1941).

29. W. B. Gould, "Prospects for Labor Law Reform: The Unions and Carter," *The Nation,* April 16, 1977, pp. 466, 467.

30. See *Republic Steel Corp. v. NLRB,* 311 U.S. 7 (1940); *H.K. Porter Co. v. NLRB,* 397 U.S. 99 (1970); *Local 60, United Brotherhood of Carpenters v. NLRB,* 365 U.S. 651 (1966); *NRLB v. Seven-Up Bottling,* 344 U.S. 344 (1953). See also *NLRB v. J.S. Alberici Const. Co.,* 591 F.2d 463 (8th Cir. 1979); and *Packing House and Industrial Services v. NLRB,* 590 F.2d 688 (8th Cir. 1978). For a general discussion of remedies, see T. St. Antoine, "A Touchstone for Labor Board Remedies," 14 Wayne State L. Rev. 1039 (1968); C. Morris, "The Role of the NLRB and the Courts in the Collective Bargaining Process: A Fresh Look at the Conventional Wisdom and Unconventional Remedies," 30 Vand. L. Rev. 661 (1977). See also *Beverly California Corp.,* 310 NLRB No. 37 (1993).

31. W. B. Gould, *Japan's Reshaping of American Labor Law* 71–81 (1984).

32. *Sure-Tan v. NLRB,* 467 U.S. 883 (1984).

33. See *Caamano Brothers Inc.,* 275 NLRB 205 (1985); *Felbro, Inc.,* 274 NLRB 1268, 1269 (1985) enforcement granted in part and denied in part *sub nom., Local 512 Warehouse and Office Workers' Union v. NLRB,* 795 F.2d 705 (9th Cir. 1986); *Del Ray Tortilleria, Inc.,* 302 NLRB No. 45 (1991) enforcement denied 140 LRRM 2826 (7th Cir. 1992). Judge Cudahy in dissent at 2831 stated: "Once an alien has crossed the border, however, employment is not an additional offense (in fact, it is no crime at all)." The dissent's view is that the appropriate distinction is between having to break the law to reach the workplace and lacking a formal legal entitlement to work. Undocumented workers may maintain an action for unpaid wages and damages under the Fair Labor Standards Act. *Patel v. Quality Inn South,* 846 F.2d 700, 28 WH Cases 1105 (11th Cir. 1988) cert. denied 489 U.S. 1011 (1989).

34. *NLRB v. General Electric Co.,* 418 F.2d 736 (2d Cir. 1969), *cert. denied,* 397 U.S. 965 (1970).

35. The Board has found bad-faith bargaining, in part, because the employer made its initial proposal after a single bargaining session and announced that major provisions of it would be implemented upon the expiration of the existing collective agreement. *American Meat Packing Co.,* 301 NLRB No. 119 (1991).

36. *NLRB v. American National Insurance,* 343 U.S. 395 (1952).

37. *Reichhold Chemicals (Reichhold II),* 288 NLRB 69 (1988) aff'd in rel. part sub nom. *Teamsters Local 515 v. NLRB,* 906 F.2d 719 (D.C. Cir. 1990).

38. *Hydrotherm,* 302 NLRB No. 153, p.12 (1991).

39. See W. B. Gould, *Japan's Reshaping of American Labor Law,* pp. 89–93 (1984).

40. *NLRB v. Wooster Division of Borg-Warner Corp.,* 356 U.S. 342 (1958).

41. *NLRB v. First National Maintenance Corp.,* 627 F.2d 596 (2d Cir. 1980).

42. *NLRB v. Wooster Division of Borg-Warner Corp.,* 356 U.S. 342, 351 (1958).

43. *Taft Broadcasting Co.*, 163 NLRB 475 (1967).

44. *Bonnano Linen Service, Inc. Charles D. v. NLRB*, 454 U.S. 404 (1982).

45. *Howard Johnson Co. v. Detroit Local Joint Executive Board, Hotel Employees International Union*, 417 U.S. 249 (1974).

46. See *Local Lodge No. 1266 etc. v. Panoramic Corp.*, 668 F.2d 276 (7th Cir. 1986). See generally W. B. Gould, "Does the Auto Union Have Any 'Rights' at Fremont," *The Los Angeles Times*, March 11, 1983, II, p. 7.

47. 351 U.S. 149 (1956).

48. *Neilson Lithographing Co. v. NLRB*, 854 F.2d 1063 (7th Cir. 1988).

49. *Concrete Pipe & Paper Corp.*, 305 NLRB No. 1 (1991); *United Paperworkers International Union v. NLRB*, 141 LRRM 2985 (6th Cir. 1992).

50. *United Steelworkers of America Local Union 14534 v. NLRB*, 142 LRRM 2177 (D.C. Cir. 1993).

51. But see *Dubuque Packing Co., Inc.*, 303 NLRB No. 66 (1991); *Mid-State Ready Mix, a division of Torrington Industry, Inc.*, 307 NLRB No. 129 (1992). Both of these cases adopt a more balanced approach than that provided in *First National Maintenance* to the issue of plant relocations in the case of *Dubuque Packing Co.* and the layoffs of nonunit employees and their replacement by nonunit employees in *Mid-State Ready Mix*.

52. 398 U.S. 235 (1970).

53. *Buffalo Forge v. United Steelworkers*, 428 U.S. 397 (1976). Justice Byron White delivered the opinion of the Court in which Chief Justice Warren Burger, Justice Potter Stewart, Justice Henry Blackmun, and Justice William Rehnquist joined. Justices John Paul Stevens, William Brennan, Thurgood Marshall, and Lewis Powell dissented.

54. W. B. Gould, "On Labor Injunctions Pending Arbitration: Recasting *Buffalo Forge*," 30 *Stan. L. Rev.* 533 (1978).

Chapter 6

1. Ramirez, *The New York Times*, July 4, 1992, p. C1, col. 1.

2. Clearly the strike replacement weapon induced the union to capitulate in the Caterpillar dispute. See Swoboda, "The Caterpillar Strike Changed the Debate over Productivity," *Washington Post National Weekly Edition*, April 27, 1992–May 3, 1992, p. 20; Rose, "Caterpillar's Success in Ending Strike Make Her Tail Unions' Use of Walkouts," *Wall Street Journal*, April 20, 1992, p. A3; Kilborn, "Caterpillar's Trump Card," *The New York Times*, April 16, 1992, p. A1; Hicks, "Anguish among Caterpillar Strikers as Jobs Are Offered to Others," *The New York Times*, April 8, 1992, p. A11. The stoppage was not, as management maintained, of limited impact; Hicks, "Caterpillar's Chief See Strike as Limited Battle," *The New York Times*, April 13, 1992, p. A11.

3. *NLRB v. Insurance Agents' International Union*, 361 U.S. 477, 80 S.Ct. 419, 419 L.Ed.2d 454 (1960).

4. 4.29 U.S.C. §158 (b)(4).

5. *Dorchy v. Kansas*, 272 U.S. 306 (1926).

6. See, for example, *Teamsters Local 695 v. Vogt, Inc.*, 354 U.S. 284 (1957).

7. See *Montgomery Ward & Co.*, 64 NLRB 432 (1945), *enforcement denied*, 157 F.2d 486 (8th Cir. 1946); *Boeing Airplane Co. v. NLRB*, 238 F.2d 188 (9th Cir. 1956); *Elk Lumber Co.*, 91 NLRB 333 (1950); *NLRB v. Blade Mfg. Corp.*, 344 F.2d 998 (8th Cir. 1965).

8. *Montgomery Ward & Co.*, 64 NLRB 432 (1945), *enforcement denied*, 157 F.2d 486 (8th Cir. 1946).

9. *C.G. Conn, Ltd. v. NLRB*, 108 F.2d 390 (7th Cir. 1939); *First Nat. Bank of Omaha*, 413 F.2d 921 (8th Cir. 1969); *Valley City Furniture Co.*, 110 NLRB 1589 (1954), *enforced*, 230 F.2d 947 (5th Cir. 1956).

10. *UAW, Local 232 v. Wisconsin Employment Relations Board*, 336 U.S. 245 (1949); *NLRB v. Blades Mfg. Corp.*, 344 F.2d 998 (8th Cir. 1965).

11. An economic strike is about economic issues and does not involve an unfair labor practice. See *NLRB v. Pecheur Lozenge Co.*, 209 F.2d 393 (2d Cir 1953) *cert denied*, 347 U.S. 953 (1957).

12. The leading case is *NLRB v. Allis-Chalmers Mfg. Co.*, 388 U.S. 175 (1967). As we shall see, subsequent Supreme Court authority limited its impact substantially.

13. *NLRB v. Mackay Radio & Telegraph Co.*, 304 U.S. 333, 58 S.Ct. 904, 82 L.Ed. 1381 (1938).

14. 138 Cong. Rec. S8228, S8230 (June 16, 1992) p. 10.

15. *United States General Accounting Office: Report to Congressional Requesters*, Strikes and the Use of Permanent Strike Replacements in the 1970's and 1980's (January 1991)

16. *NLRB v. Fleetwood Trailer Co.*, 389 U.S. 375 (1967).

17. *Laidlaw v. NLRB*, 414 F.2d 99 (7th Cir 1969), *cert. denied*, 397 U.S. 920 (1970); *American Machinery Corp. v. NLRB*, 242 F.2d 1321 (5th Cir. 1970); *Brooke Research and Manufacturing*, 202 NLRB 634 (1973). But see *Giddings S. Lewis v. NLRB*, 675 F.2d 926 (7th Cir. 1982).

18. *NLRB v. Curtin-Matheson Scientific, Inc.*, 110 S.Ct. 1542 (1990).

19. *Trans World Airlines, Inc. v. Independent Federation of Flight Attendants*, 489 US 426 (1989).

20. *Id.* at 432.

21. *Erie Resistor v. NLRB*, 373 U.S. 221 (1963).

22. *Id.* at 437.

23. *Id.* at 436.

24. *Id.* at 438.

25. *Id.* at 426.

26. *Id.* at 447.

27. *NLRB v. Allis Chalmers Mfg. Co.,* 388 U.S. 175 (1967).

28. *Pattern Makers' League of North America v. NLRB,* 105 S.Ct. 3064, 87 L.Ed.2d 68 (1985).

29. 473 U.S. 95, 105 (1985).

30. W. B. Gould, "Solidarity Forever—or Hardly Ever," 66 Cornell L. Rev. 77 (1980)

31. See, for example, *Coppage v. Kansas,* 235 U.S. 1 (1915); *Adair v. U.S.,* 208 U.S. 161 (1908); *Adkins v. Children's Hospital,* 261 U.S. 525 (1923).

32. *American Ship Building,* 380 U.S. 300 (1965).

33. *NLRB v. Brown Food Store,* 380 U.S. 278, 85 S.Ct. 980, 13 L.Ed.2d 839 (1965).

34. See, for example, *Local 825, Int'l Union of Operating Engineers v. NLRB,* 829 F.2d 458 (3d Cir. 1987) (conduct that is inherently destructive of employee rights has unavoidable consequences that the employer not only foresaw but must have intended).

35. 29 U.S.C. §159 (c)(1)(B)(1982).

36. 29 U.S.C. §159 (c)(3)(1982).

37. *NLRB v. Curtin-Matheson Scientific, Inc.,* 110 S.Ct. 1542 (1990).

38. *Erie Resistor v. NLRB,* 373 U.S. 221 (1963).

39. *Trans World Airlines, Inc. v. Independent Federation of Flight Attendants,* 489 U.S. 426 (1989).

40. *NLRB v. Brown Food Stores,* 380 U.S. 278 (1965).

41. 463 U.S. 491 (1983).

42. See *Belknap v. Hale,* 463 U.S. at 500–504 (1983) and *Hansen Brothers Enterprises,* 279 NLRB No. 98 (1986).

43. R. Lester, *Labor Arbitration in State and Local Government* (1984), p. 39.

44. J. Stern, "The Mediation of Interest Disputes by Arbitrators under the Wisconsin Med-Arb Law for Local Government Employees, 39 Arb. Journ. No. 2 (June 1984).

45. P. C. Weiler, "Promises to Keep: Securing Worker's Rights to Self-Organization under the NLRA," 96 Harvard L. Rev. 1769 (1983).

46. Employment Act of 1990, Great Britain.

47. But see *Metropolitan Edison Co. v. NLRB,* 460 U.S. 693 (1983).

48. *National Union of Seamen v. United Kingdom*, Case No. 1540 (1990).

49. See generally W. Galenson, *The International Labor Organization: An American View* (1981); E. Landy, *The Effectiveness of International Supervision: Thirty Years of I.L.O. Experience* (1966).

50. See, for example, Weiler, *supra* note 45.

51. HR 4552 (1988); see Daily Labor Report (BNA) July 15, 1988.

52. *New York Telephone Co. v. New York Dept. of Labor*, 440 U.S. 519 (1979).

Chapter 7

1. H. Phelps Brown, *The Origins of Trade Union Power* (1983) p. 235.

2. *Id.* p. 237.

3. R. Mitchell, *Solving the Great Social Problem of the Age: A Comparison of the Development of State Systems of Conciliation and Arbitration in Australia and Canada, 1870–1910*, (Univ. of Melbourne), p. 31; J. Rickard, *H. B. Higgins, The Rebel's Judge* (1984).

4. *Id.* p. 33.

5. *Id.* p. 36.

6. *The Industrial Disputes Investigation Act*, 1907, 6–7 Edward VII [1907], ch. 20; III Revised Statutes [1927], ch. 112.

7. H. Phelps Brown, *supra* note 1, p. 237.

8. See S. M. Lipset, *Unions in Transition: Entering the Second Century* (1986), pp. 442–452.

9. H. Phelps Brown, *supra* note 1, p. 240.

10. S. Barkin, *Decline of the Labor Movement* (1961); W. B. Gould, "Taft-Hartley Revisited: The Contrariety of the Collective Bargaining Agreement and the Plight of the Unorganized," 13 Labor L. J. 348 (1962); W. B. Gould, "Some Reflections on Fifty Years of the National Labor Relations Act: The Need for Labor Board and Labor Laws Reform," 38 Stanford L. Rev. 937–944 (1986); A. H. Raskin, "The Big Squeeze on Labor Unions," *Atlantic Monthly*, October 1979, p. 41; A. H. Raskin, "The Squeeze on the Unions," *Atlantic Monthly*, June 1961, p. 55; P. C. Weiler, "Promises to Keep: Securing Workers' Rights to Self-organization under the NLRA," 96 Harvard L. Rev. 1769–1827 (1983).

11. L. Troy, *Is the U.S. Unique in the Decline of Private Sector Unionism?* 11 J. Lab. Res. 111 (1990).

12. *Infra* note 14 at 8.

13. *Id.* at 17.

14. Troy's most recent article is "Convergence in International Unionism, etc. The Case of Canada and the U.S.A.," 30 British J. Ind. Rel. 1,4 (1992).

15. *Id.*

16. *Id.*

17. See W. B. Gould, *A Primer on American Labor Law* 2d ed., pp. 33–37.

18. 484 U.S. 112 (1987), 108 S.Ct. 413, 126 LRRM 3281, 98 L. Ed. 2d 429.

19. 108 S.Ct. 413, 422 (1987).

20. See W. B. Gould, *Japan's Reshaping of American Labor Law* (1984).

21. P. Bruce, *Political Parties and the Evolution of Labor Law in Canada and the United States* (Ph.D. dissertation, MIT 1988).

22. *NLRB v. Transportation Management Corp.*, 462 U.S. 393 (1983).

23. B. Murphy, "A Comparison of the Selection of Bargaining Representatives in the United States and Canada: Linden Lumber, Gissel, and the Right to Challenge Majority Status," 10 Comp. Lab. L. J. 65, 84 (1988).

24. See generally Bill 84, Labour Relations Code, 1st Session, 35th Parliament, 41 Elizabeth II, 1992 Legislative Assembly of British Columbia.

25. *Industrial Relations Act* §137.8(1), [1981] C.L.L.R. 30, 165.

26. *Stuart Olson Construction Ltd. and Stuart Olson Industrial Contractors Ltd.*, File No. L.R. 1431-T-1, (Alberta Labour Relations Board, June 1, 1983).

27. *Plateau Mills Ltd. and Int'l Woodworkers of America, Local 1-424*, [1977] 1 Can. LRBR 82 (B.C.)

28. *Id.* at 86, 87.

29. *Id.* at 87–88.

30. *Id.* at 86 (emphasis supplied).

31. *Central Broadcasting Co. Ltd. v. Canada Labour Relations Board*, (1976), 67 D.L.R. (3d) 538 (S.C.C.) at p. 541.

32. *NLRB v. Gissel Packing Co.*, 395 U.S. 575 (1969).

33. *American Federation of Labor v. NLRB*, 308 U.S. 401 (1940); *Leedom v. Kyne*, 358 U.S. 184 (1958).

34. *Cable Tech Wire Co. Ltd.*, [1978] OLRB Rep. Oct. 895.

35. *R. v. K-Mart Canada Ltd.*, (1982), 66 C.C.C. (2d) 329 (Ont.C.A.) at p. 332.

36. F. Bartosic and I. D. Lanhoff, "Escalating the Struggle against Taft-Hartley Contemnors," 39 Univ. Chi. L. Rev. 255 (1972).

37. *H.K. Porter Co. v. NLRB*, 397 U.S. 99 (1970).

38. *Tandy Electronics Ltd. (Radio Shack) v. United Steelworkers of America*, (1981), 115 D.L.R. (3d) 197 (Ont. H.C.).

39. *Id.* at 214.

40. *Id.* at 205.

41. *Dubuque Packing Co., Inc. v. UFCW Local No. 150 A*, 303 NLRB No. 66 (1991).

42. *Ex-Cell-O Corp.*, 185 NLRB 107 (1970), *enforced*, 449 F.2d 1058 (D.C. Cir. 1971).

43. 397 U.S. 99, 107 (1970).

44. *Id.*; see also *NLRB v. Seven-Up Bottling*, 344 U.S. 344 (1953) (punitive sanctions for violations of the NLRA prohibited); *NLRB v. Food Store Employees Union, Local 347, (Heck's)*, 417 U.S. 1 (1974) (litigation expenses not to be awarded unless litigation was "frivolous").

45. *United Steelworkers of America v. Radio Shack*, [1980] 1 Can LRBR 99, 129 (Ont.).

46. *Id.* at 134.

47. Memorandum from Charles McDonald to AFL-CIO National Organizing Committee (February 18, 1983) as cited by Weiler in "Striking a New Balance: Freedom of Contract and the Prospects for Union Representation," 98 Harv. L. Rev. 351, 354 (1984).

48. *An Act to Amend the Labour Code and Various Legislation*, [1983] Statutes of Quebec c. 22. See also A. P. Macdonald, *First Contract Arbitration in Canada*, School of Industrial Relations Research Essay Series No. 17 (Industrial Relations Centre, Queen's University at Kingston, 1988); C. G. Paliare, *First Contract Arbitration: A Canadian Invention* (Dept. of Industrial Relations, Laval University, Quebec City); J. Sexton, "First Contract Arbitration in Canada," 38 Labor Law J. 508–514 (1987).

49. *Review of Manitoba's First Agreement Legislation As of March 31, 1988*, Manitoba Labour Research and Planning, April 11, 1988, p. 3.

50. *Nepean Roof Truss Limited*, [1987] 13 CLRBR (NS) 64 (Ont.).

51. *Id.* at 69.

52. *Id.* at 69–70.

53. *Id.* at 70.

54. *Id.*

55. *Id.* at 70–71.

56. *Id.* at 71.

57. *Id.* at 72.

58. "Proposed Reform of the Ontario Labor Relations Act," a discussion paper from the Ministry of Labour, November 1991.

59. *United Brotherhood of Carpenters and Joiners of America, Local 2679 v. Egan Visual Inc.*, No. 1767-86-FCA (Ontario Labour Relations Board, December 1, 1986).

60. *Egan Visual Inc.*, slip op. at ¶ 3.

61. *Id.*, at ¶4.

62. See, *NLRB v. MacKay Radio & Telegraph Co.*, 304 U.S. 333 (1938); 58 S.Ct. 904; 82 L.Ed. 1381.

63. *The Becker Milk Co., Ltd.*, [1978] 1 Can. LRBR 175.

64. *Id.* at 181.

65. Labour Relations and Employment Statute Law Amendment Act (Bill 40) (1992) ss.73.1(4).

66. Report from the Ministry of Labor, p. 33.

67. More Jobs Coalition, *Facing Reality Showing Responsibility Submission to the Ministry of Labour on the Proposed Changes to the Labour Relations Act* (February 1992).

68. *Viceroy Construction Co., Ltd.*, [1978] 1 Can. LRBR 22 (Ont.).

69. *Id.* at 25.

70. *Service Employees International Union Local 224 and Focus Building Service Ltd*, unreported case no. C90/87 B.C. Industrial Relations Council (November 9, 1987).

Chapter 8

1. A. Hacker, *Two Nations: Black and White, Separate, Hostile, Unequal*, p. 201 (1992).

2. *Griggs v. Duke Power Co.*, 401 U.S. 424 (1971).

3. *Dothard v. Rawlinson*, 433 U.S. 321 (1977).

4. *Stamps v. Detroit Edison Co.*, 365 F.Supp. 87 (E.D. Mich 1973), aff'd in part, rev'd in part on other grounds sub nom. and remanded in *EEOC v. Detroit Edison Co.*, 515 F.2d 301 (6th Cir. 1975); *Williams v. Valentec Risco, Inc.*, 1992 U.S. App. Lexis 8541 (1992); *Gallagher v. Wilton Enterprises*, 902 F.2d 120 (8th Cir. 1992); *Lewis v. Federal Prison Industries*, 953 F.2d 1277 (11th Cir. 1992); *Charles Lytes v. Sara Lee Corp. & Electrolux Co.*, 905 F.2d 101 (2d Cir. 1991).

5. §1981, *Johnson v. Railway Express*, 421 U.S. 454 (1975); *Jones v. Alfred Mayer*, (1968); W. B. Gould, "Racial Equality in Jobs and Unions, Collective Bargaining and the Burger Court," 68A Mich. L. Rev. 237 (1969).

6. 490 U.S. 642 (1989).

7. *Washington v. Davis*, 426 U.S. 229 (1976).

8. *General Electric v. Gilbert*, 429 U.S. 125 (1976).

9. See, for example, *Patterson v. American Tobacco Co.*, 535 F.2d 257 cert. denied 429 U.S. 920 (1976); *Russell v. American Tobacco Co.*, 528 F.2d 357 (1975), cert. denied, 425 U.S. 935 (1976); *Acha v. Beame*, 531 F.2d 648 (1976). The leading case in this line is a district court decision, *Quarles v. Philip Morris, Inc.*, 279 F.Supp. 505 (ED Va. 1968).

10. *International Brotherhood of Teamsters v. United States*, 431 U.S. 324 (1977); W. B. Gould, "Employment Security, Seniority and Race: The Role of Title VII of the Civil Rights Act of 1964," 13 How. L. J. 1 (Winter 1967); W. B. Gould, "Seniority and the Black Worker, Reflection on *Quarles* and Its Implications," 47 Tex. L. Rev. 1039 (1969). See generally W. B. Gould, *Black Workers in White Unions* (1977).

11. 431 U.S. 324, 328 makes reference to 1972 amends. "Title VII of the Civil Rights Act of 1964, 78 Stat. 253, as amended, 42 U.S.C. §2000e et seq. (1970 ed. and Supp. V). Footnote 1 on 431 U.S. 324, 329 discusses how "Section 707 was amended by §5 of the Equal Employment Opportunity Act of 1972, 86 Stat. 107, 42 U.S.C. §2000e-6(c) (1970 ed. Supp. V).

12. Pregnancy Discrimination Act of 1978, Pub. L. No. 95-555, 92 Stat. 2076 (codified at 42 U.S.C. §2000e(k) (1992).

13. Civil Rights Attorney's Fee Awards Act of 1976, Pub. L. No. 94-559, 90 Sta. 2641 (codified as amended at 42 U.S.C. §1988 (1982). Voting Rights Act of 1965, Pub. L. No. 89-110, 79 Stat. 437 (codified at 42 U.S.C. §§1971–1973 bb-4).

14. *Local 28 of the Sheet Metal Workers' International Association v. EEOC*, 478 U.S. 421 (1986); *Local No. 93, International Association of Firefighters, AFL-CIO v. City of Cleveland*, 478 U.S. 501 (1986).

15. *Regents of California v. Bakke*, 438 U.S. 265 (1978).

16. *Wygant v. Jackson Board of Education*, 476 U.S. 267 (1986); *Johnson v. Transportation Agency, Santa Clara County, California*, 480 U.S. 616 (1987).

17. See W. B. Gould, "The Supreme Court and Employment Discrimination in 1989: Judicial Retreat and Congressional Response," 64 Tulane L. Rev. 1485 (1990).

18. *Wards Cove Packing Co. v. Atonio*, 490 U.S. 642 (1989).

19. Cf. *Connecticut v. Teal*, 457 U.S. 440 (1982).

20. *Wards Cove Packing Co. v. Atonio*, 490 U.S. 642, 657 (1989).

21. *Id.* at 642.

22. 490 U.S. 642, 659 (1989).

23. *Patterson v. McLean Credit Union*, 491 U.S. 164 (1989).

24. *Id.* at 171.

25. *Patterson v. McLean Credit Union*, 491 U.S. 164 (1989).

26. *Watson v. Fort Worth Bank & Trust*, 487 U.S. 977 (1988).

27. 487 U.S. 977, 998 (1987).

28. *Texas Dept. of Community Affairs v. Burdine*, 450 U.S. 248 (1981).

29. *Price Waterhouse v. Hopkins*, 490 U.S. 228 (1989).

30. 490 U.S. 228, 290 (1989).

31. *NLRB v. Transportation Management*, 462 U.S. 393 (1983).

32. *Mt. Healthy School District Board of Education v. Doyle*, 429 U.S. 274 (1977).

33. *Lorance v. AT&T Technologies*, 490 U.S. 900 (1989).

34. 490 U.S. 900, 912

35. *Martin v. Wilks*, 490 U.S. 755 (1989).

36. *EEOC v. Arabian American Oil Co.*, 111 S.Ct 1227 (1991).

37. *City of Richmond v. J.A. Croson Co.*, 488 U.S. 469 (1989).

38. S. A. Holmes, "Bill Would Overturn Court's Rights Decisions," *The New York Times*, p.A23.

39. J. Morley, "Bush and the Blacks: An Unknown Story," *The New York Review of Books*, January 16, 1992, p.19

40. *Watson v. Forth Worth Bank & Trust*, 487 U.S. 977 (1988).

41. *Id.* at

42. S. A. Holmes, "When the Subject Is Civil Rights, There Are Two George Bushes," *The New York Times*, June 9, 1991, p.1.

43. *Watson v. Forth Worth Bank & Trust*, 487 U.S. 977 (1988).

44. A. Clymer, "Democrats Intend to Outlaw Quotas in Civil Rights Bill," *The New York Times*, May 21, 1991, p.A10; A. Clymer, "Ban on Quotas Spurs Rights Debate," *The New York Times*, May 22, 1991, p. A14; A. Clymer, "Jobs Bill Would Allow Numbers Yet Ban Quotas," *The New York Times*, May 29, 1991, p. A8; A. Clymer, "House Democrats Hone Rights Bill," *The New York Times*, May 30, 1991, p.A16; A. Clymer, "Bush Denounces Civil Rights Bill Advocated by House Democrats," *The New York Times*, May 31, 1991, p. A1. "Even the section that supposedly outlaws quotas endorsed quotas,' Mr. Bush continued, 'It defines the 'Q' word, as it's come to be known, it defines the 'Q' word so narrowly it would allow employers to establish personnel systems based on numbers, not merit. Other sections righting the rules against employers. If the numbers aren't right, the employers are essentially helpless to defend themselves in court."p.A12.

45. T. Smart with P. Dwyer and D. Harbrecht, "The Civil Rights Brawl is Back—As Ugly As Ever," *Business Week*, March 25, 1991, p.45; S. A. Holmes, "Talks on Rights Bill Split Business," *The New York Times*, April 19, 1991, p.A10

46. See letter to the editor by W. B. Gould, "No Effective Remedy," *The New York Times*, October 19, 1991, p. E3, noting that although the Republican members of the Senate Judiciary Committee expressed skepticism about Professor Anita Hill's failure to file a sexual harassment charge with the EEOC, they voted against a damages remedy for sexual harassment prior to the Thomas-Hill hearings.

47. A. Clymer, "For Civil Rights Bill, the Name's the Game," *The New York Times*, May 5, 1991, p.1.

48. A. Clymer, "White House Attacks Compromise Rights Bill," *The New York Times*, October 24, 1991, p. A10.

49. See Opportunities Denied, Opportunities Diminished: Discrimination in Hiring (Urban Institute, August 1991)

50. C. Ness, "Attorneys Avoiding Job Bias Lawsuits," *San Francisco Examiner;* "The Hidden Impact of *Wards Cove:* The Unavailability of Legal Representation for Disparate Impact Claims," A Report by the NAACP Legal Defense and Educational Fund, Inc. May 22, 1991.

51. Civil Rights Act of 1991 102 Pub.L. 166, §101.

52. See R. Epstein, *Forbidden Grounds: The Case against Employment Discrimination Laws* (1992).

53. 137 Cong. Rec. S8983, S8984, July 8, 1991.

54. 137 Cong. Rec. S15276, October 25, 1991.

55. 137 Cong. Rec. S15234, October 25, 1991.

56. Civil Rights Act of 1991, 102 Pub. L. 166; 1991 S. 1745; 105 Stat. 1071.

57. 42 U.S.C.S. §1210.

58. 137 Cong. Rec. S8983, S8985.

59. 137 Cong. Rec. S15315. "The burden of proof issue is only part of *Wards Cove* overruled by this. In theory, more than in practice, this change is very important. But because an employer's counsel presumably puts the employer's best case forward anyway regardless of the nature of the employer's burden, this constitutes the most minor practical change in current law we could make."

60. See 137 Cong. Rec. S15315.

61. 426 U.S. 229 (1976).

62. *New York City Transit Authority v. Beazer,* 440 U.S. 568 (1979).

63. 102 Pub. L. 166, §105(c)(3).

64. 102 Pub L. 166

65. 102 Pub. L. 166 section 105(B)(i).

66. Congressional Record, S15234

67. 433 U.S. 321 (1977).

68. 137 Cong. Rec. S15474, October 30, 1991.

69. *Martin v. Wilks,* 490 U.S. 799 (1989).

70. 102 Pub. L. 166, section 109(b).

71. *West Virginia Univ. Hospitals v. Robert Casey, Governor of Pennsylvania,* 111 S.Ct. 1138 (1991); *Communication, Immigration and Naturalization Service v. Marie Lucie Jean,* 496 U.S. 154.

72. *Gilmer v. Interstate/Johnson Lane*, 111 S.Ct 1647 (1991).

73. Age Discrimination Act of 1967.

74. *Alexander v. Gardner-Denver Co.*, 415 U.S. 36 (1974).

75. *Thomas Johnson v. Uncle Ben's*, 1992 U.S. App. Lexis 14931 (July 1, 1992) 5th Cir. Ct. of Appeals; *Patricia D. Rush v. McDonald's Corp.*, 1992 U.S. App. Lexis 14925 (June 29, 1992) 7th Cir. no retroactivity; *Donthit v. The Keebler Co.*, 1992 U.S. App. Lexis 15150 (June 24, 1992) 6th Cir. no retroactivity; *Paglio v. Chagrini Valley Hunt Corp.*, 1992 U.S. App. Lexis 15399 (June 25, 1992) 6th Cir. no retroactivity; *Hines v. Vanderbile University Medical Center*, U.S. App. Lexis 14689 (June 17, 1992) 6th Cir. no retroactivity; *Luddington v. Indiana Bell Telephone*, 1992 U.S. App. 13450 (June 15, 1992) 7th Cir.

76. *Brown v. Board of Education*, 347 U.S. 483 (1954).

77. See, for instance, Treadwell, "Seeking a New Road to Equality," *The Los Angeles Times*, July 7, 1992, p.A1.

78. This makes the point propounded by Gewirtz to the effect that the legislation is not a "liberal coup" at least an arguable one. See Gewirtz, "Fine Print: The Civil Rights Bill's Lifeless?" *New Republic*, November 18, 1991, p.10.

79. *United States v. Hutcheson*, 312 U.S. 219 (1941).

80. J. Donahue, Review Essay, "Advocacy versus Analysis in Addressing Employment Discrimination Law," 44 Stan. L. Rev. 1583, 1588 (1992).

Chapter 9

1. See, for example, *The Comedy Store and American Federation of Comedians and American Guild of Variety Artists, Associated Actors and Artists of American, AFL-CIO*, 265 NLRB 1422 at 1444–45 (1982) and the cases cited therein.

2. B. Noble, "Straddling the Law on Layoffs," *The New York Times*, February 28, 1993 Business, p. 37.

3. W. B. Gould, "On Labor Injunctions Pending Arbitration: Recasting Buffalo Forge," 30 Stan. L. Rev. 533 (1978).

Index

Access to company property, 23–24, 157–158
Advisory opinions, 172, 178
Affirmative action, 28, 239, 243, 245, 254, 256. *See also* Quota issues
AFL (American Federation of Labor), 11, 45, 46
AFL-CIO, 11, 14
  and antidiscrimination laws, 57
  and associate membership, 91, 164
  and ILO conventions, 12
  and works councils view, 59–60
  on wrongful discharge legislation, 90–91, 93
AFSCME (American Federation of State, County and Municipal Employees Union), 15, 209
Age Discrimination Act (1967), 81, 83, 88, 103, 255
Air traffic controllers strike, 42, 185
Alexander v. Gardner-Denver, 81
Aliens, illegal, 26, 166–167, 260
Amalgamated Cothing and Textile Workers Union, 16, 104
American exceptionalism, 45–46
American Federation of Labor (AFL), 11, 45, 46
American Federation of Labor-Congress of Industrial Organizations. *See* AFL-CIO
American Federation of State, County and Municipal Employees Union (AFSCME), 15, 209
American Federation of Teachers, 15
American Hospital Association v. NLRB, 23, 27, 162
Americans with Disabilities Act (1990), 5, 9, 28, 83, 248, 250, 259, 262
Antitrust law, 20, 47, 50, 114, 155
  Clayton Act, 20, 47
  Sherman Act, 20, 47, 145

Application agreements, 71, 76
Aramco case (*EEOC v. Arabian American Oil Co.*) 243, 253
Arbitration, 5–6, 30, 33, 262
  in Canada, 100, 169, 170, 206, 220–230
  congressional legislation for, 182
  and duty of fair representation, 82–84
  final offer system of, 130, 169–170, 196–197
  first-contract, 169, 222–230
  NLRB compared with, 93–94, 99
  at NUMMI and Saturn, 130
  and reinstatement as remedy, 97–99
  reliance on over collective bargaining, 195, 222–223
  temptation to avoid, 83
  union as blocking claims to, 89
  unions' experience in, 93
  of wrongful discharge complaints, 81, 82–84, 99–100, 108
Associate membership in unions, 91–92, 164
At-will clauses, 71, 81, 87
Authorization cards, 162–165, 177–178, 215, 216, 217, 218

Bakke case, 238
Bankruptcy of employers, 22, 103
Beazer decision, 250–251
Becker Milk Co., Ltd., case, 231
Bieber, Owen, 112, 113, 173
Bildisco case (*NLRB v. Bildisco & Bildisco*), 22
Black, Hugo, 174
Blackmun, Harry, 193
Borg Warner decision, 170, 171, 172, 178
Bork, Robert, 235
Boulwarism, 168
Bowen v. United Postal Service, 84
Boys Market v. Retail Clerks, Local 770, 176
Brandeis, Louis, 184

Index

Brennan, Joseph, 202
Brennan, William J., Jr., 2, 22, 122, 143, 183, 188, 213–214, 242
Britain
  adversarial mentality in, 59
  Bullock Report in, 115, 145, 147
  concentration of workers in, 208
  decline of unions in, 17, 49, 51–52, 55–56
  employee protection in, 56, 88
  Japanese companies in, 130, 143
  and strike ballot, 199, 200
  and strikers' reemployment, 198, 200–201
  two-tier unionism in, 199–200
  union recognition in, 143
  and workers' participation, 123, 147
  wrongful-discharge protection in, 77
Brown Food Stores decision, 189–190, 193
Brown v. Board of Education, 256
Bullock Report, 115, 145, 147
Burger, Warren, 25, 237
Bush, George
  and Board vacancies, 159
  and 1991 Civil Rights Act, 31, 235, 236, 244–246, 253
  and quotas, 28, 235, 243–244
  and race issue, 27, 237
Bush administration, and 1991 Civil Rights Act, 2, 79, 239, 246, 254, 256

California Immigrant Workers Association (CIWA), 19
Canada, 205
  labor growth in, 55
  trade union movement in, 51, 205–213
  and Quebec, 212–213
Canadian labor law, 51, 213–219, 233–234
  and arbitration, 100, 206
  first-contract, 169, 170, 222–230
  authorization-card procedure in, 162, 163
  and collective bargaining/strikes, 230–232
  employment protection legislation, 88
  and judicial review, 164
  other areas of, 232–233
  sanctions and remedies in, 219–222
  and strike ballot, 199, 201
  and strikers' reemployment, 198, 199, 201–202
  wrongful-discharge protection in, 77–78
Carey, Ron, 6, 177
Carter administration, 165, 201
Caterpillar strike, 181–182, 186, 194, 261
Causation, and disparate impact, 249–250, 251–252

Central Broadcasting Co., Ltd. v. Canada Labour Relations Board, 218
Certification system
  and authorization cards, 162–165, 177, 215, 216, 217, 218
  and campaigning methods, 156–157
  in Canada and U.S., 213, 215–219
  and delay in Board procedures, 158–162
  and solicitation/access rights, 157–158
  and union decline, 55
Changing Situation of Workers and Their Unions, The, 23, 45, 88–89
Charles Bonnano v. NLRB, 172
Chicago Rawhide decision, 140
Chrysler bailout and union representation on board, 113–114, 144, 145, 146, 173
Civil Rights Act (1866), 236, 240, 248, 255–256
Civil Rights Act (1964), 9, 199
  and Bush, 28
  and decline of unions, 57
  1972 amendments to, 238, 249, 257
  and NLRA, 48
  and protecting of women, 106–107
  and reinstatement, 199
  title VII of, 27, 57
    and cost assumption, 98
    and damages, 29, 237, 238, 241, 246, 248
    and disparate impact, 248, 249
    and employer discretion, 78
    and foreign employment, 243
    implementation of, 256
    and job protection, 30, 102
    and 1991 Act, 235, 236, 259
    and sexual harassment or discrimination, 58, 238
  union support for, 34
Civil Rights Act (1991), 235–257, 258, 259, 262
  and affirmative action, 254
  alternative dispute resolution under, 5, 83, 254–255
  burden of proof in, 249–250
  ceiling on damages under, 28–29, 100, 246, 248–249, 257
  and collective bargaining, 9
  employer's rebuttal in, 250–253
  fight for passage of, 235–236
  and harmfulness of job loss, 75
  historical background of, 30–31, 236–247
  and job-relatedness or business necessity, 247, 251–252
  labor movement support of, 57

Index

and mixed motives, 253–254
and public awareness, 78
and quotas, 2, 27, 28, 79, 239, 243–245
retroactivity of, 255–256
scope of protection in, 248
and seniority, 254
and sexual harassment, 58
and worker participation, 148
Clayton Antitrust Act (1914), 20, 47
Clayton v. United Auto Workers, 83
Clinton administration, and NAFTA, 13
and health care reform, 256
and Family and Medical Leave Act (1993), 58
Closed shop, Taft-Hartley outlawing of, 49, 189
Codetermination, 112, 148
in Europe, 56–57, 115–116, 172–173
protecting of, 146
Collective bargaining, 31–35
Brennan on, 122
in Canada, 230–232
decentralized basis for, 35, 42–43
and decline of unions, 34–35
and job security, 63, 64, 77, 82–83, 87, 103–105
legal intervention necessary for, 230
and legislation, 6, 9
mandatory subjects for, 21, 24–25, 170–173
for minority of workers, 164–165
and partnership idea, 172–173
reasons for state intervention in, 32
and refusal to bargain in good faith, 167–170, 227
regulation of desirable, 53–55
and relative power, 32–33
and right to strike, 4–5, 6, 183–184, 187, 198, 201, 261
and seniority, 143
vs. statutory protection, 56–57, 58
and workers' participation, 116–117
and wrongful dismissal, 33, 59
Commonwealth v. Hunt, 47
Communication Workers of America, 181
Company unions, 19–20, 136
and NLRA, 7–8
and voluntary worker participation systems, 59–61
Comparable worth theory, 28
Congress of Industrial Organizations (CIO), 11, 18–19, 46, 49, 205
Cooperative efforts and model, 5, 19, 104–105. *See also* Workers' participation
and labor law, 59–61
opposition to, 110, 124, 149
and partnership idea, 172–173

Saturn project as, 127
as two-way street (pastoral letter), 109
vs. adversarial stance, 20
Cox, Archibald, 156
Craft unions, and decline of unionism, 18–19
Credit cards, and union associate membership, 90
Croson decision, 254
Curtin-Matheson Scientific decision, 190–191
Curtis Brothers decision, 50

Damage awards, 29, 30
and 1964 Civil Rights Act, 30, 237, 238, 241, 246, 248
and 1989 Supreme Court decisions, 238
and 1991 Civil Rights Act, 28–29, 102, 246, 248–249, 256–257
and procedures outside collective bargaining, 83
punitive-remedial distinction on, 166
for wrongful discharge vs. employment discrimination, 29–30
Danforth, John C., 244, 247, 249, 250, 252, 253, 255, 256
Deklewa decision, 23
Deming, Edwards, 113
Discrimination, employment, 27–29, 235. *See also* Affirmative action; Quota issues; Sexual discrimination
legislation against, 57–58 (*see also at* Civil Rights Act)
public policy against, 68–69
and Supreme Court, 238–243
testers for, 24
and wrongful discharge, 29–31, 78–79, 88, 247
Disparate impact, 238, 239, 244, 247, 248, 249, 251–252
Dole, Robert, 250, 253, 254, 255
Dothard opinion, 252
Dotson, Donald, 22
Drucker, Peter, 16, 132
Dubuque Packing Co., Inc. case, 24–25
Due process, 30, 64
Duplex Printing Press Company v. Deering, 20
Duty of fair representation, 83–84, 89
Duty to bargain, 7, 167–170, 227, 261

Eastern Airlines dispute, 121, 185
Economic or industrial democracy, 3, 32, 110, 149
Economic Justice for All: Pastoral Letter on Catholic Social Teaching and the U.S. Economy, 109

Index

EEOC (Equal Employment Opportunity Commission), 29, 48, 236
EEOC v. Arabian American Oil Co., 243, 253–254
Electoral process, union, 176–177, 262–263
Electromation, Inc. decision, 139–140, 141, 262
Emergency disputes, 195–198
Employee participation. *See* Workers' participation
Employee Retirement Income Security Act (ERISA) (1974), 9, 26, 57, 94, 103, 105, 133
Employee stock ownership plan (ESOP), 113, 132–135
Employer associations, 35
Employer-employee relations. *See also* Cooperative efforts and model; Workers' participation
  adversarial framework of, 5, 20, 59, 110, 121, 123, 173
  asymmetry of, 75–77
  collective bargaining as equalizing, 32
  equal-partnership concept of, 172–173
  new dynamic, 25–26
  and new job-security agreements, 104–105
  trust and respect needed in, 262
Employer involvement, 8
Employment at Will Doctrine, The, 90
Employment discrimination. *See* Discrimination, employment
Equal Employment Opportunity Commission (EEOC), 29, 48, 236
Equal Opportunity Act (1972), 9
Equal Pay Act (1963), 9, 27
Erie Resistor decision, 187, 191–192, 193
European codetermination, 115–117, 172–173
European Community, 12
  and workers' participation, 117–119
  works council system in, 6
European Trade Union Congress, 119
Ex-Cell-o case, 221
Executive compensation, 1, 61, 259–260

Fair Labor Standards Act (1938), 94–95
Fairness
  and seniority, 76
  workers' sense of, 30
  and wrongful discharge, 79–80
Family and Medical Leave Act (1990, 1991, 1993), 58
First-contract negotiations and arbitration, 169–170
  in Canada and U.S., 169–170, 222–230

First National Maintenance v. NLRB, 24, 128, 143, 171, 172–173, 178, 179
Flanagan, Robert, 43, 65
Flight Attendants case, 187, 190, 191, 193
Foley v. Interactive Data Corp., 63, 68, 70, 71, 72–75, 76, 77, 78, 82, 84, 86, 87, 89
Fourteenth Amendment, 20
Frankfurter, Felix, 257
Fraser, Douglas, 112, 113–114, 144, 173
Free riders, and nonunion sector, 35
Free-speech right of employers, 49, 156–157
  in Canada vs. U.S., 233
  and NLRB, 152, 156

Gade v. National Solid Waste Management Association, 107
General Agreement on Tariffs and Trade (GATT), 13
General Electric Co. v. NLRB, 168
General Motors, income-security program of, 64–65
General Motors Saturn division
  arbitration in, 130
  and cooperative model, 5, 19
  and job security, 104, 126, 128–129, 130
  and management prerogatives, 21, 127–128
  and workers' participation, 60, 123, 127–131, 137, 143, 262
General Motors-Toyota joint venture. *See* New United Motors Manufacturing, Inc.
Germany
  codetermination in, 57, 115–117, 146, 172
  as competitor, 202–203
  industrial tribunals in, 198
  temporary employment contracts in, 88
  union rebound in, 17
  U.S. firms and unions in, 35
Global competition, 11–12, 181
Global interdependence, 120–121
Gilmer decision, 81, 83, 108, 148, 255, 262
Gissel decision, 21, 162–163, 177, 218
Goldwater, Barry, 236
Gompers, Samuel, 45, 107–108, 206
Griggs v. Duke Power Co., 30, 31, 78, 237–238, 239, 240, 247, 249, 251, 252, 253, 257

Hacker, Andrew, 237, 256
Hale v. Belknap, 193–194
Hansen Brothers decision, 194
Harlan, John, 171
Hatch, Orin, 250, 253, 255

Index

Hillman, Sidney, 16
Hill-Thomas hearings, 28, 246–247, 256
History of labor movement
  and American exceptionalism, 45–46
  and current decline, 17–19, 20, 23, 25–26
  and law, 45–49
  1940s disruptions, 52–53
H. K. Porter case, 220, 221
Holmes, Oliver Wendell, 99, 156

ILO. *See* International Labor Organization conventions
Immigrant workers, 19. *See also* Aliens, illegal
Implied contract, and wrongful discharge, 69–72, 79–81, 82, 90
Industrial or economic democracy, 3, 32, 110, 149
Insurance Agents decision, 122, 131, 173, 183–184, 189
Interdependence
  global, 120–121
  of industrial operations, 53–54
International Association of Machinists, 112–113
International Brotherhood of Electrical Workers, 27
International environment, 12–13
  and trade union decline, 17
International Labor Organization (ILO) conventions, 12, 201
  and *Mackay* rule, 201
  and right to strike, 183, 198, 201
  Termination of Employment, 84, 89
International Ladies Garment Workers Union, 19
Investigatory system, in Canada vs. U.S., 214–215

Jackson, Robert, 48
Japan or Japanese companies
  in Britain, 130, 143
  collective-bargaining mandate in, 164–165
  and compensation, 131–132
  as competitor, 202–203
  and decline of unions, 17, 55–56
  and Deming thesis, 113
  and impartial tribunal, 89
  investment by in U.S., 104
  and job security, 77, 78
  and labor-management relations, 110, 148
  and labor relations board, 213
  and monetary relief, 165–167
  and severance pay, 98
  strike protection in, 184, 198
  and unfair labor practice, 170, 213, 214
  and workers' participation, 59, 119–120
Japanese-GM joint venture. *See* New United Motors Manufacturing, Inc.
Jean Country decision, 23, 154
J.I. Case decision, 48
Job security, 8, 21–22, 24–25, 63, 260
  and collective bargaining, 63, 64, 77, 82–83, 87, 103–105
  and due process, 30, 64
  and employer-employee friction, 111
  importance of, 9, 74–75
  and mandatory bargaining subjects, 21, 170–173
  and NUMMI agreement, 126, 130
  and plant-closing legislation, 58, 105–106, 171
  at Saturn project, 126, 128–129, 130
  and SUB, 64–65
  and workers' participation, 60, 78, 147, 183
  and wrongful discharge, 65–67 (*see also* Wrongful discharge litigation)
Johnson, Lyndon, 28, 237
Jointness concept, 128. *See also* Cooperative efforts and model; Workers' participation
Judicial review
  in Canada vs. U.S., 164, 218–219
  and representation process, 164
  in wrongful discharge litigation, 101
Jury trials, 82, 86, 248

Kaufman, Marcus, 72–74, 76
Kennedy, Anthony, 235, 239, 240, 251, 257
Kennedy, Edward
  on job loss through replacement, 185
  and 1991 Civil Rights Act, 245, 251–252, 252–253, 257
  and OSHA, 94, 148
Kennedy, John F., 165
King, MacKenzie, 207
Kirkland, Lane, 153
Knights of Labor, in Canada, 205–206

Labor Immigrant Assistance Project (LIAP), 19
Labor law, 3–4, 255. *See also* National Labor Relations Act
  and changing nature of employment relationships, 255
  and decline of unions, 3, 19–26, 48–50, 54, 55, 151–152
  failures of, 20
  roots of, 11
  as state control, 50
  and voluntary workers' participation systems, 60

Labor law (cont.)
    and worker-participation issues, 136–147
Labor law, Canadian. *See* Canadian labor law
Labor law reform, 3, 7, 8–9, 178. *See also under* National Labor Relations Act
    in Britain, 51–52
    and employee participation, 261
    unlikelihood of, 6
    vs. repeal, 49
    and workers' participation, 117, 142
    as prerequisite, 262
    on wrongful discharge, 80–81, 85–86, 87, 103, 108, 260 (*see also under* Wrongful discharge litigation)
Labor movement. *See* Unions and union movement
Labor policy, assumptions about, 3
Labor Reform Bill (1978), 165–166, 178
Labor Relations and the Litigation Explosion (Flanagan), 43
Landrum-Griffin Act/amendments (1959), 50, 91–92, 153, 165, 175, 176, 190, 263
Law enforcement, and union official role, 24
Layoffs, 21, 104
Lechmere v. NLRB, 24, 25, 157–158
Legal services, and union associate membership, 92
Lewis, John L., 46, 53
Lingle v. Norge Division, 83, 89, 103
Living standards, decline in, 1–2
Lockouts, 189–190, 202
Lorance v. AT&T Technologies, Inc., 242, 254
"Lordstown syndrome," 111
Lucas, Malcolm, 63, 72, 78

McDonnell Douglas Corp. v. Green, 246
Mackay (NLRB v. Mackay) doctrine, 185, 186, 188, 189, 192, 193, 194, 199, 201, 202–203, 230
Management prerogatives, 21
    and collective bargaining subjects, 21, 24–25, 143–144, 171, 173
    and financial disclosure, 174, 175
    and permanent replacements, 185, 191
    and Saturn project, 127–128
Mandatory subjects of bargaining, 21, 24, 170–173
Marshall, Thurgood, 66, 189
Martin v. Wilks, 243, 253, 255
Mass picketing, 155–156
Mazda, 19, 104
Meany, George, 45

Med-arb technique, 197–198
Mixed motives in employment disputes, 253–254
Multinational corporations, 12, 35

NAFTA (North American Free Trade Agreement), 13, 234
National Adjustment Board, 100
National Education Association, 15
National Labor Relations Act (NLRA) (Wagner Act) (1935), 11, 31, 47, 259, 260. *See also* Labor law
    attempts to replicate, 3–4
    and bankruptcy of employer, 22
    and company unions or company assistance to unions, 7–8, 19, 136–137, 138, 139–142
    and cooperative relationships, 60–61
    and decline of unionism, 3, 54, 55, 151–152, 261
    far-left view of, 49–51
    and financing of proceedings, 98
    and illegal aliens, 26
    interpretations of as concern, 3
    and management prerogatives, 143–144
    and monetary relief, 241
    and 1964 Civil Rights Act, 48
    and Norris-LaGuardia Act, 108
    and plant closing, 105
    and preemption doctrine, 213
    reform of, 151, 152, 156, 177–179 (*see also* Labor law reform)
        and authorization cards, 162–165
        and certification process, 156–157
        and delay problems, 158–161, 162, 165–166
        and employee participation, 262
        and employment discrimination law, 257
        and financial information disclosure, 171, 174–175
        and mandatory subjects of bargaining, 170–173
        and monetary relief for workers, 165–167
        and refusal-to-bargain cases, 167–170
        and solicitation/access rights, 157–158
        and successorship cases, 173–174
        and union abuses or excesses, 175–177
        and wrongful discharge, 29
    repeal of, 49–50, 151, 153–155
    and right to resign union, 22, 188–189
    and right to strike, 184
    section 10(j) requests and authorizations under, 160–161

and strikers' reinstatement, 199
and Taft-Hartley, 31, 48–49, 53 (see also Taft-Hartley Act/amendments)
on unauthorized stoppages, 200
and worker participation, 144, 148, 149
and wrongful discharge, 102
National Labor Relations Board, 3, 22–23, 48, 93, 221
and employer-free-speech controversies, 152, 157
and wrongful-discharge litigation, 93, 99
National Steel, 104
Nepean Roof Truss, Ltd., 226
New Deal, 11, 263
New United Motors Manufacturing, Inc. (NUMMI)
and arbitration, 130
and cooperative model, 5, 19
and job security, 104
as successor, 174
and workers' participation, 60–61, 123–127, 129, 130, 137, 141, 142, 143, 262
Nixon, Richard, 27, 235, 237
NLRA. See National Labor Relations Act
NLRB v. Allis-Chalmers, 188
NLRB v. Babcock & Wilcox, 157
NLRB v. Bildisco & Bildisco, 22
NLRB v. Food and Commercial Workers, Local 23, 213
NLRB v. Gissel, 21, 163, 177, 218
NLRB v. Insurance Agents' International Union, 122, 131, 173, 183–184, 189
NLRB v. Mackay (Mackay doctrine), 185, 186, 188, 189, 192, 193, 194, 199, 201, 202, 230
NLRB v. Truitt Manufacturing, 174, 175
Nonunion sector, 6, 34–35, 59
associate membership or services for, 91–93
and job security, 8
as replacements, 261
resentment in, 263
union services for, 92–95, 96
and Occupational Safety and Health violations, 94
and wrongful discharge, 92–94, 95
and worker participation, 110, 136–137 (see also Workers' participation)
works council approach in, 59
and wrongful discharge litigation, 65 (see also Wrongful discharge litigation)
Norris-LaGuardia Act (1932), 47, 48, 50, 107–108, 153, 176
North American Free Trade Agreement (NAFTA), 13, 234

No-strike clauses
at Japanese companies in Britain, 130
at Saturn and NUMMI, 130
violation of, 176, 184, 263
NUMMI. See New United Motors Manufacturing, Inc.

Occupational Safety and Health Act (1970), 9, 57, 94, 107
amendments to proposed, 94, 148, 260–261
O'Connor, Sandra Day
in *Flight Attendants* case, 187
in *Gade* case, 107
and 1991 Civil Rights Act, 257
on reinstatement gamble, 187, 201
in Watson case, 244, 251, 253, 256
Organized labor. See Unions and union movement

Packwood-Metzenbaum amendment, 4, 194–195, 198, 202, 228, 261
Parental leave legislation, 58
Participation by workers. See Workers' participation
Part-time workers, 2, 25–26, 261
and fringe benefits and health care reform, 260
as strike-breakers, 185
Pattern bargaining, 146, 181–182, 194
Patternmakers' League of North America, AFL-CIO v. NLRB, 188–189, 202
Patterson v. McLean Credit Union, 240–241, 246, 248, 255, 256
Peripheral work force, 2
Permanent replacement tactics, 4, 181–182, 185–188, 190–195, 200–201, 201–202, 261
and Canadian law, 230
and *Flight Attendants* case, 187
Perpetual bargaining approach, 130–131
Personnel manuals or handbooks, and wrongful discharge, 70–72, 90
Phelps Dodge decision, 166
Picketing
informational, 50
mass, 155–156
secondary, 153
protection of, 184
Plant-closing legislation, 58, 105–107
Plant closures, 21
and bargaining, 143, 171
Plateau Mills, Ltd., 217
Policy, public
labor policy assumptions, 3
and wrongful discharge, 67–69, 83, 86
Polygraph legislation, 57–58
Powell, Lewis, 188, 238

Index

Preemption doctrine, 107, 155, 213
Pregnancy and Disability Act (1978), 238
Price Waterhouse v. Hopkins, 242, 253
Productivity
    and labor-management relationships, 1–2
    and seniority, 76
    and workers' participation, 132–133, 135–136, 183
Profit-sharing plans, 132–136
Progressive discipline, 64
Protected activity, 192–193
Public employees
    and job security, 77
    and wrongful discharge litigation, 66, 88
Public employee trade unionism, 3–4
    in Canada, 208, 212
    membership growth in, 15
Public goods, and collective bargaining, 33–34
Public policy. *See* Policy, public

Quality of work life programs, 19, 58–59, 136, 137
Quota issues
    and Bush, 27–28, 235, 243–244
    and 1991 Civil Rights Act, 2, 27, 28, 79, 239, 243–245, 256

Racism, divisiveness of, 2
Railway Labor Act, 186–187, 195–197, 199
Reagan, Ronald, 27, 42, 106, 159, 185, 235, 237
Reagan administration, 78, 238–239
Recognition of union. *See* Certification system
Rehnquist, William H., 25, 191, 243
Remedies. *See also* Damage awards
    in Canada and U.S., 219–222
    and 1991 Civil Rights Act, 259
    and title VII, 238
    for wrongful dismissal, 97–99, 101–102
Reuther, Walter, 131, 173, 174
Reverse discrimination litigation, 79
Right to free speech. *See* Free-speech right of employers
Right to resign union, 22, 188–189
Right to strike, 4–5, 6, 183–184, 261
    as gamble (O'Connor), 187, 201
    ILO protection of, 183, 198, 201
Rojo v. Kliger, 68–69
Roosevelt, Franklin D., 53, 263

Sanctions, in Canada and U.S., 219–222
Saturn project. *See* General Motors Saturn division

Scalia, Antonin, 242, 254
Scientific management, 110, 122, 136
Secondary boycotts, 20, 153, 154
    Britain's outlawing of, 49
    Taft-Hartley outlawing of, 23, 49, 154, 184
Secondary handbilling, 50
Secondary picketing, 153
Seniority, 33, 76, 122, 143
    AFL-CIO difficulty with, 57
    courts and 1972 Amendments on, 238
    and layoffs, 65
    and 1991 Civil Rights Act, 254
    prevalence of, 63
    at Saturn plant, 128
    and women workers, 242
Service Employees Union, 15
Sexual discrimination, 69, 242, 246. *See also* Discrimination, employment
Sexual harassment, 28, 57
    public policy against, 68–69
    and remedy, 246
Sherman Antitrust Act, 20, 47, 145
Silicon Valley firms, 18, 19, 26–27
Solicitation rights, 157–158
Souter, David, 257
State regulation, 29, 106–107, 154–156
Stewart Olson case, 217
Strikes, 4–5, 202
    Canadian labor law on, 230–232
    and collective bargaining process, 183–184
    decline in power of, 42, 181–182, 261
    and emergency disputes, 195–198
    and foreign nations' reinstatement policies, 198–202
    Canadian, 198, 199, 201–202, 230–231
    and lockouts, 189–190, 202
    and *Mackay* doctrine, 185, 189, 201, 202 (*see also Mackay* doctrine)
    permanent replacements in, 4, 181–182, 185–188, 190–195, 200–201, 202, 230, 261
    protection for, 184, 192–193
    right to strike, 4–5, 6, 183–184, 187, 198, 201, 261
    unfair-labor-practice vs. economic, 171–172
    union discipline in, 188–189
Successorship cases, 173–174
    in Canada, 231–232
Sununu, John, 249
Superseniority for nonstrikers, 191
Supplemental unemployment benefits (SUB), 64
Surface-bargaining cases, 168
Sweeney, John, 16

Index

Taft, William Howard, 20
Taft-Hartley Act/amendments (1947), 31, 49, 53
   and authorization cards, 162
   and Board, 213, 220
   closed shop prohibited by, 189
   decertification procedures of, 190
   emergency strike provisions of, 195
   and Federal Mediation and Conciliation Service, 181
   and free-speech right of employers, 49, 157, 233
   injunction provision of, 32
   as lawyers' bonanza, 157
   as management tilt, 175–176
   and repeal of NLRA, 153, 154–155
   and right to strike, 184
   secondary boycott provisions of, 23, 48–49, 154, 184
Tandy Electronics, Ltd. (Radio Shack) case, 220, 222
Teamsters, International Brotherhood of, 6, 16, 31, 35, 154, 176–177, 260, 262–263
Terminable-at-will doctrine, 66, 69, 78, 85. *See also* Wrongful discharge litigation
Thatcher, Margaret, and Thatcher government, 49, 51–53, 55, 111, 118
Third-party intervention, 4, 5, 183, 195. *See also* Arbitration
Third World, textile jobs to, 16
Thomas, Clarence, 24, 247, 257
Title VII. *See under* Civil Rights Act (1964)
Toussaint decision, 70
Trade union movement. *See* Unions and union movement
Trade union movement in Canada, 205–213
Trans World Airlines Inc. v. Independent Federation of Flight Attendants, 187, 190, 191, 193
Truax v. Corrigan, 20
Truman, Harry, 52

UAW v. Johnson, 58
Undue influence, 233
Unemployment compensation, and wrongful-dismissal adjudication, 98–99
Unemployment insurance systems, and layoffs by seniority, 65
Unfair labor practices. *See also* Discrimination, employment; Fairness; Wrongful discharge litigation
   delay in deciding, 158–159, 165–166
   and *Gissel* case, 21
   and NLRA on company unions, 7–8
   sanctions and remedies for (Canada and U.S.), 218–222
   and Wagner Act, 47–48
Union organizing, 23–24, 26–27
   and certification elections, 156–157 (*see also* Certification system)
   language barriers in, 26
   and solicitation/access rights, 157–158
Unions and union movement. *See also specific unions*
   abuses in, 31–32, 175–177
   associate membership status in, 91–92, 164
   changed environment of, 11–12
   decline of, 2–3, 9, 13–25, 34–35, 42–45, 260
      and decentralization of industrial relations, 35, 42
      and delays in unfair-labor-practice decisions, 159–160
      and employee participation, 58–61
      and employee protection, 55–58
      foreign parallels to, 17, 49, 54–55
      historical parallels to, 17–19, 20, 22, 25
      and job security agreements, 77
      and law, 3, 20–25, 48–50, 151–152
      and NLRB elections, 152
      and successor contracts, 174
      and union-nonunion differential, 42, 43–44
      and worker sanctions, 188
   future prospects for, 6
   left-wing criticism of, 121
   membership in, 14–16, 34, 36–41
   and new institutions, 262–263
   regulation of, 53–54, 55–58
   reorganization needed in, 260–261, 263
   as serving nonunion workers, 92–95, 96
   and wrongful discharge, 93–94
   social benefits from, 33–34
   vs. Canadian, 208
   and worker directors, 112 (*see also* Workers' participation)
Unions and union movement in Canada, 205–213
United Auto Workers (UAW)
   in Caterpillar strike, 181–182, 186
   Chrysler board representation for, 113–114, 144, 145, 146, 173
   decline of, 15–16, 35
   and democratic procedures, 263
   and job security, 103
   "New Directions" caucus in, 110, 112
   and Saturn project/NUMMI, 60, 104, 123–131, 141, 174

Index

United Auto Workers (UAW) (cont.)
   and secondary boycott, 154
   and union discipline, 188
   and worker participation, 110, 111, 112, 122, 123–131, 137, 145, 149
United Food and Commercial Workers Union, 50, 94–95, 114, 154, 260
United Mine Workers, 42, 53
United Rubber Workers Union, 114, 122
United Steelworkers of America, 16, 35, 112, 114, 122, 149, 154

Viceroy Construction case, 233
Voting Rights Act (1965), 34

Wagner Act (1935), 11, 47, 48–49, 53, 54, 55, 136, 184. *See also* National Labor Relations Act
Wallace, George, 236
Wards Cove Packing Company v. Atonio, 238, 239–240, 241–242, 247, 250, 251, 252, 253, 255–256
War Labor Board, 11, 122
WARN (Workers' Adjustment, Retraining and Notification Act), 58, 105, 108, 260
Washington v. Davis, 250
Watson v. Forth Worth Bank and Trust, 241, 244, 251, 253, 256
Whistleblower statutes, 67, 108
Whistle blowing, and wrongful discharge, 86–87
White, Byron, 66, 240
Wildcat strikes, 200
Wisdom, John, 140
Women. *See also* Sexual discrimination; Sexual harassment
   and reproductive-hazard policies, 58, 106–107
   and title VII, 57, 238
Workers' Adjustment, Retraining and Notification Act (WARN) (1988), 58, 105, 108, 260
Workers' participation, 9, 109–115, 147–149, 262
   and codetermination in Germany, 115–117, 146
   and company assistance, 59–61, 136–142
   and current economic situation, 120–121
   and European Community, 117–119
   in Japan, 119–120
   and job security, 60, 78, 147–148, 183
   and labor law reform, 117, 142
   at NUMMI, 60, 123–127, 129, 130, 137, 141, 142, 143, 262
   obstacles to, 121, 132, 135, 144, 146
   with parallel arrangements, 131–135
   and productivity, 132–133, 135–136, 183
   and Saturn project, 60, 123, 127–131, 137, 143, 262
   and union decline, 58–61
   and worker-directors, 112, 113–115, 134, 142–147
   and workers as "managerial," 142–143
Work force
   heterogeneity of, 18
   part-time or peripheral, 2, 25–26, 185, 261
Working class, decline in living standards of, 1–2
Workplace Fairness Act (1992), 194–195, 261
   Packwood-Metzenbaum amendment to, 4, 194–195, 198, 202, 228, 261
Works council system, 6–7, 56–57, 59, 115, 117, 146, 147, 261. *See also* Workers' participation
Work standardization, 124
World Labor Board, 63
Wright Line doctrine, 214
Wrongful discharge litigation, ix, 8, 65–67, 108, 260, 262. *See also* Job security
   arbitration for, 81, 83–84, 85, 99, 108
   and at-will clauses, 71, 81, 87
   and collective bargaining, 33–34, 59
   and common law, 29–30, 81–82
   and corporate-merger displacements, 78, 85
   effect of, 85
   and employment discrimination, 29–31, 78–79, 88, 247
   and equality of employer-employee relationship, 75–77
   and foreign countries' policies, 77–78
   and layoff restrictions, 103–105
   legislation for, 80–81, 84–85, 87, 103, 108, 260
      and coverage issues, 87–90, 95, 97
      and dismissal standard, 97
      forum and remedy in, 97–103
      and importance of employment, 74–75, 77
      union support of, 90–91, 93, 103
   monetary relief for, 165–167
   and permanent replacements, 193–194
   problems for employees in
      absence of just cause standard, 86–87
      cost, 85
   and public-sector jobs, 77
   theories in support of

covenant of good faith and fair dealing, 72–74, 82
implied contract, 69–72, 79–81, 82, 90
just cause, 82, 94, 97
public policy, 67–69, 83, 86
and union services for nonunion workers, 92–94, 95

Yellow-dog contracts, 20, 46, 81
Yeshiva decision, 142–143, 260
Young people, and union membership, 14